BIG GUN MONITORS

BIG GUN MONITORS

THE HISTORY OF THE DESIGN, CONSTRUCTION AND OPERATION
OF THE ROYAL NAVY'S MONITORS

IAN BUXTON

WORLD SHIP SOCIETY — TRIDENT BOOKS

First published in 1978
by the World Ship Society and Trident Books
12 Grand Parade, Tynemouth, Tyne & Wear, England

ISBN 0 905617 06 1

Line drawings by the author

Printed in England by T. Stephenson & Sons Ltd., Prescot, Merseyside

CONTENTS

ABBREVIATIONS

Abbreviations marked * are used on illustrations

A.A.	Anti-aircraft
A.D.O.*	Air defence officer
A.E.W.	Admiralty Experiment Works (Haslar)
A.F.C.T.*	Admiralty fire control table
A.F.D.	Admiralty floating dock
A.N.C.X.F.	Allied Naval Commander, Expeditionary Force
A.P.	Aft perpendicular
A.P.C.	Armour piercing, capped (projectile)
B.	Barbette (mounting)
B.H.P.	Brake horsepower (diesels)
BISCO	British Iron and Steel Corporation
B.L.	Breech loading (gun)
B.L.O.	Bombardment liaison officer
B.P.	Between perpendiculars (length)
C.	Cemented (armour)
Cal	Calibre (length of gun)
C-in-C	Commander-in-Chief
C.L.*	Cable locker
C. & M.	Care and maintenance
C.N.F.	Common, nose-fuzed (projectile)
C.O.	Commanding officer
C.O.W.	Coventry Ordnance Works
C.P.	Centre pivot (mounting)
C.P.	Common, pointed (projectile)
C.P.C.	Common, pointed capped (projectile)
C.P.O.	Chief petty officer
c.r.h.	Calibres radius of head (projectile)
C.S.A.*	Chloro-sulphonic smoke apparatus
D and D.1	Designation of Admiralty special high strength steel
D.C.B.	Distance-controlled boat
D.C.H.Q.*	Damage control headquarters
D.N.C.	Director of Naval Construction
D.N.O.	Director of Naval Ordnance
D.O.*	Diesel Oil
D.R.*	Dressing room
D.S.	Detached Squadron
E.C.M.	Electronic counter-measures
e.f.c.	Equivalent full charge
E.H.P.	Effective horsepower
E.O.C.	Elswick Ordnance Company (Armstrong, Whitworth)
F.O.B.	Forward observer, bombardment
F.O.O.	Forward observation officer
F.P.	Forward perpendicular
FR.*	Frame
F.W.*	Fresh water
GM	Metacentric height (distance between centre of gravity and metacentre)
H*	Hatch
H.A.	High angle
H.A.C.P.	High angle calculating position
H.A./L.A.	High angle/low angle
H.E.	High explosive (projectile)
H.E.T.F.	High explosive, time fuze (projectile)
H.M.S.	His Majesty's Ship
H.P.	Horsepower
H.Q.	Headquarters
H.T.	High-tensile (steel)
H. & W.	Harland and Wolff
I.H.P.	Indicated horsepower (steam reciprocators)
kW	Kilowatt
L.A.	Low angle
L.C.G.	Landing craft, gun
L.C.M.	Landing craft, mechanised
L.C.T.	Landing craft, tank
L.S.I.	Landing ship, infantry
L.S.T.	Landing ship, tank
MAG.*	Magazine
MD	Modified (cordite)
Mk	Mark
M.L.	Motor launch
M.P.	Member of Parliament
M.V.	Muzzle velocity
N.C.	Non-cemented (armour)
N.C.T.	Nitro-cellulose, tubular (propellant)
O.F.T.*	Oil fuel tank
P.	Pedestal (mounting)
pdr	Pounder (gun)
P.O.	Petty officer
P. & O.	Peninsular & Oriental (Steam Navigation Co.)
P. & S.*	Port and starboard
Q.F.	Quick-firing (gun)
R.A.F.	Royal Air Force
R.F.C.	Royal Flying Corps
R.F.W.	Reserve feed water
R.G.F.	Royal Gun Factory (Woolwich)
R.M.	Royal Marines
R.N.	Royal Navy
R.N.A.S.	Royal Naval Air Service
R.N.V.R.	Royal Naval Volunteer Reserve
R.P.C.	Remote power control
r.p.g.	Rounds per gun

r.p.m.	Revolutions per minute
R.U.L.*	Ready use locker
S.A.*	Small arms
S.A.P.	Semi-armour piercing (projectile)
S.B.*	Shell bin
SC	Solventless carbamite (cordite)
S.F.C.P.	Shore fire control party
S.G.*	Steering gear
S.H.P.	Shaft horsepower (turbines)
S.L.*	Searchlight
S.R.*	Shell-room
ST.*	Store
T.*	Tank
T.N.T.	Tri-nitro-toluene (high explosive)
T.P.D.*	Tons per day
T.P.H.*	Tons per hour
T.S.	Transmitting station
U.K.	United Kingdom
U.P.	Unrotated projectile (rocket)
U.S.S.	United States Ship
W.*	Winch
W.B.*	Water ballast
W.C.*	Water closet
W.L.*	Waterline
W.O.*	Warrant officer
W/T	Wireless telegraphy
W.T.C.*	Watertight compartment
W.T.D.*	Watertight door
WW1	World War 1
WW2	World War 2

PREFACE

On one day in August 1965, I spent many hours aboard Britain's last big gun monitor *Roberts* after she had arrived for breaking up at Inverkeithing. When later I tried to find out more about these unusual but relatively little known warships, I found that very little information was available. There were brief entries in *Jane's Fighting Ships*, a few paragraphs in official histories and a page or two in a handful of other books. The only full length book on monitors turned out to be a novel — *H.M.S. Saracen* by Douglas Reeman.

The paucity of published material appears to stem largely from the 'hostilities only' character of the monitors rather from any lack of potential interest. In wartime, their construction and operations were shrouded in secrecy, while in peacetime, they were soon paid off and either scrapped or relegated to subsidiary duties, away from the public gaze. I determined therefore to fill the gap and to publish an account of the origins, design, construction and operations of the 42 British monitors which served between 1914 and 1965.

The history of the monitors is more than an account of some special ships built for bombardment of enemy-held coastlines. Their requirement for the heaviest guns, up to 18-inch calibre, had an influence on the battleship building programmes, where availability of heavy ordnance was a determining factor. The monitors' intensive bombardments pushed the science of naval gunnery to its limits in terms of accuracy and sustained fire. Not many of such topics have been previously discussed publicly in print, so putting together a comprehensive history required some ten years of research among many original sources of material.

The relaxation of the closed period for official records from 50 to 30 years opened up much new material after 1972, especially on the Second World War. Similarly many original records such as drawings and official handbooks are now available in the National Maritime Museum or the Imperial War Museum. Many who served in the monitors in both World Wars were able to provide invaluable assistance as noted in the Acknowledgements.

I have taken great pains to verify all numerical data — in some cases finding errors in official publications. Where precise figures were not available, estimates have been made as carefully as possible; for example there is no accurately measured range for the 18-inch gun as installed in two of the monitors. If the reader finds an above average measure of discussion on technical and economic aspects of ships and ordnance, this not only reflects my outlook as a professional naval architect, but is a measure of how important these factors are in the design and construction of any novel type of ship.

Nevertheless my intention has been not only to fill a gap in the naval literature, which was not recognised by the major publishers in the field of naval history, but to make the account one of interest to the general reader as well as a definitive reference for the specialist.

I. L. B.

The two warship types mounting the heaviest ordnance — capital ships and monitors — are seen under construction at Clydebank. The upper view taken in July 1916 shows Erebus *having her 15-inch turret erected under the 200-ton hammerhead crane at John Brown's shipyard, with battlecruiser* Repulse, *destroyers* Romola *(alongside forward) and* Peregrine *(aft), and submarine* E.35 *in the foreground. The lower view taken about March 1941 shows* Roberts *awaiting her 15-inch turret. The battleship fitting out is* Duke of York *and the destroyer* Piorun *(ex-*Nerissa*). The only significant change visible in the shipyard in the intervening quarter of a century is the addition of the large tower crane to cover the upper end of the longest slipway on which the* Queens *were built.*

CHAPTER I

THE ORIGINS OF THE BRITISH MONITOR

"MONITOR — one who admonishes another as to his conduct"

Shorter Oxford English Dictionary

In a letter to the Assistant Secretary of the United States Navy during the American Civil War, the Swedish engineer John Ericsson claimed for his new design of ironclad ship:[1]

> "The impregnable and aggressive character of this structure will admonish the leaders of the Southern Rebellion that the batteries on the banks of their rivers will no longer present barriers to the entrance of the Union forces. The ironclad intruder will thus prove a severe monitor to those leaders. ....On these and many similar grounds, I propose to name the new battery *Monitor*."

The wooden ships of the Federal forces had been unable to overcome the batteries guarding the way to the Confederate strongholds above Hampton Roads. Construction of Ericsson's ironclad began in October 1861 and she was completed just in time to counter the destruction that the newly converted Confederate ironclad *Virginia* (ex-*Merrimack*) had been wreaking amongst the blockading Federal ships. The 987-ton ship was named U.S.S. *Monitor,* her principal features being: a powerful armament of two 11-inch smooth-bore muzzle-loading guns in a rotating armoured turret, a well protected low freeboard hull presenting a very small target, and no rig or sails, as she relied entirely on steam propulsion to provide her modest 6-knot speed. The inconclusive action between the *Monitor* and *Virginia* on 9 March 1862 has been recounted many times; neither ship was seriously damaged owing to the protective value of their iron plates. Such a radically new design of fighting ship had a significant influence on warship development, making obsolete at a stroke virtually all the vulnerable wooden sailing vessels whose design had changed little over the centuries — although it must be recognised that the trend towards the turret and iron-cladding was already apparent in contemporary European designs.

The use of special ships to attack well-defended targets has a long history. Both the British and French used bomb vessels at the end of the 17th Century to bombard forts, as at Tripoli, Algiers and Genoa in 1682-84. From time to time, bomb and mortar vessels continued to be used as required for coast offence purposes. The first serious attempt to ally this type of vessel with the new developments of steam propulsion and iron protection occurred during the Crimean War. In July 1854, the French Emperor Napoleon III ordered ten ironclad floating batteries to be constructed, which could be used against the Russian Crimean and Baltic forts. Five vessels were built in Britain and five in France, each of about 1600 tons, mounting sixteen 68-pdr or 50-pdr muzzle-loading guns. Four-inch wrought iron plating covered the sides of their hulls, which could steam at about four knots.

During the 1860s, the unprotected broadside-armed sailing vessels and wooden screw battleships of the major navies were rapidly superseded by a wide variety of steam-propelled ironclad designs. The principles of Ericsson's *Monitor* found favour amongst the smaller powers for coast defence vessels, but low freeboard made the type unsuitable for overseas operations. Even the mighty Royal Navy embarked on building vessels suitable only for coast defence, starting with the *Prince Albert* in 1862. Over the next decade, a motley fleet of some dozen such vessels was built. Apart from the three designed for colonial defence, these ships were almost valueless. It was strategically unsound for a major power to build coast defence vessels. The best defence against attack or invasion was the destruction of the enemy fleet, in effect making the enemy's own shores the defence perimeter of the British Isles. Subsequent development of armoured ships for the Royal Navy therefore concentrated on well armed, well protected vessels with a reasonable speed and capable of keeping the seas in all weathers. Such ships were necessarily large and could not be afforded in great numbers. When coast offence vessels were needed, as at the Bombardment of Alexandria in 1882, the regular ships of the line were employed. Thus for some forty years, the Royal Navy built neither coast offence nor coast defence vessels, although the latter remained popular with most of the smaller navies. The United States continued to build monitors up to 1903 when the last of a line of 71 vessels ordered was commissioned, the 3225-ton U.S.S. *Florida.* Several navies also built river monitors, in effect shallow draft armoured gunboats, but they were intended only for service on rivers like the Danube or Amur, not the open sea.

With the outbreak of World War I in August 1914, the Royal Navy was committed to its first full scale war for a century. The Grand Fleet's role was that of neutralising

[1] *The Life of John Ericsson* by W. C. Church, p.254

the German High Seas Fleet, so enabling Britain to keep command of the seas and her overseas communications. Germany's rapid thrust on land through Belgium towards Paris had been brought to a halt by October, when the war was already showing signs of dragging on for a year or more. In addition to the main belligerents of Britain, France and Russia on the one hand, and Germany and Austria-Hungary on the other, attempts were made to persuade other nations to join either the Allied Powers or the Central Powers. At the end of October, it was plain that Turkey would join the latter bloc, but Italy could not yet be persuaded to join the former.

When Lord Fisher replaced Prince Louis of Battenberg as First Sea Lord on 30 October 1914, it was clear that some form of naval initiative would be desirable to break the impending stalemate on land and attempt to strike Germany decisively in a vulnerable spot. Winston Churchill, First Lord of the Admiralty, and Fisher had been mulling over various possibilities. Fisher had long been a proponent of a Baltic strategy, where an offensive against the Pomeranian coast could enable a landing to be made with Russian support only 90 miles from Berlin. To be successful, such a scheme required the prior disablement or neutralisation of the High Seas Fleet, which otherwise could emerge from the Kiel Canal and wreak havoc amongst the invasion fleet. The shallow waters of the Baltic were easily mined, which would hamper and endanger the deep draft big gun ships of the Royal Navy. It would therefore be necessary to undertake the hazardous operation of seizing some form of advanced base across the North Sea in the Friesian Islands or off the Danish coast, either to force the High Seas Fleet out of its well protected base at Wilhelmshaven and enable the Grand Fleet to destroy it by battle, or to permit surface forces and submarines to blockade movements from the German bases.

The stabilisation of the Western Front on the Belgian Coast also offered opportunities for landing forces under the cover of heavy guns to turn the enemy's flank and prevent ports like Zeebrugge from being used as submarine bases by the Germans. Any hostilities against Turkey would probably entail an attempt to force the Dardanelles to open the direct supply route to Russia. Ships of the Grand Fleet could not be risked from their vital strategic role for such operations, while most of the older British ships had insufficiently powerful guns or were of too deep draft for working close inshore near strong shore defences. The makeshift fleet which had bombarded the Belgian Coast at the end of October (see p. 83) had demonstrated the potential of coast offence vessels, as it had been instrumental in stemming the German advance towards the French Channel ports.

All of these possibilities for coastal bombardment, some more practical than others, were at the back of Churchill and Fisher's minds when an important visitor called at the Admiralty on Tuesday, 3 November 1914. The visitor was Charles M. Schwab, President of the Bethlehem Steel Corporation, who had left New York a fortnight earlier in the White Star liner *Olympic* to try to sell arms and munitions to Britain. In addition to steel and armour plate, Bethlehem manufactured ordnance as well as owning several shipyards. After some delay because the passengers on the *Olympic* had witnessed the sinking of the British battleship *Audacious*, mined off the north coast of Ulster on 27 October, Admiral Sir John Jellicoe, Commander-in-Chief of the Grand Fleet, permitted Schwab to travel to London, when he learned that Schwab had arranged to see Lord Kitchener at the War Office and that Bethlehem had submarine building capacity available. At the Admiralty, the new construction programme was discussed and agreement was reached with Schwab to build 20 submarines for Britain in the United States. That evening, Schwab was asked by Churchill and Fisher if he had any other naval material which might be of use to Britain. He then disclosed that he had four twin 14-inch turrets nearing completion, which had been ordered for the Greek battlecruiser *Salamis*, then building in Germany. As the British blockade would obstruct their delivery, he was quite willing to sell them to Britain instead.

At this moment of time, the British monitor was conceived. A supply of modern heavy ordnance was the main prerequisite for building coast offence vessels. While hulls and machinery could be constructed quite quickly, heavy gun mountings took well over a year to build. The only source of supply in Britain would have been the requisition of mountings ordered for some of the battleships of the 1912 and 1913 new construction programmes. Any such diversion would have a serious effect on the completions which were needed to ensure an adequate margin of capital ship numbers over the High Seas Fleet. Schwab's offer opened up the prospect of rapidly obtaining a significant coast offence capability, so Churchill and Fisher eagerly accepted.

After the meeting, the Third Sea Lord, Rear-Admiral F. C. T. Tudor, who was responsible for naval construction, immediately minuted to the Director of Naval Construction (D.N.C.), Eustace Tennyson d'Eyncourt:[1]

> "To design immediately 2 Armoured Monitors, to be built in 4 months — each to carry 2-14" guns or equivalent. Draft 10 feet. Speed 10 knots. To have crinoline. An armoured conning tower. Armoured deck. Who could build them?"

A design to satisfy these requirements was worked up very quickly, as detailed in the next chapter. It was a revolutionary design in that it owed nothing to previous ship designs, unlike the normal evolutionary process of naval achitecture. By the standards of Ericsson's original design, the British concept was not strictly a 'monitor', but over the intervening half-century, the term could reasonably be considered as having expanded somewhat to embrace a new type which still owed something of its characteristics to the first monitor. Within the Royal Navy, the description 'monitor' would be distinctive and unambiguous, while not giving away too much as to their expected operational role.

Over the next four months, a total of 33 vessels were authorised; thus, with the two vessels ordered later, the

[1] D'Eyncourt papers, National Maritime Museum.

Royal Navy had by 1916 a fleet of 35 monitors, 16 large and 19 small, mounting guns from 6-inch to 15-inch calibre. Incuding three ex-Brazilian river gunboats and two ex-Norwegian converted coast defence ships, a total of 40 vessels saw service during World War I. Further vessels were built exclusively for river work, the so-called China gunboats of the *Insect* and *Fly* classes but, as they were not intended primarily for bombardment operations, they are only mentioned in passing in this history of British big gun monitors.

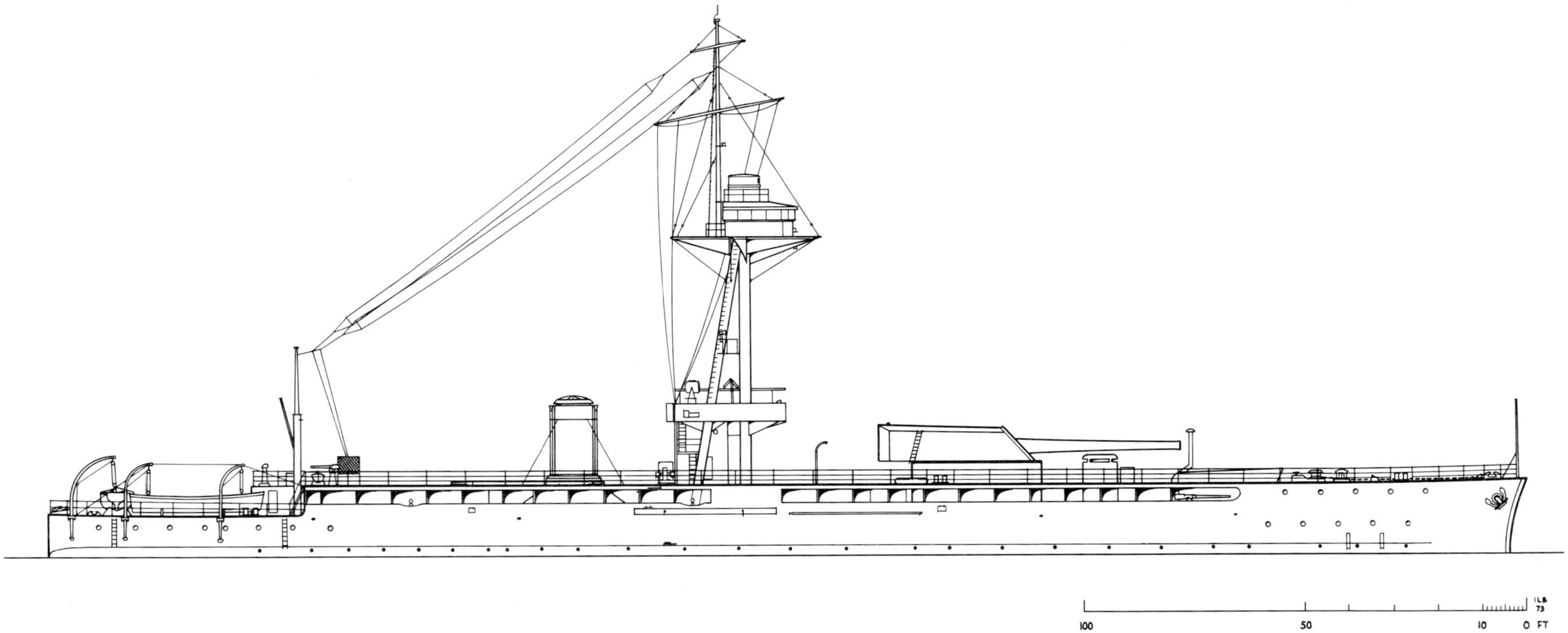

H.M.S. Roberts. *The first monitors to be completed were simple in their essentials — a Bethlehem twin 14-inch turret mounted on a low hull with a tripod mast and single funnel. Unlike* Abercrombie *and* Havelock, Roberts *and* Raglan *had the folding midship ammunition derrick post shown, but the latter had no seaplane derrick posts aft. Later modifications included a lengthened funnel, removal of the topmast, and additional secondary armament.*

CHAPTER II

THE 14-INCH GUN MONITORS

H.M.S. ABERCROMBIE, HAVELOCK, RAGLAN, ROBERTS

§1 Design of the First British Monitor

Churchill and Fisher were in their element in November 1914, planning a vast new fleet of ships. The projected cruisers, destroyers and submarines were all relatively well established types, but the monitors were a totally new concept. While some of the latter's characteristics might be similar to coast defence vessels or river gunboats, neither of these types formed a suitable basis for designing seagoing vessels. The main requirements could be summarised:—

- (i) Twin 14-inch turret to be carried on a good gun platform
- (ii) 10-foot shallow draft, to get close inshore
- (iii) Maximum protection against mines and torpedoes, with reasonable protection against gunfire
- (iv) Hull and machinery as simple as possible for rapid construction
- (v) Modest speed of 10 knots
- (vi) Reasonable seagoing capability.

By the time Schwab returned to the Admiralty on 6 November to discuss further details of the proposed contracts, a Constructor, A. M. Worthington, had sketched out a preliminary specification of a monitor of about 6000 tons displacement. After the weekend, formal instructions were given on the 9th to a young Assistant Constructor, Charles S. Lillicrap. It was a challenging task even for a talented man who was later to become D.N.C. himself — a totally new type of ship to be designed and built with the greatest urgency, with the formidable Fisher continually appearing in the office to hasten progress.

Unfortunately no Ship's Cover (the file kept by D.N.C. Department recording the design of each new class of ship) was prepared for the early monitors, probably owing to Fisher's impatience and to the secrecy surrounding them. However it is possible to glean something of the considerations applied in the monitor design from the calculations recorded in Lillicrap's calculation workbooks. The turret was the heaviest single item, about 620 tons revolving weight, plus about 350 tons for ammunition and barbette armour. Such a concentrated weight would have to be placed nearly amidships to avoid problems of trim. The width of the hull would need to be about 60ft to contain the turret comfortably and its magazines. Protection spaces were to be fitted outboard, as a monitor was the ideal vessel on which to demonstrate d'Eyncourt's newly developed design of an anti-torpedo bulge. The bulges, sometimes called blisters, were added outside the hull proper, being 15ft wide on each side, as described on p.17. The breadth of the ship would thus be about 90ft; anything wider would severely restrict the number of drydocks that could be used. The hull needed only to be long enough to provide the necessary internal space for the turret, machinery, accommodation and stores. The depth of the ship (height of deck above keel) was established from the length of the turret trunk containing ammunition hoists and working machinery, the height of the engines and boilers, and the need for adequate freeboard forward.

The dimensions which resulted from a consideration of all these factors were: length between perpendiculars (B.P.) 320ft, moulded breadth over bulges 90ft, depth to upper deck $18^1/_2$ft (i.e. the uppermost continuous deck) on top of which was added a forecastle deck 7ft high, draft 10ft forward and aft. The hull form amidships was composed of a rectangle for the main hull, with the bulges added below water at each side, as illustrated on pages 24 and 42. The form was parallel-sided for over half the length, before tapering in towards the very bluff ends considered acceptable owing to the low speed. The resulting effective block coefficient[1] was the highest of any British warship type at 0.84, compared with a normal 0.55 to 0.65. By Archimedes' principle, the buoyancy of this hull in seawater was about 7000 tons, but as the bulges contained compartments open to the sea, the net figure was reduced to about 6150 tons.

Part of the naval architect's skill lies in achieving balance between a ship's weight and its buoyancy at the designed draft. Once the underwater hull form has been established, the buoyancy at any given draft is fixed. If the completed ship is to float at the correct waterline, the weight of all materials built into the ship together with fuel, ammunition, stores etc. must exactly equal the buoyancy. The weight of a warship (and thus its displacement of water) can be regarded as being made up of:—

- (i) Armament and ammunition
- (ii) Hull structure and fittings
- (iii) Machinery and fuel
- (iv) Armour and protection
- (v) Crew, stores, equipment etc.

For the monitors, (i) had already been specified. (ii)

[1] Block coefficient is the ratio between the underwater volume of a ship's hull and the rectangular circumscribing block having the same length, breadth and draft.

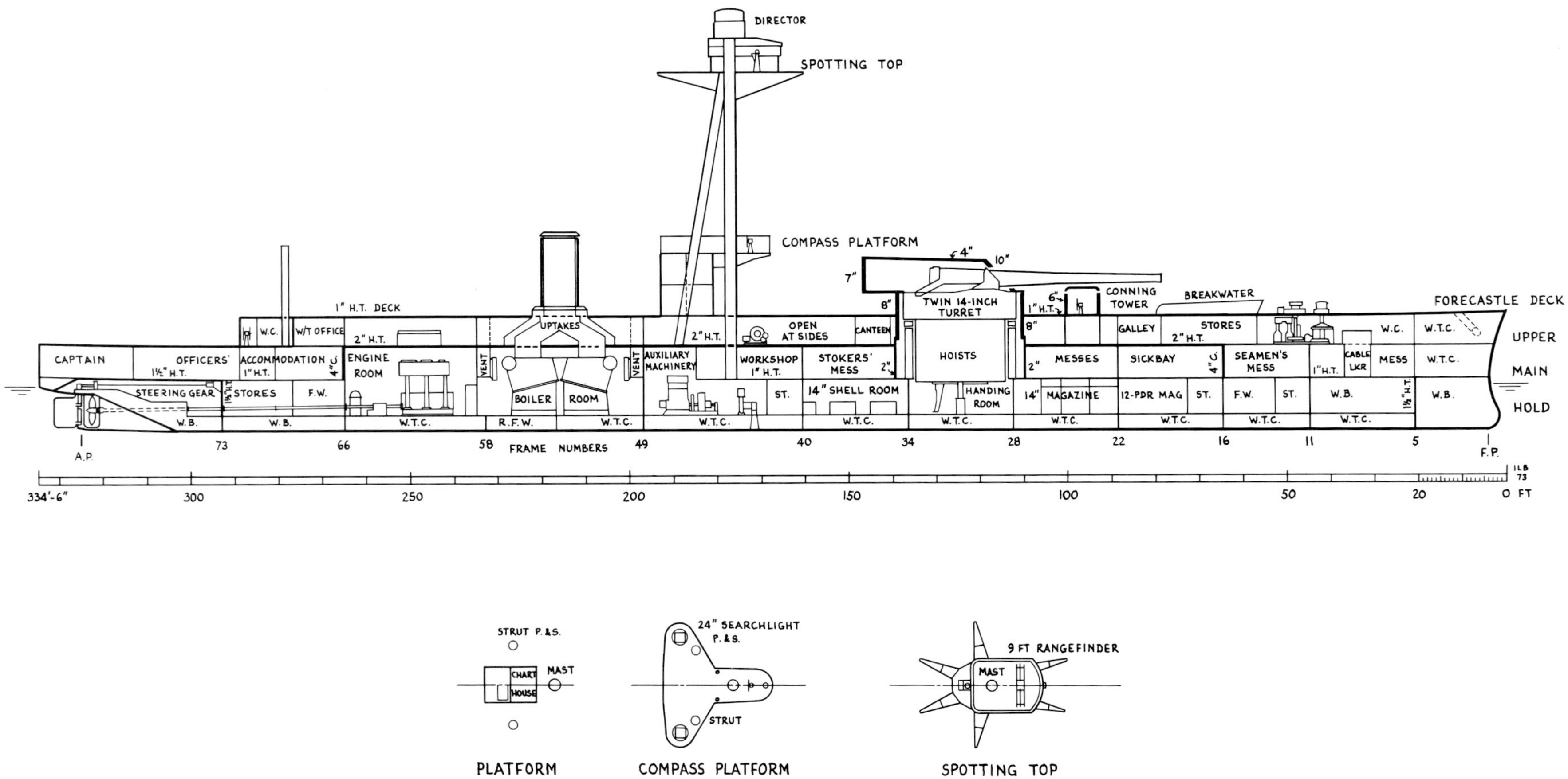

Roberts' *inboard profile and upperworks. A section of the centre-line of the 14-inch monitors shows that half the length was devoted to main armament and machinery. The accommodation, working spaces, stores and watertight compartments filled the rest of the hull. Frames were spaced 4ft throughout, from No. 1 at the fore perpendicular to No. 81 at the aft perpendicular. Abbreviations are listed on page 7.*

largely depended upon the proposed hull dimensions. (iii) was determined mainly by the power of the machinery and the endurance requirements, both low for monitors. As (v) was relatively small, the protection that could be afforded tended to be the balancing item, using up all the remaining buoyancy after deduction of the other items.

Lillicrap finalised the hull form by 17 November, so he was able to give an outline of its shape to the Admiralty Experiment Works (A.E.W.) at Haslar near Portsmouth. Here the Superintendent, R. E. Froude, son of the pioneer of scientific ship model testing, would arrange for a scale model to be made and towed along the test tank to measure the resistance at various speeds and hence deduce the horsepower required for the actual ship. As it would take a few weeks to make full tests, a preliminary estimate had to be made from data for existing ships. Unfortunately there had never been any other British naval vessel of remotely similar form, so that it was difficult to estimate not only the resistance of such an unusual design, but also its propulsive efficiency. The best estimate that could be made from existing data suggested that about 2000 horsepower would be required for a speed of 10 knots, which would easily be obtained from steam reciprocating machinery. The shallow draft and very full form aft limited propeller diameter, so it was necessary to have twin screws no larger than about $7^1/_2$ feet in diameter.

Having established the arrangement of the turret, magazine and propulsion machinery, the remainder of the ship features could then be worked in. On the lower decks: coal bunkers around the boiler room, auxiliary machinery between the magazine and boiler room, stores and accommodation for the crew of about 200 — officers aft, men forward. The upper deck was open at the sides, containing galleys and washplaces together with the barbette structure surrounding the ammunition trunks to the turret. The forecastle deck, which ran over three-quarters of the length of the ship, was comparatively bare: a huge tripod mast amidships carrying the gunnery spotting top and director, the heavy turret forward of the mast, with a small armoured conning tower nestling beneath its guns, and a stumpy funnel abaft the mast. The great expanse of deck abaft the funnel provided sufficient space to arrange stowage for two observation seaplanes, making the monitors the first ships designed from the outset to carry aircraft.

The protection of these first monitors was arranged primarily against torpedo and mine attack, secondarily against gunfire, thirdly against air attack. The threat of torpedoes came both from destroyers and U-boats, although the danger from the latter would be reduced by operating principally in shallow coastal waters, while the modest draft offered a chance that torpedoes would pass harmlessly underneath the hull without exploding. The main protection however came from the underwater bulges which, contrary to popular belief, were not fitted to improve stability. The bulges were divided into two compartments by a vertical longitudinal bulkhead, the outer being 10 feet wide and watertight, the inner 5 feet wide and open to the sea via holes in the top and bottom. The principle was that a torpedo would detonate against the outer chamber some distance away from the main hull, while the inner flooded chamber absorbed the splinters and distributed the energy of the explosion over a larger area of the main hull. The structure of the latter at this point consisted of a strong protective bulkhead formed of two thicknesses each of $^3/_4$-inch high-tensile (H.T.) steel. Behind this was another watertight compartment to contain any leakage resulting from deformation of the protective bulkhead. Although the bulge was intended mainly as a defence against torpedoes, it also afforded some protection against mines. In order to prevent moored mines being carried under the less well protected bottom before exploding, tripper mine-catcher wires were fitted along the outer edge of the bulge. The 14-inch monitors were the first new construction ships to have these underwater protection features.

The main protection against gunfire was provided by a sloping belt of 4-inch cemented armour[1] 12 feet wide fitted inside the main hull, stretching from the ship's side at the waterline up to the upper deck, closed at the ends by 4-inch transverse bulkheads, proof against 6-inch gunfire. An armoured citadel was thus provided which would preserve flotation if the ends of the ship were damaged. One-inch H.T. steel extended over the full area of the forecastle deck to detonate any shells or light bombs, while the 2-inch H.T. steel upper deck would take care of any resulting splinters. The armour and protective plating amounted to a considerable weight — about 1850 tons, or about 30% of the displacement, as shown in the Technical Particulars at the end of the chapter (p.39).

As soon as Froude received the drawings of the monitor hull, he was aghast at its shape. The very full form with steep buttock lines along which the water flowed from underneath the hull upwards towards the propellers would have an appalling hydrodynamic performance compared with the usual fine-lined warship. He wrote immediately to d'Eyncourt, pointing out that the resistance would be very high, the propulsive efficiency very low and the steering unsatisfactory. Work on making the 1/36th scale wax model was nevertheless put in hand, all other work being suspended owing to the urgency; the first runs in the tank were made on 27 November. Over the next few days, tests continued at different speeds and drafts. All of Froude's fears were confirmed; the resistance was even higher than expected, while the steering resembled that of the circular *Popoffkas,* which steamed sideways almost as readily as forwards. The measurements showed that in order to overcome the towing resistance alone, about 2000 effective horsepower (E.H.P.) would be needed at 10 knots. The power required to be supplied by the engines would have to be considerably greater, due to the inherent losses of propellers in converting engine torque into propulsive thrust. Froude estimated that the

[1] Cemented armour (C.) had a specially hardened face to resist initial impact but a tough back. Non-cemented armour (N.C.) was more ductile and intended to deflect projectiles attacking obliquely, e.g. for deck protection. Armour plating was ordered by weight in pounds per square foot. The weight of one square foot one inch thick was nominally 40lb, but was actually 40.8lb. Thus '4-inch' armour ordered as '160lb' was actually 2% thinner, 3.92 inches.

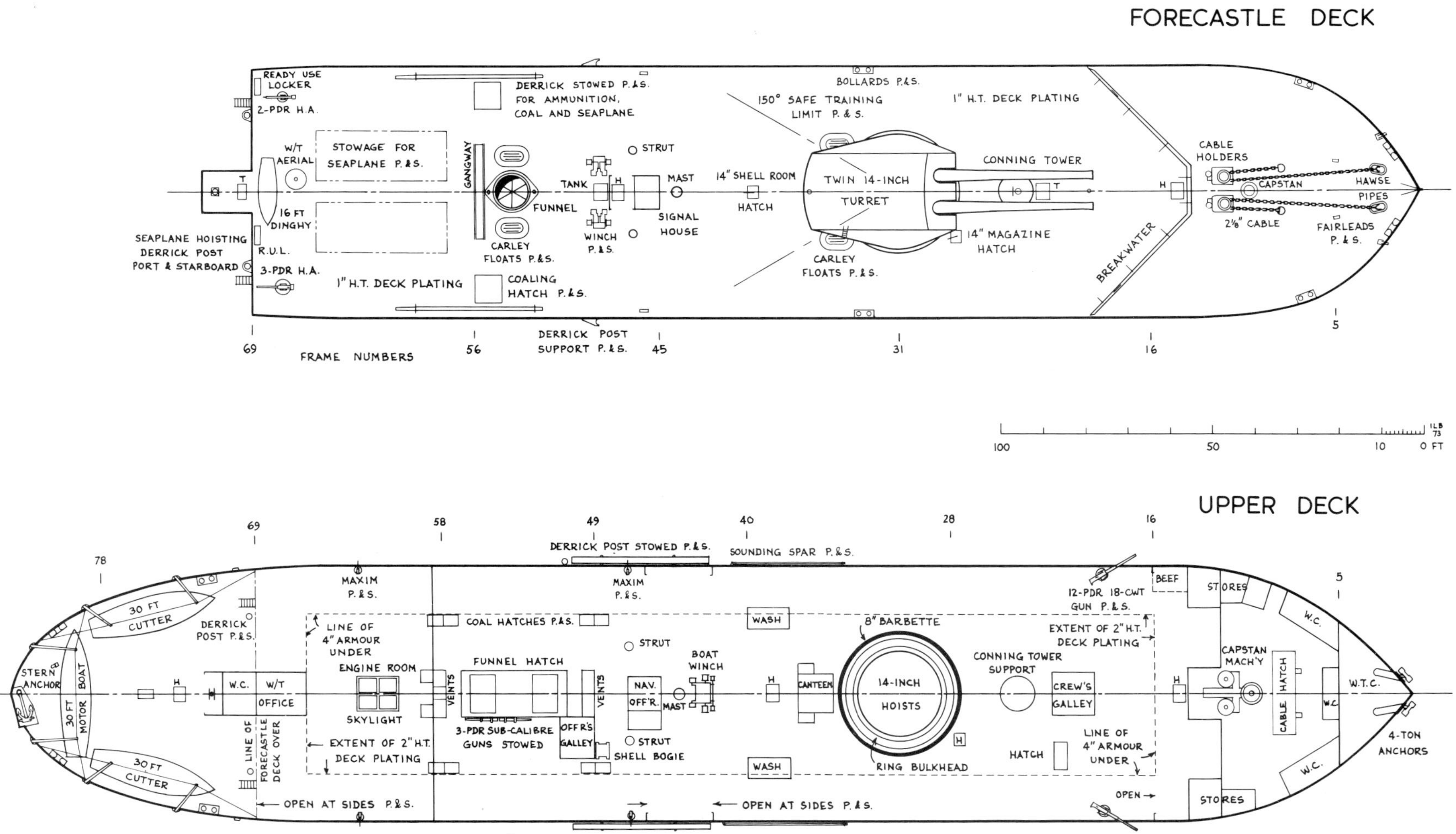

Roberts' *forecastle and upper deck. The forecastle deck was uncluttered, leaving plenty of space for the planned stowage of two seaplanes. The upper deck was open at the sides above bulwark height for most of its length, but a number of small compartments also served to support the forecastle deck. Both decks were painted steel except for the planked quarterdeck.*

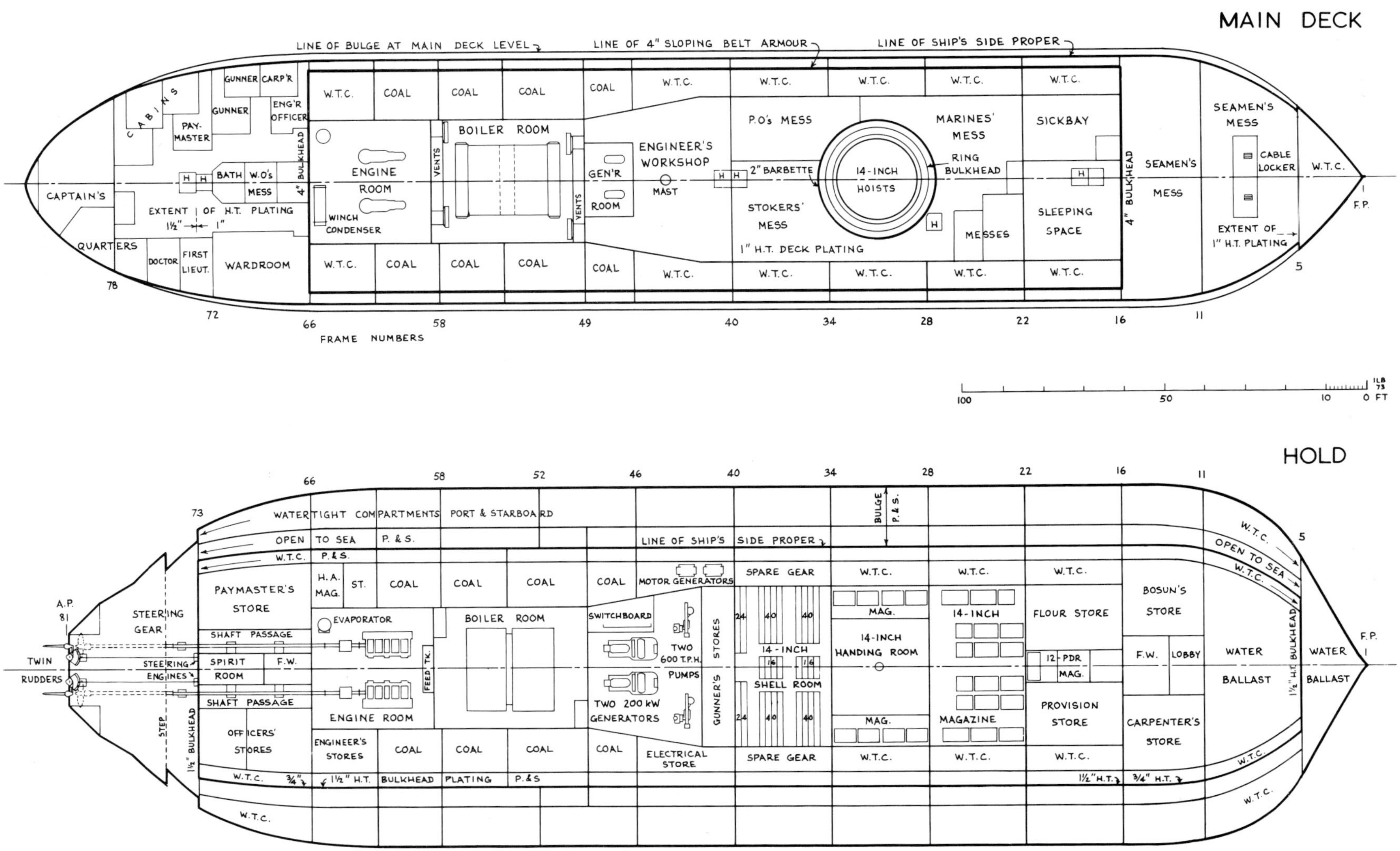

Roberts' *main deck and hold. The hold plan clearly shows the beamy below water hull, the bluff angle of entrance and the extensive watertight subdivision. Accommodation spaces were floored with linoleum, other areas were painted steel.*

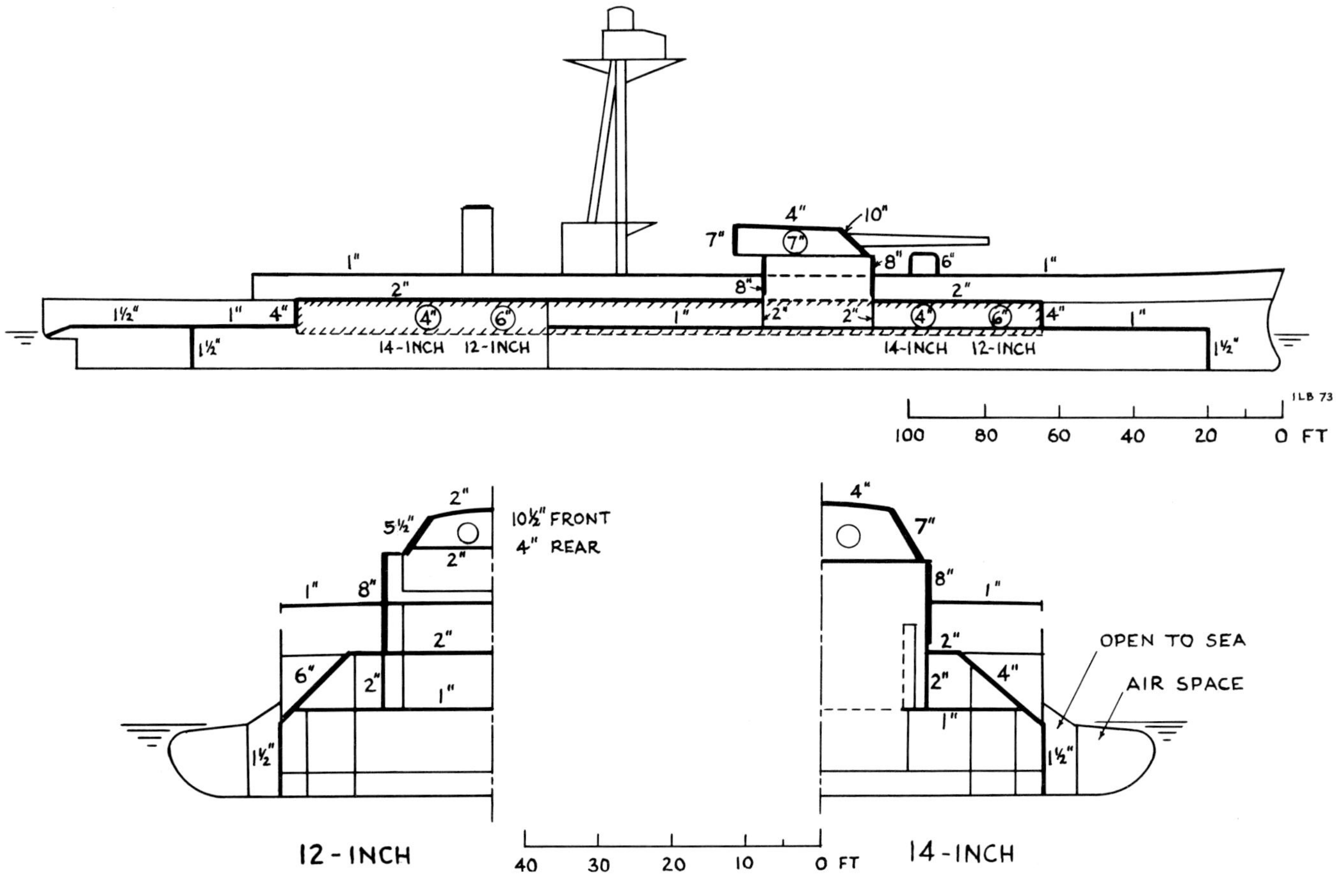

The principal hull protection for the 14-inch monitors was provided by a 4" sloping belt, a 2" upper deck and a $1^1/_2$*" longitudinal bulkhead, covering magazines and machinery. The 1" forecastle deck provided splinter protection. The main anti-torpedo and mine protection was provided by the bulge with its air and water spaces — the latter open to the sea at top and bottom through holes in the shell plating. Turret protection was the same as in the original battleship design. The protection for the 12-inch monitors was identical except for the turret and the 6" sloping belt.*

propulsive efficiency would be well under the 50-60% typical of warships of this period, so that appreciably more than 4000 H.P. would be needed for 10 knots, which was double the power being proposed by D.N.C.

Froude had telegraphed the preliminary results to d'Eyncourt on 27 November, following up with full results and comments a week later, pointing out the reasons for the poor performance and proposing modifications to the afterbody lines. But it was too late to change the design of the hull, the first ship already having been laid down. However much the constructors would have liked to improve the lines or increase the power of the engines, Fisher would permit no delays in construction. The design was committed; the monitors' speed would have to be accepted whatever it was.

§2 Armament

The Greek Government ordered the 19,500-ton battlecruiser *Salamis* from Germany in 1912, with her four twin 14-inch turrets to be supplied by Bethlehem Steel to a design generally similar to the U.S. Navy 14-inch. The battlecruiser was launched at Hamburg on 11 November 1914, having been renamed *Vassilefs Giorgios.*[1] Meantime, the first gun had been proof-fired in March 1914, and construction of the mountings was progressing well. By the outbreak of war, *Salamis'* armament had been nearly completed but then, as described earlier, Schwab offered it to Britain, as it would not be permitted through the British blockade. A new contract was therefore quickly signed on 10 November with the Admiralty for the eight 14-inch guns, four twin mountings, their turret shield armour and two sets of 8-inch barbette armour, plus 500 rounds of ammunition per gun.

The R.N. designated the 45-calibre guns as 14-inch B.L. Mark II.[2] Their range was 19,900 yards at the maximum elevation of 15°. The design of both gun and mounting differed appreciably from current British practice; for example, the propellant was nitro-cellulose compared with the R.N.'s cordite. Being electrically instead of hydraulically worked, two 200kW generators were required — double the capacity of a cruiser. Magazine arrangements were also different, stowage for the 120 projectiles per gun being arranged vertically, nose down. The magazine and shell room were arranged on

[1] The ship was never completed, but her hulk was usually referred to as *Salamis* until it was scrapped in 1932.

[2] Breech loading guns have their propellant charge in a silk case, the gas-tight seal being formed by an elastic obturator pad on the breech block itself.

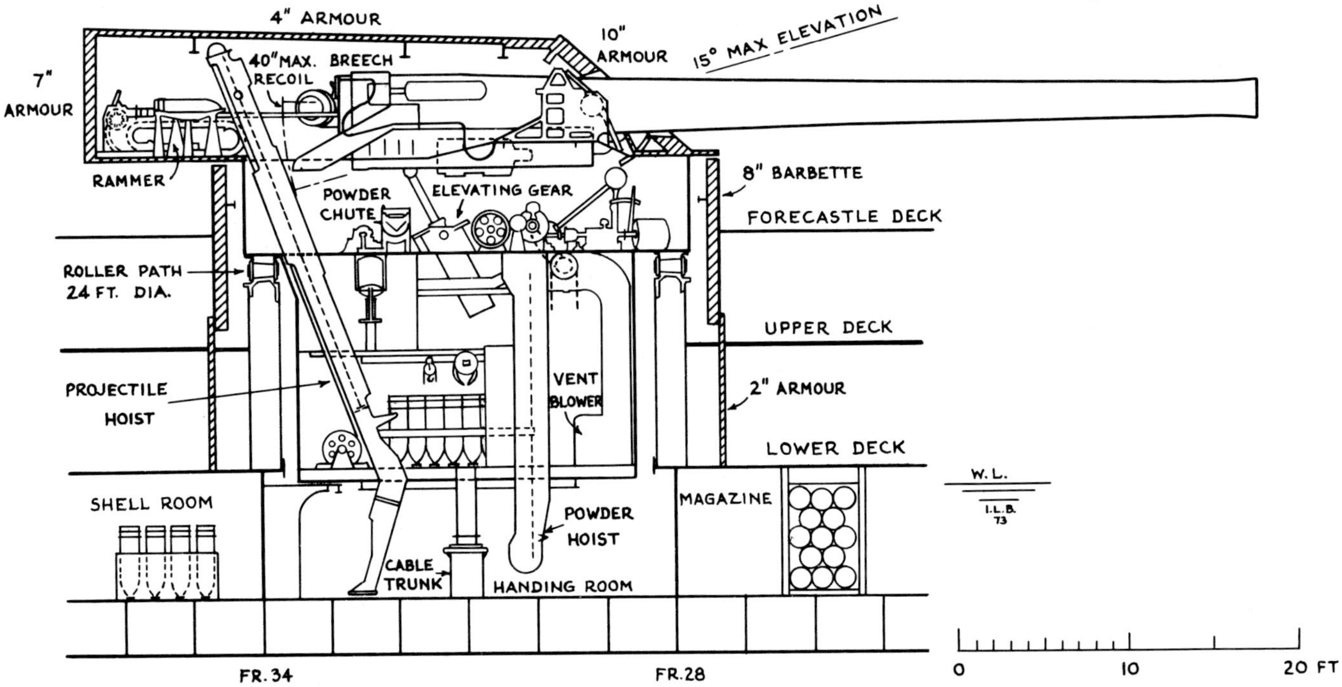

The Bethlehem-built 14-inch 45-calibre guns and four twin turrets intended for the Greek battlecruiser Salamis *followed the same basic arrangement as the U.S. Navy pattern in the* New York *class battleships. The arrangement differed appreciably from contemporary British practice: electrically instead of hydraulically worked, nitro-cellulose propellant ('powder' in U.S. parlance) in place of cordite, projectiles stowed and hoisted nose down (compared with horizontally) and fixed angle loading.*

one level to keep them below the waterline as far as possible. Further details of the 14-inch guns are given on p.188.

A light secondary armament of 3-inch or 4-inch guns was proposed, sited on the upper deck to repel torpedo craft. Four, later reduced to two, 12-pdr 18-cwt Q.F. guns[1] were therefore selected — a weapon normally mounted in the older battleships. Later, high-angle (H.A.) guns were added at the after end of the forecastle deck. Although their main target was expected to be airships and not aeroplanes, the designers were far-seeing in appreciating the conditions under which the monitors were likely to operate close to hostile shores exposed to air attack. The British monitor stands out as being one of the first warships to take aircraft into account at the design stage, with their two seaplanes, two H.A. guns and protected forecastle deck. The anti-aircraft (A.A.) weapon chosen was the new 3-inch 45-calibre gun but, owing to shortage of supply, alternative weapons were actually fitted as detailed later.

Although only local control was fitted for the secondary armament, the main guns had director control. The gunnery director was placed on the roof of the spotting top, which also contained the rangefinder. The director housed the gunlayer's and trainer's sights, whose movements were passed electrically to the layer and trainer in the turret. The system was similar to that being fitted in British capital ships but, as it had been designed primarily for direct fire at other ships, it was not entirely suitable for shore bombardment, where the target was usually invisible from the ship; nor was a transmitting station fitted. Consequently, new fire control techniques had to be developed as described in Chapter X, §7.

[1] In quick-firing guns, the propellant is contained in a brass cartridge case which forms the gas-tight seal at the breech.

§3 Construction

While full details of the monitors' design were being worked out, arrangements were being made to find suitable shipbuilders to undertake construction. Very wide building berths would be necessary for the beamy hulls but, because most ships of that period had breadths of about 40-60ft, only a few shipyards would be capable of building them. There were less than a dozen British shipbuilders who regularly built broad ships: capital ships and passenger liners.

Fisher called a meeting of all the important shipbuilders at the Admiralty on 11 November 1914 to allocate orders for his massive new construction programme, mostly destroyers and submarines, but also including the first monitors. None of the regular builders of large warships had a slipway free for the monitors, as they all had capital ships in hand already. One other major builder, Harland and Wolff (H. & W.) of Belfast, could offer quick delivery since, although they had full order books, their contracts for large vessels were all passenger liners. Since the outbreak of war, the passenger and emigrant trade had slumped disastrously with the threat of enemy sinkings of merchant ships, so shipowners were not pressing for delivery of their new tonnage. So H. & W. would be able to switch their resources to building monitors, even though they had not built a warship at Belfast since completing a number of

Admiral Farragut, *later* Abercrombie, *on 15 March 1915, a month before her launch at Belfast. The crane is lowering a 4-inch slab of the sloping side armour into place. In the left foreground, the stern of* General Grant *can be seen; in the background the pre-dreadnoughts* Mars *(left) and* Magnificent *(right) are about to have their turrets removed for the 12-inch monitors.*

gunboats in the 1870s. However in 1912, they had taken over the London & Glasgow Company's shipyard at Govan, Glasgow, which had recently built a number of cruisers and destroyers. H. & W. had a massive order book totalling 400,000 gross tons, mostly for passenger-cargo liners, spread between their Belfast and Clyde yards. Two of the orders were for the Belgian Red Star Line, a subsidiary of J. P. Morgan's giant shipping combine International Mercantile Marine, which also owned White Star Line. As Belgium had just been overrun by the Germans, including Red Star's home port of Antwerp, the company had little use for its 27,000-ton liner *Belgenland,* nearly ready for launching, and even less for its as yet unnamed 35,000-tonner which had been laid down earlier in the year. However not very much steel had been erected for this second vessel, H. & W.'s Number 469, so it would be possible to clear the 860ft × 99ft No. 2 slipway fairly quickly. H. & W.'s chairman Lord Pirrie could therefore offer to build two monitors; Fisher eagerly accepted. Thus were placed the orders for the first two monitor hulls, H. & W.'s Numbers 472 and 473.

Arrangements for the other two vessels took a few days longer. Nine shipbuilders were circulated with invitations to tender for the construction of either one or two monitors. Tenders were also invited from engine builders for the supply of twin screw steam reciprocating machinery. As a result, orders were placed on 21 November: one ship with Swan, Hunter & Wigham Richardson at Wallsend-on-Tyne, who also had had merchant ship orders suspended, the other with H. & W.'s Govan yard, to be numbered 476. Swan Hunter's large covered berth next to that on which the *Mauretania* had been built would be freed after the forthcoming launch of the cruiser *Comus,* so capacity was available to start work almost immediately on a monitor. The machinery contracts were also allocated: H. & W. were to build the machinery for their first two monitors at Belfast, while McKie & Baxter were to engine H. & W's third ship, their works at that time being near to the Govan yard. Swan Hunter received the machinery contract for their monitor, which was allocated to their Neptune Engine Works as No. 984, although the hull was to be built at the Wallsend yard as No. 991. H. & W.

arranged to build their engines with quadruple expansion, each set developing 1000 indicated horsepower (I.H.P.). The other two engine builders chose triple-expansion engines of slightly less power, 800 I.H.P. each for McKie & Baxter, 900 I.H.P. for Swan Hunter, as the Admiralty had not specified any precise power to be installed.

The ships were described as 'monitors' from the very beginning, so it was necessary to change the name of the destroyer *Monitor* then building at Thornycroft's to *Munster*. In the period before names were selected, the four monitors were identified by numbers only, *M.1* to *M.4*. Churchill, Fisher and Schwab used the codeword 'Styx' to describe the vessels in correspondence.

The urgency of construction was paramount. The builders were instructed by Fisher that there were to be "no fall-lalls or comforts of any kind", as it was not expected that the ships would survive long in their intended role of bombarding heavily defended coastlines. The first keel, *M.3* at Govan, was laid on 1 December and that of the last, *M.4* at Wallsend, on 17 December, the day after *Comus* was launched. The two Belfast ships, *M.1* and *M.2,* were laid down simultaneously on the same slipway, that on which the White Star liners *Olympic* and *Britannic* had been built. As virtually all work had ceased on merchant ship construction, it was possible for H. & W. to devote a large proportion of their resources to the monitors. Work went on round the clock seven days a week but, as they were still early days in a war which was not expected to last long, it was sometimes difficult to persuade the night-shift workers that the customary procedure of taking naps on the job was no longer appropriate. With the long hours of overtime, riveters were able to make £13 a week, compared with about £2 to £3 in normal times. Most of the hull was of simple construction, with much of the plating a standard ½-inch in thickness. Merchant ship quality fittings were used wherever possible, while only the quarterdeck was planked, all other exposed decks being bare or painted steel.

The monitors were allocated names in February 1915. In recognition of the United States being the source of

ESTIMATED COST OF A 14-INCH MONITOR

1. *Actual Cost Records for Swan Hunter's No. 991* (Roberts)			
Item	Tons	£/ton	£
High tensile steel plates	1182	10.02	11,852
Mild steel plates and sections	1979	7.01	13,880
Miscellaneous steel and rivets	227	15.50	3,515
Total purchased steel	3388		29,247
Labour on steel hull			31,567
Labour on outfitting			20,119
Outfit materials and subcontractors			21,131
Overhead charges			8,101
Total cost of hull to shipbuilder			110,165
2. *Estimated Costs for Other Items*			
Engines, boilers, auxiliaries and installation			33,000
Shipbuilder's profit margin on hull and machinery			15,000
Armour plating, belt, bulkheads etc.			43,000
Items of Admiralty supply, boats, small guns etc.			6,000
Admiralty overheads and incidentals			8,000
Total cost of ship excluding main armament			215,000
3. *Estimated Cost of Main Armament if Built in U.K.*			
Twin 14-inch mounting			85,000
Two 14-inch guns			26,000
Barbette armour			17,000
500 rounds of ammunition per gun			110,000
Total cost in U.K.			238,000
4. *Estimated Price of Armament Charged by Schwab (40% extra)*			335,000
5. *Estimated Total Cost of Monitor to the Admiralty*			550,000

General Grant *on 28 April 1915, the day before her launch. Her name was changed before completion to* M.2, *finally becoming* Havelock *in mid June. The full lines aft of the early monitors produced both a high resistance and a low propulsive efficiency. The mine-catcher wires can be seen underneath the bulge.*

General Grant*'s launch on 29 April 1915 provides an excellent view of the monitors' bulged hull form. As the monitor was built at the head of the same slipway as* Admiral Farragut, *the drag chains were placed well aft as seen in the photograph above, connected by wires running under the hull to the hawsepipes. The launch was the only occasion on which any of the early monitors achieved their designed speed of 10 knots!*

their main armament and the original *Monitor,* they were named after American Civil War leaders, *M.1 to M.4* becoming respectively: *Admiral Farragut* (originally just *Farragut*), *General Grant, Robert E. Lee* and *Stonewall Jackson.* The compliment was ill received. The U.S. Government was anxious to maintain its neutral status and to confine any shipments of war material to relatively minor items. A roundabout way of delivering Schwab's submarines had to be found, and these arrangements rather diverted attention from his other deal. The 14-inch guns were safely shipped across the Atlantic in British ships in February 1915. When the monitors were given names so unusual for British warships which drew attention to the origin of their armament, the Americans were indignant. After representations from the American Ambassador in London, the names were changed in May, as detailed later.

While construction of the hulls and machinery was progressing, arrangements were being made to erect the turrets in the monitors. Because of its proximity on the Tyne, Armstrong Whitworth's Elswick Ordnance Company (E.O.C.) were to erect *M.4*'s turret, while Coventry Ordnance Works (C.O.W.)[1] handled the three H. & W. ships, all under the supervision of Bethlehem staff. H. & W. and Swan Hunter tied for the launch of the first monitor; both *Admiral Farragut* and *Stonewall Jackson* were sent down the ways on 15 April 1915, just four months after their keels were laid, the other pair following a fortnight later. Such rapid construction constituted a remarkable achievement for the builders, especially as the monitors were launched in a relatively complete state. Most of the machinery, armour and superstructure was aboard, leaving only the final outfitting and the shipping of the armament to be done afloat.

With delivery of the ships so urgent, formalities were kept to a minimum. No detailed cost records exist in Admiralty files, apart from Churchill's estimate to the Cabinet in December 1914 of £2,207,000 for the four vessels, i.e. £551,750 each. From a few surviving records at Swan Hunter's, plus comparative cost rates for other ships of this period, it is possible to estimate the likely breakdown of total costs as shown in the Table. As Bethlehem have no record of the value of Schwab's deal, it is also necessary to estimate likely costs based on comparable ordnance. The cost of naval construction in the United States was about 25% higher than in Britain at this period, when the pound was worth about $4.87 and had a purchasing power about 10 to 12 times greater than the late 1970s. Schwab would certainly have demanded a substantial premium for his immediately available guns, possibly about 10-20%, so that total contract value per ship would have been about 40% above the equivalent British costs based on the comparable 13.5-inch gun, say about £335,000. Ammunition alone comprised nearly half the total, as not only was it necessary to buy about four outfits but nitrocellulose was an expensive propellant. The final probable cost of each 14-inch monitor to the British taxpayer of about £550,000 was thus close to Churchill's estimate.

§4 As Completed

Four weeks after launch, *Admiral Farragut* was the first big monitor to be commissioned, Captain H. M. Doughty assuming command on 12 May 1915. There were twelve officers in all: Captain, First Lieutenant cum Gunnery Officer ('First and G.'), Navigating Officer, two Lieutenants, Surgeon, Paymaster, Mate, Artificer Engineer, two Gunners and Shipwright. The last five were Warrant Officers, men of long experience promoted from the lower deck, most of whom had been standing by the ship for several weeks and preparing to receive the ship's full complement. The 186 ratings, largely reservists, were from Chatham, 89 in the Seaman branch, 45 Engine Room, 15 Artisans, 14 Stewards and Miscellaneous, together with 23 Royal Marines to man the secondary armament. The total complement of 198 for a ship carrying two big guns was in proportion to that of a battleship with about 900 to 1000 men for eight to ten big guns.

The crew quickly settled in to their somewhat spartan quarters. Conditions were similar to most R.N. ships — large communal mess-decks used for sleeping, eating and recreation. Each man had a place to sling his hammock, a space on the bench at the wooden tables and a small kit locker. Heating was by means of a small coal stove, ventilation by a mechanical supply fan with natural exhaust through hatches, skylights and sidelights. The officers were much better off for space; each had his own cabin, complete with portable bath, the Captain having a separate day cabin, sleeping cabin and bathroom. The Warrant Officers had a mess separate from the wardroom, as it was considered that their pay was too low for them to afford the additional expenses of wardroom messing.

Three days after commissioning, she was ready for her steam trials. The intention was to steam the ship at full power for four hours continuously and, during this time, make a number of runs up and down the measured mile in Belfast Lough. The trials were not a success. After $3^1/_2$ hours, the ship could only make about six knots in place of the designed ten, although developing 1864 I.H.P., not far short of the designed power. Such a poor result came as no surprise to Froude at A.E.W., who had predicted from the beginning that the performance would be bad. D'Eyncourt thought that the low speed might have been due to the bulge being so close to the surface or due to the trim of the ship in the trial condition. Froude was not impressed with these explanations and re-emphasised that the low speed was due to the steep buttock lines aft producing not only a high resistance but also a low propulsive efficiency, owing to the poor flow of water past the propellers.

While a 6-knot speed might just be sufficient to get along in fine weather, in bad weather, or with a heavily fouled hull, or against wind, tide or current, the ship would make little headway at all. The hull form could not

[1] C.O.W. was established in 1905 to enable a group of shipbuilders to compete with Vickers and Armstrong's, particularly on foreign contracts, by supplying armaments as well as hull, armour and machinery. Ownership was shared between John Brown, Cammell Laird and Fairfield. Naval mountings were built at Scotstoun, Glasgow, guns at Coventry.

now be altered, but two small changes could be made which might increase the speed a little. New propellers could be tried and the mine-catcher wires with their high drag removed. New propellers were therefore ordered with four blades of increased area compared with three, diameter reduced by three inches to 7ft 3in and pitch reduced by twelve inches to 7ft 6in, thus permitting the engines to run closer to their designed r.p.m. and reducing the propeller loading. After the wires were removed, a further trial on 22 May showed a slight increase of speed to about $6^1/_2$ knots. Other trials of the ship were also carried out: anchoring, turning, stopping, running astern, compasses. The all-important gun trials took place that same day, four rounds being fired from each 14-inch gun, with only a few minor defects appearing. After a further week of ammunitioning, storing and fitting temporary additional coal bunkers on the upper deck, H.M.S. *Admiral Farragut* was handed over by her builders and left Belfast on 29 May.

The other ships all commissioned within a fortnight of each other: *Stonewall Jackson* on 21 May under Captain P. N. Garnett, *General Grant* on 26 May under Commander G. Hamilton, and *Robert E. Lee* on 3 June under Captain C. D. S. Raikes. The last ship was actually commissioned as H.M.S. *M.3,* as on 31 May had come a directive from the Admiralty that the names were to be changed, as a result of American pressure. All four ships thus reverted to their original numbers, *M.1* to *M.4.* This change did not last long: it was appreciated that it was inappropriate for such large ships to be identified by numbers only. With King George V's approval, new names were selected on 19 June, this time of former British military leaders. *M.1,* late *Admiral Farragut,* became *Abercrombie,* named after Major-General Sir Ralph Abercromby of the Napoleonic era. This was the second use of the name for a British warship, perpetuating the mis-spelling first adopted on a third-rate of 1809. *M.2,* late *General Grant,* became *Havelock,* named after Major-General Sir Henry Havelock, a hero of the Indian Mutiny fighting. *M.3,* late *Robert E. Lee,* became first *Lord Raglan,* then on 23 June simply *Raglan,* named after Field-Marshal Lord Raglan, who had fought with Wellington and in the Crimea. *M.4,* late *Stonewall Jackson,* became *Earl Roberts,* shortened on 22 June to *Roberts,* named after Field-Marshal Earl Roberts, who had fought in nearly every campaign in the latter half of the 19th Century, and who had died only the previous year. During their lives, the ships were sometimes referred to erroneously as *Lord Raglan, Earl Roberts* or *Lord Roberts,* while the title *General* was likewise occasionally added to *Abercrombie* and *Havelock.*

The trial performance of the three later ships was also disappointing. *Havelock* managed 6.32 knots on 29 May but *Raglan,* who had now been fitted with higher powered engines by H. & W. (see p.42), produced the best performance of the class with 7.64 knots. *Roberts* had only been able to achieve 5.70 knots, handicapped by overpitched propellers.

Little official data has survived on the characteristics of the monitors as completed. Displacement, dimensions, armament, speed, stability and most technical features usually differ slightly from the designed figures, owing to changes during construction and to the difficulty of making fully detailed calculations from the limited information available at the design stage. The Technical Particulars list the details of the ships, distinguishing where possible between the 'designed' and 'completed' conditions. No record of the actual displacement as completed can be found in either Admiralty or builders' records, but it can be estimated from the drafts recorded in service that the deep displacement (i.e. fully loaded) was almost exactly as designed — about 6150 tons compared with 6157 tons with a full load of coal.

Although all the ships were intended to be identical, there were the usual minor differences between each vessel as completed. All except *Raglan* were fitted with two derricks at the after end of the forecastle deck for hoisting the seaplanes in and out. The aircraft were not aboard when the ships were completed and, to preserve secrecy, they were referred to on plans as 'boxes', with overall dimensions corresponding to their size with folded wings, 31ft long × 12ft wide × 13ft high — probably a Sopwith 807. All ships were initially fitted with the very tall topmasts needed to support the aerials of the long-range battleship-type wireless transmitter. The actual H.A. armament fitted was a single 3-pdr semi-automatic and one of the new 2-pdr pom-poms, each on specially designed H.A. mountings.

§5 The Deployment of the First Monitors

The first large monitors had been conceived and ordered in great haste without any detailed plans being made for their employment. Fisher's original intention had been to use them for his Baltic plan but Churchill regarded the North Sea area or the Dardanelles as more promising. By January 1915, it was clear that there were very serious dangers in the Baltic scheme, not least from mines, while nothing could be done until the High Seas Fleet had been neutralised. A memorandum prepared by Churchill on 27 January 1915 included the following paragraph:[1]

> "Between the beginning of April and the end of July we shall also receive 14 heavily armoured, shallow draft Monitors; 2 armed with two 15-inch guns, 4 armed with two 14-inch guns, and 8 armed with two 12-inch guns. These last 8 will be armed by taking the turrets out of 4 of the *Majestics.* It is this force which it is proposed to use for special services and for bombarding as may be necessary from time to time in furtherance of objects of great strategic and political importance, among which the following may be specifically mentioned:—
>
> 1. The operations at the Dardanelles;
> 2. The support of the left flank of the Army;
> 3. The bombardment of Zeebrugge; and later on
> 4. The seizure of Borkum."

The priorities listed reflected the current military and political situation. It was already evident to Churchill that the stalemate on the Western Front in France was likely to continue indefinitely. A strongly defended line

[1] *The World Crisis 1915* by W. S. Churchill, p.161

In this rare view of Raglan *being towed past Clydebank on 21 June 1915 after having left H. & W's Govan yard, she is still bearing the name* M.3 *(on the quarter, not visible in this view), although she had already been renamed* Lord Raglan *that very day, before becoming plain* Raglan *on 23 June. The essential simplicity of the early monitors' design is apparent. The destroyer* Moon, *recently completed by Yarrow's, is overtaking.*

was held from neutral Switzerland to the Belgian Coast. With the high losses resulting from frontal attacks, it was vital to turn one of the enemy's flanks. Long before the entry of Turkey into the war in early November 1914, Churchill had appreciated that the Dardanelles, the gateway to Constantinople (now Istanbul), would be a key objective. The rewards for the seizure of this strategic waterway would be many, including the opening of a direct supply route to the ally Russia, the relief of Turkish pressure on the Suez Canal and a favourable influence on the Balkan states.

Compared with the prize of the Dardanelles, the support of the Army's left flank was of secondary importance. Useful work had been done by the makeshift bombarding fleet of October-December 1914 and this work could be continued, provided that the German shore defences did not become too strong. The bombardment of Zeebrugge and Ostende was desirable to discourage their use as advanced bases for German destroyers and U-boats, although there was little possibility of backing up the operations by landings at that time. The seizure of Borkum could be considered when the necessary naval and military forces had become available, although an attempt to capture and retain the island as a forward base against strong German opposition would be a most hazardous undertaking.

The Dardanelles scheme was officially approved in January and the campaign began on 19 February with a naval bombardment of the Turkish forts by British and French ships, which included the newly completed battleship *Queen Elizabeth.* A major naval offensive was launched on 18 March to try to force a passage; some progress was made for the loss of three pre-dreadnoughts from mines. As with so many WW1 operations, the opportunities were not followed up. No Army landing was made nor any sustained naval attack continued while the Turkish defences were still weak. It was not until 25 April that troops were landed on the Gallipoli peninsula, with gunfire support from the warships. The Army was able to make little progress ashore in the very difficult conditions; it became clear that additional forces were required. Churchill telegraphed Vice-Admiral John M. de Robeck, the Allied Fleet commander, on 12 May:[1]

> "Two more infantry divisions with other reinforcements leave about 17th and 30th. Meanwhile arrival of German submarines in Turkish waters makes it undesirable to expose *Queen Elizabeth.* We are therefore sending you at once instead *Exmouth* and *Venerable,* and also, before the end of the month, the first two new monitors, *Admiral Farragut* and *Stonewall Jackson,* with 2 14-inch guns apiece, an effective range of 20,000 yards, firing a 1,400-pd high-explosive shell, 10-feet draught, and special bulges against mine and torpedo. You will be able to use the two monitors much more freely for all purposes, as they have been specially built for this work."

Kitchener and the Army were disturbed at the prospect of losing the support of the *Queen Elizabeth,* but Fisher was adamant that she should be brought home, especially after the news was received that the pre-dreadnought *Goliath* had been torpedoed in the Dardanelles that same day. The monitors were expected to be able to play a valuable role, not least because they were considered

Abercrombie *anchored at Kephalo on the island of Imbros, soon after her arrival at the Dardanelles. Wind scoops are visible in the scuttles to improve ventilation below decks. The remains of the painted false bow wave can still be seen.*

relatively expendable, both in support of Army operations and in forcing a passage of the Dardanelles. Loss of a monitor would have less psychological effect than loss of a battleship, even though an obsolete pre-dreadnought.

The anticipated departure date was optimistic; the monitors were not ready until well into June. Churchill was determined that they should be used to the fullest extent. On 14 May, he minuted:[2]

> "The following nine heavy monitors should go in succession to the Dardanelles, as soon as they are ready:— *Admiral Farragut, General Grant, Stonewall Jackson, Robert E. Lee, Lord Clive, Prince Rupert, Sir John Moore, General Craufurd,* and *Marshal Ney.* The first six of the 9.2-inch monitors should also go, unless the Admiral [de Robeck] chooses to have two of their guns for work on shore, in which case the first four only will go."

The first four named carried two 14-inch guns, the next four two 12-inch and *Ney* two 15-inch, while the 9.2-inch were small monitors with a single gun. In addition, the four old *Edgar* class cruisers were to go — *Edgar, Endymion, Grafton* and *Theseus* — each now carrying twelve 6-inch and fitted with bulges. Against this fleet of well protected vessels, the U-boats would be less of a menace.

During the preceding weeks, Fisher had become increasingly opposed to any extension of the Dardanelles operation, including anything involving the vessels intended for his specially created Baltic fleet. Disagreements between Churchill and Fisher had been building up for some time and matters came to a head on 15 May, when Fisher resigned. Churchill and others tried to dissuade him, but the old man was determined. A train of political changes was set off; Churchill was forced out as First Lord and was succeeded by Arthur J. Balfour on 25 May. There followed a dangerous hiatus between Fisher's resignation and the settling-in of the new Government in June, when the whole question of reinforcing the Dardanelles had to be reconsidered. On 7 June, it was agreed to send a monitor fleet: the four 14-inch vessels, together with eleven small monitors and a number of other vessels.

§6 At the Dardanelles

Now that the despatch of the monitors had been finally agreed, additional preparations had to be made for the 3000-mile voyage. *Abercrombie* had to be drydocked at Avonmouth — which had one of the few graving docks sufficiently wide to take her — to have her new propellers fitted. She then undertook a full power trial in Milford Haven on 6 June, making 7.04 knots — a gain in speed of about one knot. Further work at Pembroke included the replacement of her underpowered steering gear and the loading of the 170 tons of coal into the temporary bunkers. She sailed on 24 June for the Dardanelles, with *Theseus* giving her a tow to speed her up. After *Havelock* had also got modified propellers, she departed from Pembroke on 30 June, assisted by a tow from the old cruiser *Juno.* After a call at Plymouth, *Roberts* was taken in tow by *Endymion* on 28 June, while *Raglan* also left that same day from Pembroke in tow of the old cruiser *Diana. Abercrombie* arrived on 12 July at the main British naval base in the fine natural harbour of Mudros on the Greek island of Lemnos, some 50 miles west of the Dardanelles (see map on p.111).

The monitors' arrival was particularly welcome to the troops at Gallipoli. For several weeks, U-boats had made it dangerous to expose heavy ships to give close support bombardment to supplement the Army's limited

[1] *The World Crisis 1915,* p.347
[2] *The World Crisis 1915,* p.355

artillery, but now it became possible to deploy extremely powerful guns without the same risk of loss. *Abercrombie* was inspected by de Robeck shortly after her arrival at the anchorage at Kephalo on the south-east corner of the island of Imbros. Although barely ten miles from Cape Helles (see map on p.34), the south-western point of the Gallipoli peninsula, Kephalo was just out of range of the Turkish batteries on the mainland. The same day she hoisted Rear-Admiral Nicholson's flag, the commander of the supporting forces, and fired her first 12 rounds at the enemy. Her targets were Turkish ammunition dumps at Eren Keui on the Asiatic shore of the Dardanelles, but no hits were reported after the 50-minute bombardment. The Turks were not slow to reply; a 150-mm (5.9-inch) shell hit *Abercrombie*'s quarterdeck, penetrating the Captain's cabin, fortunately without exploding.

Roberts arrived on 15 July and was allocated to bombard the batteries on the Asiatic side of the Dardanelles which were severely harrassing the British and French troops on the European side. As the slowest monitor, she was anchored on the 23rd south of Rabbit Island (Mavro Island), four miles from the Turkish coastline. Hidden behind the island's cliffs, she and one of the small monitors engaged the enemy at leisure protected by anti-submarine nets, with aiming marks erected on the island and connected by telephone to the Naval Observation Station on shore at Cape Helles. She continued in this stationary role for five months, suffering the occasional minor shell hit and bombing attack by enemy aircraft. However, de Robeck had warned General Sir Ian Hamilton, commanding the Allied Armies, not to expect too much:[1]

> "The presence of naval monitors at Rabbit Island will no doubt assist a little to neutralise the Asiatic batteries, but owing to the distance involved (18,000 yards) large guns with a consequent small supply of ammunition will be required, and it is not to be expected that direct hits will be obtained; moreover it will not be possible to reach the batteries beyond In Tepe."

Meanwhile both *Havelock* and *Raglan* arrived on 22 July and were quickly in action. The Army reinforcement programme culminated in the Suvla Bay landings on 6-7 August, which were supported by the monitors, large and small, and the bulged cruisers. During the simultaneous offensive from Anzac just to the south, *Havelock* was assigned to deal with any enemy ships that might fire from the Narrows, while *Abercrombie* and *Raglan* were further south firing at Krithia village and the heights of Achi Baba, where large numbers of Turkish troops and guns were ranged against the British Helles position. The guns were mobile and difficult targets amongst the smoke and dust of the bombardments, as only a direct hit would silence them completely. *Abercrombie* did manage to hit one Turkish redoubt, which according to an eye-witness sent "whole Turks whirling in the air". Most of the fire in direct support of the Allied troops came from the cruisers *Bacchante, Endymion, Grafton* and *Theseus,* backed up by the small monitors. On one unfortunate occasion, one of *Raglan*'s guns went off prematurely whilst still at a low elevation and the shell landed amongst British troops, killing one man and wounding three. Such episodes had occurred before the monitors arrived and discouraged the Army from calling on the full weight of naval bombardment support available.

Havelock moved into Suvla Bay on 8 August to give closer support, firing occasionally and with a clear view of the fighting ashore. On the 12th, she was hit four times by Turkish shells, three men being injured. During the Suvla landings, the large monitors had fired 138 rounds of 14-inch H.E. (high explosive) in two days. Such a rate of expenditure was considered excessive for the available

Roberts *arriving at Malta on 10 July 1915 on her way to the Dardanelles. The planked-in parts of the upper deck housed temporary coal bunkers.*

targets and the limited stocks of ammunition. Thereafter the monitors' big guns were ordered to be used only with the Senior Officer's permission against specific targets out of range of other guns and when spotting conditions were favourable. Generally, Army forward observation posts on shore were used for spotting, but aircraft and balloon spotting were also being experimented with. An officer from the firing ship would often be embarked in the aircraft, although it was some time before effective wireless communications and spotting code procedures were developed. Although the monitors were designed to carry two spotting seaplanes, they rarely ever carried even one, as the shore-based Royal Naval Air Service (R.N.A.S.) aircraft were found to be more suitable. During September, *Roberts* embarked a Short 166 seaplane, which was quite effective, although there were problems as the plane had to be hoisted off whenever the guns were fired, to avoid blast damage. On one occasion, *Abercrombie* experimented with a Sopwith Schneider. *Raglan* also embarked a Short 166 for several days for her bombardment in company with small monitors of enemy lines of communication and flour mills near Gallipoli town on 12 October. The weather turned out too poor for successful spotting and it proved difficult to handle the seaplane on board and in the water.

The monitors usually anchored close offshore for their bombardments, using aiming marks on the rocky coastline. In these exposed positions, they were vulnerable to return fire from the Turkish batteries

[1] Public Record Office (P.R.O.) file ADM 137/177

This view of Roberts *shows her with a Short 166 embarked with wings folded, as planned in the original monitor design. The seaplane was however only carried for a short period during September 1915. The three bands of the funnel identify the monitor as* Roberts. *Awnings are spread over the ammunitioning derricks, presumably as a form of shelter.*

between Suvla and Helles. Fortunately the Turks were not very good shots and their shells prone to be duds. By keeping nearly all the monitors' crews under cover, the shell hits caused little injury. On 8 September, *Abercrombie* was hit several times by 75-mm (2.95-inch) shells, which damaged a winch and severed rigging. *Roberts* was hit on two occasions in October, the first time on the forecastle, the second on the port bulge. Fragments of one of the shells showed that it was a 4.7-inch made by Bethlehem Steel in 1910, indicating that Schwab's munitions were now being used by both sides.

The Suvla landings were not followed up with vigour ashore and failed to break the stalemate, although a link was made with the Anzac position to the south. The Allied troops were thus confined to two small areas, unable to break past the dominating ridges to the Narrows to open the way for the ships. With the decline in demand for heavy gun support following the landings, it was possible to review the monitors' performance to date. De Robeck reported to the Admiralty:[1]

> "Each class of monitor has her own particular trouble; 14", the steering engines are too weak; 9.2", the exhaust fumes in the funnel; 6", weakness of decks under the guns; but they are mostly being successfully dealt with by *Reliance,* where Engineer-Captain Humphreys is worth his weight in gold and never makes a difficulty. We must not expect too much from these monitors, especially the 14", which could not navigate the Dardanelles without tugs, so the question of forcing the Narrows with monitors is, I am afraid, for the present not a workable proposition."

A Special Squadron for bombardment was organised, with the First Division comprising the four 14-inch monitors; the Second the ten small 9.2-inch monitors *M.15* to *M.23* and *M.28*; the Third the six 6-inch monitors *M.29* to *M.33* (see Chapter VII) plus the ex-Brazilian river monitor *Humber*, and the Fourth the four bulged cruisers. Over the remaining months of 1915, *Abercrombie* continued to support the left flank of the Helles position, generally firing against the Turkish redoubts on the northern slopes of Achi Baba, which were hidden from shore artillery fire. *Roberts* remained off Rabbit Island, while *Havelock* made an occasional bombardment of the Narrows, firing right over the peninsula. Her bombardment of the iron foundries at Chanak (now Cannakale) from 17,000 yards on 3 October was quite successful: 15 rounds in 45 minutes, 11 reported hits, two missed short and two duds. In reply, 33 rounds were fired at her, which included four hits by 12-pdr shells. With practice, all the ships greatly improved their bombardment performance, the large monitors eventually proving themselves good platforms for firing accurately close to Allied troops. During all these operations, none of the monitors were attacked by U-boat, an immunity partly due to the extensive use of anti-submarine nets at their anchorages.

Separate suggestions by Churchill and by Commodore Roger Keyes, de Robeck's Chief of Staff, to use a fleet of old battleships and monitors to force the Dardanelles were turned down by the Admiralty; not only were the losses of 18 March too well remembered, but the monitors' slow speed and poor manoeuvrability would give them little chance of getting past the Turkish forts. No further attempts were made to use the monitors in other than a purely harrassing role at Gallipoli, a modest enough contribution compared with Churchill's original ambitious plans for devastating the Turkish defences and breaking into the Sea of Marmara.

Meanwhile, in an effort to assist Serbia, British and French troops had landed at Salonika (now Thessaloniki) in October, Bulgaria already having thrown in her lot with the Central Powers. *Raglan* spent a month with the British squadron at Salonika from 14 November, but there was little for her to do there. At the same time, *Havelock* and *M.18* were at Milo in the southern Aegean from 22 November, where a number of ships was being held ready to put pressure on Greece not to interfere with Allied operations, if the political situation so demanded. By this time, the monitors' firing had improved to the point where VIII Army Corps at Helles could signal on 16 November:[2]

> "The Corps Commander wishes me to express to you his appreciation of the excellent shooting of the cruiser and monitors yesterday [*Edgar, Abercrombie* and *Havelock*], which undoubtedly contributed very largely to the ease with which our troops seized two very important positions in the enemy's line and added enormously to the moral effect and material damage done to the enemy. All who saw it agree as to the accuracy and value of the

[1] *Winston S. Churchill,* Volume III, by M. Gilbert, p.542

[2] Quoted by Captain E. Altham in "Monitors in Modern Naval Warfare", *Journal of the Royal United Services Institution,* November 1923

monitors' fire, but the chief point is that it has been established that co-operation in an attack has now become a practical reality, and that a system has been established which with further development will prove a powerful factor both in attack and defence."

Abercrombie's firing was also commended unofficially by one of the naval observers ashore, "You have, I think, got the best shooting monitor out here (between ourselves that is)". On *Raglan*, another officer's comment was less complimentary, "*Raglan* in his usual inconsequential fashion dropped half a dozen shell anywhere on the same continent as Krithia."

All four 14-inch monitors, the two 12-inch which had just arrived (*Sir Thomas Picton* and *Earl of Peterborough*, see p.59), plus most of the small monitors were concentrated off the Dardanelles in December, after it had been decided to evacuate the Gallipoli peninsula, starting with the northern positions at Suvla and Anzac. *Havelock* took over *Roberts'* Rabbit Island berth on 16 December, while the latter retired to Mudros having fired about 150 rounds since July, some of them at a range of 22,000 yards requiring the ship to be heeled about five degrees by flooding the bulges on one side to increase the guns' elevation. The other four large monitors supported the diversionary attacks being made on the Turkish lines at Helles; their powerful guns wrought a heavy execution on the Turkish counterattacks. The monitors did not escape unscathed; *Raglan* was hit six times on 17 December but was only slightly damaged. The evacuation of Suvla and Anzac went off without the loss of a single man, being completed on the night of 19/20 December.

At the end of the month, it was decided to evacuate the remaining position at Helles early in the New Year, so all six large monitors again foregathered. *Roberts, Peterborough, Picton, M.18* and *M.31* were stationed at Rabbit Island in early January to neutralise the Turkish Asiatic batteries. *Raglan* and *Havelock* were with the reserve squadron at Imbros ready to move up in close support off Helles as necessary, while *Abercrombie* was in her usual position off the left flank. An unexpectedly heavy Turkish attack was launched on the British lines on 7 January, supported by fire from across the Dardanelles. *Abercrombie, Havelock, Raglan* and *Peterborough,* together with three bulged cruisers and several destroyers, moved in to pour a heavy fire onto the Turkish lines and the Asiatic batteries. The ships amply compensated for the previous withdrawal of a high proportion of the Army's artillery, the attack being beaten off with many Turkish casualties. The evacuation was completed on the night of 8/9 January 1916 with the loss of only one man, although a considerable amount of stores had to be abandoned.

Roberts *fires at the Turkish batteries on the Asiatic shore of the Dardanelles from her berth at Rabbit Island. She is heeled to starboard to increase gun elevation and maximum range. The left gun is just recoiling after firing, while the right gun appears to have already been reloaded.*

Thus ended the only major Allied attempt to make a decisive thrust away from the stalemate of the Western Front. Despite Churchill's high hopes for the monitors, plans for forcing the Dardanelles by sea were not really practicable by the time the ships were ready. There was very little more that they could have done beyond their purely supporting role from July 1915 onwards, and even this was limited until bombarding technical efficiency had been built up.

§7 The Rest of the War

With the withdrawal from Gallipoli, there was no need to keep six large monitors in the Mediterranean. Accordingly, after final bombardments of the Turkish and Bulgarian coastlines, *Roberts* (the slowest monitor) and *Havelock* (the most junior C.O.) were sent back to Britain. Both ships departed from Mudros on 14 February, under tow by a collier most of the way, and arrived at Portsmouth during April for overhaul.

The Lowestoft Raid by German battlecruisers on 24 April aroused public indignation over the vulnerability of our East Coast towns, but it was very difficult for the Royal Navy to defend the lengthy British coastline against such 'hit-and-run' operations, with the major Fleet bases far away to the north. However Balfour was able to write to the Mayors of Lowestoft and Yarmouth in a letter also published in *The Times* of 10 May 1916, assuring them that steps were being taken to discourage such raids by redistributing naval forces. In addition to moving some pre-dreadnoughts and cruisers further south, "submarines and monitors, which form no portion of the Grand Fleet, are now available in growing numbers for coast defence". In consequence, *Havelock* and *Roberts* were ordered to Lowestoft and Yarmouth respectively as guardships at these patrol craft bases. The only alternative deployment for them would have been off the Belgian Coast, but their 14-inch guns would have been even further outranged than were the 12-inch monitors' guns by this time. *Havelock* arrived on 14 May, securing in the Hamilton Dock just north of the harbour entrance. Here she remained until the end of the war, apart from a short drydocking in the big 32,000-ton Admiralty floating dock in the Tyne in July 1917. Although her anti-aircraft guns were occasionally in action, there was little for her to do, except for endless drills, the occasional target practice firing and a few false alarms.

Roberts' subsequent career was hardly more exciting.

In an effort to reassure public opinion after the Lowestoft Raid in April 1916, journalists are shown round Havelock, *moored as a floating battery in the Hamilton Dock at Lowestoft. One 14-inch gun is at the maximum 15° elevation. The unsuitability of the conning tower for navigation is evident; the searchlight platform has been built up to serve as a bridge, with splinter protection visible.*

She arrived at Gorleston at the entrance to Yarmouth harbour on 27 May 1916. Her new C.O. was Commander K. G. B. Dewar, a clear-thinking but outspoken gunnery specialist who was none too pleased with his new static command. She was camouflaged at her moorings so that from a distance she merged with the background. Searchlight and observation posts were set up on shore, so that good bearings and range could be obtained on any attacking ships. The posts were linked by telephone to the ship, which was always at short notice for fire. On 28 November, the Zeppelin *L.21* passed close overhead, so that *Roberts'* new 6-inch H.A. was able to get off two or three rounds. Shortly afterwards, *L.21* came down in flames, but the credit belonged to the pursuing fighters. During June 1917, *Roberts* was drydocked in the Tyne and then moved to the Thames Estuary. She joined the monitor squadron which was preparing for the Great Landing, as a reserve vessel (see p.54). She returned to Yarmouth in October, where she remained until the end of the war, apart from a refit at Portsmouth in July 1918. Although she came to "Action Stations", she had no opportunity to open fire during the minor German raid on the East Coast on 14 January 1918.

The two monitors remaining in the Mediterranean had a more varied life. In early 1916, the Admiralty orders for the Aegean Squadron were "to watch the Dardanelles, and safeguard Greek islands in our occupation, to maintain the blockade and submarine patrols in the Aegean, and to support the Army at Salonica".[1] In the weeks following the evacuation of Gallipoli, *Abercrombie* continued to be based on Imbros, now an almost deserted island, whence she could harrass Turkish troops picking over the abandoned stores on the peninsula. She made occasional bombardments of Turkish shipping lying in the Narrows and generally kept the Turkish batteries on their toes, but there were few worthwhile targets.

Abercrombie also formed part of the squadron at Kephalo detailed to prevent a break-out by the German battlecruiser *Goeben,* which initially included pre-dreadnoughts such as *Russell.* She was anchored out of sight behind cliffs, her guns trained over the land towards the Dardanelles entrance. Fire control depended on shore spotting stations and she had to remain ready to open fire at short notice, even though her H.E. projectiles would be of limited value against an armoured ship. In May 1916, she sailed to Malta for a well earned rest, refit and drydocking, then returned to Imbros and a quiet life through the hot summer months. She sailed north on 5 October to bombard the railway line connecting Constantinople to the Salonika front, which had already been the target for the small monitors twelve months earlier (see p.108) and for *Raglan* and *Havelock* in January. She anchored with *M.32* off the small Bulgarian port of Dedeagatch (now Greek Alexandroupolis), taking her time to select aiming marks and organise the spotting aircraft. The resulting fire was very accurate from a range of about 18,000 yards. The fifth round was a direct hit on the rail switch at Bodoma Junction a few miles inland, the mean error of the 17 rounds fired being only about 20 yards. This was one of the last large shoots that *Abercrombie* carried out; she had already fired over 500 rounds of 14-inch in about 15 months.

The remainder of her time was spent in a variety of places in the Aegean with the various Detached Squadrons (see p.109), generally for a few weeks at a time. For the closing months of 1916, she was at Port Iero in the island of Mitylene (now Lesbos) with ships blockading Smyrna (now Izmir) and the Turkish coast. The Squadron also tried to keep the Turks at a high pitch of readiness in expectation of another landing, as well as discouraging the use of the ports as submarine bases. She returned to Kephalo early in 1917 to the *Goeben* watch. In April she went north to Stavros, 40 miles east of Salonika at the north-west corner of the Gulf of Strimon, on the right flank of the Allied Balkan front. As Lieutenant-Commander L. A. W. Spooner, her 'First and G.', later wrote, "This was a most peaceful war zone, and it seemed a great pity to disturb it by bombardment". So *Abercrombie* fired only a few rounds before departing for refit at Malta in May 1917. She returned to Stavros, staying until September, and then pottered around the islands off the Turkish coast — Samos, Imbros, Mitylene, Khios — until January 1918. After the loss of *Raglan* (see §8), she became the only large monitor available to support the Salonika front, so she spent virtually the whole of 1918 at Stavros, making brief visits to Mudros for bunkers and rest. At the end of August, she was near-missed by the U-boat which torpedoed *Endymion,* although the cruiser's bulges saved her from sinking. She returned to Mudros after the Bulgarian Armistice on 29 September, until Turkey also

[1] *Naval Operations,* Volume IV, by J. S. Corbett and H. Newbolt, p.128

The view shows a number of the ships of the Aegean Squadron used to blockade the Turkish coast anchored at Port Iero on Mitylene. In the nearest row are Triad, *the C-in-C's H.Q. ship, left, and* M.22 *(probably) right. In the next row are* Roberts, *left, and* Canopus, *right. Behind* Canopus *is* Raglan, *while the two small vessels furthest off are probably* M.16 *and* M.30. *Although the original photograph is undated, study of the logs of the ships present puts it at between 26 and 29 January 1916.*

surrendered. On Armistice Day, 11 November 1918, she joined the Allied Fleet steaming up the Dardanelles and she anchored off Chanak, unmolested by the batteries she had been bombarding over the preceding years.

Abercrombie's war was over; she had been the hardest worked of all the 14-inch monitors. Although it had not been possible to put into effect the ambitious plans of her creators, she had performed much useful service in her shore bombardment role and, in her patrol work, she had relieved vessels which could be better employed elsewhere.

Raglan's last two years were rather more exciting than *Abercrombie*'s. In February and March 1916, she enlivened the Mitylene patrols with bombardments of Smyrna and the Turkish west coast, supporting the small monitors off Long Island (see p.108). She transferred to the Salonika front in April and occasionally fired a few rounds at targets on the Bulgarian coastline, sometimes setting fire to crops. Kitchener's nephew, Viscount Broome, took command in May. After a refit at Malta, she returned to Imbros in October, taking over the *Goeben* watch from *Abercrombie*. In December, she relieved *Peterborough* at Stavros and continued to support the Allied Armies ashore, occasionally being fired on or attacked by aircraft but without result. From this time on, there were only two large monitors out of the original six in the Aegean, so they concentrated on the Imbros and Stavros patrols, backed up by small monitors.

Raglan remained on watch off the Dardanelles for several months in mid 1917, interspersed with bombardments of the Turkish coastal batteries around Smyrna. She moved to Port Said in September, where she prepared to assist General Edmund Allenby's forthcoming offensive from Egypt against the Turks in southern Palestine. A Short 184 spotter from the seaplane carrier *City of Oxford* was embarked on top of her 14-inch turret, when she joined the other ships at the anchorage of Deir el Belah, nine miles south-west of Gaza. A naval feint attack was to be made north of Gaza, while the main Army thrust was to be inland at Beersheba. On 30 October, *Raglan* began to bombard the railway station and bridge four miles inland at Deir Seneid, while four of the small monitors tackled other targets as described on p.112. The bombardment continued on and off for a week, as the land attack pushed forward. An ammunition dump was exploded, bridges hit and the supply railway damaged. As the Turkish line broke and fell back northwards, *Raglan* moved up to Askalon in support but, as the Army penetrated inland, possible targets were soon out of range of her guns. She spent the next few weeks at Port Said

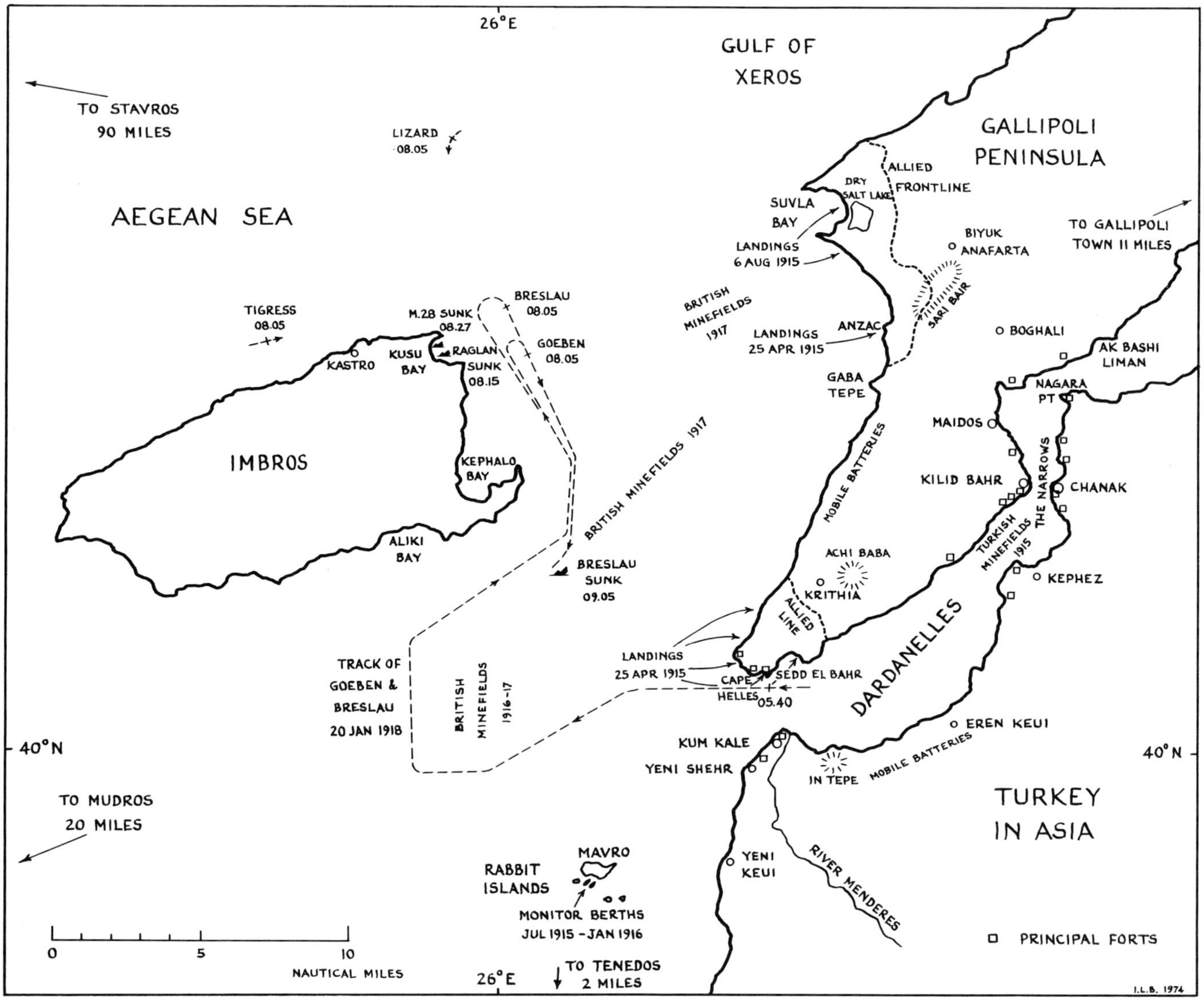

The map of the Dardanelles shows the area of operations of the large and small monitors during the First World War. The whole of the Aegean area is shown on the map on p.111.

before returning to her old base at Imbros. According to the direction of the prevailing weather and the harrassing gunfire from the Turkish batteries, she moved between the netted anchorages at Kephalo, Aliki on the south coast and Kusu on the north-east coast of Imbros.

§8 The Loss of RAGLAN and M.28

The German battlecruiser *Goeben* and the light cruiser *Breslau* had been bottled up above the Dardanelles since taking refuge in Constantinople in August 1914. Although given Turkish names — *Yavuz Sultan Selim* and *Midilli* respectively — the German crew members remained on board, and several sorties were made into the Black Sea. The British had taken precautions against a sortie into the Mediterranean by these two vessels, which included the laying of extensive minefields off the Dardanelles from April 1916 onwards. Towards the end of 1917, there were indications that such a sortie might be made, although it was thought that it would be preceded by minesweeping, thus giving sufficient warning to permit concentration of superior British forces. The ships available included the 12-inch pre-dreadnoughts *Lord Nelson* and *Agamemnon* based at Mudros, together with three cruisers, destroyers and supporting forces, usually including *Abercrombie* or *Raglan* as well as small monitors.

Following her bombardments off Palestine, *Raglan* had returned to Imbros on 26 December 1917, anchoring frequently in Kusu Bay, 15 miles from the entrance to the Dardanelles and out of range of the batteries on Cape Helles. Together with the small 9.2-inch monitor *M.28,* four destroyers and other vessels, she formed the Second Detached Squadron of the Aegean Squadron.

In January 1918, highly secret preparations were being made for *Goeben* and *Breslau* to attack British ships in their Aegean bases and to destroy any vessels on patrol. In the half-light of the early morning of 20 January, the two ships slipped out of the Dardanelles. The lookouts on

Mavro Island (see map) failed to spot the enemy ships in the poor visibility before sunrise on that misty winter Sunday morning. Half an hour later when they were ten miles to the westward, *Goeben* struck a mine; the Germans had misjudged the full extent of the minefields. However her damage was not serious so, after seeing that the Aliki anchorage was empty, the two ships turned north up the east coast of Imbros, bombarding the wireless station at Kephalo on the way. The destroyer *Lizard,* patrolling north-east of Imbros, was the first to sight them at 07.20, *Breslau* steaming ahead of *Goeben.* Owing to enemy wireless jamming, it was several minutes before she could get in visual contact with *Raglan* and flash "GOBLO", the signal that *Goeben* was out. Almost simultaneously, *Raglan* sighted the ships herself, as did the net drifters and shore lookouts. At 07.35, *Raglan* managed to get off a wireless message to *Agamemnon* at Mudros, passed on to Rear-Admiral, Aegean, A. Hayes-Sadler at Salonika, where he had unwisely taken his flagship *Lord Nelson* four days earlier.

Meantime *Raglan* came to "Action Stations" and started raising steam on her second boiler. Her twin 14-inch turret and single 6-inch trained round to port but withheld their fire temporarily, as it was thought that she might not have been spotted by *Breslau* against the background of cliffs. It was a forlorn hope; after some well-directed shots to prevent *Lizard* from launching torpedoes, *Breslau*'s first salvo of 150-mm (5.9-inch)[1] from 10,000 yards crashed into the sea 1000 yards short of *Raglan.* The latter's 6-inch then opened fire in local control, the first round missing. *Breslau*'s second salvo was 500 yards short, but by this time *Raglan*'s 14-inch had opened fire, the single round falling astern of the German. *Breslau*'s third salvo landed 400 yards over but with a very small spread of shot. In *Raglan,* a correction was applied before firing the second round but it too missed. *M.28* also opened fire with her 9.2-inch at a range of 11,500 yards.

Breslau's fourth salvo included a lucky shot that hit *Raglan*'s spotting top, killing the Gunnery Officer, wounding Broome and wrecking the control gear. Now that *Breslau* had the range, she began firing rapid salvoes, knocking out the 6-inch ammunition supply party. The engine room was hit twice, putting all telephones and lights out and damaging the port engine. Before running out of ready-use ammunition, the 6-inch got off seven rounds, one of which was reported by the drifters to have hit *Breslau* and another *Goeben,* but German accounts mention no damage. The latter ship had just appeared round the southern headland of Kusu Bay to add her 280-mm and 150-mm fire.[2] On board *Raglan* attempts were being made to get the 14-inch turret into local control. Just as the guns were reloaded, a 280-mm shell from *Goeben* penetrated the barbette armour on the port side below *Raglan*'s turret and ignited the charges in the hand-ups. Although the flash did not reach the magazine, several of the turret's crew were killed, the impression being that one of the guns had burst. The survivors escaped out of the back of the turret, including the First Lieutenant. The latter, on seeing the ship's hopeless position and presuming the C.O. killed, gave the order to abandon ship.

After nine salvoes at *Raglan, Breslau* turned her attention to *M.28,* hitting her amidships with her second salvo, which ignited her cordite and her oil fuel tanks in one fierce flash. The two British monitors were now helpless, caught at anchor close to the shore, their armament out of action and their hulls on fire; *Lizard* had been driven off. The German fire was rapid and accurate at a range which had now shortened to only about 4000 yards. *Raglan* received more hits forward, the resulting fire reaching the 12-pdr magazine which then blew up. She sank quickly by the head at about 08.15, the incoming water preventing the fire from reaching the 14-inch magazine. She settled on an even keel in about 40 feet of water with her mast, funnel and part of the bridge projecting above the water. A drifter was able to come alongside the spotting top to take off Broome and the other survivors. When *M.28*'s C.O., Lieutenant-Commander D. P. Macgregor saw that *Raglan* was sinking, he ordered his whaler over to pick up survivors.

Raglan *at Mudros, probably late 1916 or early 1917. She is sporting a camouflage scheme on her upperworks, including her newly installed 6-inch gun visible abaft the funnel. One of her 12-pdr can be seen on its new H.A. mounting abreast the turret.*

Meantime *M.28*'s 9.2-inch had got off its second round, but no further charge could be loaded, owing to the flames in the magazine welling up through the hatch in the deck. A shell from *Breslau* then hit *M.28*'s gun, killing most of its crew and the C.O. who was standing close by, and blowing others into the water. The whaler then returned to assist and had just moored alongside aft when the fire reached the shell room and *M.28* blew up at 08.27 with a huge explosion, scattering debris and bodies over *Lizard* who was approaching to help.

Goeben and *Breslau* then made off to the south, intending to bombard Mudros Harbour, although by now the alarm had been raised in British ships all over the Aegean. Both vessels were again caught in the minefield and *Breslau* soon struck a mine, followed shortly by *Goeben* hitting another. *Breslau* found herself right in the

[1] *Breslau* now carried eight 150-mm, in place of her original twelve 105-mm (4.1-inch)

[2] *Goeben* carried ten 280-mm (11-inch) and ten 150-mm

middle of the minefield under attack from British aircraft and she hit four more before finally sinking at 09.05. All German plans to continue the sortie had to be abandoned, *Goeben* turning back to the Dardanelles. Despite striking a third mine and suffering more serious damage, she reached the safety of the Narrows, but ran aground off Nagara Point.

Continuous attempts were then made to bomb her from the air but, despite many attacks, no serious damage was inflicted. On 23 January, Hayes-Sadler sent a telegram to the Admiralty,[1] "Suggest there is a fair prospect of completely disabling *Goeben* by gunfire if a 15-inch monitor could be sent." This was a curious request: firstly, he had a perfectly adequate 14-inch monitor available. *Abercrombie* had left Samos on the 20th and arrived at Mudros on the 22nd, departing the next day for Stavros. Although muzzle velocity had been falling off, her guns were still quite capable of reaching *Goeben* if she went fairly close in to the peninsula, but she was never called upon to try. Secondly, Hayes-Sadler should have been well aware that the R.N. had only three 15-inch monitors, that they were all based at Dover and that, given their slow speed, it would take at least three weeks for one to reach the Dardanelles. Not surprisingly, the Admiralty turned down his request but did offer him the 12-inch monitors from the Adriatic.

Overwhelmed by the gunfire of Goeben *and* Breslau *on 20 January 1918,* Raglan *lies on the bottom of Kusu Bay on Imbros. The bulged cruiser* Edgar *is assisting salvage operations.*

Raglan *on an even keel in 40 feet of water in Kusu Bay. The wreck is being inspected by naval divers to salvage as much equipment as possible.*

However one of the more immediately available small monitors was used instead. *M.18* was immobilised at Mudros by engine repairs, so *M.17* was called up from Stavros. She arrived at Kusu on the night of 23/24 January and moved up to the peninsula the following evening. She anchored bow and stern in 240 feet of water and opened fire on *Goeben* shortly before 22.00. The haze made air spotting of her indirect fire difficult and she was harrassed by shore batteries. Only ten rounds were got off, without any visible result. No further attempts were made to bombard the battlecruiser from the sea before she was finally towed off on 26 January, returning safely to Constantinople.

Back on Imbros, the wounded from *Raglan* and *M.28* were being treated and a start was made on salvaging equipment from the ships. In all, 127 of *Raglan*'s crew had been killed, leaving 93 survivors, while *M.28* lost eight killed out of 66 on board at the time. The then customary Court Martial following the loss of an H.M. ship in questionable circumstances took place on 31 January. Evidence was given by Broome and the other survivors on board *Lord Nelson*. There was no disputing the surprise of the attack and the overwhelming odds of ten 280-mm and eighteen 150-mm guns against two 14-inch, one 9.2-inch and one 6-inch. Although unprepared, the monitors' crews had put up a reasonable fight against superior forces, so they were all acquitted. The report to the Admiralty stated:[2]

> ". . . . . loss [of *Raglan* and *M.28*] was due to overwhelming gunfire causing fire and explosions, and that the conduct of the survivors was in accordance with the traditions of the Service, and that blame is not attributable to any of them."

Without sufficient warning allowing superior forces time to concentrate, the two monitors were doomed against *Goeben* and *Breslau*. With longer warning, the monitors would certainly have been better prepared, but their loss would still have been almost inevitable. Without *Breslau*'s lucky hit on *Raglan*'s spotting top, the latter could have kept up her fire longer, inflicted greater damage on the enemy and possibly given the other ships a chance to arrive. Although the pre-dreadnoughts were too slow to catch an undamaged *Goeben* and the cruisers were not powerful enough to sink her, it might have been possible to cause sufficient damage to restrict seriously any further operations. As it was, *Goeben* had re-entered the Dardanelles almost before *Lord Nelson* had cleared the fog present at Salonika, *Agamemnon* having left Mudros to rendezvous with her.

Nonetheless, the outcome was on balance favourable to the British, although not fully appreciated at the time. The two German ships had long been a potential menace to British forces, especially the vessels supplying the

[1] [2] ADM 116/1348

Salonika Army. Now one was sunk, the other damaged, for the loss of two relatively expendable British vessels. The British surface patrols could be reduced and even greater reliance placed on air reconnaissance, especially as the minefields were to be reinforced. A number of the ships so relieved could make a greater contribution strengthening the convoy system then being introduced into the Mediterranean.

§9 Performance in Service

The speed of the 14-inch monitors on their first trials had been very low, and they continued to be handicapped in service by their poor performance. Fresh from drydock with newly painted bottoms, they were capable (except *Roberts*) of a shade over six knots without forcing in good weather. With several month's fouling on their broad underwater areas, the average speed dropped to about $5^1/_2$ knots. Even the modest 700 miles from Mudros to Malta used to take *Abercrombie* and *Raglan* five days if conditions were good but over a week if they were bad.

A.E.W. had followed up their preliminary reports on the proposed monitor hull form in December 1914 with a full analysis of subsequent model tests in March 1915, which confirmed all their earlier predictions. Subsequent experience bore out their pessimism. Although nothing was done to modify the 12-inch and first 15-inch monitors which immediately followed the 14-inch, the lessons learnt were used to improve all subsequent designs of large monitor.

Despite the monitors' modest speed, their fuel consumption was considerable. Steam reciprocating engines supplied with saturated steam did not have a high thermal efficiency (only about 8%), while there was additional extensive steam consumption by the auxiliary machinery, which included the two high-powered 600 tons per hour ballast pumps. Each of the two 200-kW generators was driven by a steam engine of about 300 H.P., in total nearly one-third of the main engines' power. On trials, the specific fuel consumption was about 2.25lb of coal per I.H.P. per hour (equivalent to about 1.6lb of oil), corresponding to about 48 tons of coal per day in *Abercrombie* and *Havelock*. In service, the ships generally consumed about 40 tons of coal a day at sea, and in harbour about 6-8 tons; fresh water consumption was about 5-9 tons per day. Coal capacity limited endurance to only about eight days without emergency bunkers; consequently any voyage had to be undertaken in stages of a few hundred miles — *Abercrombie* required five intermediate bunkering stops on her way home from the Dardanelles in 1919. Bunkering was usually done from colliers sent out from Britain to supply the ships of the Fleet. As the monitor lay at anchor in Mudros or Kephalo harbour, the collier would come alongside. About 150 to 200 tons of best Welsh steam coal would be slung aboard from derricks in 2-cwt sacks at the rate of about 50 to 70 tons per hour.

While the speed in fine weather was just about sufficient for the monitors to carry out their bombarding duties, there was no margin at all for bad weather. The very full form was quite unsuitable for pushing through heavy seas as, in addition to increased hull resistance, the wind resistance was appreciable too. The shallow draft allowed little immersion for the propellers, which were liable to emerge from the water when pitching in the short Mediterranean seas. In beam winds, considerable leeway was made so that progress was distinctly crabwise. Against moderate wind and sea, speed dropped rapidly to two to four knots, at which point it was not unknown for small Greek sailing craft to overhaul them. In anything over Force 7, speed dropped further to one to two knots and, even when a tow was available, no appreciable headway could be made until the weather moderated. Returning home early in 1916, *Roberts* tried rigging fore and mizzen staysails, thus using three means of propulsion simultaneously: engines, sails and towline from a tug. In the heavy weather of the Bay of Biscay, this combination of propulsive power yielded a speed of just $3^1/_2$ knots!

Although the loss of speed was inconvenient, the ships were safe enough in a seaway. With their broad flat bottoms, most rolling and pitching were damped out, which made them good gun platforms. The hulls would slap the sea however, causing much spray over the forecastle and onto the upper deck through the sidescreens. The top of the bulge was just about submerged at deep load, so causing a broken wave profile and a considerable wake. In harbour, the top of the bulge was usually dry enough for men to work alongside the hull for painting, repairing boats 'docked' by heeling the ship under them, or even for bathing.

As was to be expected, the steering characteristics remained unsatisfactory. A hull with a length-breadth ratio of 3.7 is not well endowed with directional stability, especially when the rudders operate in an irregular wake. The ships were hard to manoeuvre, difficult to control and required great skill in helmsmanship, especially when entering or leaving harbour. To add to the monitors' troubles, the steering gear was underpowered. Their performance does not bear thinking about had only a single rudder been fitted.

Ammunition and stores were received from store-ships or lighters which came alongside in Mudros. Here also, maintenance and minor damage repairs could be undertaken by the repair ship *Reliance*. The food was adequate but limited by the lack of refrigerated stores and bakery. Bully beef and biscuit was a frequent menu, with some vegetables available from Egypt. Although fresh water could be distilled on board for feed water and drinking, the crews preferred the tanks to be filled from a shore supply. The ships' boats were used continually as the monitors spent much time at anchor. Three 30-foot boats were slung in davits aft, one being a motor boat, the other two pulling cutters; there was also a 16-foot dinghy stowed on the deck abaft the funnel. The motor boat was hard-worked and its engine none too reliable, so two motor boats and one pulling boat would have been a more useful outfit.

Despite their not being regarded as real Navy ships, the monitors were popular with their crews. Most of the officers were young and were holding positions of responsibility much earlier than they would have expected normally. For the men, the less formal routine and moderate numbers made for reasonable conditions. Living quarters were spacious by warship standards, although they could become hot in the Mediterranean, even when the steel decks were cooled by fire hoses. Under these conditions, sleeping on the upper deck with its open sides was preferred.

Taken overall, the performance of the first monitors was barely adequate for their role in service. As the first of a totally new type built in great haste, any shortcomings were understandable, and did lead to modifications to existing vessels and to improved design of the later monitors.

§10 Modifications

The 14-inch monitors underwent fewer changes than most of the later vessels, which were largely deployed in the more demanding conditions off the Belgian Coast. The most obvious change was the lengthening of the funnel by about 12 feet. As the conning tower was badly sited for normal navigation, the exposed searchlight platform halfway up the mast was preferred. Unfortunately it was just level with the top of the funnel so, as the ships were so slow, it only required the lightest of breezes from abaft the beam to cover the watchkeepers in smoke. At the first refit therefore, an extension was added to the funnel of the same diameter as the inner casing, resulting a somewhat stovepipe appearance. *Havelock* however had a superior version with a double casing, which was not as tall as the other three. At the same time, the navigating position was provided with some modest shelter.

Apart from general overhauling on their annual refits, modifications were also made on these occasions to the secondary armament. In order to relieve the 14-inch guns of routine harassment fire, a 6-inch B.L. XII[1] was added to the two Mediterranean monitors, similar to the guns in *M.29* and *M.33*. It was fitted on the forecastle deck abaft the funnel in the space originally allocated for seaplane stowage. *Raglan*'s gun was fitted in 1916 and was one of the pair salvaged from *M.30* (see p.109); *Abercrombie*'s was fitted a year later. *Roberts* had a 6-inch Q.F. I on an improvised H.A. mounting fitted on the starboard side aft, the mounting being fixed to the upper deck, but the trunnions and the gun itself projecting through the forecastle deck, from which it was loaded. The gun was found to be too heavy, slow and unwieldy to make a successful A.A. weapon, yet it remained in *Roberts* for the rest of her life.

Other more useful changes were made to improve the monitors' A.A. armament. The 12-pdrs were moved from their restricted position on the upper deck and remounted on the forecastle deck on mountings modified for H.A. firing. *Abercrombie*'s 2-pdr automatic had been one of the first ever made of that design; calling it a 'pom-pom' was a distinctly optimistic description, as its usual mode of operation was merely to 'pom', much coaxing being needed to persuade it to fire more than one round at a time! The armament changes are summarised below, showing the ships' armaments as finally fitted towards the end of the war:—

Abercrombie	2—14″, 1—6″, 2—12 pdr H.A., 1—3″ H.A., 1—3pdr, 1—2pdr
Havelock	2—14″, 2-12pdr H.A., 2—3″H.A.
Raglan	2—14″, 1—6″, 2—12pdr H.A. 1—3pdr, 1—2pdr
Roberts	2—14″, 1—6″ H.A., 2—12pdr H.A., 1—3″ H.A., 1—3pdr, 2—2pdr

The elaborate camouflage painting schemes common to some ships in home waters were not used. In *Raglan*, only the bridge, funnel, turret and spotting top had a modest disruptive pattern, *Abercrombie* simply having very light coloured upperworks, with a slightly darker grey hull beneath. Whilst all four ships were in the Mediterranean together, each carried identification bands on the funnel, three for *Roberts*, two for *Raglan*, one for *Havelock*, none for *Abercrombie*. The false bow wave painted on the monitors when new to give an impression of speed to mislead U-boats was soon removed.

Minor internal changes were made in all ships, including the provision of secondary armament magazines and rearrangement of the stores and accommodation spaces, the crew number having been increased slightly to 208 to man the additional guns.

§11 Post-War Careers

Following the Armistice in November 1918, there was no further need for monitors as guardships, nor was there a role in the post-war fleet for most of those engaged on patrol and bombardment work. Accordingly, in February 1919 *Abercrombie* set off on the long voyage home, arriving at Devonport on 19 April. After de-ammunitioning, she was sent round to Immingham with a Care and Maintenance (C. & M.) party. There she joined eight other monitors already on the Disposal List, as there was insufficient berthing accommodation at the dockyards; she finally paid off on 9 May. *Havelock* arrived at Immingham from Lowestoft shortly afterwards, paying off on 14 May, while *Roberts* arrived from Yarmouth, paying off on 26 May.

By the summer of 1920, there was capacity at the dockyards to take the monitors in hand for de-equipping. *Abercrombie* and *Havelock* were towed to Portsmouth in June to have their 14-inch guns and secondary armament removed. *Roberts* followed in October but retained her guns. All three vessels were put on the Sale List and formed part of the massive purchase of warships for scrap by T. W. Ward of Sheffield. On 9 May 1921, the Admiralty sold them 113 obsolete naval vessels at the flat rate of £ 2½ per ton. The purchase included five battleships, 12 cruisers, 88 destroyers and torpedo boats, as well as three 12-inch monitors (*General Wolfe, General Craufurd* and *Prince Eugene*) and two of the ex-Brazilian river monitors (*Severn* and *Mersey*), totalling about 300,000 tons in all. The effective price for one of the large monitors was thus about £15,000. The Admiralty had reserved the right to withdraw any of the vessels if required and to substitute others, and the three 14-inch

[1] B.L. XII = Breech loading gun, Mark XII

monitors were in fact retained. They remained laid up in Spithead or in Portsmouth Harbour until 1927, when *Abercrombie* and *Havelock* were resold to Ward's and scrapped that same year, as detailed in the Technical Particulars.

Roberts was retained for experimental purposes for a number of years. Consideration had been given about 1925 to converting her for use as a mobile mooring mast and fuelling station for airships. In the early 1930s, she was involved in trials for new designs of underwater protection. In order to correlate model experiments with large scale results, a structure representing a proposed double bottom and bulge was built on to *Roberts.* With her 10-foot draft, the structure was one-third the full scale for a battleship. Various charges representing different sizes of bomb were exploded against her; the results provided information for the design of the aircraft carrier *Ark Royal* and battleship *King George V.*

After WW1, Roberts *was used for experimental purposes, including tests of new designs of underwater protective structure. This view shows her later at Portsmouth in July 1928 in a poor state, with part of the bulge removed amidships.*

By 1936, she was of no further use, so she was handed over to Ward's with some twenty old destroyers in part exchange for the White Star liner *Majestic*. Ward's had recently purchased the latter for scrap, but now the Admiralty wanted her to provide accommodation for young artificers under training at Rosyth. The total exchange value was about £140,000 of which *Roberts* constituted about one-sixth. *Roberts* was allocated to Ward's Preston yard, leaving Portsmouth on 10 September in tow of the tug *Seaman.* Some weeks after arrival, she broke adrift during a December gale and was blown down the River Ribble to strand off Lytham, later being towed back. She had outlived all of her sisters and her near-sisters the 12-inch monitors, and it was to be only three years before a new *Roberts* was to be designed, who would herself become the last to survive of all the large monitors (see Chapter IX).

THE 14-INCH MONITORS — TECHNICAL PARTICULARS

Displacement and Dimensions 6150 tons legend, 6150 tons deep. Length 334′-6″ overall, breadth 90′-2″, draft 10′-0″

Weight Distribution Armament 650 tons, ammunition 195, armour plating 682, protective plating 1170, hull structure 2091, hull fittings 393, general equipment 220, machinery and reserve feed water 376, coal (nominal) 200. Designed total 5977 tons.

Complement 12 officers, 186 men.

Armament (As completed) 2—14″ (twin) (120 H.E. + 15 practice rounds per gun), 2—12pdr 18cwt (200 r.p.g.), 1—3pdr Vickers H.A. (500 r.p.g.), 1—2pdr H.A. (1000 r.p.g.), 4—0.303″ Maxim machine guns (5000 r.p.g.).

Protection Forecastle deck 1″ high-tensile; upper deck amidships 2″ H.T.; main deck, forward and aft 1″ H.T.; sloping internal belt 4″ C.; bulkheads at end of belt 4″ C.; torpedo protective bulkhead 1½″ H.T. (1″ at ends); steering gear 1½″ H.T.; barbette 8″ C.; gunhouse 10″ front, 7″ sides and rear, 4″ roof; conning tower 6″ sides, 2½″ roof, cast steel; spotting top 1″ H.T. sides and floor.

Machinery Twin screw steam reciprocating engines. Two Babcock & Wilcox watertube boilers, 200lb/sq in. *Abercrombie* and *Havelock*: two quadruple-expansion 2000 I.H.P. at 175 r.p.m. *Raglan*: two 4-cylinder triple-expansion 2310 I.H.P. at 200 r.p.m. *Roberts*: two 3-cyl triple-expansion 1800 I.H.P. at 180 r.p.m. Coal 380 tons maximum. Endurance 1340 miles at 6 knots.

Speed 10 knots designed, 6½ service. Trials: *Abercrombie* 7.04, *Havelock* 7.35, *Raglan* 7.64, *Roberts* 5.70 knots.

Construction Harland & Wolff, Belfast: *Abercrombie* laid down 12 Dec 1914/launched 15 Apr 1915/completed 29 May 1915; *Havelock* 12 Dec 1914/29 Apr 1915/18 Jun 1915. *Raglan* H. & W. Govan 1 Dec 1914/29 Apr 1915/24 Jun 1915. *Roberts* Swan Hunter, Wallsend 17 Dec 1914/15 Apr 1915/14 Jun 1915.

Disposal *Abercrombie* scrapped Ward, Inverkeithing 29 Jul 1927; *Havelock* scrapped Ward, Preston 20 Jul 1927; *Raglan* sunk 20 Jan 1918; *Roberts* scrapped Ward, Preston 19 Sept 1936.

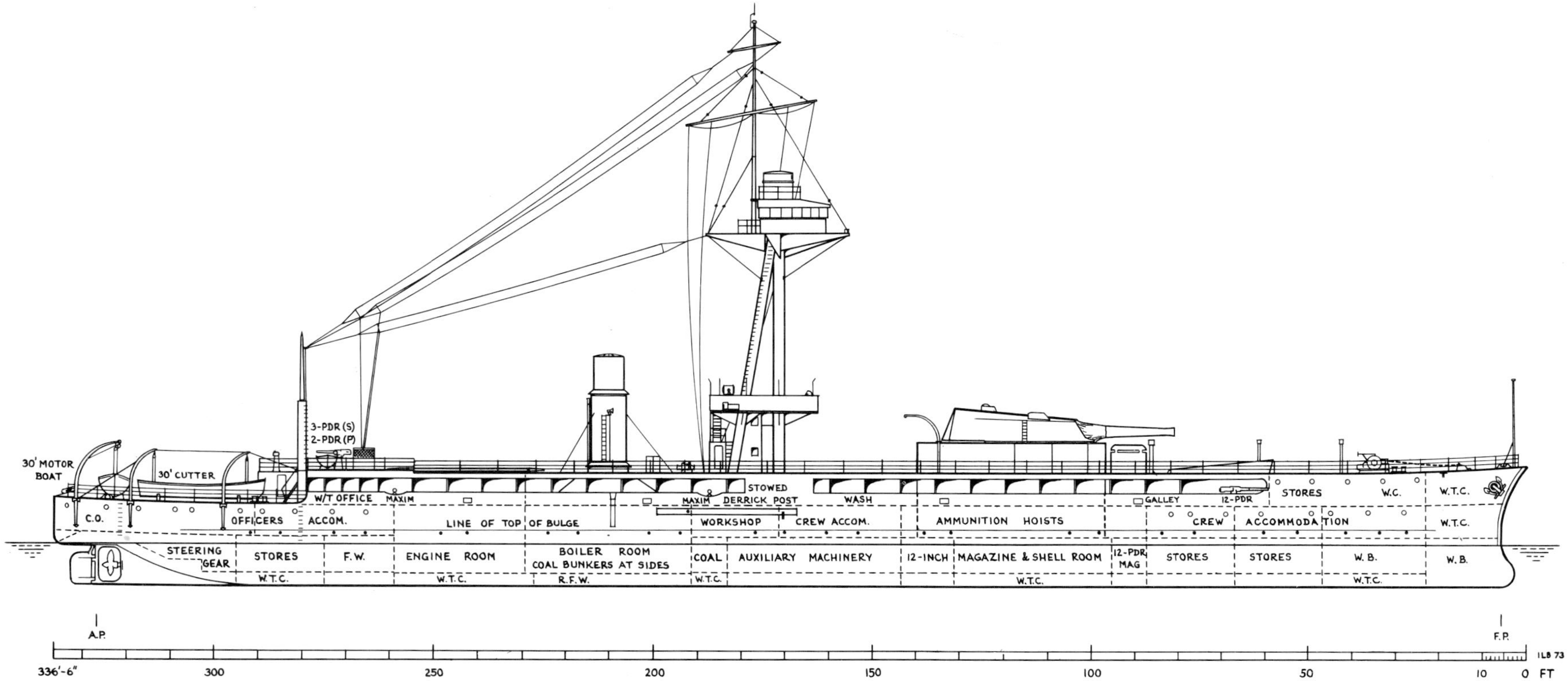

Prince Rupert *as completed. The design of the 12-inch monitors was almost identical to the 14-inch vessels, except for the turret and magazine arrangement. The extension to the funnel was fitted to all ships before entry into active service to keep smoke away from the navigating position. Most of* Rupert*'s sisters were one foot shorter in overall length as completed. The topmast and long range wireless aerials were removed from the six ships based at Dover. Later modifications included the addition of two or four 6-inch guns on the forecastle deck abreast the mast, more H.A. guns and a small two-level enclosed bridge structure. Derrick posts were later removed from most vessels.*

CHAPTER III

THE 12-INCH GUN MONITORS

H.M.S. LORD CLIVE, PRINCE RUPERT, SIR JOHN MOORE, GENERAL CRAUFURD, PRINCE EUGENE, EARL OF PETERBOROUGH, SIR THOMAS PICTON, GENERAL WOLFE

§1 Design

The rapidity with which construction of the 14-inch monitors got under way, plus the extent of the coastal bombardment opportunities beginning to present themselves with Turkey's entry into the war, encouraged Churchill to plan further big gun monitors. On 11 December 1914, he minuted to Fisher and the Secretary to the Admiralty:[1]

> "We ought without delay to order more 'Styx' class for heavy in-shore work. There are, for instance, the four reserve 13.5-inch guns of the *Audacious,* which should certainly be mounted in new monitors. It should also be possible to draw from the reserve of 15-inch guns, and to make in a short time 15-inch or 18-inch howitzers. We require now to make ships which can be built in 6 or 7 months at the outside, and which can certainly go close in shore and attack the German Fleet in its harbours. These are special vessels built for a definite war operation, and we must look to them in default of a general action for giving us the power of forcing a naval decision at latest in the autumn of 1915.
>
> Our thought is proceeding independently on the same lines. I propose, as a basis of discussion, that in addition to the 4 Schwab monitors, we prepare 8 more at a cost of not more than £700,000 apiece. These vessels should be armed either with 13.5-inch or 15-inch guns, two or four in each as convenient. Or, alternatively, they should be armed with four 18-inch howitzers in separate cupolas sunk low on their heavily-armoured turtle backs. They should draw 8 feet at most, and be propelled entirely by internal combustion at a speed not exceeding 10 knots; no funnels; three or four alternative telescopic masts for fire observation; strong crinolines 20 feet away all round to make them immune from mine and torpedo, etc. A third alternative variant would be two heavy guns in turrets in the centre and two mortars in 'cupolad' pits on each side of the deck."

Fisher was also in favour, so the idea was passed to the Third Sea Lord for examination by D.N.C. and the Director of Naval Ordnance (D.N.O.), Rear-Admiral Morgan Singer. The loss of *Audacious* had indeed released spare 13.5-inch guns, and there was also one spare mounting kept for each ship. But in the context of heavy non-transferable ordnance, 'mountings' meant only the elevating parts, i.e. one gun cradle, slide and fittings, not the complete turret and equipment. Thus there was no installation suitable for use and it would take at least a year to build one. Similarly with 15-inch guns; it was not enough to possess spare guns, cradles and slides, which were useless without the complete mounting for loading, training and elevating. 15-inch howitzers were a possibility, but it was considered that their range would be insufficient when matched against shore defences.

Although none of Churchill's suggestions for armament were found to be practicable, there remained one further possibility — taking mountings from existing ships. There were still a fair number of pre-dreadnoughts in service carrying 12-inch guns, which were now of limited value. The oldest class comprised the nine *Majestic*s designed in 1893, which were now being used largely for coast defence purposes. Each ship carried two twin 12-inch mountings of a pattern which marked a big step forward in naval ordnance at the time, as described on p.181. It was therefore proposed that eight new monitors could be armed by disarming four of the battleships. Admiral Sir Percy Scott, who had done so much to improve the Navy's gunnery before the war and who had now returned to the Admiralty from retirement, appreciated that the range of the *Majestic*s' 35-calibre 12-inch Mk VIII at its maximum elevation of $13^1/_2°$ was only 13,700 yards. While this was adequate for the 1890s, it was well below the range of modern coast defence guns, so he pointed out that if 30° elevation could be obtained, over 21,000 yards was possible. Elswick confirmed that 30° was feasible without major modifications to the turret, so Fisher immediately approved Scott's suggestion.

Meantime, design of the hull had been going ahead, but leaving sufficient space for whatever armament was likely to be fitted. The design was virtually a repeat of the 14-inch monitors, as it was not found possible to adopt Churchill's other suggestions. A draft of only 8 feet was insufficient to provide the required buoyancy, so 10 feet was substituted, while 20-foot crinolines became 15-foot bulges. Diesel engines were still in their infancy for marine propulsion, so it was quite impossible to provide eight sets of 2000-H.P. machinery in as little as six months. Steam reciprocators were the only practicable propulsion units, although machinery of slightly greater than 2000 H.P. was sought.

The proposed armament and its ammunition was

[1] *Winston S. Churchill,* Companion Volume III, p.305

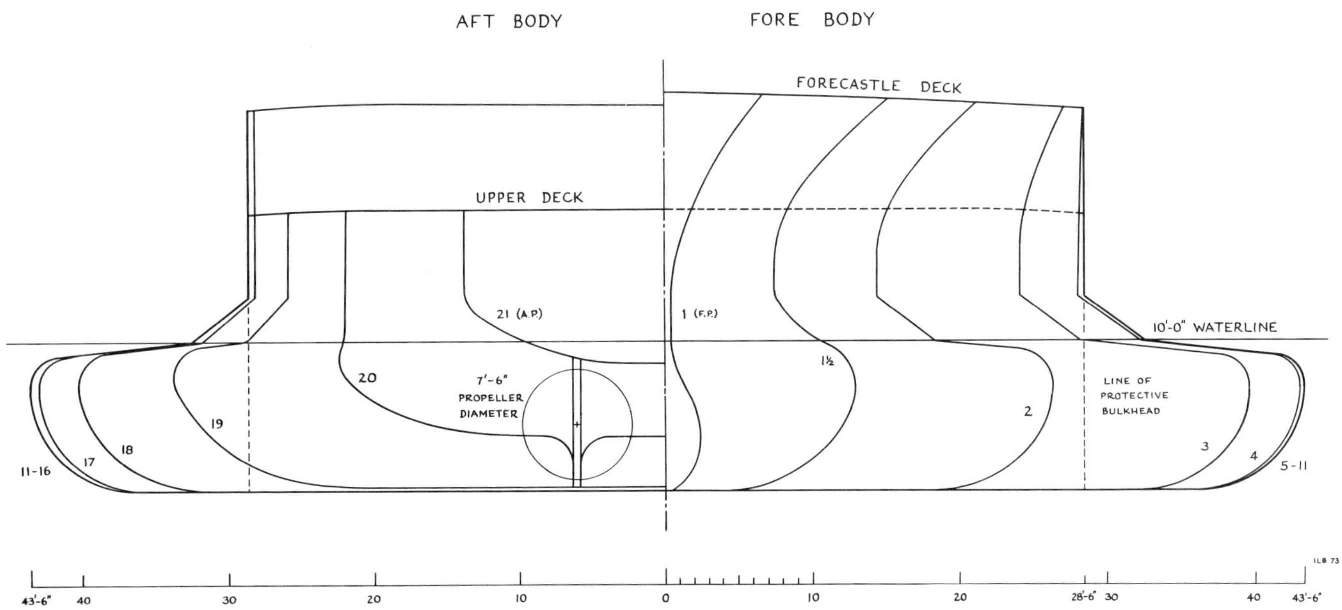

The body plan of the 12-inch monitors shows the cross-sections of the hull at the 21 constructional stations, each one-twentieth of the 320-ft length B.P. apart (16ft). Station No. 1 was at the fore perpendicular and No. 21 at the aft perpendicular. The hull was parallel-sided from Station No. 5 to No. 16, or 176ft, over half the ship's length. The rectangular cross-section of the main hull and the large area of flat bottom simplified construction, as did the angled transition between bulge and main hull.

about 367 tons lighter than the 14-inch, so the hulls of the 12-inch monitors could be made slightly narrower. A reduction from 90 to 87 feet would also simplify the problem of finding sufficiently wide building berths. The only other significant change was to increase the thickness of the sloping armour belt from four inches to six — see diagram on p.20. The resulting designed displacement was 5599 tons compared with 5977 in the earlier class, the difference being nearly all due to the lighter armament. There was no time to make a detailed cost estimate, but in seeking Cabinet approval it was anticipated that the combined cost of all eight monitors would be about £3½ million, i.e. about £437,500 each. This figure is almost certainly too high as it would have been based on the estimate for the 14-inch monitors with their expensively purchased armament. As the 12-inch monitors' armament already existed, the major components of their cost would be hull and machinery, and it is unlikely that actual expenditure exceeded about £260,000 each.

§2 Construction

It was no easy problem to find the shipbuilding capacity to tackle a further eight beamy ships, at a time when most shipyards with wide berths were already fully occupied. However with more shipowners postponing their passenger liner orders, Pirrie could offer to build five more monitors as Nos. 477 to 481: two on Berth 1 at Belfast following the launch of Red Star's *Belgenland* on 31 December, two on Berth 3 after the modest amount of steel erected for White Star's *Homeric* had been dismantled, and one more at Govan. The three other berths were provided by Clyde yards after tenders were received: Scotts of Greenock, Hamilton of Port Glasgow and Fairfield of Govan. With the postponement of so many big ships, H. & W's engine works also had considerable spare capacity. They offered to produce a special design of twin screw triple-expansion machinery for the monitors, developing a total of 2310 I.H.P. Each engine actually had four cylinders, an arrangement which gave better balancing characteristics than three cylinders. There were two low pressure cylinders 30in bore each, high pressure 15in, intermediate pressure 25in, with a stroke of 24in. Although H. & W. only needed five sets for their 12-inch ships, they could easily manage a sixth and fit it in *M.3 (Raglan)* at their Govan yard. So McKie & Baxter's existing contract for *M.3*'s 1600-I.H.P. machinery was transferred to the Hamilton monitor, as the latter company had no engine works, unlike Scotts who were to engine their hull. The switch was a sensible one as the more powerful machinery would be more usefully deployed in a monitor armed with modern 14-inch guns rather than one with old 12-inch guns. McKie & Baxter also received the order for the machinery of the Fairfield ship, but the power was increased to 2500 I.H.P. Orders to build went out about 23 December 1914. Following the transfer of the battlecruiser *Repulse* from Palmer's to Clydebank and acceleration of *Renown* at Fairfield's, the latter yard's monitor order and its machinery was transferred to Palmer's on 6 January, although their shipyard at Hebburn-on-Tyne, rather than the main yard at Jarrow a mile downstream.

The eight ships had been given provisional *M* numbers, the Scott's ship being *M.5*, Palmer's *M.9*, Hamilton's *M.10*, while the H. & W. ships filled the gaps up to *M.12*. Names of British generals were chosen early in 1915 and, after some reconsideration as to the exact titles[1], those finally selected in March were:—

M.5: Sir John Moore, of Peninsular War fame.

M.6: Lord Clive, the soldier-statesman who established British domination in India.

M.7: General Craufurd, of the Peninsular War (whose name was frequently mis-spelt).

M.8: Earl of Peterborough, of the War of the Spanish Succession.

M.9: General Wolfe, the victor of Quebec.

M.10: Prince Rupert, the English Civil War Royalist leader.

M.11: Prince Eugene, the Savoy prince who fought with Marlborough.

M.12: Sir Thomas Picton, of the Peninsular War and Waterloo.

The decision as to which four pre-dreadnoughts were to surrender their armament had been made on 1 January 1915. Early in February, *Mars* and *Magnificent* arrived at Belfast, *Hannibal* at Dalmuir on the Clyde and *Victorious* at Elswick. The work of conversion was done aboard ship and the mountings then lifted out and placed on the dockside to await re-erection, although the barbette armour was not transferred, new flat plates being provided. Conversion was divided amongst the big three ordnance companies as follows:

Ship	*Conversion by*	*From*
Prince Rupert	E.O.C.	*Victorious*
General Wolfe	E.O.C.	*Victorious*
Lord Clive	C.O.W.	*Magnificent*
General Craufurd	C.O.W.	*Magnificent*
Prince Eugene	C.O.W.	*Hannibal*
Sir John Moore	Vickers	*Hannibal*
Earl of Peterborough	Vickers	*Mars*
Sir Thomas Picton	Vickers	*Mars*

Prince Rupert had the shortest time on the berth, being laid down on 12 January, launched on 20 May and then towed up to Clydebank where her turret was shipped using John Brown's heavy crane. Back at Greenock, J. & G. Kincaid finished installing her machinery and she was ready for trials on 1 July, 24 weeks after construction started. McKie & Baxter had delivered her engines as early as February, as not only did their ex-*M.3* contract precede that of the hull by one month, but the design was a repeat of the machinery supplied to the steamer *Lampo*. *Rupert*[2] was the first to go out on gun trials, but several faults showed up. The additional elevation had greatly

[1] For example, *M.9* was first to have been *Wolfe*, then *Sir James Wolfe*, finally *General Wolfe*.

[2] The names were often abbreviated in everyday use by dropping the titles.

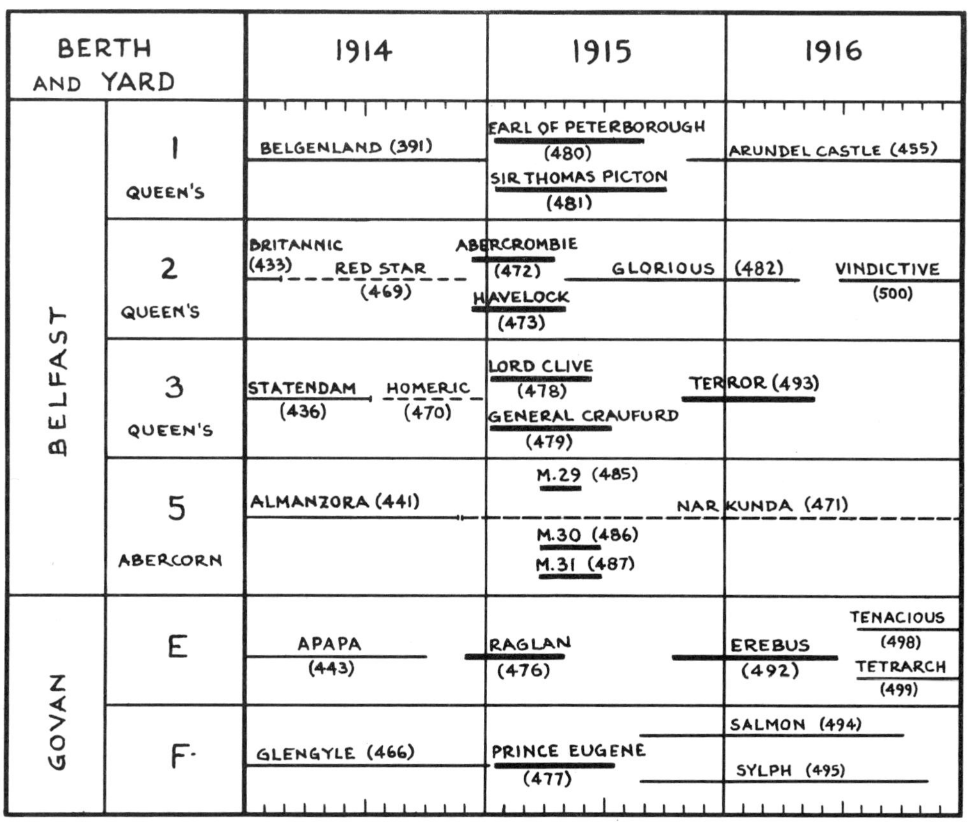

This portion of Harland & Wolff's berth chart shows how merchant ship construction rapidly gave way to monitor construction after the outbreak of war. The monitors are shown as heavy lines from keel laying to launching, with their hull numbers. Not shown are the small 6-inch monitors M.32 *and* M.33 *(488-9) subcontracted to Workman, Clark. Berths 2 and 3 were the pair under the large gantry in the Queen's yard, seen in the photograph on p.24. There were also merchant ships on the other four berths at Belfast and the other seven at Govan, on which work was suspended throughout 1915. No. 469 was never recommenced, No. 470 was re-ordered post-war as the smaller* Laurentic *built on another berth, while* Narkunda*'s keel was transferred to Berth 8 in the Abercorn yard in 1917. None of the berths on the chart are now in use, as the Queen's, Abercorn and Govan yards of H. & W. were dismantled in the 1960s.*

Prince Rupert *was towed to John Brown's Clydebank shipyard following her launch at Port Glasgow on 20 May 1915 to have her twin 12-inch turret installed by Elswick Ordnance Co. This fine view, typical of the work of Clydebank's resident photographer, shows the roof plates being fitted. The original short funnel is fitted, which was lengthened soon after entry into service. The vent holes in the bulge water space are clearly seen — more closely spaced than in most of the monitors. In the background, the battleship* Barham *is seen completing. The gap in her main deck shows where one of the 6-inch guns which was used to arm the small monitors was to have been fitted.*

increased firing stresses, which caused the gunmetal run-in and run-out ram to distort. This was cured by fitting a steel ram, but then other faults appeared, particularly in the hydraulic piping. Considerable pressures were developed, especially at maximum elevation, which soon produced leaks from inadequately brazed joints.

After the fiasco of the 14-inch monitors' speed trials, care had been taken to redesign the propellers and leave the mine-wires off the later ships, but even so there was no chance of their making the originally specified 10 knots. As anticipated with her particularly low-powered machinery, *Rupert* turned out to be slowest ship, just making 7 knots. *Wolfe, Clive* and *Eugene* all made 8 knots, the latter claiming to be the fastest at 8.2 knots, but this was probably an overestimate of about 0.6 knot as the speed had been assessed from a towed log, not a measured mile. So *Clive* must be reckoned the fastest of the class on trials with her 8.02 knots. All ships except *Clive* and *Rupert* ran their trials with the increased funnel height found necessary on the 14-inch monitors.

Rupert was the only one of the class to have an accurate check made on stability and displacement as completed. This indicated that the light displacement was 5033 tons and the deep was 5683 tons, which compared well with the estimated 5755 tons after allowing for the full stowage of coal. Design calculations of the stability characteristics had been less accurate, the measured vertical centre of gravity being two feet above the estimate at 13.6ft above the keel — a serious error in a normal ship, but nothing to worry about in a monitor with its broad beam and ample stability. The corresponding metacentric height, GM, (see p.126) was 13.4ft, much the same as the 14-inch monitors. As with the 14-inch monitors, insufficient 3-inch guns had been completed for them to ship their designed H.A. armament of two 3-inch, so they were generally equipped with one 3-pdr and one 2-pdr. There were a few minor differences between ships of the class as completed, such as in details of rig and in bow profile.

As mentioned on p.28, *Prince Rupert, Sir John Moore, Lord Clive* and *General Craufurd* were initially intended to go out to the Dardanelles. These orders were

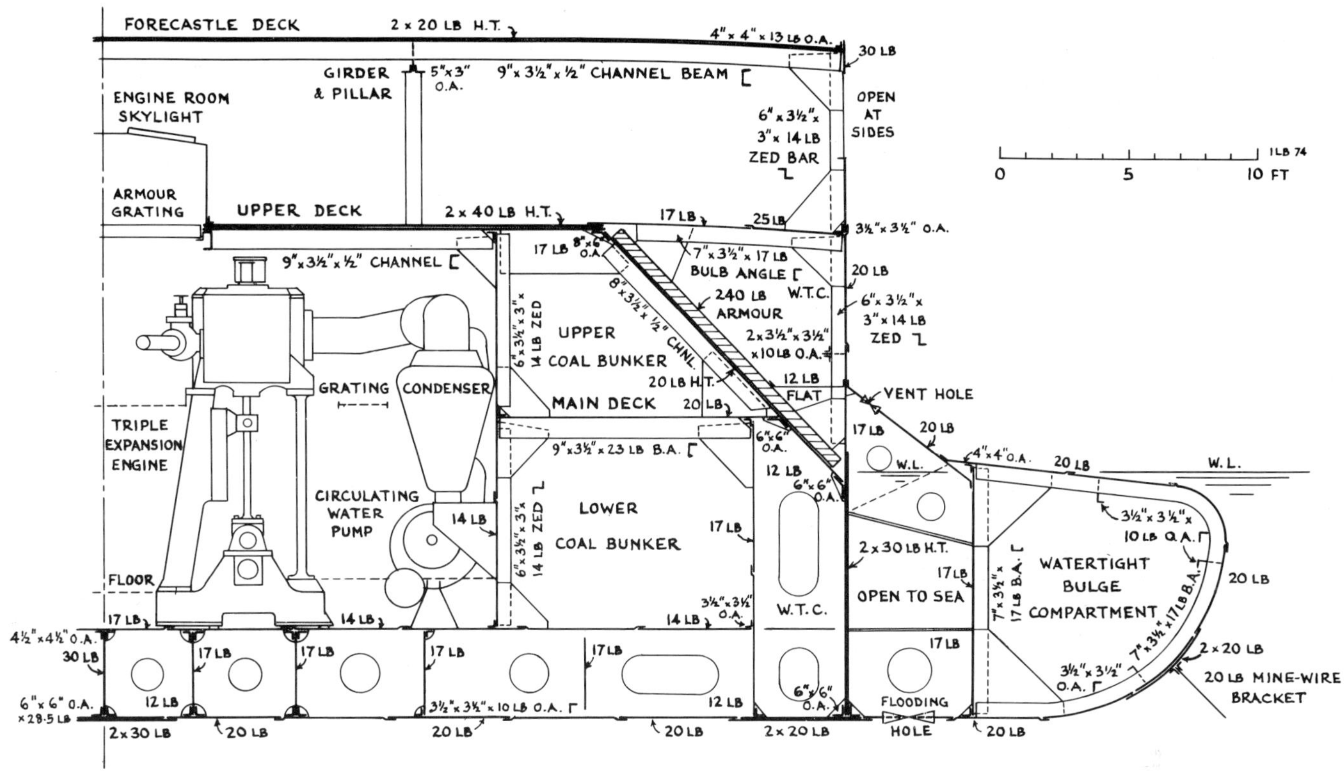

The cross-section through Sir John Moore*'s engine room shows the port side looking aft, with the scantlings of the riveted main structure. Plating thicknesses are given in pounds per square foot: 20lb corresponds to ½-inch (actually 0.49in). Stiffeners are given as web and flange breadths, with weights in pounds per foot run. Frames and beams are spaced 4ft apart. (H.T. = high-tensile steel; B.A. = bulb angle; O.A. = ordinary angle).*

cancelled by the new Board and the ships were allocated to the Dover Squadron, where the German-occupied coast of Belgium offered tempting targets for bombardment. *Clive* was the first to leave her builder's on 10 July having been commissioned on the 4th by Commander N. H. Carter. *Rupert* followed two days later under Commander H. O. Reinold, having commissioned on 22 June. Both vessels put into Devonport for three weeks, where the dockyard ordnance department sorted out all the minor problems which had shown up on trials. Commander S. R. Miller had commissioned *Moore* on 1 July and was anxious to press on to Dover so, although she did not leave Greenock until 22 July, she was the first ship to join the Monitor Squadron when she arrived at Dover on the 27th. The other five commissioned at their builder's yards, with C.O.s and dates as shown:—

General Craufurd	Cmdr. E. Altham	19 Aug.
Prince Eugene	Capt. E. Wigram	21 Aug.
Earl of Peterborough	Capt. H. G. C. Somerville	21 Sept.
General Wolfe	Cmdr. N. W. Diggle	27 Oct.
Sir Thomas Picton	Capt. W. R. Napier	31 Oct.

There had been some competition to get command of a monitor, as it was expected that they would see plenty of action. Although some of the C.O.s selected were relatively young, others were older men passed over for further promotion, who were glad to get such a command.

§3 Wartime Service in Home Waters, 1915-1916

Churchill had identified the Belgian Coast and the area covered by the Dover Squadron as second only in importance to the Dardanelles for the monitors, as it would permit support of the Allied Armies' left flank, the bombardment of U-boat bases such as Zeebrugge and the possibility of seizing Borkum as a forward base. Following the "Race to the Sea" in October 1914 and the naval gunfire support which helped stabilise the Allied line (see p.83), occasional bombardments had been made during the early months of 1915 by the pre-dreadnought *Venerable* and the gunboats *Excellent* and *Bustard,* although their guns were of limited range. The Germans now held 27 miles[1] of the Belgian Coast from Nieuport, eight miles east of the French border, right up to neutral Dutch territory at the mouth of the Scheldt. Two important ports were held: Ostende and Bruges — the latter being eight miles inland and connected by canal to the North Sea at Zeebrugge. From these bases only 60 miles from the Kent coast, U-boats and destroyers menaced British control of the narrow seas by torpedo, mine and gun. The all-important transports crossing the Straits of Dover to supply the Armies in France were particularly vulnerable, necessitating keeping strong forces of British ships in the Dover area. In order to protect their bases and their Army's flank, the Germans had strongly fortified the Belgian Coast.

[1] See map on p.46. All distances in this book are given in nautical miles (1.15 statute miles, 2025 yards or 1.85 km)

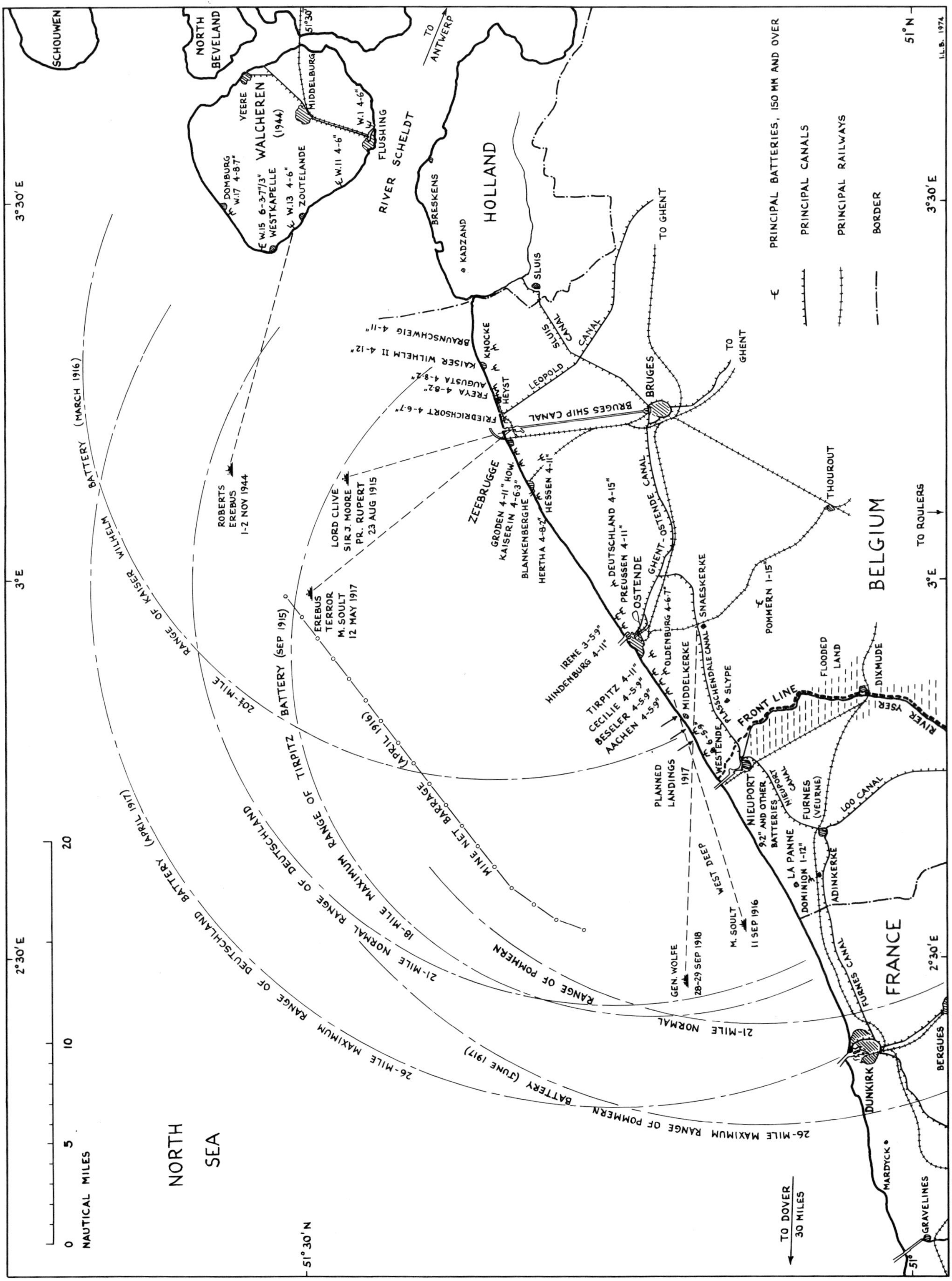
NORTH SEA
NAUTICAL MILES
0 5 10 20
SCHOUWEN
NORTH BEVELAND
WALCHEREN (1944)
VEERE
MIDDELBURG
FLUSHING
DOMBURG W.17 4-8.7"
W.15 6-3.7"/3" WESTKAPELLE
W.13 4-6" ZOUTELANDE
W.11 4-6"
W.1 4-6"
RIVER SCHELDT
TO ANTWERP
HOLLAND
BRESKENS
KADZAND
SLUIS
TO GHENT
BRAUNSCHWEIG 4-11"
KAISER WILHELM II 4-12"
KNOCKE
FREYA 4-8.2"
AUGUSTA 4-8.2"
HEYST
FRIEDRICHSORT 4-6.7"
LEOPOLD CANAL
SLUIS CANAL
BRUGES
BRUGES SHIP CANAL
ZEEBRUGGE
HESSEN 4-11"
GRODEN 4-11" HOW.
KAISERIN 4-6.3"
BLANKENBERGHE
HERTHA 4-8.2"
THOUROUT
TO ROULERS
DEUTSCHLAND 4-15"
PREUSSEN 4-11"
OSTENDE
GHENT-OSTENDE CANAL
SNAESKERKE
POMMERN 1-15"
BELGIUM
IRENE 3-5.9"
HINDENBURG 4-11"
OLDENBURG 4-6.7"
MIDDELKERKE
PLASSCHENDALE CANAL
SLYPE
TIRPITZ 4-11"
CECILIE 4-5.9"
BESELER 4-5.9"
AACHEN 4-5.9"
WESTENDE
FRONT LINE
FLOODED LAND
DIXMUDE
RIVER YSER
NIEUPORT
9.2" AND OTHER BATTERIES
NIEUPORT CANAL
FURNES (VEURNE)
LOO CANAL
LA PANNE
DOMINION 1-12"
ADINKERKE
FURNES CANAL
FRANCE
DUNKIRK
BERGUES
MARDYCK
GRAVELINES
TO DOVER 30 MILES
ROBERTS EREBUS 1-2 NOV 1944
LORD CLIVE SIR J. MOORE PR. RUPERT 23 AUG 1915
EREBUS TERROR M. SOULT 12 MAY 1917
PLANNED LANDINGS 1917
WEST DEEP
M. SOULT 11 SEP 1916
GEN. WOLFE 28-29 SEP 1918
MINE NET BARRAGE (APRIL 1916)
20½-MILE RANGE OF KAISER WILHELM BATTERY (MARCH 1916)
18-MILE MAXIMUM RANGE OF TIRPITZ BATTERY (SEP 1915)
21-MILE NORMAL RANGE OF DEUTSCHLAND BATTERY (APRIL 1917)
21-MILE NORMAL RANGE OF POMMERN
26-MILE MAXIMUM RANGE OF DEUTSCHLAND BATTERY (JUNE 1917)
26-MILE MAXIMUM RANGE OF POMMERN
PRINCIPAL BATTERIES, 150 MM AND OVER
PRINCIPAL CANALS
PRINCIPAL RAILWAYS
BORDER
51°30'N
51°N
3°30'E
3°E
2°30'E
I.L.B. 1974

The Royal Navy faced conditions which were quite different from the Dardanelles. A short length of heavily defended coastline was flanked by shallow waters abounding in tricky tidal currents. The shore was low-lying and offered few visible points of aim for bombardment. Many of the most important targets were in areas still occupied by Belgian civilians. Weather conditions were notoriously unpredictable; poor visibility and gales could severely limit operations. All the time there hovered in the background the threat of a sortie by the High Seas Fleet, considerably nearer at Wilhelmshaven than the Grand Fleet at Scapa Flow.

Vice-Admiral Reginald H. Bacon took over the Dover Command from Rear-Admiral H.L.A. Hood in April 1915. He brought a fresh and ingenious mind full of technical innovations, but their implementation was not helped by his autocratic tendencies and a refusal to delegate. Having been a previous D.N.O. (1907-09) and more recently Managing Director of Coventry Ordnance Works (1909-14), it was natural that he should devote much of his attention to bombardment operations. While waiting for the monitors to arrive, Bacon had been busy making plans for their use. The problem was that of obtaining hits at long range against small targets invisible from the sea. This required an accurate knowledge of the position of both ship and target, as well as the development of reliable spotting methods. Experiments had been carried out in April by Altham before his posting to *General Craufurd,* using seaplanes to observe firings from the pre-dreadnought *Revenge*[1] in the Thames Estuary. Portable tripod observation islands were also prepared, to be carried by ship and dropped in shallow water at suitable points off the coast. The danger of mines was to be reduced by sweeping operations prior to a bombardment, while the U-boat menace was to be countered by surrounding the firing area with drifter-laid nets. Bacon's book *The Dover Patrol 1915-1917*[2] is one of the few published works which give monitors any more than the briefest of passing references. He gives considerable detail of his plans and operations, especially the initial bombardments from which so much was expected.

After *Lord Clive* and *Prince Rupert* had joined *Sir John Moore* off Sheerness on 9 August 1915, bombardment practice could start in earnest in the broad waters of the Thames Estuary. For a fortnight, the three ships put their newly converted 12-inch mountings through their paces. These trials proved a great disappointment to the keen young Gunnery Officers; a story of continual breakdown, makeshift repair and endless re-tests on the 20-year old equipment, with Bacon lending an experienced hand to get the guns right. A replica of some of the principal features of the Belgian Coast near Zeebrugge had been laid out in the Thames, thus permitting the monitors to practise their manoeuvring and spotting arrangements. For the latter, Bacon had two observation tripods, which were to be positioned in the sea about six miles offshore prior to bombardment. The signals from the two groups of observers, coupled with the monitors' own spotting, would give three bearings from which to fix the fall of shot. Bacon considered that spotting from seaplanes alone was not yet sufficiently reliable for such operations.

By 21 August, all was deemed ready for the first bombardment of German-held territory by big gun monitors, one month after the 14-inch monitors had opened fire on the Turks. A considerable fleet of supporting vessels was required: ten escorting destroyers, nine minesweepers, the seaplane carrier *Riviera*, four observation tripod handling ships and no less than 50 drifters to manoeuvre the explosive anti-submarine nets around the monitors. Bad weather delayed departure on the 21st, so that operations had to be postponed 24 hours. During the night of 22/23 August, the ships took up their stations about ten miles off Zeebrugge (see map on p.46). Marker buoys were laid, tripods were lowered into position and nets were laid around the monitors on all sides except to landward, where it was considered that shoals would prevent any U-boat approach. These activities were not accomplished without difficulty; some of the positions laid were inaccurate, while the enemy had

[1] Renamed *Redoubtable* in August 1915 after the new battleship *Revenge* was launched

[2] Two volumes published in 1919; concise revised volume in 1932

(Opposite) *The map of the Belgian Coast shows the area of operation of the large and small Dover monitors during WW1, as well as the 1944 Walcheren assault. Apart from a small loss of Allied territory at the mouth of the Yser, the front-line remained static from 1914 to 1918. The German defences were continually being strengthened; the map shows them as in 1918, although more coast defences were still under construction. The maximum range of the German 15-inch could only be attained with special ammunition.*

McKie and Baxter received an order for a pair of 800 I.H.P. triple expansion engines (Nos. 807-8) in November 1914. Originally intended for Raglan, *they were re-allocated to* Prince Rupert *in December. This view shows the engines (looking aft) in the company's Glasgow works nearly ready for shipping, at a weight of 18 tons each.*

General Craufurd on her way to trials in Belfast Lough on 21 August 1915. It is possible to see right across the upper deck through the open side-screens.

observed the drifters' operations and proceeded to drop some shells amongst them, fortunately none being hit.

Moore with Bacon aboard, *Clive* and *Rupert* then anchored by the stern within the zareba of nets and opened fire at 05.36 on the 23rd. Their primary target was the locks of the Zeebrugge Canal leading to the naval base at Bruges, but a secondary target was nearby industrial works. From 18,000 yards *Clive*'s guns quickly found the range, so she kept up a steady fire for $1^1/_2$ hours dropping 31 rounds in the vicinity of the locks. She then switched to the works, firing a further 11 rounds at maximum range on the gun-sights. *Moore* was less fortunate; after 9 rounds, which included some misfires, the leather in one of the walking pipes blew. As these pipes carried the hydraulic fluid from the fixed to the revolving part of the mounting, the turret was effectively put out of action for the rest of the operation. *Rupert* was scarcely more fortunate; the electrical connections from the director to the turret broke down and training had to be undertaken by verbal message. She was thus only able to get off 19 rounds before the cease-fire was ordered. Although none of the German batteries could reach the monitors, Bacon judged two hours a sufficient exposure to risk off Zeebrugge. It had been hoped to go on to bombard Ostende, but with the turret troubles, this was not possible and the fleet returned safely to Dover. Preliminary reports indicated considerable damage from the bombardment, including two submarines and two dredgers sunk, one lock damaged and part of the works destroyed.

German accounts however show that these reports were much exaggerated, damage being limited to two barges sunk, some buildings and works damaged, two Belgian civilians killed and some German workmen wounded. Although the locks were not hit, Admiral A.D. Jacobsen, commanding the marine artillery in Flanders, later wrote commending the good British shooting in which shells had landed close all around the target. With short range batteries of old-fashioned guns transferred from Germany and no U-boats ready for action, the enemy were powerless to retaliate. Jacobsen wrote:[1]

> "We stood there with clenched fists, gritting our teeth, and had to let the onslaught roll over us. After we had expended so much effort on building our coastal batteries, the enemy simply remained outside their range and could do just as he liked."

From the British viewpoint, the operation could be regarded as reasonably successful for a first attempt and, if the technical difficulties could be overcome, promised well for the future.

Plans were then made for a second bombardment, this time of Ostende, whose dockyard was being used as a forward base for German torpedo-boats and U-boats.. Westende, seven miles west, was also included; it was nearer the front-line and contained numerous small batteries and observation posts. Following the weak retaliation at Zeebrugge, no great enemy response was anticipated, although several 150-mm (5.9-inch) batteries had been located, together with the Hindenburg battery, which mounted four relatively short range 280-mm (11-inch) guns east of Ostende. Meantime, *Moore* and *Rupert* had retired to Chatham to have their turrets and steering gear overhauled, *Clive* remaining at Dover. *General Craufurd* had just arrived from Belfast on 30 August, so that by early September there were four large and one small monitor (*M.25* carrying one 9.2-inch gun) ready to bombard Ostende. Arrangements remained basically similar to the Zeebrugge operation, except that the ships would fire whilst underway. The force was

[1] *Trutzig und Treu*, p.49 (see Bibliography)

All six of the Dover 12-inch monitors in line ahead, taken from Prince Rupert, *showing (left to right)* Sir John Moore, Prince Eugene, General Craufurd, General Wolfe *and* Lord Clive. *The date and purpose of the operation are not known, but may have been support of the Allied offensive in France in September 1916.*

divided into two divisions, the first with the monitors going to Ostende, the second with *Redoubtable, Excellent* and *Bustard* to Westende.

Two false starts were made; bad weather both on 2 September and on the 5th forced the 87-ship fleet to return to Dover. The weather cleared on the 6th so, by early morning on the 7th, the fleet was in position off Ostende, the mines swept and the nets laid. Unfortunately the weather was clear everywhere except over the target, where a haze prevented observation. Rather than risk exposure to the enemy shore batteries, Bacon ordered the fleet to retire until visibility improved. Attacks by German U-boats and aircraft were made, but the monitors sustained no damage. By mid-afternoon, the weather had cleared and the monitors again took up their positions. However it was found that the observation tripods could not be used effectively after their temporary withdrawal in the morning, so they were unable to provide any worthwhile spotting information. Fortunately the shore spotting posts near Nieuport had not yet been located by the Germans, and these could also be supplemented by three Short seaplanes put up by *Riviera*.

At 15.30 *Lord Clive* opened fire with a ranging shot at Ostende lighthouse from 17,500 yards but, as the other monitors started to shoot, a hitherto unsuspected shore battery began to drop heavy shells close to *General Craufurd*. The enemy fire soon switched to the flagship *Clive*, and there ensued a very lively half-hour. The Germans had the range accurately as they were using an observation balloon, so proceeded to surround *Clive* with an alarming number of near-misses. In an endeavour to open the range, she turned to steam out to sea but, as her speed was so slow, the shells continued to follow and fall all around her. At about 15.50 she received four hits in quick succession; one on the port bulge aft; one on the starboard 2-pdr, but fortunately this shell did not explode although it knocked the gun down on to the quarterdeck; one hit alongside the bulge forward and another on the bows, which severely shook the turret. It was obvious to Bacon that it would not be long before one of the steeply plunging shells would hit *Clive* fair and square and penetrate right through her decks to explode near her keel; furthermore, falling rigging had severely injured Carter, so he gave the order to retire.

Meantime the other monitors had got off a few rounds, but *Moore*'s hydraulic pump had broken down after only two rounds. In all only 14 rounds had been fired between the four ships, one setting fire to part of the dockyard. The enemy fire slackened as the monitors waddled out of range, but the ships were unable to reply as their turrets would not train far enough aft. During this time, the seaplanes had had a grandstand view from 7000ft; not only could they see the gunflashes, but they could even watch the individual shells passing through the air on their way towards their targets and landing with a splash that almost obscured the monitors.

The strength of the enemy defences in this sector had come as a nasty surprise. It was afterwards discovered that the damage had been wrought by 28 rounds from the newly installed Tirpitz battery, two miles south-west of Ostende, mounting four 280-mm coast defence guns in single mountings which had originally been ordered by Belgium from Krupp. The guns could normally range about 31,000 yards, although this was later increased to about 36,000 yards using special ammunition. Fortunately the Germans ceased firing at only 25,000 yards, as the guns had only just been installed and the fire control equipment had not been completed. Although *Clive*'s damage was little more than scratches, it was evident that Bacon's system of nets and tripods would not work within range of such powerful shore batteries. Once again it was demonstrated that ships were at a severe handicap in a duel with shore guns.

Prince Eugene had arrived at Dover on this same day, followed shortly after by *Marshal Ney*. With the latter's longer range 15-inch guns, it was considered possible to bombard Ostende docks and the Tirpitz battery from the West Deep, an offshore channel between Dunkirk and Nieuport, which was thought to be outside the training sector of Tirpitz' guns and which would be too shallow for U-boats. *Lord Clive* and *Sir John Moore* would again tackle Ostende targets, while *Prince Eugene* and *Marshal Ney* attempted to suppress the batteries' fire. After another postponed start, the ships set off on 19 September, but *Eugene* had to drop out as she had depleted her bunkers waiting. *Ney*'s activities are related

Sir John Moore *coaling in Dover harbour from a collier alongside. Two of the four 6-inch added as secondary armament in 1916 can be seen. A flexible voice-pipe runs from the spotting top to the turret to supplement the telephone system.*

on p.72, but *Clive* had little more success than on the last occasion. The enemy guns were found to be quite capable of all-round training and quickly drove her out of range, although later in the afternoon she managed a few retaliatory rounds.

The Allies' autumn offensive was due to start on 25 September and Sir John French wished the Germans to keep as many of their troops as possible tied up at the coast, away from Champagne and Artois where the main blow was to fall. Bacon therefore planned a feint landing and arranged for the monitors to bombard near Nieuport to cover an imaginary advance and near the Dutch border as if covering a landing. So on the 25th, *Craufurd* and *Eugene* shelled the coast near Zeebrugge, while *Clive, Moore* and *Ney* bombarded Westende. 194 rounds in all were fired that day, but such a rate of fire could not long be maintained as ammunition stocks were limited; so also was the supply of spare gun barrels. An intermittent fire was kept up till the end of the month, then bad weather interfered with operations. A final bombardment to support the Army was made at night on 3 October by *Moore, Eugene* and *Rupert*.

The monitors had come under attack from shore batteries, from the air and from U-boats but, by keeping on the move, they avoided damage. The effect of these bombardments was not known at the time, but in fact the Germans did reinforce their troops in the coastal sector as they feared a British landing; they also put in hand the construction of additional coastal batteries. During October, the batteries near Westende were fired at on several occasions but, although the shells fell close and one battery was temporarily evacuated, no gun positions were actually destroyed. Under the strain of these repeated firings, some of the 12-inch guns were beginning to give trouble, necessitating their replacement as described on p.183.

General Wolfe, the last 12-inch monitor to be completed, arrived at Dover on 12 November, bringing the squadron up to six 12-inch and two 15-inch gun ships, plus four small monitors. For operations off the Belgian Coast, the monitors normally used Dunkirk as a forward base. At night, one of them would usually anchor off Nieuport to deter enemy torpedo-boats from raiding Dunkirk or the Army's left flank or laying mines, but the Germans in fact considered such operations too risky.

With winter setting in, the daylight hours fading and the gales increasing in frequency, it was time to take stock of operations to date. Two major difficulties had arisen: (i) the lack of satisfactory observation methods, and (ii) the outranging of the monitors' guns by the shore batteries. As a result of earlier experience with the *Revenge* trials, Altham was sent to the Thames Estuary with *Craufurd* and *Riviera* on 15 November. A series of trials were undertaken to develop the use of wireless in seaplanes and to practise methods of spotting the simultaneous fire of several ships. The observers were required to learn the positions of all the topographical features surrounding each target, so that corrections could be more accurately translated into "yards, left or right, over or short". With the keen co-operation of the R.N.A.S., the trials were successfully completed, but bad weather prevented the adoption of the new methods in service until January 1916.

The problem of the shore batteries remained, as they were sited to protect the most important targets. Smokescreens showed promise for shielding the monitors, so experiments were made with different types of smoke producer. To date the Germans were not very impressed by the monitors' performance. A report on 5 December by the Commander of the Flanders Naval Corps, Admiral von Schröder, stated:[1]

> "They always took good care to keep out of range of our coastal guns, for if they had not done so, the danger of being hit was far greater for them than the prospect of hitting anything themselves; as soon as they were under fire they steamed off again. At the long ranges thus made necessary, spotting and sufficient hitting power were not possible. In fact hitting was merely accidental. Long range coast artillery practically nullifies the navigational advantage possessed by these ships in their light draft; the completion of the new battery at Knocke will therefore be of great importance to Zeebrugge section. Again the immunity of the monitors from

[1] *Der Krieg zur See, Nordsee,* Vol. IV, p.328

mines and submarine attacks is only relative. At all events the English obtained better results with the old cruisers and battleships in which they first appeared off our coast than they now get with the new type of ship."

During December and January, all the Dover monitors except *Wolfe* were ordered to the Thames Estuary to try to intercept Zeppelins coming in from over the North Sea to raid London. The intention was for the small monitors to fix the Zeppelins in their searchlights, while the large monitors fired 12-inch shrapnel at maximum elevation. However lacking any form of high angle fire control, hitting such a target was almost impossible; in the event, the few Zeppelins sighted were far out of range.

During these quieter spells, Bacon's thoughts were turning towards other means of restricting German use of the bases at Ostende, Bruges and Zeebrugge. Three plans were considered, all fully described in *The Dover Patrol*:—

(i) Landing on the mole (breakwater) at Zeebrugge and blowing up the lock gates of the Bruges Canal
(ii) Closing the entrance to Ostende harbour with blockships
(iii) Landing a force of 10,000 men at Ostende to capture the Tirpitz battery and link up with Allied forces advancing from Nieuport.

In all these operations, it was planned to use the large and small monitors both as bombardment ships and as landing vessels. Upon detailed examination, the first scheme had to be abandoned until an effective type of smokescreen had been developed. The second planned to use an old cruiser to manoeuvre two blockships across the narrow harbour entrance. The scheme was well advanced when the Army vetoed it; it was considered unwise to block a harbour which the Allies might need after a subsequent advance into Belgium. In addition, it was realised that no blocking could be permanent; it would not take the Germans long to salvage the blockships. The third scheme replaced the second; it was intended that all six 12-inch monitors would force their way right into Ostende harbour, together with three of the small monitors and 90 troop-carrying trawlers. Planning and co-operation with the Army was going well, when early in 1916 came news of the installation of a new German battery at Knocke near Zeebrugge, named after Kaiser Wilhelm II. Following the first bombardment of Zeebrugge, the Germans had pressed on with the construction of a battery there which could outrange the monitors. With four 305-mm (12-inch) guns with a range of 41,000 yards capable of reaching Ostende, the position of any British ships forcing a way into the harbour would become completely untenable. Reluctantly, the plan had to be abandoned.

The monitors continued to meet short-term calls on their services. During January 1916, Marshal Foch requested a demonstration to support Army operations. Here was the chance to put into effect the newly developed air spotting procedures. Bacon set off in *General Wolfe* on the 25th accompanied by *Lord Clive, General Craufurd, Prince Eugene, Marshal Ney, M.25* and *M.27. Wolfe* was now commanded by Captain J. A. Moreton, who had previously served under Bacon as a pioneer submariner. The monitors anchored in the mid-afternoon of the 26th and, from an extreme range of 21,000 yards, proceeded to bombard the batteries around Westende. The ships fired in rotation so that shells landed at roughly 20-second intervals, thus permitting corrections to be signalled to individual ships. The spotting proved reasonably effective but, as might be expected, *Craufurd* was the most efficient at making use of the corrections. Each large monitor fired about 11 rounds, meeting with little response from the enemy during the half-hour operation.

This proved to be the last bombardment for seven months, until the faster 15-inch monitors *Erebus* and *Terror* joined the squadron. In the interim, the 12-inch monitors remained based at Dover, undertaking a multitude of activities. The opportunity was taken to refit each ship at Chatham or Portsmouth, where 6-inch guns were added on the forecastle deck to strengthen their anti-destroyer defences and supplement short range bombardment capability. Early in April, *Craufurd* started ferrying spare naval guns from Chatham to Dunkirk to be used as heavy shore artillery in France. Initially one 12-inch Mk X weighing 58 tons, was brought over, followed in July by two others, and then by three 9.2-inch Mk X, each 28 tons. Bacon describes in detail how the guns were chocked up on the forecastle deck amidships, whence they could be rolled down a special timber platform on to the quayside without the need for heavy cranes, as shown in the photograph.

During the summer of 1916, General Craufurd *was used to ferry 12-inch Mark X guns from Chatham to Dunkirk, whence they could be moved to the front near Nieuport. This view shows the first of the guns being unloaded at Dunkirk on 5 April 1916 and being rolled on to the quayside, there being no crane heavy enough for the 58-ton lift.*

On 24 April, a net barrage was laid off the Belgian Coast, with the object of restricting the passage of U-boats to and from their bases. *Eugene* and *Wolfe* were allocated to cover the operation, which involved drifters laying nets fitted with mines, backed up by further lines of moored mines. The barrage ran for 20 miles between Nieuport and Zeebrugge, about 12 miles offshore. During the afternoon, Tirpitz battery fired on *Wolfe* from 32,000 yards, straddling her with four salvoes.

Earl of Peterborough*'s 12-inch turret covered by sandbags to give protection against aircraft bombs while in the Adriatic. The short 35-calibre guns are at maximum elevation. The hatch and davit are for loading shells into the magazine.*

Wolfe retreated at full speed but, as she could only cover about 200 yards a minute, it was some time before she was out of range. Enemy aircraft then appeared on the scene, but their bombing was ineffective. Possibly *Wolfe*'s 12-inch fire scared them off, as it produced an impressive burst of black smoke as well as a hail of shrapnel balls. Later in the afternoon, enemy torpedo-boats were sighted, so the escorting British destroyers set off in pursuit. In the ensuing fight, German shore batteries hit *Melpomene* but she was extricated under the covering fire of *Wolfe* and *Eugene*.

In order to prevent the Germans clearing the nets and sweeping the mines, a continuous patrol of large and small monitors, destroyers and drifters was maintained all through the summer of 1916. The monitors served as rallying points for the destroyer patrols, as they were reckoned almost invulnerable to anything below a cruiser. German destroyers appeared on numerous occasions, especially during May, June and July. A strong force of 12 ships was turned back on 8 June by the combined fire of *Clive, Moore, Soult* and destroyers. The Germans soon acquired a healthy respect for 12-inch gunfire and usually retreated out of range on seeing the flash of the guns, while U-boats dived rapidly if spotted on the surface; the barrage and its patrols were a considerable nuisance to them. Occasionally Kaiser Wilhelm battery would open up at the monitors, but at such long ranges the monitors were very small targets — although any hit would probably have been fatal. The most serious threat was from enemy aircraft; bombs were frequently dropped all around the monitors, but fortunately without success. On those occasions when there were no British aircraft on patrol, the monitors' A.A. guns could usually keep the German planes high enough to spoil their aim. Air raids on the monitors' bases at Dover and Dunkirk were commonplace, but damage was usually slight, although alarming to the civilian population.

By early July, the first of the 12-inch guns which *Craufurd* had brought over had been erected in the Dominion battery at Adinkerke near the Franco-Belgian border. Fire was opened on the Tirpitz battery from 27,000 yards on the 8th. Elaborate precautions had been taken to conceal the battery during its erection in dummy farm buildings, but it was also essential not to give away its position during firing, thus inviting retaliation. So Bacon arranged both for French 240-mm (9.45-inch) guns ashore and *Clive* offshore to fire simultaneously to mislead the Germans as to the true source of the gunfire. *Clive* was rigged out with a dummy second funnel to make her appear as a newly arrived monitor, and she fired blanks in unison with the shells of Dominion battery. The Germans were not deceived by this ruse and retaliated at the French guns. The firings were technically successful on this and the next day but, although some 40 shells landed all round the Tirpitz battery temporarily damaging No. 2 gun, no direct hits were scored on the actual mountings. The Germans soon developed a smokescreen to hide the battery, which severely hampered spotting and they also located and returned Dominion's fire.

During August, *Craufurd* continued her role as guinea-pig ship with night bombardment trials using a gyro receiver to help train the turret to predetermined bearings. She fired 38 rounds at Middelkerke in the early hours of the 16th. Shore spotting aircraft were not able to reach the area in time but, observing that the night was clear and moonlit, Altham reported that if a seaplane had been carried on board, there would have been no difficulty. Four nights later, he arranged with the Commodore in charge at Dunkirk to hoist aboard a Short 184. The seaplane was stowed on the forecastle deck abaft the funnel in the position provided for in the original design, the only difference being that the wings could not fold. Unfortunately low cloud prevented the seaplane from providing any useful reports. When Bacon heard of this trial, he was furious that his express permission had not been sought first. Altham was reprimanded in writing, Bacon's open letter to the Squadron ending, "In future, experimental work will be undertaken by ships other than *General Craufurd*." This rather childish response was typical of Bacon, a difficult commander who allowed his officers little scope for initiative, but one suspects that the main reason for his displeasure was that he had not first thought of the idea of using seaplanes at night.

On land, the Armies had been completely bogged down in virtually static trench warfare for nearly two years. In an attempt to break the stalemate, a major British offensive was planned for the summer of 1916, the Somme campaign opening on 1 July. Later General Sir Douglas Haig, commanding the British forces, requested operations by the Navy to simulate a landing between Middelkerke and Westende. As in the previous autumn, ships apparently associated with possible landings were exercised in the area, while the monitors softened up the enemy defences. From 8 September until Haig's offensive opened on the 15th using some of the first tanks, all the big gun monitors were in action off the Belgian Coast. Reinforcing *Soult* and the 12-inch stalwarts were the newly completed *Erebus* and *Terror*.

These bombardments were now being undertaken in quite a different manner from the opening rounds of twelve months earlier. The nets and spotting tripods had disappeared, but in their place considerably improved air and shore spotting techniques had been developed, as further described in Chapter X, §7. Smoke-producing motor-launches (M.L.s) were used to lay screens from behind which the monitors fired, invisible to the enemy spotters ashore. Although the 12-inch ships contributed their quota of nearly 200 out of over 300 rounds fired during this period, they also assisted the 15-inch monitors by acting as offshore aiming marks, especially for night firings. *Clive* notched up 74 rounds during the week, having taken over *Craufurd*'s experimental role, but the latter was only permitted to fire seven, Altham still being in disgrace. Generally three or four monitors would anchor offshore in the early evening and lay down a barrage for half an hour, each firing every two minutes. No great number of hits was observed, but the principal object was to tie down enemy forces and keep them occupied, especially the numerous 150-mm batteries around Westende.

After a week of intensive operations, normal duties could be resumed. On 23 September *Moore* completed her interrupted trials of the small Zero submarine scout airship, to discover whether it could be towed from ships for gunnery spotting, but the results were not very encouraging. The weather soon turned wintry, limiting any further operations during 1916. The monitors were despatched in turns to Southampton during October and November, where they could be drydocked two at a time in the large 900ft × 100ft Trafalgar Dock. As *Rupert*'s guns had been giving trouble during the recent bombardment, including three prematures at 1000 yards, and she was the slowest of the 12-inch monitors, she was banished to guardship duties similar to the two 14-inch monitors. After her refit, she took up a berth on 5 November at the mouth of the River Tees to protect Middlesbrough and Hartlepool, the latter having been bombarded by the Germans during the Scarborough Raid in December 1914. The patrol of the Belgian Coast barrage was abandoned for the winter, but 12-inch monitors maintained anti-destroyer patrols most nights during the early months of 1917 off Calais and the Downs.

§4 Home Waters 1917-1918

Two major schemes had been maturing in Bacon's mind for some time, one concerned with checking the activities of the U-boats using Belgian bases, the other a landing at Middelkerke to outflank the German front-line. The former operation involved putting out of action the lock gates on the Bruges Canal but, as the bombardment was planned to be made by the 15-inch gun monitors, it is described on p.74. The role of the 12-inch ships was merely that of acting as aiming marks. The landing operation was intended to link up with an Army advance from Ypres. The 12-inch monitors were recognised as now being of little direct value in bombardments as their guns were completely outranged by the shore batteries. They could thus be spared for operations which, although risky, would offer worthwhile advantages if successful.

The menace of the Germans using Belgian bases during wartime was all too apparent, but the Admiralty was equally concerned about the danger of their continuing to

Coaling in progress on board Sir John Moore, *with 2-cwt sacks being hoisted aboard from a collier alongside. A typical coaling rate was about 60 tons per hour, or ten sacks a minute.*

The monitors' bulges had many uses besides torpedo protection. Here a diver goes down to inspect Sir John Moore*'s hull. The C.P.O. is standing on one of the fenders added for the Great Landing operations.*

Prince Rupert *(left) and* Prince Eugene *(right) linked together with one of the three 540ft pontoons for the Great Landing, from which a division of men were to have been landed in August/September 1917, had the Allied Ypres offensive progressed well. Smoke producing gear can be seen in front of the spotting tops.*

hold the coast after any possible armistice. If they did so, they would dominate the approaches to London and much of the southern North Sea, as well as surrounding Holland from all sides on land. During the latter months of 1916, Bacon had thought out a new plan, in which troops would be put ashore between Nieuport and Ostende. They would have the opportunity of turning the German flank, destroying the coastal batteries and linking up with British forces advancing from the south. The shallow sandy coastal waters would require the use of long piers to disembark the troops, so Bacon's plan, described at length in his book, was for these to be formed by floating pontoons, which would be pushed into place by the 12-inch monitors.

An initial pontoon design was completed at the end of 1916: 540ft long, 30ft broad and a draft tapering from 20in forward to 9ft aft, the latter being the forward draft of the monitors. Such a pontoon displaced 2500 tons and could carry several thousand men, as well as tanks, guns and transport equipment. One was hurriedly constructed at Chatham Dockyard, during which time other preparations were made for the landings: coastal surveys, Army liaison, tank landing experiments and modifications to the monitors. The first pontoon was completed in March 1917 ready for trials. *Clive* and *Moore* had been undergoing their modifications at Southampton and arrived at the Swin off Foulness on 28 March, where they would be out of sight of any watchers ashore. The two monitors were lashed alongside each other and the pontoon was manoeuvred so that it fitted between their bows, projecting forward some 500 feet, as shown in the photograph. The trials showed that using the monitors to push the pontoons was perfectly practicable.

Orders were immediately given for two more similar pontoons and detailed planning with the Army went ahead. Haig was anxious to proceed with the operation which, apart from clearing part of the coast and fulfilling the Admiralty's request to strike a blow at the U-boat bases, would relieve pressure on the weakened French lines further south. His objective was first the capture of the commanding Messines Ridge about five miles south of Ypres, and then an advance north-east towards the important railway junction of Roulers on the way to the Belgian Coast ports. At this point the Navy would land 1 Division of 13,750 men at three places about one mile apart between Westende and Middelkerke. Each of the groups or columns comprised a pair of monitors, a pontoon, a brigade of men, three tanks, four 13-pdr field guns, two 4.5-inch howitzers and transport. A large supporting fleet of cruisers, destroyers, 15-inch and small monitors, minesweepers, motor-launches and lighters was also required to cover the landing and the subsequent supply operations. The three 15-inch monitors would bombard shore batteries, *M.25* would carry the Army H.Q. staff and the four other small monitors would act as general escorts.

The monitors joined the three pontoons at South West Reach in the Thames in mid-July. *Clive* and *Moore* were again paired, taking the pontoon which would make the centre landing, while *Wolfe* and *Craufurd* took the eastern and *Eugene* and *Rupert* the western pontoon. *Rupert* had been recalled from the Tees to make up the numbers, and *Roberts* had been withdrawn from Yarmouth to act as reserve ship in the event of breakdown. During the last two weeks of July, the monitors practised their manoeuvres, either at night or in cloudy weather to prevent observation by German aircraft. No leave was permitted and communications with the shore were strictly limited. Similarly 1 Division was restricted in a special camp near Dunkirk, which port was to be used for final embarkation of troops and equipment onto the monitors and pontoons. Embarkation was planned to take place three days before the scheduled landing, whose own date would depend on progress of the Army inland.

The Third Battle of Ypres opened with high hopes on 31 July 1917. Almost immediately however, the weather broke and the rain and mud of Flanders, allied to strong German defences, severely hampered progress. The monitor crews and soldiers waited in vain all through August for the news that Roulers had been taken and the landing could go ahead. The September offensive was undertaken in better weather, but progress remained obstinately slow; by 20 September the British forces had advanced only two of the necessary ten miles. By this time, suitable daylight hours, favourable tides and expectations of reasonable weather were all rapidly disappearing. In order to salvage something from all the elaborate preparations, Bacon put forward the suggestion of a modified landing operation with the limited objective of destroying enemy guns in the Nieuport-Middelkerke area. But Haig was not prepared to co-operate with such a different plan, so on 2 October the monitors and pontoons were dispersed.

Thus ended the only serious attempt to use amphibious power on the Western Front during WW1. Subsequent assessments showed that the landing, spearheaded by tanks, stood a fair chance of success, particularly if carried out whilst the enemy was being hard pressed by Allied forces further inland. The covering of the actual landing by smokescreens would have reduced the effectiveness of the German batteries' fire. Jacobsen later wrote that he considered the landing itself would have been successful, but that the various lines of defence inland would have halted a further advance. Although casualties would have been heavy, it seems strange that an Army leadership which could countenance the resulting slaughter of Passchendale (which included 1 Division) was reluctant to risk one division and six relatively expendable ships in an operation which might have helped turn the enemy flank, seriously weaken his hold on the Belgian Coast and its naval bases, and open up new hope to the stalemated Allied Armies.

The six 12-inch monitors all arrived at Portsmouth on 4 October for drydocking in pairs. On completion, *Rupert* was sent back to the Tees, where she remained for the rest of the war, apart from a month refitting at Jarrow in April 1918. Before coming south for the Great Landing, she had been relieved by *Moore* off Redcar Wharf at the end of May 1917 whilst she was in the Tyne for Smith's Dock to add teak fenders and extra mooring fittings. In mid-June *Moore* provided a similar service for *Roberts* at Yarmouth, taking the opportunity of using the shore observation stations to recalibrate her guns.

During July, a barrage similar to that of 1916 was laid off the Belgian Coast. Owing to the absence of the 12-inch monitors preparing for the Great Landing, most of the patrols were carried out by the 15-inch monitors. As related in Chapter VIII, they made good use of their opportunities for bombarding Ostende. The 12-inch

Prince Eugene *after being taken in hand for conversion by Portsmouth Dockyard to carry a single 18-inch gun abaft the funnel. As the mounting was not yet ready, she returned to service in April 1918 without the gun. The upper deck has been completely plated up at the sides and its after part strengthened for the gun. A rail has been fitted on the bulge to stop distance-controlled explosive boats hitting the main hull.*

monitors took up patrols again in November, firing on distant enemy destroyers and submarines as occasion offered, and in their turn being shelled by shore batteries and bombed by aircraft. These actions were inconclusive; only on rare occasions was even minor damage inflicted on either side. The barrage patrols continued throughout the winter, the monitors giving support to the smaller vessels guarding the anti-submarine minefields. Until April 1918, this burden fell mainly on *Craufurd, Wolfe* and *Moore*, as the other two were undergoing conversion at Portsmouth Dockyard to carry an 18-inch gun. As described in more detail in §6 and p.184, three 18-inch guns were available after *Furious*' conversion into an aircraft carrier. *Clive, Eugene* and *Wolfe* were each selected to receive one gun, to be installed at the after end of the forecastle deck. Considerable modifications were required to prepare the ships for their massive new armament. *Clive* underwent her structural modifications between 5 December 1917 and 6 April 1918 and *Eugene* between 13 December and 7 April. Owing to delays in converting the gun mountings, their new armament was not ready for shipping by April, so the two monitors returned to normal service. *Clive* got a new C.O., Commander R.J.N. Watson, who had spent the previous year in command of *Marshal Ney* at the Downs. The dockyard then took the third ship *Wolfe* in hand on 5 April.

Meantime Bacon had continued to make new plans for action against the U-boat base at Bruges. Although the 18-inch guns would be able to reach inland to bombard Bruges, he was anxious to mount another operation which could be put into effect rather sooner to limit the U-boat activities which had been causing increasing merchant ship losses during 1917. He planned for two 12-inch monitors to go alongside the outer wall of the mole at Zeebrugge under cover of a smokescreen. While troops disembarked from *Sir John Moore* to overwhelm German defences in the immediate vicinity, *General Craufurd* would fire her 12-inch guns directly at the lock gates of the Bruges Canal 2000 yards distant. Bacon submitted his plan to the First Sea Lord, now Admiral

Lord Clive*'s 384-ton 18-inch mounting caused a trim by the stern of $4^1/_2$ feet. The two large 36-inch searchlights, the pom-poms on the 18-inch gunshield and the 18-inch director offset to port where it could train on the aiming mark ship out to sea, can all be seen.*

Jellicoe, on 4 December but the latter, whilst in general agreement, suggested combining it with a blocking operation across the canal entrance. Bacon was doubtful of the efficacy of blocking; even if blockships could be accurately placed in position under heavy defensive fire, it would not be difficult for the enemy either to make a channel around them by cutting away the canal bank or to demolish their above-water structure sufficiently to allow the relatively shallow draft submarines to pass over the obstructions on the top of the tide. With some reluctance however, he acceded to Jellicoe's request and included blockships in his plan.

At the same time and unknown to Bacon, the newly appointed Director of Plans at the Admiralty, Commodore Keyes, had been preparing his own plan for blocking Zeebrugge and Ostende. As the number of U-boats passing through the Dover Straits had been seriously worrying the Admiralty for some time, Bacon was summoned to the Admiralty on 18 December in connection with the plans for patrolling the anti-submarine minefield across the Straits and for blocking Zeebrugge. At the meeting, the discussion was outspoken; Keyes criticised Bacon's plan and advocated his own, while Jellicoe overruled Bacon's views on the patrols. But great changes in personnel and organisation at the Admiralty were being proposed at the same time. Neither the Prime Minister, Lloyd George, nor the First Lord, Sir Eric Geddes, had been satisfied with Jellicoe's uninspired record as First Sea Lord, so they arranged to replace him with Vice-Admiral R.E. Wemyss. Similarly, Admiralty confidence in Bacon's handling of the Dover Command had waned, particularly in regard to the continuing passage of U-boats, so Wemyss lost no time in replacing him by Keyes on 28 December.

Keyes immediately took steps to put his own plans into effect and to develop a more offensive spirit in the Dover Squadron. Extensive night patrols of the Straits minefields were instituted, the small craft being backed up by large and small monitors. Detailed planning of his own scheme for blocking Zeebrugge and Ostende went ahead rapidly. This plan required of the monitors simply that they should act as a covering force to suppress the German coastal batteries. Full details are given in Keyes' memoirs[1] as well as in *Naval Operations* Volume V, although the former does not give sufficient credit to Bacon's preparations and the latter exaggerates the importance and results of the subsequent operations.

The 12-inch monitors were allocated to cover only the Ostende blocking force; *Prince Eugene* and *Lord Clive*'s targets being Tirpitz and Aachen batteries, *General Craufurd*'s Hindenburg, while *Sir John Moore* remained in the Dover Straits supporting the anti-submarine patrols. *Marshal Soult* was also in the force; her target was the Deutschland battery which had been installed in 1917 three miles east of Ostende, mounting four naval 380-mm (15-inch) guns with a normal range of 42,000 yards but a maximum range of 52,000 yards using special ammunition. The attempt on 11 April was called off after the blocking fleet was already at sea, the wind direction having changed, but by this time *Soult, Clive, Eugene* and *Craufurd* had fired off 50 rounds in all. After a second attempt was also abandoned due to bad weather, the four monitors set out again on the 22nd. They anchored in the West Deep and opened fire on their principal targets at 23.10 using *M.24* and *M.26* as aiming marks, later shifting to 150-mm batteries on the coast. Enemy return fire was accurate, some of the monitors being spattered by shell splinters. *Soult* fired a total of 87 rounds of 15-inch, the others about 50 rounds of 12-inch apiece, plus some 6-inch secondary. Meantime *Erebus* and *Terror* covered the Zeebrugge force as related on p.129.

When the blocking ships went in to Zeebrugge and Ostende in the early hours of the 23rd, the monitors were able to draw some of the fire of the coastal batteries. Although carried out with outstanding gallantry and providing a much needed morale-booster during a particularly bad time for the Allies, neither raid was successful in its principal objective of denying the enemy the use of the bases. The blockships only partially blocked the canal entrance at Zeebrugge, so a passage round them was soon made, first for the smaller German vessels, then for the larger. The attempt to block Ostende was a complete failure as the blockships grounded some distance from the harbour entrance.

The middle of 1918 did indeed see a reduction in U-boat successes, but this owed little to the operations against Ostende and Zeebrugge. By this time the convoy system had become fully effective, while the deep minefields and surface patrols in the Dover Straits were making hazardous this short cut to the favourite hunting areas. In retrospect, it is clear that much heavier aerial bombing would have been a more effective weapon against Bruges, but insufficient effort was devoted to such attacks.

This period also saw the fruition of developments set in train by Bacon which improved bombardment efficiency. In his memoirs, Keyes claimed that the Belgian Coast monitors had a good deal to learn from the experience of the Dardanelles bombardments, but this ignores the fact

[1] *The Naval Memoirs of Admiral of the Fleet Sir Roger Keyes. Scapa Flow to the Dover Straits 1916-1918*

that conditions for the monitors off the Belgian Coast were totally different and vastly more difficult than at the Dardanelles. At Gallipoli, there were visible targets, weak shore batteries, easy location of relative ship and target positions, better weather, deep water and lack of tides, together with Allied naval and air superiority. The improvements included more accurate charts permitting better position finding and ranging, and new longer range projectiles. In place of the old 2-calibre radius of head (c.r.h.)[1] 12-inch projectiles, 4 c.r.h. had already been introduced, but a newly designed 8 c.r.h. was planned to become available during 1918, with a long pointed cap to reduce air resistance. While not sufficient to match the range of the 15-inch guns, the increase to 26,000 yards for the 8 c.r.h. was worth having, as it would enable the 12-inch monitors to range again on Ostende and Zeebrugge from outside the line of mine nets.

The 12-inch monitors were more active during 1918 than at any time since 1915. Apart from covering the blocking operations, April saw several other bombardments mainly from the 15-inch monitors, including night action against coastal batteries. Standing orders allowed for emergency bombardment of certain specified locations on receipt of a call from the Army. *Eugene* and *Moore* were on patrol on 3 May when such a call was received. Between them they dropped 30 shells near Middelkerke from behind a smokescreen. D.H.4 aircraft of No. 202 Squadron of the newly formed Royal Air Force spotted the fall of shot, which was being used to calibrate the firing of the new 8 c.r.h. projectile. A second attempt to block Ostende was made on the night of 9/10 May. The monitors were out again to support the operation, *Craufurd* buoying the approach track, while *Eugene* and *Moore* fired on the smaller coastal batteries to the west of Ostende amidst clouds of enemy star-shells. Unfortunately the old cruiser *Vindictive*, who played such a gallant role at Zeebrugge, was not fully blocking the entrance channel when she was scuttled.

A new ship joined the monitor squadron in June — the ex-Norwegian coast defence ship *Gorgon* armed with two long range 9.2-inch guns, as described in Chapter VI. During July, *Clive* relieved *Roberts* at Yarmouth for five weeks while the latter refitted. On 16 August *Clive* arrived at Portsmouth to have her 18-inch gun and mounting fitted. The first gun had been allocated to *Wolfe*, whose conversion had now been completed, and she now returned to the Dover Squadron on 15 August with a new C.O., Commander S.B. Boyd-Richardson. It was not until late September that she had an opportunity of using her 18-inch gun against the enemy, although not at Zeebrugge as originally intended.

The Allies' recent attacks had found a weakened enemy with little capacity for resisting a sustained offensive. The Northern Armies, comprising British, French and Belgians under the command of the latter's King Albert, attacked along the coast in the early hours of 28 September. They were supported by seven of the Dover monitors, i.e. all the large ships except *Clive* and *Soult*, who were in dockyard hands. Initial night bombardments were made near Ostende and Zeebrugge to mislead the enemy into thinking that a landing might be attempted. By dawn, the monitors had all taken up new positions from which they could harass the German lines of communication inland. Division II, consisting of *Eugene, Moore* and *Craufurd*, anchored near the West Deep, while Division III with *Wolfe* and *Gorgon* were farther out. *Erebus* and *Terror*, comprising Division I, were in the same area, but were allocated enemy howitzers for targets. A continuous fire was planned to be kept up all day, supplemented by the monitors' secondary armament. Division II also had the subsidiary role of entering Ostende harbour to land troops, if the town showed signs of being evacuated.

During the morning, a regular fire was kept up, each ship firing at about 3-minute intervals. The weather was

[1] The c.r.h. figure denoted the radius of the ogive forming the head of the projectile, e.g. 2-calibre or 24-inch radius indicated a relatively short blunt projectile.

The two 18-inch monitors Lord Clive *(right) and* General Wolfe *seen at Dover in October 1918.* Clive *does not have the smoke producer which was fitted in* Wolfe *in front of the spotting top.* Clive's *secondary armament comprised four modern 4-inch, two 3-inch H.A. and three 2-pdr.*

A port broadside of General Wolfe *showing the rear of the open 18-inch mounting, the 18-inch ammunition derrick abaft the funnel, the cordite tanks (the shells were stowed horizontally on the upper deck beneath) and the anti-D.C.B. rail.*

poor, but some spotting was possible which reported good shooting. Division II were old hands, so their effort during the day in each firing about 100 rounds of 12-inch, plus their 60 rounds of 6-inch or 4-inch during the previous night, needs no further description. However *General Wolfe*'s activity is worth describing in some detail, as it is sometimes doubted whether she ever fired her 18-inch in action. The gun was fitted in a semi-fixed athwartship mounting projecting over the starboard bulge, capable of only a very limited amount of training. It was therefore necessary to anchor the ship at bow and stern broadside on to the target. In the tidal currents off the Belgian Coast, this presented some difficulty, so good weather was desirable for accurate shooting. Aiming marks were set up to seaward of the monitor, where they could be seen from the second director, fitted beneath and to port of the spotting top. The director passed signals to control training and elevation as well as to the main capstans to shift the ship if larger movements were required. The recoil of firing was found to produce not only a bodily sideslip with the shallow draft hull but also an appreciable roll. Thus an interval of some minutes was necessary between rounds, which gave time for the heavy work of reloading to be completed.

At 07.32 she opened fire from 36,000 yards on the important railway bridge at Snaeskerke, four miles south of Ostende. In doing so she made naval history: firing the heaviest shell from the biggest gun at the longest range ever used to date in action. The enemy batteries soon returned her fire, but with little effect. Despite assistance from the tug *Lady Brassey, Wolfe* was soon in trouble maintaining her position broadside on to wind and tide, as her anchors started to drag. Nevertheless, she managed to keep up over two hours of 'rapid' fire, dropping in all 44 shells near their target. The rate of fire was much better than anticipated — one round per 2min 38sec in place of 4 minutes on trials. Later in the day she fired a further eight rounds, thus virtually exhausting her outfit of sixty 18-inch. The monitors then all retired to Dunkirk for the night after the heaviest shore bombardment of the war — some 550 large shells. News was received that the Armies were making good progress, and that *Moore* had scored a direct hit on an ammunition dump.

The bombardment continued for the next five days, although not as heavy as on the 28th. *Wolfe* fired a further eighteen rounds on the 29th, three on 2 October, six on the 3rd; as before, the target was Snaeskerke. However air spotting conditions were unfavourable, as the weather had worsened, limiting the accuracy and value of the bombardment. The advance of the Allied Armies ashore ground to a halt once more in the Flanders mud. Not until 14 October were they able to make any further advance; the Germans began to withdraw to the east. The same targets were allocated to the monitors, but this time *Wolfe* was joined by *Lord Clive*, newly arrived with her 18-inch gun from Portsmouth the day before. Firing commenced at 07.10 on the 14th from 34,000 yards, but *Clive* fired only a single round at this time, receiving no spot. The other monitors were also firing, while one of the Great Landing pontoons was towed off the coast to give the impression of an imminent landing. Later in the day, *Clive* again tried her 18-inch. Three rounds were got off, again all unspotted, before the order to cease fire came to avoid hitting advancing Allied troops. *Wolfe* fired only two 18-inch rounds as she received no air spots either, but the other monitors fired 174 12-inch.

Another sortie was made on the 17th to assist the Army but, although well within range of the shore batteries, the monitors drew no fire from the enemy. Within 48 hours, the whole of the Belgian Coast had been evacuated. The batteries which had menaced the monitors for so long were now silent, having been blown up before evacuation. Armistice negotiations had been under way for some weeks and on 11 November the cease-fire came into effect. Meanwhile *Prince Eugene* had been despatched to Portsmouth on 19 October to have her 18-inch gun fitted, but three days later came orders to stop all further work. So she received neither mounting nor gun and was removed from drydock, paying off on 12

December. The other 12-inch monitors paid off in quick succession at Sheerness: *Craufurd* on 15 November, *Wolfe* on the 19th, *Clive* on the 26th and *Moore*, first of the monitors to arrive at Dover and last to leave, on 16 January 1919.

Thus ended the operations of the hard worked Belgian Coast 12-inch monitors. In the days before they were severely outranged, they had provided a useful bombardment capability which no other vessels could do satisfactorily. In subsequent years, they were outclassed by *Erebus* and *Terror*, but they continued to make a useful contribution as maids of all work. The monitors' harassment and the fear of landings forced the Germans into fortifying the Belgian Coast ever more strongly, so that by the end of 1918 it contained the strongest coastal defences anywhere in the world with around a hundred guns between 105-mm (4.1-inch) and 380-mm (15-inch) calibre. Resources of men, material and heavy guns had to be diverted for this purpose, which would have been more value at the front; conversely the Allies were enabled to dispense largely with such measures on their own coastlines. The monitors also provided a deterrent value against raids by German surface vessels in the Channel area and, in the event of an attempt by the High Seas Fleet to break through the Straits, might have helped delay them long enough for the Grand Fleet to arrive. For their crews, life was certainly more interesting than the dull routine of the big gun ships of the Grand Fleet far away to the north.

§5 Wartime Service in the Mediterranean

Churchill had originally planned that four of the 12-inch monitors should go to the Dardanelles, but this plan was cancelled after he left the Admiralty. Although the first five had been allocated to Dover, it was possible to send the sixth and seventh to be completed, *Earl of Peterborough* and *Sir Thomas Picton,* out to the Mediterranean where they could assist at Gallipoli and at the newly opened Salonika front. *Peterborough* set off from Devonport under her own steam on 19 October 1915 and arrived at Mudros on 13 November. She moved to a position off Suvla Bay and was soon in action, as the earlier successes of the 14-inch monitors and bulged cruisers had by now encouraged the Army to call on naval support with increasing frequency. Meanwhile *Picton* followed, arriving at Mudros on 15 December. She was briefed by *Abercrombie*, and then attached to the southern squadron which was to harass the Turkish positions on the Helles front during the Suvla and Anzac evacuations. On 19 and 20 December, she fired her first 50 rounds of 12-inch, while *Peterborough* undertook similar duties off Suvla. The two monitors also gave close support during the Helles evacuation as described on p.31.

By the middle of January 1916, new dispositions had been made for the monitors remaining in the Mediterranean. *Picton* moved off to Port Said, then steamed up the Suez Canal to Ismailia on 4 February to provide heavy gunfire support if the Turkish forces on the east side of the Canal should make another attempt to cross, such as had been tried twelve months earlier.

Sir Thomas Picton *leaves her builder's yard on 4 November 1915, already fitted with temporary coal bunkers for the long voyage to the Dardanelles.*

Following the paying off of *Marshal Ney* (see p.73), Captain Hugh Tweedie arrived to take command in April. Despite the availability of troops released from Gallipoli, the Turks were in no position to attempt a serious attack on the Canal so far from their bases across the wastes of Sinai. After several weeks, Tweedie became impatient to adopt a more active role and, as the Turks seemed increasingly unlikely to attack the Canal again, *Picton* was allocated in May to the *Goeben* watch at Imbros, relieving *Abercrombie*. Tweedie considered his ship quite unsuited to such a role, being not only vastly inferior in armament, but quite likely to be temporarily out of action for boiler cleaning or turret repairs. He reported accordingly to the C-in-C, but with no effect; 19 months later, *Raglan*'s loss proved him right.

In February 1916, *Peterborough* had been transferred to the Mitylene squadron at Port Iero, blockading the Turkish coast. Occasional bombardments were made on Turkish shore batteries protecting Smyrna, for which she sometimes carried her own spotting seaplane. Brief interludes occurred with a visit to Salonika in March, and also to Milo in June and August. The island of Milo, 80 miles south-east of Athens, was being used to harbour the Anglo-French squadron of battleships and other vessels, including *Peterborough* and *M.17*, gathered as a show of force against the Greek Government to accede to Allied requests concerning the prosecution of the war on the Salonika front against the Bulgarians. The Greek Navy put up no resistance at the end of August when the Allied ships, now including *Peterborough, M.29* and *M.33*, took over their Fleet.

The whole of 1916 saw an integration of the operations of the four remaining Mediterranean large monitors and the small monitors. One large vessel was always near Imbros on the *Goeben* watch, another at Stavros supporting the Allies' Salonika right flank, a third with the Mitylene squadron and the fourth refitting. *Picton* relieved *Raglan* at Stavros in August where she remained until December. These four months were more active for her, particularly after the Bulgarians occupied that part of the Greek coastline to the east. Stavros was close to the Allied right flank which reached the sea near the mouth

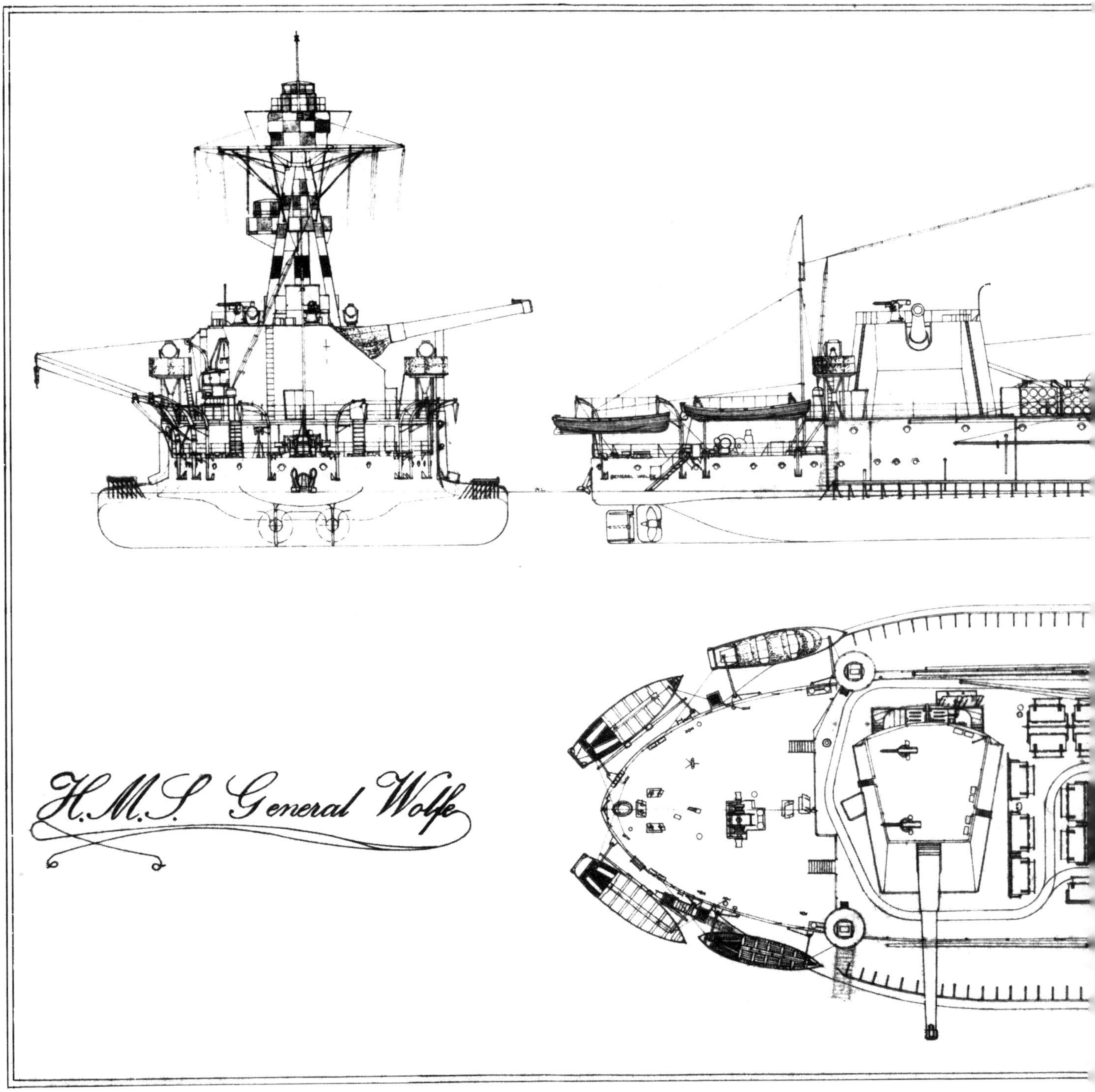

This drawing by A & A Plans shows General Wolfe *in August 1918 after her 18-inch gun had been installed. Other changes included the 18 cordite stowage tanks on the forecastle deck and the bogie track, the anti-D.C.B. rail on the bulge and the additional director*

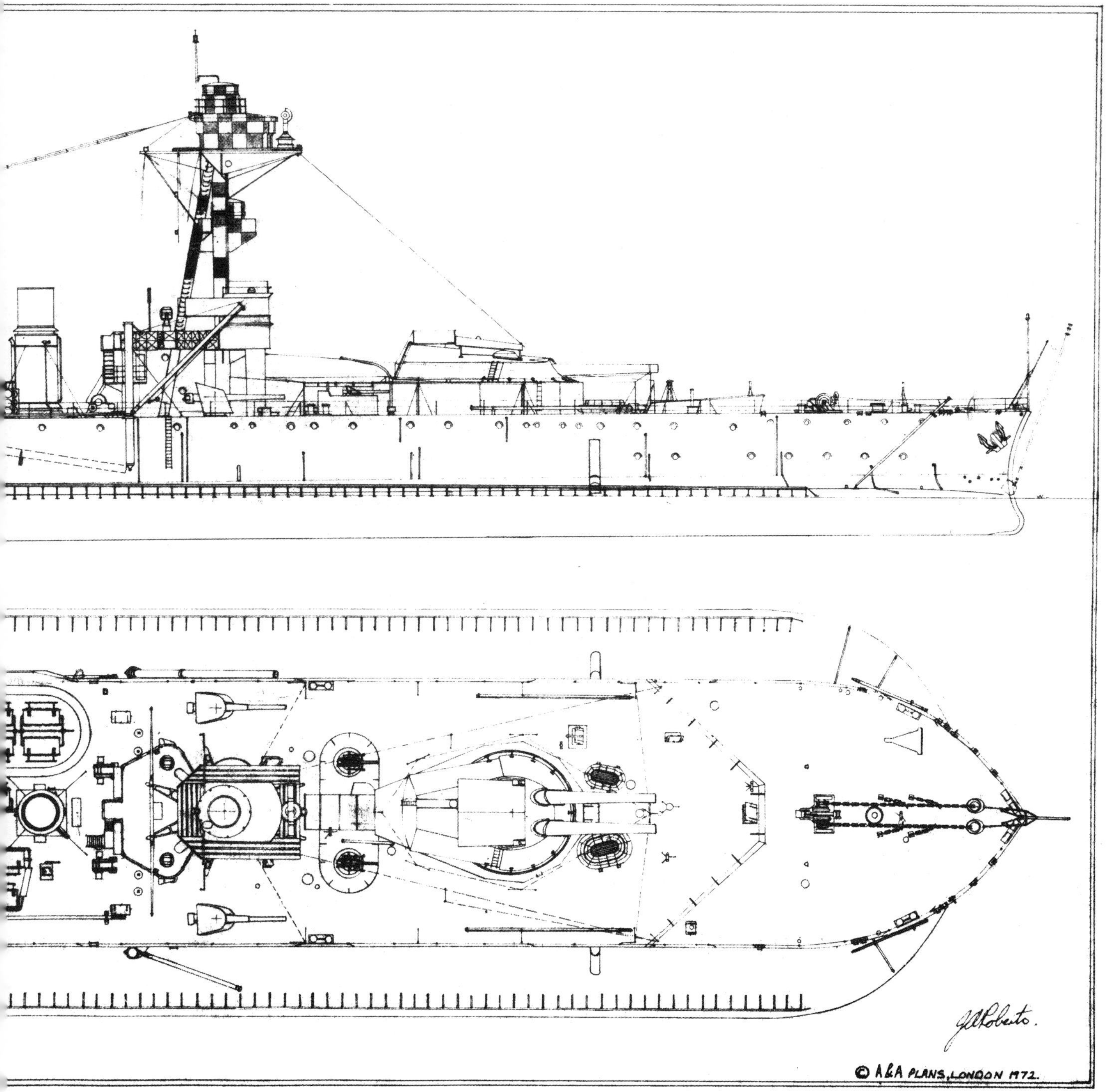

for the 18-inch to port on the foremast below the spotting top — painted in a chequer pattern. Lord Clive *was generally similar, apart from her secondary armament of four 4-inch in place of two 6-inch, and three instead of two single 2-pdr.*

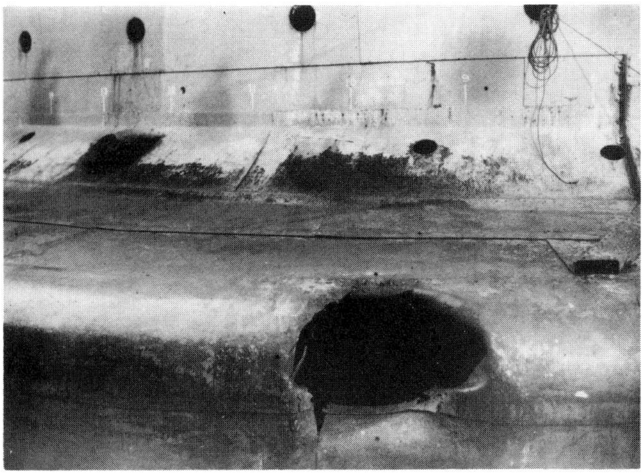

Exposed close off enemy-held coastlines, nearly all the monitors received shell hits at one time or another, but most were minor scratches like this one on Sir Thomas Picton's *forward bulge, received off the Salonika front in 1916.*

of the River Struma. Although the enemy was not very adventurous, the British squadron, which usually included a bulged cruiser and four or five small monitors, was able to assist feint attacks which were intended to tie down enemy troops, the Allied forces only having light artillery. The monitor was usually anchored bow and stern, and could readily engage in indirect fire, as by this time the calibration of the guns was accurately known.

Anchoring so close to the enemy was not without its risks; on the night of 4 September an enemy mobile battery had approached unobserved and at daylight proceeded to drop shells on to *Picton*. Before she could weigh anchor, she had received six hits, suffering nine casualties. Fire was exchanged but, by the time she returned after landing the wounded, the battery could not be relocated. Support was also given during the Allies' autumn attack which eventually took Monastir (now Bitolj) in southern Serbia. During mid-September a Short 184 from the seaplane carrier *Empress* was embarked for spotting duties. After a month at Salonika, *Picton* was back at Malta in February 1917 to have her guns changed.

Meanwhile *Peterborough* had been allocated in November 1916 to the British Adriatic Squadron at the request of the Italians and had arrived at Venice on 4 December. The Italians had entered the war against Austria-Hungary in May 1915, the Austrians withdrawing to a strong defensive line in hilly country to the east of the River Isonzo at the head of the Gulf of Trieste. Throughout 1916, the Italians had made little progress; the battle front remained as static as the Western Front. As the southern Austrian positions barring the way to Trieste were within range of naval guns, it was hoped to use monitors in situations where British and Italian battleships could not be risked owing to the danger of submarines and the nearness of the Austrian Battle Fleet at Pola. The Italians were building or converting a number of monitor type vessels; although some mounted 15-inch guns, they were smaller, slower and much less seaworthy than the British monitors. The Italian Army was short of heavy artillery so, with the withdrawal of the British pre-dreadnoughts from the Adriatic in early 1917, it was thought that the monitors would prove useful.

Picton was sent to join *Peterborough* as soon as she was available, arriving at Venice on 22 March 1917. The Italians were not very keen to expose ships near the Austrian naval bases, so the first real opportunity to use *Peterborough* and *Picton* offensively did not arise until May, when the Tenth Battle of the Isonzo was being planned. The Italian C-in-C, Count Cadorna, asked for a naval bombardment on Austrian lines of communication in the Gulf of Trieste. Rear-Admiral Mark Kerr, commanding the British Adriatic Squadron, arrived from Taranto to take charge of the operation but had some difficulty persuading the local Italian Admiral that the operation was not unduly risky.

After considerable delays, *Peterborough* and *Picton* sailed from Venice on 23 May to bombard the railway line out of Trieste and the important Austrian airfield at Prosecco. They arrived in the firing position at 05.30 on the 24th, intending to fire off 50 12-inch shells each. The monitors kept up a steady fire on the airfield unmolested for half an hour, but then shore batteries opened up, although their rounds fell short. Then eight enemy aircraft appeared and attacked fiercely, dropping bombs all around the monitors, splashes and splinters landing continuously on board. One 50-kg (110-lb) bomb landed on *Peterborough* blowing a hole in the forecastle deck abaft the turret and injuring Kerr, the only casualty. She got her revenge when her newly modified 12-pdr H.A. damaged an enemy plane, enabling Italian fighters to finish it off. After blasting the airfield with a good proportion of hits, the monitors turned their fire onto the Austrian headquarters and railway station. The spotting aircraft reported good shooting here also; the Italians were much impressed by the monitors' cool performance so close to strong enemy bases. The two monitors then returned safely to their berths at Venice for another three quiet months.

The Eleventh Battle of the Isonzo also gave the monitors a good chance to display their capabilities. Moving up to the forward base of Grado on 19 August, both vessels lay off the dominating Mount Hermada, which was being attacked by the Italian Third Army. After a few rounds of unspotted fire in poor visibility in the morning, the arrival of spotting aircraft permitted *Peterborough* and *Picton* to open rapid fire all afternoon on enemy dugouts and ammunition dumps. Six direct hits were obtained at about 16,000 yards out of about 60 rounds fired. Shore batteries returned a desultory fire, but their range was too short to do any damage. A repeat performance was undertaken on 21 August at the longer range of 19,000 yards which, with well-worn guns, necessitated heeling the monitors to gain additional elevation. Eleven hits were obtained out of 65 rounds. Spotting aircraft were able to provide a good service, as they were covered by Italian and French fighters.

The Italian monitors *Faa Di Bruno* and *Alfredo Cappellini* also added their 15-inch fire but, even with their support, the troops ashore could make little headway against the strongly defended Austrian positions. On 23 August, the British monitors switched to bombarding lines of communication. Results were less satisfactory as the 12-inch mountings were beginning to break down under the strain of repeated firings. The chances of hitting precise targets such as railway viaducts were slight; out of 54 rounds, only three hits were obtained and these only on large targets such as villages.

During September, the monitors shuttled between Venice and Grado; in October it was the Austrians' turn for the offensive. The blow fell on Caporetto on 24 October. The ill prepared Italian Second Army could not resist and fell back in rapid retreat, forcing the Third Army on the coast to withdraw also. *Peterborough* and *Picton* helped evacuate Grado on the 28th; between them they took to Venice 1200 people as well as guns from the forts. The Austrian advance was so rapid that the Italians were not able to make a stand before reaching the River Piave, less than 20 miles east of Venice. The monitors were withdrawn on 3 November to Chioggia but, when the Italian line had stabilised on the Piave, moved up again to give support.

The Austrians did their best to force crossings of the Piave, using floating pontoon bridges. The monitors could get within range by steaming up the shallow San Felice channel to the north-east of Venice. *Peterborough* started the firings on 18 November from about 19,000 yards. Her early attempts to hit such small targets were not very successful; after 28 rounds, all she had to show for her efforts were weed-choked condensers. On the 20th, she scored four hits and set fire to one of the bridges, in spite of the difficulties of spotting where enemy aircraft continually harassed the spotting planes. She was relieved by *Picton* soon afterwards; the latter continued the good shooting, obtaining hits on the narrow 10-foot wide bridges at the end of November. In December, the Austrian attacks eased off, though *Picton* ventured up the channel again on the 10th to bombard Passarella, using three-quarter charges for the reduced 15,000-yard range.

The two monitors remained at short notice until January 1918, when the situation appeared to have stabilised. In early February, and again in early March, they returned to the San Felice channel to bombard the Austrian positions. They both set off down the Adriatic on 18 March for the Italian west coast, where leisurely refits were undertaken: *Peterborough* at Spezia, *Picton* at Genoa. The monitors were still refitting during the Battle of the Piave in June 1918 but on completion they were sent to Valona in Albania at the western flank of the Allied Balkan front. The Italians were preparing an offensive, so on 7 July *Peterborough* and *Picton* fired on the Austro-Bulgarian positions near the coast, earning the thanks of the Italian C-in-C.

During the next few weeks they were at Valona, Brindisi and Ancona available for support if required. No further action occurred before the Armistice was signed, firstly with Bulgaria, finally with Austria on 3 November. Both monitors then proceeded up the now submarine-free Adriatic in easy stages, *Peterborough* going to

A view of Earl of Peterborough *in 1918, probably off Venice, showing her modifications, including heat-shield over the turret, 12-pdr converted to H.A. firing and closed-in upper deck. She was the only 12-inch monitor not to get a 6-inch secondary armament and she retained her topmast and yards for wireless aerials.*

Venice and *Picton* to Fiume as guardship at the Austrian naval base. Both ships were sent to Malta on 2 February 1919 to prepare for the voyage home, finally arriving in Britain in mid-March to pay off and join the other monitors laid up at Immingham in May.

§6 Modifications and Performance

The 12-inch monitors underwent rather more frequent modification than the 14-inch vessels, as conditions off the Belgian Coast were continually changing and dockyards more readily available. It was soon recognised that their weak secondary armament of two 12-pdr would not prevent a 'cutting-out' attack by destroyers from bearings and ranges which the 12-inch could not reach. It was also appreciated that a more powerful secondary armament would provide a supplementary medium range bombardment capability. Accordingly either two or four 6-inch Q.F. were fitted abreast the funnel on the forecastle deck of each of the Dover monitors, most of the guns being removed from the pre-dreadnought *Illustrious.* Chatham and Portsmouth dockyards carried out the installations early in 1916. *Wolfe, Moore* and *Craufurd* got four guns each, *Clive, Eugene* and *Rupert* two.

Minor changes were continually being made, especially to the H.A. armament. Topmasts were struck on the Dover ships, where long range wireless aerials were not needed, and the aircraft handling derricks removed. The navigating bridge structure was extended from the original bare searchlight platform that had been the only alternative to the inconvenient conning tower under the guns. The actual arrangement of the bridge differed in each ship, providing a useful recognition feature later. The changes to the Mediterranean pair were fewer than the Dover ships; *Picton* got only a single 6-inch B.L. XII abaft the funnel as in the 14-inch monitors.

Extensions were also required to the accommodation

as the numbers of the crew increased. From 194 as completed, numbers rose to 215 for ships with two 6-inch and to 232 for ships with four. Fortunately it was a simple matter to plate in parts of the side of the upper deck to make more cabin and mess space. This process continued until by 1918 the whole side was plated in all ships except *Moore, Rupert* and *Craufurd.* During 1917, further modifications included fitting smoke-making apparatus in front of the spotting top in the Dover ships, giving the appearance of a large rangefinder. The upperworks were often painted in a grey and white chequer pattern, although the hulls remained grey. The Adriatic monitors were painted khaki to match the colour of the water. 2-pdr and Maxims were often mounted on the turret and similar platforms for shooting-up the numerous mines found drifting off the Belgian Coast, as well as distance-controlled boats (D.C.B. — see p.128). The 6-inch Q.F. were gradually replaced by the more modern 6-inch B.L. VII, as the latter had a range of 13,500 yards compared with only 11,000 for the Q.F.; these in turn were later replaced by 4-inch B.L. IX in *Moore* and *Clive.*

The really big changes came in 1918 with the conversion of three ships to take the 18-inch gun. Because of the dual-purpose nature of the duties proposed after removal from *Furious*, i.e. capable of being mounted on land or on ship, a completely different design of mounting to the normal revolving turret was selected, as detailed on p.184. The whole mounting weighed about 384 tons, including the 149-ton gun, but nearly double when ammunition, equipment and supports were included, presenting quite a problem in mounting aboard a 6000-ton ship. Bacon's proposals for fitting the 18-inch in the monitors were put forward in the summer of 1917 and included strengthening the forecastle deck abaft the funnel to take the mounting, but leaving the existing armament undisturbed. As there was insufficient space below decks, stowage for enough projectiles for a day's firing would have to be on the upper deck, with cordite in cases on the forecastle deck. A light shield over the mounting would be arranged to represent armour plating, allowing elevation to 45°.

The only place to fit the mounting with its structural supports without removing the 12-inch turret was abaft the engine room. The large trimming moment due to this concentrated load aft would increase the draft aft to over 14 feet, seriously reducing the freeboard to only about 4 feet. The most satisfactory solution to reduce the resulting trim was to close up watertight the after inboard bulge compartments, which were normally open to the sea. Even so, the ship's drafts as finally converted became 8ft 9in forward and 13ft 2in aft, corresponding to a displacement of 6850 tons. The after part of the bulge was fully submerged, increasing the risk of a torpedo or D.C.B. riding over the bulge and exploding against the main hull proper, so a heavy steel deflector was built on top of the bulge.

The actual ships to be converted to take the 18-inch gun were easily selected: simply those with the three most senior C.O.s — *Lord Clive, Prince Eugene* and *General Wolfe.* The plan was to take the first two vessels in hand at Portsmouth in December 1917, fit the heavy supports in January and ship the mounting in March. After trials, they would return to service in May, while the third vessel started her conversion. But delays in converting the mountings meant that work on the hulls of the first two vessels was completed long before the mountings were ready. When the first mounting finally arrived at Portsmouth, it was fitted into the third ship *Wolfe*; the gun itself being lifted aboard in drydock on 9 July. After coaling and ammunitioning, *Wolfe* was ready for gun trials, which were carried out successfully off the Isle of Wight on 7 August.

General Wolfe's appearance had substantially altered. The huge box-like shield over the 18-inch gun gave rise to the nickname "Elephant and Castle" for the ship. The closing-in of the sides of the upper deck gave the hull a more businesslike appearance. The quarterdeck was considerably cramped by an extra boat, a proper stern

A starboard broadside of General Wolfe *shortly after her 18-inch had been installed in August 1918. Her twin 12-inch turret, complete with sunshield, was retained.*

anchor and windlass, and the extension aft of the forecastle deck. Apart from the two pom-poms on top of the 18-inch shield, the secondary armament was all concentrated forward — two six-inch B.L. VII abreast the bridge and two 3-inch H.A. abreast the 12-inch turret. Smaller changes included installing two 36-inch searchlights aft, replacing the two 24-inch on the mast, a slim mainmast to support the wireless aerials, bow defence gear (modified paravanes) for the bulged hulls, removal of the armoured conning tower, siting the 18 cordite stowage tanks and associated rail tracks abaft the funnel on the forecastle deck, a new ammunitioning derrick on the port side for the 18-inch and a more substantial bridge structure. Internally, the after half of the upper deck was given over to the 18-inch shell stowage and their transporters plus the extensive structural supports for the mounting. The latter cramped the officers' accommodation, so the warrant officers were moved up to cabins on the upper deck, where crew berthing was increased for the new complement of 278. The wireless room was moved to the hold where it would be better protected, as was the new gyro compass; magazines and stores were also re-arranged.

Clive returned to Portsmouth in August 1918 for her missing gun, which was finally shipped on 7 September, trials being carried out on 13 October. The war was over before *Eugene* received her gun, so she retained her rather bare aft end appearance with the plated-in hull and clear forecastle deck aft.

Changes to the 12-inch monitors' armament were more extensive than any of the other classes during WW1; they are tabulated below as existing at the end of the war:—

Lord Clive	1—18", 2—12", 4—4", 2—3", 3—2pdr
General Wolfe	1—18", 2—12", 2—6", 2—3", 2—2pdr
Prince Eugene	2—12", 2—6", 2—3", 2—2pdr
Sir John Moore	2—12", 4—4", 2—12pdr H.A., 2—3", 2—2pdr
General Craufurd	2—12", 4—6", 2—12pdr H.A., 2—3", 2—2pdr
Prince Rupert	2—12", 2—6", 2—12pdr H.A., 2—3", 1—2pdr
Sir Thomas Picton	2—12", 1—6", 2—12pdr H.A., 1—3", 1—3pdr
Earl of Peterborough	2—12", 2—12pdr H.A., 2—3", 1—2pdr.

During 1918, the corresponding official outfit of ammunition for each gun comprised:—

18-inch:	60 H.E. (high-explosive)
12-inch:	90 H.E., 10 C.P.C. (Dover); or 120 H.E. (Med)
6-inch:	150 H.E., 10 C.P.C. (common, pointed capped), 40 shrapnel
4-inch:	150 H.E., 10 C.P. (common, pointed), 40 shrapnel
3-inch:	240 H.E., 60 incendiary, 32 C.P.
12-pdr:	150 H.E., 50 C.P.
2-pdr:	480 C.P., 320 C.N.F. (common, nose fuzed)

In addition, 30 rounds of star-shell were carried per ship, generally for the 3-inch or 4-inch guns.

Four calibres of gun visible on Lord Clive *in 1918: the 18-inch aft, twin 12-inch forward, 4-inch to starboard of the bridge, 2-pdr on the turret.*

Seagoing performance of the 12-inch monitors was similar to the 14-inch ships, but the extra few hundred horsepower gave the slightly higher cruising speed of about 7 knots clean, except for the underpowered *Prince Rupert* at 6½. Mileage steamed at Dover was modest, *Moore* covering only 5600 miles in her first year, requiring coaling about once a week. Coal consumption was around 50 tons a day at full speed, giving a nominal endurance of about 1100 miles, but the official figure was about 960. This probably took account of the subsequent loss of two of the bunkers to make room for 6-inch magazines. *Wolfe* was the fastest of the ships in normal service and, under ideal conditions, could even better her 8-knot trial speed by a whisker, but needed 70 tons of coal a day to do so. After her 18-inch conversion, speed dropped appreciably with the extra displacement

Lord Clive*'s 18-inch at its maximum 45° elevation, which had a range of up to 40,100 yards, depending on type of ammunition. Some of the eighteen cordite tanks with their lifting rails can be seen, each of the twelve compartments holding two 105-lb one-sixth charges. Steam heating pipes can be seen at the base to keep the water-filled tanks at an even temperature. The fitting on the 18-inch muzzle was for pulling through to clean the gun bore. Also visible are shields of two of the 4-inch B.L. guns.*

— she made only 6.7 knots on trial in August 1918. Manoeuvring was always a problem with their unsympathetic hull forms and underpowered steering gear. In the crowded conditions of Dover Harbour, there were few ships who did not show some signs of a brush with one of the monitors — dents in the hull, twisted guardrails or splintered boats and fittings.

§7 Post-War Careers

Only one ship of the class had a post-war career of any special interest — *Lord Clive*. After 19 months laid up at Immingham, she was towed to Portsmouth in September 1920 to be converted to carry three 15-inch guns for trial purposes. The design of the projected 1921 battlecruisers included triple 16-inch guns, but the R.N. had no information on the effects of firing three-gun salvoes from a single turret. Interference and throw-off (the effect produced by firing an off-centre gun on a multiple mounting) needed to be investigated, so it was arranged to mount three 15-inch guns on one of the monitors. *Clive*'s 18-inch and secondary armament were therefore removed, and additional strengthening fitted. The three guns were then installed on a fixed mounting covered by a canvas screen, pointing out to starboard as illustrated below. The new mounting weighed 520 tons complete with guns, rather heavier than the 18-inch. *Clive* recommissioned on 15 December 1920, but she was not ready to leave Portsmouth until 1 February. She was towed round to the Nore, for the next month firing off her test rounds up the Shoeburyness range. The trials showed that there were no serious problems with a triple mounting, so *Clive* paid off again in August 1921, remaining laid up at Portsmouth until sold and scrapped in 1927.

Three other ships saw very limited post-war service. *Prince Rupert* remained in the Tees as a temporary tender to the submarine depot ship *Vulcan*. In September 1919, she joined the other monitors laid up at Immingham. In May 1920, she went to Chatham to serve as a hulk for the dockyard police, also providing accommodation for boats' crews and serving as a lashing hulk. Two years later, she took over from *Achilles* (originally an ironclad of 1863) as parent ship of the naval depot, being renamed *Pembroke*. She was sold in May 1923 to Beardmore's, as their Dalmuir shipyard was going through a very bad patch, so *Rupert* was bought to provide work to help keep a nucleus of men together.

General Craufurd and *Sir John Moore* remained at the Nore after the war, and in January 1919 were recommissioned as gunnery tenders to the First Fleet firing service and to keep alive experience of bombarding techniques. Later in the year, *Craufurd* was offered for sale to Roumania, but nothing transpired. Both ships were paid off again in the spring of 1920 and were put on the Sale List. The remaining four ships, *Prince Eugene, General Wolfe, Sir Thomas Picton* and *Earl of Peterborough* were all laid up at Immingham from spring 1919 to winter 1920-21. They were then towed round to Portsmouth where guns and useful fittings were removed by the dockyard, after which they were moved to lie at moorings in Spithead until finally sold. *Wolfe, Eugene* and *Craufurd* all formed part of Ward's massive purchase in May 1921 (see p.38) and were broken up in 1922-23. *Picton, Moore* and *Peterborough* were all sold to the Slough Trading Company on 8 November 1921. This company was acting on behalf of German shipbreakers, so all three were towed away and broken up in Germany in 1922.

In 1920, Lord Clive*'s 18-inch was removed and three 15-inch guns were substituted in a fixed athwartship mounting to test the effects of firing three guns simultaneously.* Clive *is seen here entering Portsmouth in March 1921.*

During trial firings of Clive*'s three 15-inch guns at the Nore in March 1921, a faulty A.P.C. projectile exploded prematurely in the bore, bursting the jacket and wrecking the gun. The gun cradle is seen on the right, together with some of the fractured wire winding.*

THE 12-INCH MONITORS — TECHNICAL PARTICULARS

Displacement and Dimensions 5900 tons legend, 5683 tons deep. Length 335′-6″ o.a., breadth 87′-2″, draft 9′-7″ deep.

Weight Distribution Armament 335 tons, ammunition 143, protection 1824, hull 2486, equipment 220, machinery and R.F.W. 391, coal (nominal) 200. Designed total 5599 tons.

Complement 12 officers, 182 men.

Armament 2—12″ (twin) (60 C.P.C. + 60 H.E. r.p.g.), 2—12pdr (200 r.p.g.), 1—3″ 20cwt H.A. (*Eugene* and *Craufurd*) (300 r.p.g.), 1—3pdr Vickers H.A. (except *Eugene*) (500 r.p.g.), 1—2pdr H.A. (except *Craufurd*) (1000 r.p.g.), 4—0.303″ Maxim (5000 r.p.g.).

Protection As 14-inch monitors except: sloping belt 6″ C.; gunhouse $10^1/_2$″ front, 4″ rear, 2″ roof and floor (nickel steel), $5^1/_2$″ sides (Harveyed).

Machinery Twin screw triple-expansion. *Wolfe*: two 4-cyl 2500 I.H.P. at 180 r.p.m. *Moore*: two 3-cyl 2500 I.H.P. at 200 r.p.m. *Rupert*: two 3-cyl 1600 I.H.P. at 180 r.p.m. Others: two 4-cyl 2310 I.H.P. at 200 r.p.m. Coal 356 tons. Endurance 1100 miles at $6^1/_2$ knots.

Speed 10 knots designed, 7 service. Trials: *Clive* 8.02, *Craufurd* 7.42, *Peterborough* 7.66, *Picton* 7.4, *Eugene* 8.2, *Rupert* 7.06, *Moore* 7.75, *Wolfe* 8.01 knots.

Construction Harland & Wolff, Belfast: *Lord Clive* laid down 9 Jan 1915/launched 10 Jun 1915/completed 10 Jul 1915; *General Craufurd* 9 Jan/8 Jul/26 Aug 1915; *Earl of Peterborough* 16 Jan/26 Aug/12 Oct 1915; *Sir Thomas Picton* 16 Jan/30 Sep/8 Nov 1915. *Prince Eugene* H. & W. Govan 1 Feb/14 Jul/2 Sep 1915. *Prince Rupert* Hamilton 12 Jan/20 May/12 Jul 1915. *Sir John Moore* Scotts 13 Jan/31 May/22 Jul 1915. *General Wolfe* Palmer, Hebburn Jan/9 Sep/9 Nov 1915.

Scrapped *Clive* MacLellan, Bo'ness 17 Nov 1927; *Craufurd* Ward, New Holland Oct 1922; *Peterborough* Slough Trading, Hamburg 1922; *Picton* Slough Trading, Bremen 21 Dec 1922; *Eugene* Ward, Preston 10 Aug 1923; *Rupert* Beardmore, Glasgow 1923; *Moore* Slough Trading, Bremen Jul 1922; *Wolfe* Ward, Hayle 1923.

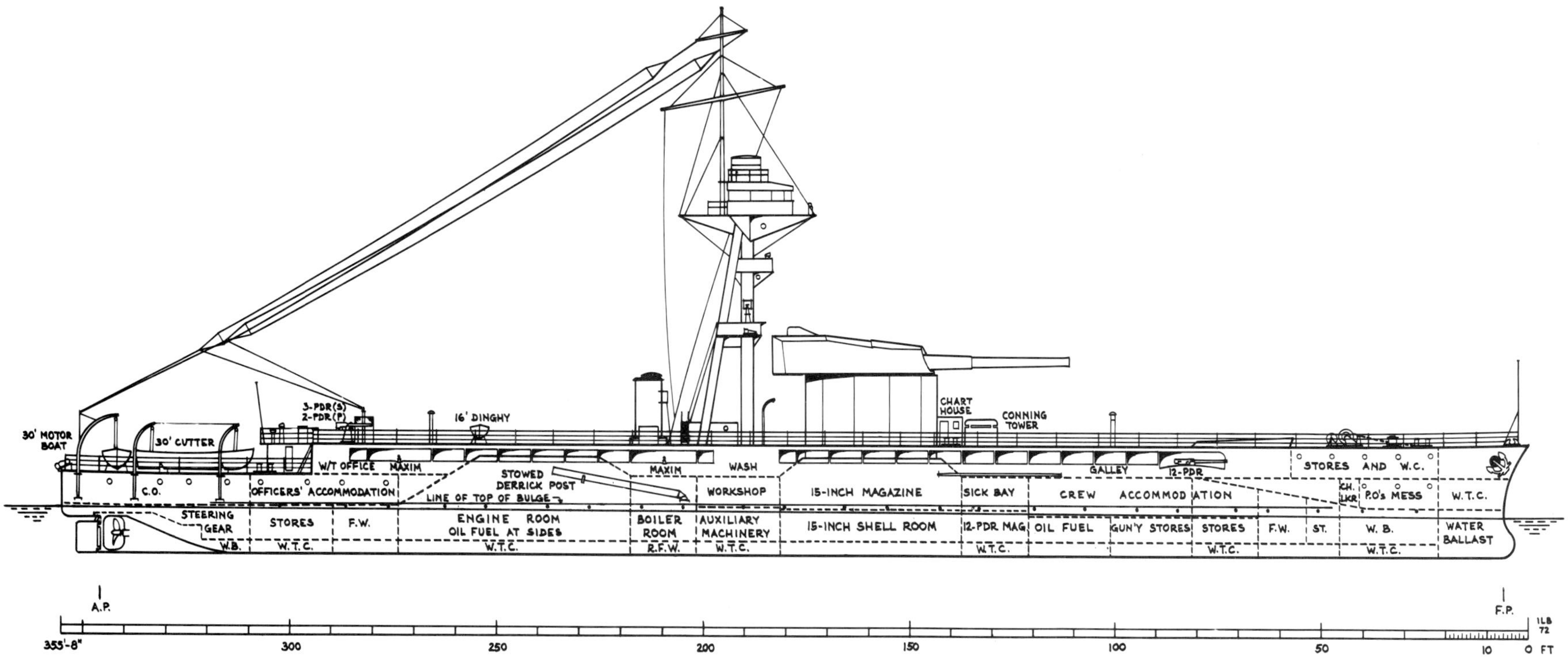

Marshal Soult *as completed — the ugliest of all the monitors with a disproportioned profile. The later 14-foot increase in* Soult's *funnel height worsened an already bizarre appearance. The tall barbette was necessary owing to the minimum length of the turret ammunition trunk.* Marshal Ney *was almost indistinguishable from her sister as completed, although after removal of the 15-inch turret, her later armaments of 9.2-inch and then 6-inch guns readily distinguished the two vessels.*

CHAPTER IV

THE FIRST 15-INCH GUN MONITORS

H.M.S. MARSHAL NEY and MARSHAL SOULT

§1 Design

Following the Battle of the Falkland Islands, two eight-gun battleships of the 1914 Programme were converted into the 32-knot battlecruisers *Renown* and *Repulse*, mounting six 15-inch guns. With two spare 15-inch turrets now available, Churchill and Fisher planned to build two more monitors, whose guns could hurl a 1920-lb projectile 23,400 yards. So in January, for the third time in two months, Lillicrap was called upon to design another class of monitor, provisionally identified as *M.13* and *M.14*. A twin 15-inch turret weighed about 760 tons, but including barbette armour and ammunition was some 300 tons heavier than a 14-inch installation. A hull rather larger than the two previous classes was therefore called for, but draft had to be kept at 10 feet. Breadth remained fixed at 90ft from drydocking considerations, the main hull being 62ft wide, so length was the only dimension that could be increased; it went up to 340ft B.P. to provide the necessary displacement of 6670 tons.

Meanwhile D.N.O. had been examining the detailed problems of installing the 15-inch Mk I mounting in a relatively shallow hull. Much to Fishers' annoyance all-round fire could not be achieved as the turret could not train more than 300° owing to the arrangement of the hydraulic supply pipes. It was also found impossible to shorten the ammunition trunk below the length required for a battleship's aftermost turret, namely 43 feet from gun axis to shell room floor. As a result, the barbette had to project 17 feet above the forecastle deck, and had to be heavily armoured to protect the turntable and working chamber, being formed of 12 flat plates eight inches thick in place of the usual circular shape, to speed production.

Fisher pressed the case for diesel propulsion, as Churchill had suggested for the 12-inch monitors. Although such relatively complex engines normally took much longer to build than steam reciprocators, there were under construction two oilers with diesel engines. The 2400-ton deadweight oilers *Trefoil* and *Turmoil* were being built at Pembroke Dockyard; two of a number of oilers being fitted with alternative makes of diesel engine, so that the performance of this new form of propulsion could be compared using non-combatant ships as test-beds. *Trefoil*'s machinery had already been installed and she was about to start her trials, but it would be possible to remove her engines and transfer them into a monitor, while *Turmoil's* engines had just completed shop trials at their maker's works and were ready for despatch to the dockyard. Here indeed was a fine chance to obtain two sets of diesel engines quickly, as they appeared to be the ideal prime mover for the low powered monitors. The oilers were designed for 12 knots, requiring about 1500 B.H.P.,[1] which was to be provided by two 750-B.H.P. engines driving twin screws. This power was slightly less than installed in the earlier steam monitors, so it was expected to give a speed of about 9 knots, allowing for the increased displacement.

Trefoil's 88-ton engines had been designed and built by Vickers at Barrow, being a development of their submarine engines. By contrast, *Turmoil*'s 68-ton engines had been designed by M.A.N. of Ausburg but built by J. Samuel White of Cowes in the Isle of Wight. The contracts for the complete machinery installations were worth about £40,000 for each ship, about double that for steam reciprocators. The advantage lay in the much reduced fuel consumption of only about 0.4 tons of oil per hour, compared with 1.3 tons of oil or 1.9 tons of coal using steam. The corresponding daily fuel costs would have been about £96 for the diesel burning shale oil at about £10.00 per ton for Admiralty supplies during WW1, £110 for oil-fired steam reciprocators (fuel oil at £3.55) and £75 for coal-fired (Welsh coal at £1.65). Although a smaller bunker capacity could be arranged, slightly longer machinery spaces were needed compared with the steam monitors. Two small oil-fired boilers were required to power the steam-driven electric generator, the turret hydraulic pump, the steering engines, the fresh water evaporators, the capstans and the ballast and other pumps.

The other design features followed the pattern established by the earlier monitors, including ignoring completely A.E.W.'s advice about fining the hull lines aft, with consequences that were to be most serious. The decision to substitute 1500-B.H.P. engines in place of the equivalent of about 2000 B.H.P. in the slightly smaller 12-inch monitors had already meant the loss of about one knot in speed. D.N.C.'s judgement was at fault in rejecting Froude's advice on redesigning the afterbody lines, especially as it would not have delayed construction.

§2 Construction

The choice of a builder for *M.13* and *M.14* was not difficult. With *Repulse* transferred to Clydebank and *Resolution* launched on 14 January 1915, Palmer's two

[1] Brake horsepower. The ratio of B.H.P. to I.H.P. was a measure of the mechanical efficiency, typically about 80% at that time.

A view of Marshal Soult *under construction on 12 June 1915 at Palmer's shipyard at Jarrow, with* Marshal Ney *in the background.* Ney *was almost ready for launch, going down the ways five days later.* Soult *has reached the stage where her protective deck is being completed, consisting of two 1-inch thicknesses of high-tensile steel at upper deck level, sloping down to the bow and sideways to the bulge, where the 4-inch armour has yet to be fitted. The erections above the upper deck include the turret ring bulkhead, conning tower support and hump aft over the diesel engines. Shipyard equipment visible includes the two famous gantries whose cableways spanned the length of the two main berths until the yard closed in 1933. Timber uprights are for supporting staging for access to the ship's side. Plates were bolted on before being riveted up, with rivets heated at the braziers on deck. The bow of the battleship* Resolution *can be seen at the right.*

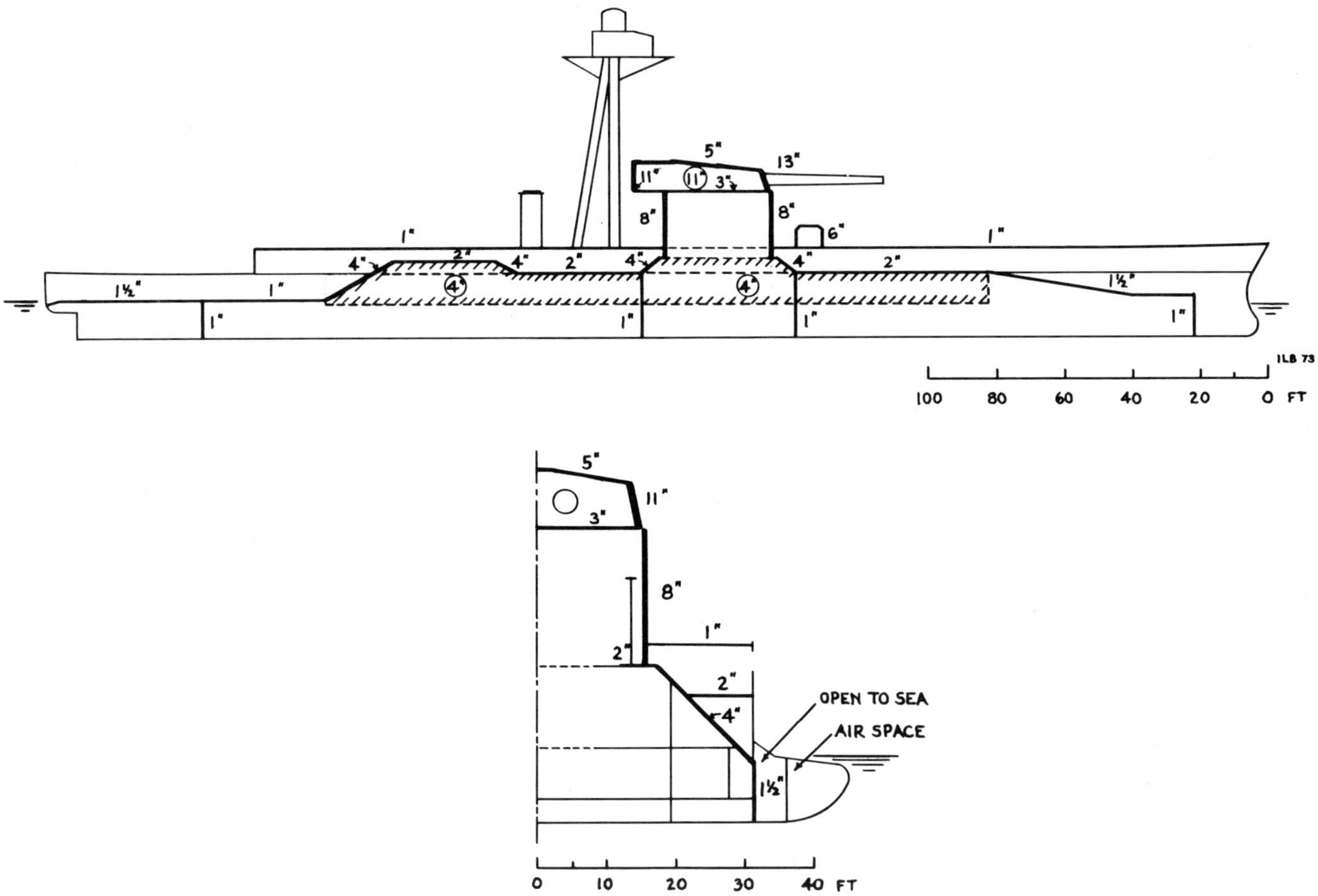

The protection of the Marshals *was basically similar to the 14-inch monitors, except for the turret and the hump necessitated by the height of the diesel engines. The sloping main deck forward, visible in the photograph opposite, saved a little weight compared with a closing vertical bulkhead.*

large building berths at Jarrow were now available, so contracts were rapidly placed. The first monitor was laid down at the end of January, while the second followed in mid-February on the adjacent berth. With completion expected in six months, it was not possible to await delivery of *Renown* and *Repulse*'s fourth turrets, which were not due until 1916. As described on p.177, the deficiency was made good by transferring two of the turrets allocated to *Resolution*'s sister *Ramillies*. The cost of the turrets was not charged to the monitors, so the ships' estimated cost was only £270,000 each, compared with a probable £440,000 if built wholly from new.

Arrangements were made with Vickers' and White's to transfer the oilers' engines to Jarrow, where they were installed before the hulls were launched. Construction had been proceeding rapidly until the night before the launch of the first ship. In the early hours of 16 June, the Zeppelin *L.10* raided the Tyne area. Attracted to Jarrow by the lights of Palmer's ironworks and workshops on night-shift, she dropped 12 bombs. Severe damage and casualties were caused in the engine shops, while splinters hit the monitors. Damage here was slight and the launch postponed only one day. Captain H. J. Tweedie's wife launched *Marshal Ney* on 17 June, naming her after one of Napoleon's generals in tribute to Britain's WW1 ally.

From Dover, Bacon repeatedly pressed for delivery as soon as possible; *Ney* was ready for trials on 26 August. Gunnery trials went off satisfactorily but her steering proved atrocious, as discussed later. Her M.A.N. engines were found to be extremely difficult to start, exhausting a whole series of air bottles before success was achieved. Even when once started, they were liable to stop whenever any change of load or speed occurred. The trials programme called for four hours' continuous steaming at full power, but this proved impossible to attain. When the news of *Ney*'s dismal performance reached the Admiralty, serious consideration was given to cutting their losses with the 15-inch monitors by transferring their guns to other ships, as described later. Eventually after several days' abortive trials, it was agreed to give *Ney* a chance to prove herself in service by accepting her from her builders if only one hour's continuous steaming could be obtained with both engines running. Her Engineer Officer, Lieutenant D. Swan R.N.V.R., who had been transferred from *Turmoil*, pulled out all the stops and got three hours' steaming out of her on the afternoon of 31 August. However only about six knots was obtained — like the steam monitors about three knots less than anticipated. The builder's men then left the ship, at 16.45 the tug *George V* took her

Marshal Ney *with her turret trained to its maximum bearing of green 150°. Both red and white ensigns fly from the yardarm, as she is still in her builder's hands.*

in tow and together the pair set off for Dover at six knots. Thus departed for action the Royal Navy's first diesel-powered surface warship; her ungainly profile and utterly functional design, consisting only of one huge turret, tall mast and diminutive funnel projecting above the low hull, attracting astonishment wherever she went.

The second ship was named *Marshal Soult* after another of Napoleon's generals. She followed about two months behind *Ney*, her engines proving much more reliable on trials. She could only make about five knots as her engines were unable to develop full power at the designed r.p.m., having been fitted with wrongly pitched propellers. No official record of her displacement as completed exists but analysis of the drafts recorded in her Log show that her deep displacement was about 6900 tons, with a draft about five inches deeper than designed. On this basis, *Ney* would have been about 50 tons less, owing to her lighter engines. *Soult* left the Tyne on 3 November 1915 under Captain W.D. Paton, her future and that of her sister still under consideration.

§3 Wartime Careers

As with the first of the 12-inch monitors, the original plan for sending *Marshal Ney* out to the Dardanelles had been cancelled and she had been allocated to the Dover Squadron. Her maiden voyage from the Tyne was an exciting one as engine trouble continued to to plague her; more often than not one or other of her engines was out of action. Her difficulties were accentuated by underpowered steering gear and poor response to the helm so that, despite tug assistance, she was continually sheering off course, at times even making a complete 360° turn before control was regained. She eventually arrived at Sheerness on 3 September, going straight on to calibrate her guns on the Shoeburyness range, to adjust the sights so that both guns fired to the required distance.

It had been discovered by this time that the 12-inch monitors were outranged by the Tirpitz battery. Bacon was therefore anxious to get *Ney* into service as soon as possible to use her longer range guns, so she was prepared for her first operation, that described on p.50. She was to steam inshore between Dunkirk and Nieuport, where it was thought that Tirpitz' guns could not bear. After waddling across to Dunkirk, she joined the other monitors on 19 September in attempting to smother the fire of the coastal batteries. About midday *Ney* opened fire on Westende from 15,000 yards but she received no spotting reports as the only spotting station ashore could not obtain proper bearings from its acute angle to the line of fire. Tirpitz' guns soon showed that *Ney* was still within their arc of fire, so she was forced to withdraw out of range after only seven rounds. She returned later in the afternoon even closer off the beaches of La Panne and obtained rather better results, one hit being signalled out of 16 rounds and the Germans being forced to evacuate temporarily the Aachen battery of four 150-mm guns. Unfortunately the heavy blast from her guns blew the securing slip off the port anchor and the cable ran out whilst the ship was under way, bringing her to a complete halt. It proved impossible to heave the cable back in, neither could the starboard engine be started. Under power of the port engine, she grounded lightly while, to add to her discomfort, Tirpitz had now found her range and proceeded to surround her with uncomfortably close shell bursts. She soon got off the sandbank only to find that her rudders had jammed and that the only motion possible was slow circling. Tweedie dared not stop his one remaining engine, so the destroyer *Viking* was ordered to tow her out of danger. This was successfully achieved under cover of a smokescreen, the passage back to Dunkirk being made at twice her normal speed.

She was back in action again on 25 September supporting the big Army offensive. This time the Westende batteries were her target, receiving 17 rounds before *Viking* again had to tow her away. A week later, both engines again broke down prior to another bombardment. It was now abundantly clear that if her great firepower was to be properly exploited, considerable modifications would be needed to her engines and steering gear to obtain reliable performance. So on 20 October, she was drydocked at Southampton where her rudders were modified and new steering gear was fitted. She then went across to Cowes to give her engine builders a chance to improve the starting and reversing characteristics of her diesels.

Meantime *Marshal Soult* had arrived at Dover on 6 November but had been despatched immediately to Portsmouth for a new set of propellers and to have her mine-wires removed. On her new trials she managed $6^1/_2$ knots, without any trouble from her Vickers' engines. She joined the Dover Squadron as an effective unit on 28 November and saw her first action on 23 December when she bombarded the area around Westende Casino with six rounds. Two more similar sorties were made in late December, while on 15 and 26 January, she again bombarded Westende, on the latter occasion in company with four of the 12-inch monitors.

Ney had arrived back at Dover on 13 December, as Bacon wanted her for supporting his planned attacks on Zeebrugge and Ostende (see p.51). But the next few weeks showed that her troubles had not really been cured; she remained as unmanageable as ever and her engines could never be relied upon, either to start or, once started, to continue running. Finally the ever-optimistic Swan had to admit defeat when a cylinder exploded, blowing parts of the engine through the deckhead. As *Soult* had shown herself a much more satisfactory performer, the Admiralty at last decided to cut their losses with *Ney*. By transferring her turret to one of the new fast monitors then building, they hoped to get her powerful armament back into service quickly. Accordingly *Ney* was despatched to the Tyne under tow, arriving at Elswick on 29 January 1916 where her turret was removed for transfer to *Terror* under construction at Belfast. She returned to Portsmouth in April where she was fitted with a reduced armament consisting of a single 9.2-inch and four single 6-inch. Back in commission on 16 June, new trials were undertaken with a moderate degree of success, so she returned hopefully to Dover. But her performance in service proved as bad as ever; her engines and steering prevented her from becoming an effective unit of the Squadron. She was sent back to Portsmouth, paying off for the second time on 15 August.

General patrol work occupied most of *Soult*'s time during 1916, involving occasional brushes with enemy aircraft and destroyers. It was September before she again used her 15-inch guns in earnest, supporting Haig's Somme offensive. Between 8 and 13 September, she fired 37 rounds of C.P.C., mostly at enemy 150-mm coastal batteries. By firing from behind a smokescreen, the safe firing range could be brought down to about 22,000 yards. Shortly afterwards, she was hit by a bomb whilst alongside at Dunkirk. By this time, both *Erebus* and *Terror* had entered service, so *Soult* could be spared to have her gun mounting altered to give 10° extra elevation up to 30°, similar to the two new ships. She left for Elswick, arriving on 6 November and was returned to Dover on 12 March 1917 with her guns now capable of nearly 30,000 yards.

Meantime, further modifications had been made to *Ney* at Portsmouth. White's had another go at her engines, which performed quite well in basin trials at Portsmouth in December. But these were too late to save her from being relegated to a stationary role as a guardship. Merchant traffic along the south and east coast of England all passed through the special anchorage at the Downs off Ramsgate, where examination of vessels for blockade-running cargoes took place. Vessels also used the anchorage to lay up overnight or when enemy sorties or unswept minefields presented temporary dangers. Such a collection of ships formed a tempting target, which had to be well protected by destroyers and drifters, backed up by a 12-inch monitor when necessary. The need for strong protection was borne out when German destroyers raided the Downs in February and March 1917. Rather than employ one of his more active monitors, Bacon decided to convert *Ney* to a full-time guardship at the Downs, fitting her with six 6-inch guns. Her good underwater protection made her almost immune from U-boat attack, while her armament was still strong enough to drive off destroyers. She took up her station at the north end of the Downs on 5 April 1917, and was soon in action. On the morning of the 19th, six German seaplanes appeared over the Goodwin Sands and two, which were carrying torpedoes, calmly circled *Ney* amidst a barrage of A.A. fire. One torpedo was dropped from low level but fortunately missed *Ney*, passed under a nearby dredger and embedded itself in the mud of Ramsgate Harbour. *Ney*'s chance came on 27 April when she returned the fire of several destroyers shelling Ramsgate, who retired in the face of this strong opposition. Thereafter things became rather quieter as German destroyer raids

Marshal Ney *with her turret trained on the broadside, probably on gunnery trials. Blast bags are fitted to each gun to prevent the blast entering the turret through the gun ports.*

F

virtually ceased, but she often used her H.A. guns against the night-time aircraft and Zeppelin raids. Not until after the Armistice did she leave her anchorage, where she had performed a dull but important service, being towed round to Sheerness on 12 December 1918.

In contrast, *Soult* saw considerable action over the next 18 months, as Bacon was determined to make full use of his three 15-inch monitors. From early February 1917, he had been making detailed plans to bombard the lock gates of the Bruges Canal, which if damaged would seriously restrict the use of the important naval base at Bruges. It is worth describing the operation in some detail as it well illustrates the difficulties the monitors faced in bombarding small targets on strongly defended coastlines. First the target: to put the lock out of action, both gates needed to be hit, as otherwise passage could be made using only one gate which could be opened for about two hours around high water. Each gate was only about 90ft × 30ft in size and invisible from the sea. Bacon calculated the chances of hitting such a target from 13 miles as 1 in 63, but he halved the chances to allow for the difficulty of accurately laying a gun subject to all the motions of a ship. About 250 rounds would thus be required to hit both main lock gates, even before any consideration could be given to the spare gate kept nearby. Second the opportunity: to fire 250 rounds would take about $1^1/_2$ hours with three monitors each firing one round per minute. Such a rate was not difficult for the ships, but would be quite a strain on the spotters. But conditions had to be just right; a calm sea to prevent excessive rolling, no cloud or mist over the target so that the spotting aircraft would have a clear view, and the tide running along the coast to allow the ships to anchor broadside on to the target. Third and most important of all, opposition: the monitors would have to fire from within the 41,000-yard range of the Kaiser Wilhelm battery. This meant that an onshore wind was required so that the M.L.'s smokescreen would continue to shield the monitors from view; that a dawn operation was desirable to achieve surprise before the enemy could retaliate seriously, jam the spotting wireless or cover the target with defensive smokescreens; that strong air patrols would be needed to prevent enemy aircraft or balloons spotting for their return fire, and to guard the British spotters. All in all, the chances of getting exactly the right conditions and then actually hitting the targets were slight, but Bacon judged the risks worthwhile to curb the U-boats by sealing one of their bases. His plan was to anchor the three 15-inch monitors near to a predetermined position off Zeebrugge and for them to use a 12-inch monitor as a back aiming mark. To keep their approach within the hours of darkness, a speed of at least 9 knots was required of the fleet, so each fast monitor would have to tow one of the slow ones.

A close-up of Marshal Soult*'s turret showing the raised axis of the 15-inch guns permitting 30° elevation. Ammunitioning is in progress at Dunkirk, with cordite cases lying on deck, each holding two 107-lb quarter charges. The two 4-inch visible and the two 2-pdr on platforms aft date the photograph as the spring of 1918. The conning tower has ceased to be used, the original searchlight platform being expanded instead. The chequer pattern was intended to confuse German rangefinders ashore and to blend into the M.L's protective smokescreens.*

All was ready by 25 March, but mist came down forcing a postponement of the operation. A fortnight elapsed before the tides were once more suitable but again on 8 April the weather proved too bad. On 18 April, the start was delayed by *Erebus* fouling her propeller at Dunkirk and then, after the flotilla had got under way, *Soult* sheered off whilst being towed by *Terror*, breaking her towline. Further attempts during April were frustrated by the weather or other factors. Not until 11 May did everything again appear promising, when the 41-ship flotilla set off from Dover at about 18.00; *Terror* flying Bacon's flag and towing *Soult* at 10 knots, *Erebus* towing *Sir John Moore*, followed by *M.24* and *M.26*, ten destroyers, six paddle minesweepers and nineteen M.L.s. They anchored in the firing position at about 04.20 on the 12th but poor visibility forced *Moore* to anchor only 4200 yards off instead of the planned 12,000 yards, thus seriously multiplying any errors of bearing. Of the three spotting aircraft, two had reported mechanical trouble and had been forced to land again, while the third had arrived as early as 03.00 and was running short of fuel by the time the monitors were in position.

Fire was opened at 04.45 from about 26,000 yards, *Soult* and *Terror* taking the south gate as their target while *Erebus* took the north. The first ranging shots fell short but were soon corrected, and shooting settled down to a steady 20-second rhythm. Not all of the rounds could be spotted after their 54-second flight, as several did not burst, but the spotter reported hits with *Soult*'s 12th round and *Erebus*' 26th. The Germans put up smoke to screen the locks but fortunately it was wrongly placed and did not hamper the British fire. By now, Kaiser Wilhelm had begun to open fire, but the British smoke-screen and strong air patrols prevented any worthwhile spotting so, after four rounds, the Germans gave up. The thick white screen completely covered the ships from the shore, even hiding the red-brown cordite puffs and the occasional black smoke from their funnels. The spotting aircraft stayed as long as possible but had to leave at 05.30, having run seriously short of fuel. Thereafter the monitors estimated their own corrections and ceased fire at 06.00 when the wind changed direction, but before a relief spotter could take over. The flotilla then retired to Dover, feeling that a good morning's work had been done: 175 rounds fired of which *Soult* had contributed 51. Subsequent reports and aerial photographs were disappointing as they showed that, although several shells had fallen very close, 21 of them within 50 yards, no damage had been inflicted on the actual gates or pumphouses. The only results of this major effort were three enemy killed, four wounded, temporary damage to the lock pumphouse and some churned-up roads and railways, plus the confirmation that the chances of hitting such small targets from long range in the face of a host of practical difficulties were slim indeed.

The summer months of 1917 were spent on patrol, particularly from July whilst the 12-inch monitors were preparing for the Great Landing. This "B.O. Patrol" consisted of one of the 15-inch monitors, two small monitors, a light cruiser and about nine destroyers. Arrangements were made for M.L.s and spotting aircraft to be on hand if conditions were favourable for bombardment. *Soult*'s first opportunity came on 4 September when she put 28 rounds into Ostende Dockyard, firing at maximum range whilst under way. She had another go at Ostende on 21 October, firing 19 rounds and damaging some ships and exploding the magazine of a nearby A.A. battery, before the thickness of enemy smokescreen prevented further shooting. For a short period at the end of October, she found herself the only large monitor available for service, the other eight all being in dockyard hands. Favourable conditions for bombardment had largely disappeared with the onset of winter so with the return of the other monitors, *Soult* could be spared for a long refit at Portsmouth which lasted from January to April 1918.

Soult's role in the forthcoming Zeebrugge raid was a relatively minor one of diversionary bombardment with three of the 12-inch monitors described on p.56. While waiting for the operation to take place, she went out on the night of 17/18 April to fire on coastal batteries west of Ostende with *Erebus, Terror* and *Prince Eugene,* using *M.26* as an aiming mark. Following up the Zeebrugge raid, a bombardment was made on 9 June by *Soult* and *Terror* with *M.21* to harrass enemy dredgers and salvage craft which were attempting to remove the blockships. The monitors opened fire from 27,000 yards at 13.08 but, as the wind direction was unfavourable, no smokescreen could shield them. The enemy return fire soon became uncomfortably accurate so, after 25 rounds each, the monitors retired to Dunkirk. *Soult*'s last bombardment of the war came on 29 July when she and *Gorgon*, again with *M.21* as aiming mark, took on the Tirpitz battery in co-operation with Allied artillery ashore. Although the target was only 28,500 yards off, her guns had fired 210 e.f.c. (equivalent full charges) each and could only reach this distance by heeling the ship. Flooding the bulges increased the effective gun elevation to 33° and she was able to fire 10 rounds before a combination of inadequate stern anchor, fautly firing mechanisms and about 30 retaliatory rounds from Tirpitz forced her to retire.

The next few weeks were mainly spent on the Dover Barrage patrol, guarding the deep anti-submarine minefields. She was back at Portsmouth for docking on

The Royal Navy's first 15-inch monitor Marshal Ney *leaves the Tyne for trials at the end of August 1915. Details visible include the 12-pdr forward and the 3-inch H.A. aft.*

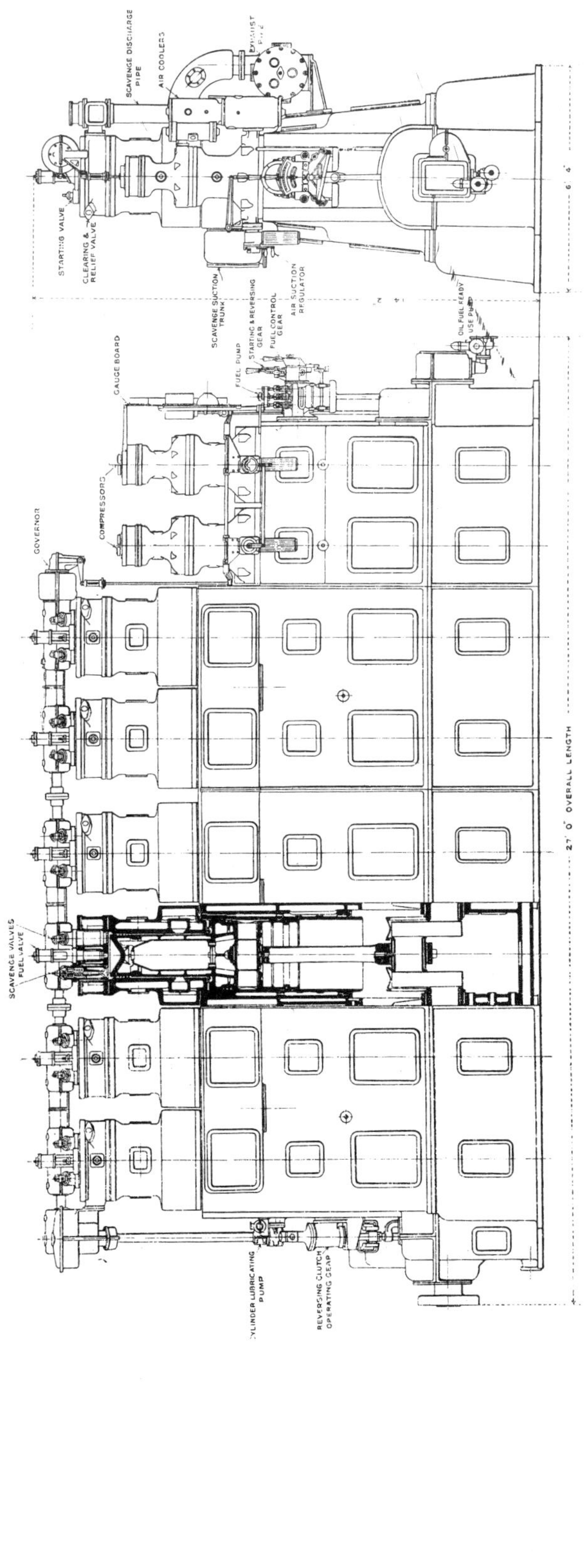
SCAVENGE DISCHARGE PIPE
AIR COOLERS
EXHAUST PIPE
STARTING VALVE
CLEARING & RELIEF VALVE
SCAVENGE SUCTION TRUNK
STARTING & REVERSING GEAR
FUEL CONTROL GEAR
AIR SUCTION REGULATOR
OIL FUEL READY USE PUMP
GAUGE BOARD
FUEL PUMP
COMPRESSORS
GOVERNOR
6' 4"
27' 0" OVERALL LENGTH
SCAVENGE VALVES
FUEL VALVE
CYLINDER LUBRICATING PUMP
REVERSING CLUTCH OPERATING GEAR

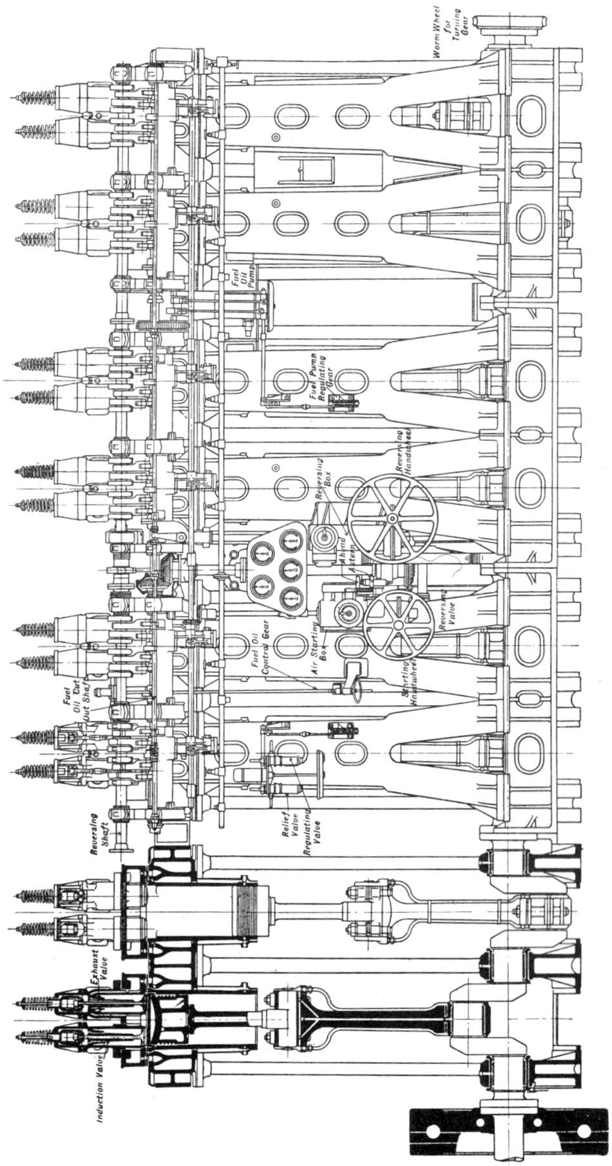
Worm Wheel for Turning Gear
Fuel Oil Pump
Fuel Pump Regulating Gear
Reversing Handwheel
Reversing Box
Ahead
Astern
Reversing Valve
Fuel Oil Control Gear
Air Starting Box
Starting Handwheel
Fuel Oil Cut Out Shaft
Reversing Shaft
Relief Valve
Regulating Valve
Exhaust Valve
Induction Valve

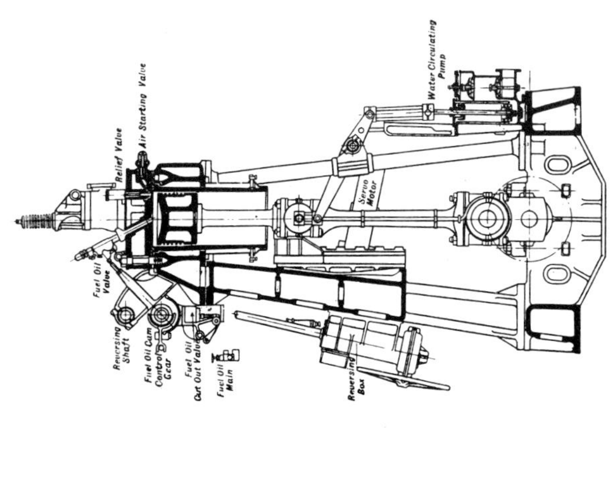
Relief Valve
Air Starting Valve
Water Circulating Pump
Servo Motor
Fuel Oil Valve
Reversing Shaft
Fuel Oil Cam Control Gear
Fuel Oil Cut Out Valve
Fuel Oil Main
Reversing Box

Following her 1918 refit, Soult *emerged as one of the Navy's ugliest ships, with her lengthened funnel and gawky appearance. Her armament now includes eight 4-inch, two 12-pdr H.A. (under the 15-inch guns), two 3-inch H.A. and two 2-pdr. She is seen here at Devonport in 1920.*

13 September and thus missed the heaviest bombardment of the war. By the time she was back at Dunkirk, the Germans had evacuated the Belgian Coast, so she was sent round to Chatham to await a decision on her future, where she arrived on 25 October 1918.

§4 Performance and Modifications

The news of *Marshal Ney*'s trials had come as a great disappointment to the Admiralty. Here was a ship, carrying two of the most powerful guns afloat, which was not only even slower than the earlier 7-knot monitors, with machinery incapable of continuous running, but which was not even able to steer a defined course. As early as September 1915, Tudor, a gunnery specialist, had suggested removing her turret and installing it in a new monitor. Admiral H. B. Jackson, the new First Sea Lord, was in agreement about removing *Ney*'s turret, but suggested re-arming both *Ney* and *Soult* with the 12-inch twin mountings from the pre-dreadnoughts *Caesar* or *Illustrious.* The alternative solution of re-engining *Ney* with steam reciprocating machinery was also considered. The existing engine and boiler rooms could accommodate a twin screw installation of about 3600 I.H.P., but even this roughly doubled power would give at most eight knots, while it would do nothing to improve the steering.

However, Bacon's urgent need for ships with guns of longer range than the existing 12-inch overrode these plans for modifying the *Marshals*. *Ney* was temporarily reprieved, while it was appreciated that *Soult*'s different engines might turn out to be more satisfactory. In service however, *Ney*'s performance was quite as bad as her trials had foreshadowed. She could neither steam nor steer with any degree of certainty. The steering problems arose largely from the bluff lines aft, which produced a deadness of flow around the rudders and propellers. As a result, she possessed neither directional stability nor any ability to correct a swing once induced by excessive use of the helm. Despite her M.A.N. engines running faultlessly on their 96-hour test-bed trials at Cowes in December 1914, in service there was found to be a fault in the design of the reversing gear, which partly accounted for the engines' erratic performance. Various modifications were tried, but the engines never proved sufficiently reliable for regular service.

Tweedie remained cheerful in the face of all these difficulties but his crew were bitterly disappointed. On occasion, he himself would take the helm under tricky conditions, such was his feel for the ship. Life aboard *Ney* during her brief offensive career was certainly hectic, but there was always time to entertain visiting French officers whilst based at Dunkirk. The latter, on spotting the framed wardroom picture of Marshal Ney, would leap to their feet, don their kepis and stand to attention in front of the portrait, saluting and solemnly intoning, "Le Maréchal Ney, le brave des braves." On the first occasion, the British officers were somewhat disconcerted, but scrambled to their feet, hunted for their own caps and sheepishly mumbled, "Le brave des braves" in their best French accents! Thereafter, the picture was usually removed temporarily whilst French officers were aboard.

The modifications that were eventually made to *Ney* in 1916 were not as extensive as originally envisaged. Although her turret was transferred to *Terror*, her diesel machinery was retained. In place of the 15-inch twin mounting, a much lighter mounting was fitted — one of

(Opposite) *The upper drawing from* The Shipbuilder *shows one of* Marshal Ney*'s two 750-B.H.P. M.A.N. 2-stroke diesel engines. The two smaller cylinders provided the compressed air for the oil fuel blast injection for the six propulsion cylinders. Despite its businesslike appearance and satisfactory test-bed performance, it never operated successfully in service. The lower drawing from* The Engineer *shows to the same scale one of* Trefoil*'s 750-B.H.P. Vickers 4-stroke airless injection engines, which was transferred to* Marshal Soult. *Despite the comparatively primitive appearance of the 8-cylinder engine, somewhat resembling a steam reciprocating engine, it performed well in service.*

the two single 9.2-inch Mk VIII 40-calibre guns which had recently been removed from the old 1st class cruiser *Terrible*, the other being earmarked for *Soult*, although never fitted. Four single 6-inch Q.F. were also transferred from *Terrible* and sited two on either side abreast the funnel. The director and topmast were removed, but a modest bridge structure was added to improve navigational facilities. She did not remain long in this state and another extensive refit took place during 1916-17. The 9.2-inch was removed and mounted ashore in France, and *Ney* was given a uniform armament of six single 6-inch B.L. XI removed from the pre-dreadnought *Hibernia*. Two were sited on the centre-line, one forward and one aft, while the other four were placed abreast the mast; each gun had 100 rounds of ammunition. A fully enclosed bridge structure was provided — no doubt much appreciated by the cold and bored watchkeepers

Soult *seen here in Basin No. 3 at Chatham as a stationary Turret Drill Ship in July 1936. Three V class destroyers in reserve are berthed alongside, including* Velox *(inboard).*

during the long months she lay at the Downs. The 12-pdr were removed and two new 3-inch H.A. fitted aft to augment her existing 2-pdr. The only other noticeable change was the emergence of the bulge above the waterline, as the removal of some 1100 tons net reduced her displacement to about 5780 tons deep and her drafts to 7 feet forward and 10 feet aft.

Soult's service performance was an improvement on *Ney*'s, though hardly spectacular. A maximum cruising speed of only $5^1/_2$ knots, in waters where tidal currents reached 3 knots and gales were frequent, meant that sometimes the quickest progress could be made by anchoring and waiting for better conditions, as otherwise she was inclined to be driven astern, or at least sideways. The two *Marshal*s were often bracketed together when maligning diesel propulsion, but in fact *Soult*'s Vickers' engines proved extremely reliable, quiet and free from vibration.

Soult's visible modifications during 1916-17 were relatively few: two 6-inch Q.F. (one from *Ney*) and a 3-inch H.A. added on the forecastle deck, and the topmast struck. A better navigational position was built on the tripod mast above the turret level, painted in distinctive grey and white chequers. The main modification was not readily apparent; the raising of the axis of the 15-inch guns about two feet to permit them to elevate to 30°. 1918 saw further modifications; first four single 4-inch B.L. IX replaced the 6-inch. The 4-inch had not only a longer range than the 6-inch but a much faster rate of fire. Then later in the year came the really startling changes which transformed her from being merely bizarre in appearance into what must surely have been the ugliest ship in the Royal Navy. The most offending feature was a funnel doubled in height yet of the original diameter. Its proportions were thus those of a 30-foot long cigarette, totally disproportionate to the size of ship. Two 36-inch searchlights were added on tall lattice platforms abaft the funnel to replace the two 24-inch on the tripod mast. A control position was fitted aft and the conning tower removed. The latter was replaced by a platform carrying the two 12-pdr, now converted to H.A. The secondary armament was increased to eight single 4-inch distributed along the sides of the forecastle deck. Two single 2-pdr were retained on their platform aft, as well as two 3-inch H.A. at the break of the forecastle.

The problems of *Marshal Ney* formed one of the elements of the Churchill-Balfour controversy in the House of Commons in March 1916. Returning from France to make a speech in the Navy Estimates debate, Churchill attacked Balfour and the new Board of the Admiralty for the slowing down in the rate of construction. He compared the rapidity with which the monitor fleet had been completed with the subsequent delays in battleship construction. While stretching a point when he claimed that the monitors had been finished in six months (the average time was eight months) there was some substance in his accusation. None of the five *Royal Sovereign*s had been completed, although contract completion dates had all been at the end of 1915. Balfour was stung to reply at length the next day, 8 March. He ridiculed Churchill for claiming credit for the speedy construction of the monitors while in the same breath criticising the delay with the battleships, pointing out that the former had only been achieved by using guns and mountings ordered for the latter. Balfour's excuse about diversions of gun mountings was a bit thin as it only applied to two out of the fourteen big gun monitors — the *Marshal*s — and he was quickly taken up on this point by Sir A. Markham, Liberal M.P. for Mansfield, who pointed out that the monitor guns had come from America. Yes, conceded Balfour, but not all of them.

Although his case was scarcely any stronger than Churchill's, Balfour proceeded to wade in with further criticism of the monitor fleet. Although they were doing good service, they added nothing to the strength of the Grand Fleet and, furthermore, they had design faults. "So hastily was the design of some of these vessels and so ill were they contrived to carry out their purpose that even now it has not been found possible to use some of them for the purpose for which they were originally designed. They are in process of being remodelled or remodelled so as to make them suitable for this amphibious warfare. The design was hasty, the execution was hasty and the result is therefore as might easily be expected not always satisfactory."[1] To speak of "some" of the monitors having to be remodelled was quite unfair, as such a description could only be applied with any accuracy to but one vessel, *Marshal Ney*. Markham again came to Churchill's rescue, saying although alterations had been made, they were not due in any way to the latter's "hasty action" but rather to "another cause," which he did not specify. Presumably he meant that it would be unfair to blame Churchill for not foreseeing the failure of *Ney*'s diesels. However it could reasonably be argued that it was rather foolhardy of Churchill and Fisher to authorise such an untried form of prime mover for a combatant ship in wartime. The outcome of this particular aspect of the debate was inconclusive, but at least 1916 did see the completion of six more capital ships.

§5 Twilight Careers

Even before the Armistice was signed, the Admiralty realised that in *Marshal Soult* they had a very suitable ship for gunnery instruction. She carried an example of the Navy's latest big gun mounting, while her poor seagoing characteristics were no handicap for a harbour-based ship. Her upkeep costs would be modest compared with a battleship, yet she had all that was necessary for turret and director instruction. She left Chatham on 14 November 1918 to become a tender to H.M.S. *Excellent*, the gunnery training school at Portsmouth. Four months later, she was transferred to Devonport for similar duties. There she remained as Director and Fire Control Ship until March 1921, when she paid off and was put on the non-effective list. After *Glorious*, who had relieved her, had been taken in hand for conversion to an aircraft carrier, *Soult* was reinstated for gunnery instruction. She started a £35,000 refit at Portsmouth in May 1924 to bring her up to the mark and, by March 1925, she was back at Devonport as Turret Drill Ship.

Proposals for the defences of the new base to be created at Singapore were discussed in 1923 by the Admiralty and War Office. Consideration was given to stationing all three 15-inch monitors there (*Soult, Erebus* and *Terror*) but rejected in favour of shore batteries. *Soult* and *Erebus* exchanged places in April 1926, when the former berthed in No. 3 Basin at Chatham, which remained her home for the next 14 years, apart from brief trips to Portsmouth for drydocking. In addition to her drill ship role, her duties also included Senior Officer Reserve Fleet, Royal Naval Reserve Training Ship and Accommodation Ship at the Nore, for which her official complement was 203. In the event of mobilisation, it was intended that she would pay off so that her crew could be drafted to active ships.

Marshal Ney was also put to good use after the war, although nominally on the Disposal List. In February 1919 she was base ship for M.L.s at Queenborough in the Medway. In September she moved back to Sheerness as an accommodation ship. She was sent round to Portsmouth in August 1920 to act as submarine school depot ship at Fort Blockhouse in place of the old cruiser *Arrogant*. For this role she was completely disarmed and her tripod mast removed. On 12 July 1922 she arrived at Devonport to replace *Harlech* (originally the 1893 cruiser *Cambrian*) attached to the Stoker Training Establishment and was renamed *Vivid* after the R.N. Barracks whose tender she officially was. She remained at Devonport for the rest of her service life — another 35 years. In her later days, she became almost unrecognisable as a former monitor, her forecastle deck being buried under a mass of huts providing additional accommodation. For most of this time she remained in the dockyard, taking the parent name *Drake* in 1934. She saw out World War 2, providing valuable accommodation when the Barracks were bombed. She was renamed yet again in 1947, this time *Alaunia II*, as she formed part of the stoker training establishment, which included the repair ship *Alaunia*, a recently converted ex-Cunarder. She was finally disposed of in 1957, being handed over to BISCO[2] who allocated her to

Marshal Ney *is seen here in her final WW1 appearance with six single 6-inch, two 3-inch H.A. and two 2-pdr, plus an enlarged bridge structure. The view shows her as a motor launch base ship in the Medway early in 1919.*

T. W. Ward for scrapping at Milford Haven. Thus departed the least successful but longest lived of all the large monitors.

Following the outbreak of WW2, the question of putting *Soult* back into active service was considered. However a survey showed that her hull was not worth refitting and it would be better to transfer her turret to a new hull. This was carried out as described in Chapter IX, so one of the turrets originally intended for *Ramillies* continued in service in a second *Roberts* for another quarter-century. *Soult* was towed to Portsmouth for the removal of her turret, arriving on 11 March 1940, where Vickers-Armstrongs[3] refitted the turret before it was despatched to the new monitor building on the Clyde. *Soult* took up her new role as base ship for naval trawlers in December, providing administrative and maintenance

[1] Hansard, 8 March 1916, p.1567

[2] After WW2, British warships were not sold for breaking up but were handed over to BISCO — the British Iron and Steel Corporation (Salvage) — who then allocated them to an appropriate shipbreaker and returned the net proceeds of the sale of scrap material to the Exchequer.

[3] Vickers and Armstrong merged in 1927, retaining the joint title until 1965, when it reverted simply to Vickers.

Marshal Ney *almost unrecognisable under a mass of accommodation huts as* Alaunia II *at Devonport in 1957.*

facilities from her berth in the pocket of No. 3 Basin. During the heavy German air attacks of 1941, she proved a popular ship as her armoured decks made her a first class air raid shelter. She was only hit once during these attacks, receiving a bomb forward on the forecastle deck on 11 March, but suffering only splinter damage. She remained a trawler base ship all through the war, succouring in addition kindred vessels such as motor minesweepers and motor fishing vessels. She finally paid off on 31 March 1946, and four months later was towed to Troon on the Firth of Clyde for breaking up.

THE MARSHALS — TECHNICAL PARTICULARS

Displacement and Dimensions 6670 tons legend, 6900 tons deep. Length 355′-8″ o.a., breadth 90′-3″, draft 10′-5″ deep.

Weight Distribution Armament 850 tons, ammunition 290, protection 2140, hull 2600, equipment 220, machinery 450, oil fuel (nominal) 100. Designed total 6650 tons.

Complement 13 officers, 174 men.

Armament 2—15″ (twin) (100 C.P.C. r.p.g.), 2—12-pdr (200 r.p.g.), 1—3″ H.A. (*Ney*) (300 r.p.g.), 1—3-pdr Vickers H.A. (*Soult*) (500 r.p.g.), 2—2-pdr H.A. (1000 r.p.g.), 4—0.303″ Maxim (5000 r.p.g.).

Protection As 14-inch monitors except: upper deck over 15-inch magazine 4″ N.C.; main deck forward 1½″ H.T.; gunhouse 13″ C. front, 11″ C. sides and rear, 5″ N.C. roof, 3″ H.T. floor.

Machinery Twin screw diesels. *Ney*: two 6-cyl M.A.N., 1500 B.H.P. at 185 r.p.m. *Soult*: two 8-cyl Vickers, 1500 B.H.P. at 150 r.p.m. Oil fuel 226 tons. Endurance 2080 miles at 5½ knots (*Soult*).

Speed 9 knots designed, 6 service. Trials: *Ney* 6.3, *Soult* 6.61 knots.

Construction Palmer, Jarrow: *Marshal Ney* laid down Jan 1915/launched 17 Jun 1915/completed 31 Aug 1915; *Soult* Feb/24 Aug/2 Nov 1915.

Scrapped *Ney* Ward, Milford Haven 6 Oct 1957; *Soult* West of Scotland Shipbreaking, Troon 5 Aug 1946.

CHAPTER V

THE EX-BRAZILIAN RIVER MONITORS

H.M.S. SEVERN, HUMBER, MERSEY

§1 Origins

The small Brazilian river monitors taken over at the beginning of WW1 had been one of the catalysts which brought the larger monitors into existence, but both in their conception and subsequent deployment they differed considerably from their successors. The naval rivalry between South American countries and the profits from rubber exports formed the basis of a large expansion of the Brazilian Navy. Late in 1911, negotiations were undertaken with Vickers, Son & Maxim at Barrow for vessels for the inland waters of the River Amazon. Three shallow draft river monitors were required, to be well armed and well protected for their size. Vickers' design was for a vessel of about 1200 tons carrying two 6-inch 50-calibre guns in one twin turret forward, on a draft of 4ft 6in. In order to obtain such a shallow draft, a very beamy hull was necessary, 261ft 6in B.P. by 49ft. The magazine and machinery spaces would be protected by 3-inch side armour, with 1-inch deck protection, the double bottom extending up behind the belt. Twin screw steam reciprocating machinery to be built by Vickers with dual coal/oil-fired boilers was designed to give a trial speed of about 12 knots. A powerful secondary armament was also fitted: two single 120-mm (4.72-inch) howitzers aft, four 3-pdr and six machine guns. The main hull was only a single deck deep (8ft 6in), but with the wide superstructure there was sufficient space for accommodation well equipped for extended operations, complete with sickbay, refrigerated stores and even a prison cell.

Vickers' proposal was accepted by the Brazilians in January 1912. The three vessels were built broadside on to the water. All were named after tributaries of the Amazon: *Javary, Solimões* and *Madeira. Javary* was the first to be completed, steaming off to the Clyde in October 1913 for drydocking and trials. Although she proved capable of exceeding her contract speed of $11^1/_2$ knots going ahead, it was found impossible to manoeuvre her astern. As the diameter of her propellers was greater than her draft at normal load (5ft 7in vs. 4ft 9in), they were arranged to work in a tunnel swept up into the hull. The shape was found to be such that a proper flow of water could not be obtained going astern, but the problem could be overcome by arranging a hinged flap to drop over the stern when required. Gun trials were also undertaken at the same time. The compact twin 6-inch turret was an improved version of that fitted in the British *Monmouth* class cruisers.

All three monitors were completed by February 1914 and ready for their delivery voyage to Rio, but the Brazilians were now not in a position to be able to pay for the ships. Rubber prices had dropped dramatically in 1913 with competition from the newly established Malayan plantations, and Brazil could no longer afford the luxury of expanding her navy. The three monitors were put up for sale at about the same time as the battleship *Rio de Janeiro*, which was sold to Turkey. But river gunboats were not such a saleable proposition as battleships during the pre-war frenzy of capital ship construction amongst all the naval powers, large and small, so they remained laid up in the Devonshire Dock at Barrow. Just prior to the outbreak of war, Churchill expressed his concern about the possibility of their falling into enemy hands. Immediate arrangements were made to take them over for the Royal Navy on 3 August, a price of £155,000 being agreed with Vickers for each vessel as made up as follows:

	£
Armament	28,000
Machinery	23,667
Hull and protection	103,333
Total	155,000

The price was high at about £120 per ton, comparable with a destroyer, reflecting the elaborate fittings and the special weight-saving construction techniques.

Although no specific use was envisaged for the monitors, they had the advantage of being complete and ready for service, while of course they would be denied to other possible belligerents. Things moved fast: the declaration of war on the 4th, arrival of the C.O.s and crews at Barrow on the 5th and commissioning on the 8th. The new names chosen were those of English rivers with initial letters as near to the Brazilian as possible: *Solimões* became H.M.S. *Severn*, *Madeira* H.M.S. *Mersey* and *Javary* H.M.S. *Humber*. The Senior Officer of the squadron, Commander E. J. A. Fullerton, took *Severn* as his ship, Commander A. L. Snagge *Humber* and Lieutenant-Commander R. A. Wilson *Mersey*. By 25 August, they had been prepared for R.N. service and were manoeuvred out into the Walney Channel with tug assistance. New speed trials were carried out but, instead of her reputed 12 knots, *Humber* could only manage 9.67, over two knots less than she had done ten months earlier. The explanation was twofold: a much deeper draft and the

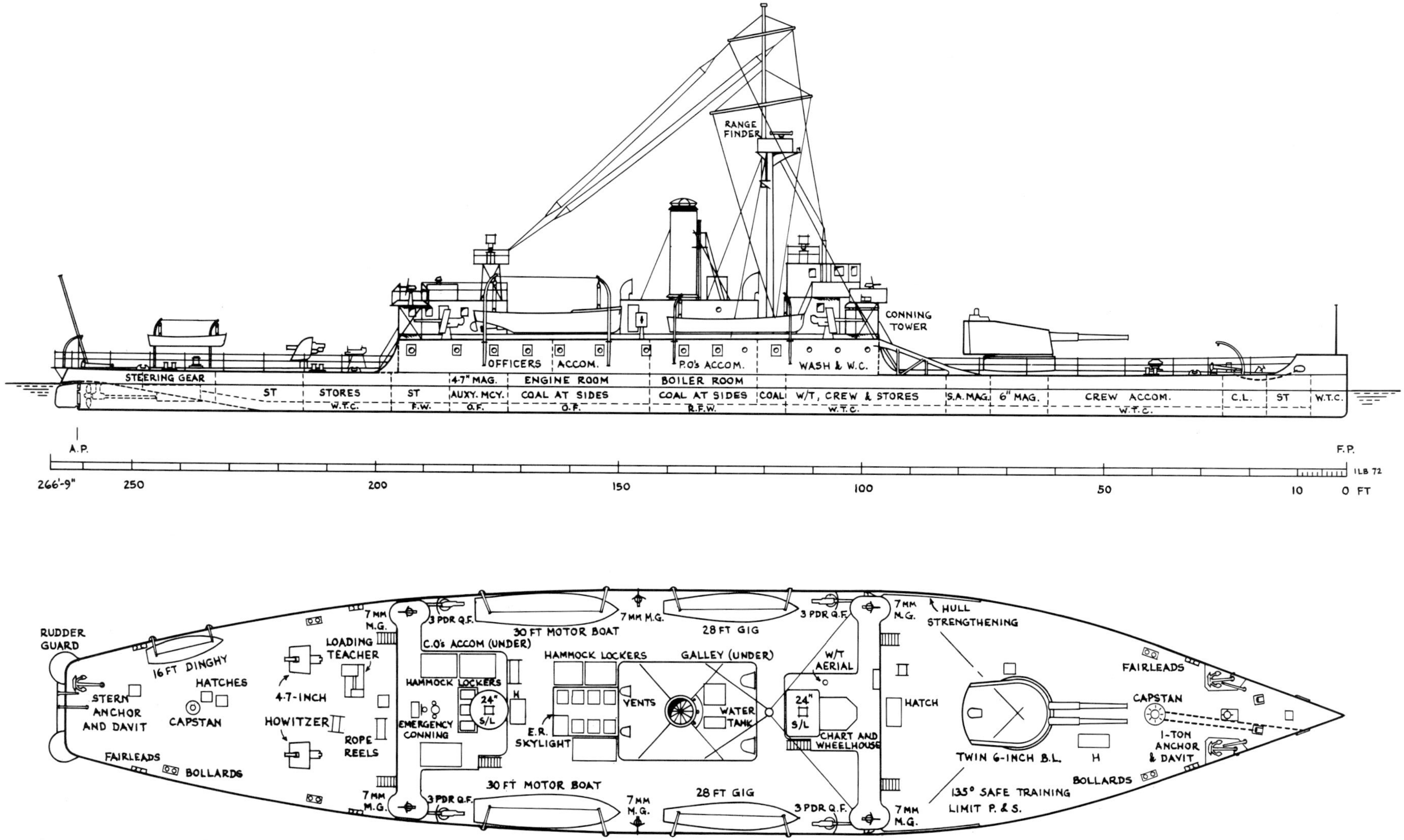

Severn, Humber *and* Mersey. *The drawing shows the Brazilian river monitors as taken over by the R.N. At the end of 1914,* Severn *and* Mersey*'s turret was replaced by a single 6-inch gun, while all three ships had a single 6-inch fitted on the quarterdeck. As with all the profiles in this book, the waterline shown is that corresponding to the service draft in the deep condition, not the designed draft — which emphasises the low freeboard. The propellers operated in a tunnel between the rudder skegs, as their diameter was greater than the draft. There is a builder's model of the class in the Science Museum, London.*

A rare view of Javary *passing Clydebank on her way down-river after drydocking at Glasgow in October 1913. Ordered from Vickers by Brazil in January 1912, she was taken over by the R.N. in August 1914 and renamed* Humber.

fouling that had taken place during her long lay-up. Subsequent experience showed that it was almost impossible for the monitors to reach double figures even under the most favourable conditions, yet all official publications continued to show their authorised speed as 12 knots.

The three ex-river gunboats were initially allocated to the Dover Patrol, responsible for protecting from any German attacks the Straits and the shipping to France and around the English coast. *Severn* and *Mersey* departed in company from Barrow immediately after completion of their trials, while *Humber* proceeded independently. The $3^1/_2$-day voyage to Dover turned out to be a nerve-wracking introduction to navigating river craft outside sheltered waters. The monitors demonstrated quite clearly that they were unsuited to open sea operation and that in any force of wind they were blown all over the surface of the water. They eventually reached Dover on 29 August after a most uncomfortable voyage averaging only $7^1/_2$ knots.

§2 Wartime Operations

No sooner had the three monitors arrived at Dover than they were ordered to Ostende to embark Marines being evacuated to England. Early on 31 August, they left Dover, undertaking gunnery trials on the way. After arriving at Ostende late in the evening they found that the Marines had already been evacuated. They were sent back to the Medway, whence they carried out patrols in the Thames Estuary for the next six weeks. The opportunity was taken for Chatham Dockyard to add an extra inch of deck protection over the 6-inch magazine, making two inches in all.

Meantime the "Race to the Sea" was taking place in France as the Allied and German armies each attempted to envelop the other's flank after the initial rapid German advance had been finally halted on the River Aisne north-east of Paris. Following the fall of Antwerp on 9 October, other German forces were racing westwards towards the Channel ports and soon virtually the whole of Belgium had been overrun right up to Ostende. The Belgian Army was attempting to hold the line of the River Yser, about ten miles east of the French border, from the sea at Nieuport inland towards Ypres, where the British Expeditionary Force was being equally hard pressed by the Germans.

On 10 October *Severn, Humber* and *Mersey* had left Sheerness in response to orders to provide naval cover off the Belgian Coast and to prevent any enemy landings behind the Allied lines. They anchored off Ostende the next day to assist troop withdrawal by sea before the town was finally overrun. A squadron, which included the light cruiser *Attentive*, the three monitors and several other vessels, was then formed under Rear-Admiral Hood, hitherto Churchill's Naval Secretary, who had just arrived to take over the newly created Dover Command. Requests for assistance on their sea flank had been received from the hard pressed Belgians, so on 16 October the squadron was ordered up in close support. But the weather was too bad for the low freeboard monitors to proceed safely from Dover, and it was not until the 18th that they arrived off Nieuport. Their principal duties were to break up any movements of German troops, particularly along the coastal road from Ostende to Nieuport, and to prevent any enemy movements by sea. By mid-morning the Belgium Army was asking for naval gunfire to be directed at inland targets east of Nieuport. From 2000 yards offshore, the shallow draft monitors were able to pour a heavy fire from their 6-inch guns and 4.7-inch howitzers onto enemy forces advancing on Westende, only two miles north-east of Nieuport. The enemy returned fire with field guns and, although none of the monitors received a direct hit, shrapnel wounded several men aboard *Humber* and *Mersey*. The monitors then lengthened the range to 10,000 yards where they were out of reach of the

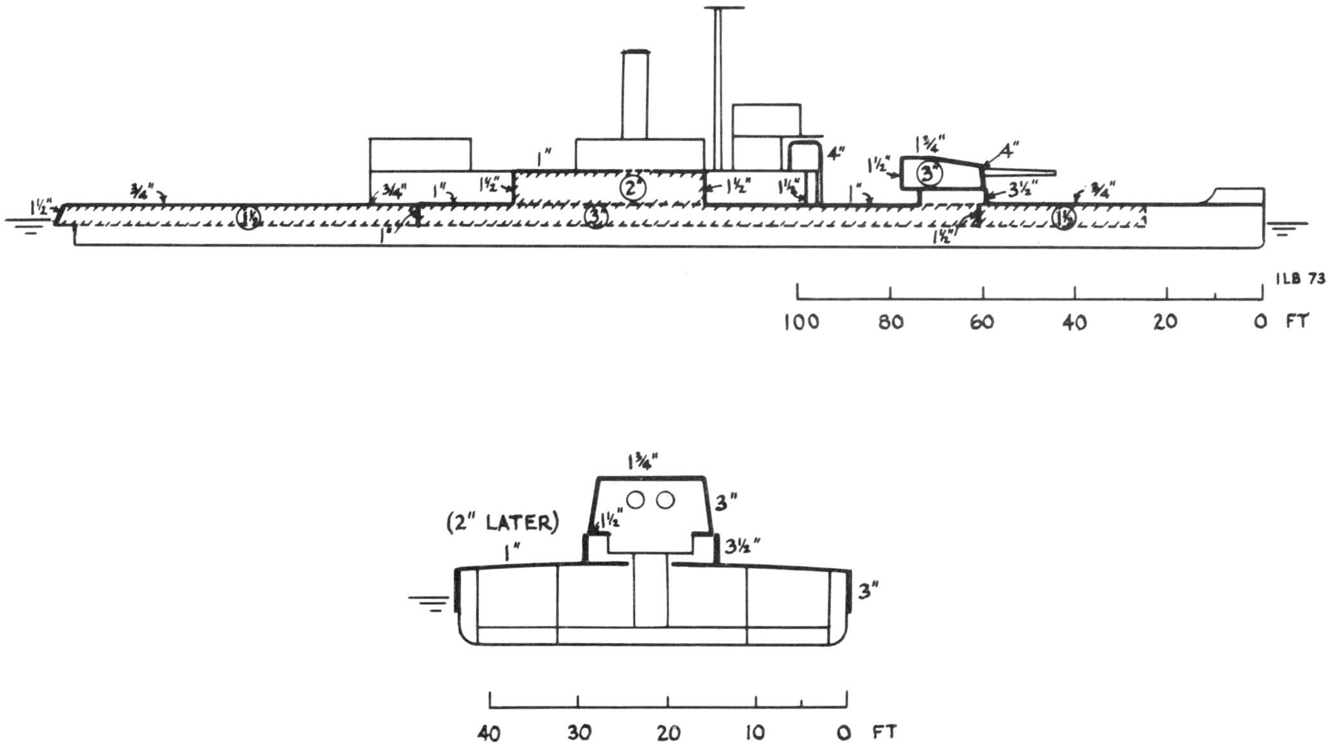

All the hull protection in Severn, Humber *and* Mersey *was worked structurally except for the 3-inch belt. A further inch was added at the end of 1914 to the deck protection over the 6-inch magazine forward.*

enemy guns. For the rest of the day continuous fire was kept up, directed by wireless messages from the Belgian headquarters, as the targets were out of sight from the sea behind the sand dunes and no proper spotting facilities yet existed. Firing continued the next day at various targets, including howitzers at Slype which were severely harrassing the Belgians. In the afternoon a Belgian officer arrived in *Severn* to assist co-operation, reporting that the bombardment had put fresh heart into the Belgian troops to defend the last remaining corner of their homeland.

On the 20th, machine gun parties were landed from the monitors, while the ships themselves were heavily engaged in repulsing the attack on Westende. By the afternoon, all their ammunition had been shot off and the monitors retired to Dunkirk to replenish. They were back in action on the 22nd, the squadron having been reinforced by a makeshift collection of bombarding vessels, including the old cruisers *Brilliant* and *Sirius*, sloops *Vestal, Rinaldo* and *Wildfire* and the ancient gunboats *Hazard, Excellent* and *Bustard.* For the next ten days, fire was kept up whenever the opportunity arose and the weather permitted. The arrival of the pre-dreadnought *Venerable*, with her four 12-inch guns, helped stabilise the position later but not before Westende had fallen. The bombardments from the sea had however caused the Germans considerable concern; they requested as many U-boats as possible to be sent to attack the British ships.

By now the monitors were feeling the strain of continuous action, both crews and hulls. *Mersey*'s turret had broken down on the 28th, *Severn*'s left 6-inch was badly scored and high rates of fire were overheating the guns, rapidly shortening their life and causing over 2000 yards' reduction in maximum range. As the enemy entrenched themselves more firmly along the coast, heavier guns were brought up which soon inflicted damage on several of the other bombarding vessels as well as near-missing *Severn* and *Humber.* By 1 November the position ashore had fully stabilised, French reinforcements had arrived and the Nieuport sluice-gates had been opened, flooding low lying areas to restrict further German advances. Although the German thrusts had been halted, the Allied counterattacks were unable to make any progress towards recovering Ostende, still less Antwerp. There was little more the monitors could do so, as the U-boats were becoming more active, *Severn* and *Mersey* returned to the Medway on 3 November. *Humber* followed a week later after a final bombardment of Westende on the 7th in support of a French attack. The Germans later testified that the presence of the bombarding fleet had played a vital part in stabilising the Allied line during those critical October days, preventing a German advance to Dunkirk, Calais and Boulogne, whose loss would have been a severe handicap to British support of subsequent naval and military operations.

The next few weeks were spent in Chatham Dockyard replacing worn-out guns. As there were no spare 6-inch Mk XIV and XV — as the R.N. designated the right and left hand versions of the Vickers' design — consideration was given to replacing the entire turrets with the spare mountings for the *Monmouth* class. The necessary conversion work was found to be too extensive, so the turrets were removed altogether from *Severn* and *Mersey* and two single 6-inch B.L. VII substituted, which had a very similar performance, one forward behind a steel breastwork and one aft. Two of the guns had been salvaged from the pre-dreadnought *Montagu*, which had been wrecked on Lundy Island in 1906. Ammunition stowage was increased from 150 to 225 rounds per gun. As *Humber*'s guns were not so badly worn, she kept her turret. The 4.7-inch howitzers were moved from the quarterdeck to the boat deck and a single Hotchkiss 3-pdr H.A. added in place of the after 24-inch searchlight, the latter moving to a new platform further aft.

An invasion scare blew up during November, a possible landing being suspected in the shallow waters of the Wash. The heavily armed light draft monitors would be ideal for resisting such an operation, so all three were hurried round to the Lincolnshire port of Boston, where they remained for three weeks until the scare receded in mid-December. *Severn* and *Mersey* then returned to Dunkirk in response to French requests for naval support, while *Humber* was taken in hand at Chatham for modifications including the addition of a single 6-inch B.L. VII aft, also salvaged from *Montagu*, giving her a total of three 6-inch, one hardly used and two well-worn.

It was hoped that the two shallow draft monitors would be a useful supplement to the deep draft pre-dreadnoughts, but the severe winter weather and the limited range of their guns restricted their operations. Furthermore, Hood was only in favour of using his ships in conjunction with land offensives which would justify the risk of damage from shore batteries, and not for casual bombardment. The monitors therefore returned to the Medway on 11 January 1915, while Belgian Coast operations were reduced to a low key until the first large monitors arrived in August.

Early in March came orders to prepare the ships for service again, this time overseas. If the plans to force the Dardanelles were successful, it would be necessary to have vessels capable of going up the River Danube for operations against Austria-Hungary. The 3000-mile voyage out to the Mediterranean would not be possible under their own steam, so arrangements were made to tow the monitors. Their crews would be evacuated to another ship and their hulls specially strengthened and upperworks boarded over, as they would be continually washed by green seas on passage. Each monitor was taken in tow by a pair of tugs when the squadron left Sheerness on 11 March. The crews embarked in the fleet messenger *Trent*, a liner taken over from the Royal Mail Steam Packet Company, when the ten ships set off from Devonport three days later at $6^1/_2$ knots. Malta was safely reached on 29 March, where the monitors were readied to go on to Mudros to prepare for the forthcoming Allied landings at Gallipoli, scheduled for 25 April. Bad weather delayed their sailing for so long that insufficient time remained to tow them the 700 miles and then complete the expected fortnight's work of putting them back into shape again, so the monitors stayed at Malta. Then on 19 April came new orders which were to split up the squadron for the next three years.

There had been a number of German cruisers overseas when war had broken out, most of which were quickly accounted for by the Royal Navy. The 3400-ton cruiser *Königsberg* did however still remain afloat as, after operations against British shipping in August and September 1914, she had taken refuge amongst the shallow channels of the Rufiji River delta in German East

Intended for operations up the Danube should the Gallipoli Expedition be successful, the three river monitors are seen here at Malta in April 1915. From left to right are Mersey, Severn *and* Humber *berthed alongside their depot ship* Trent.

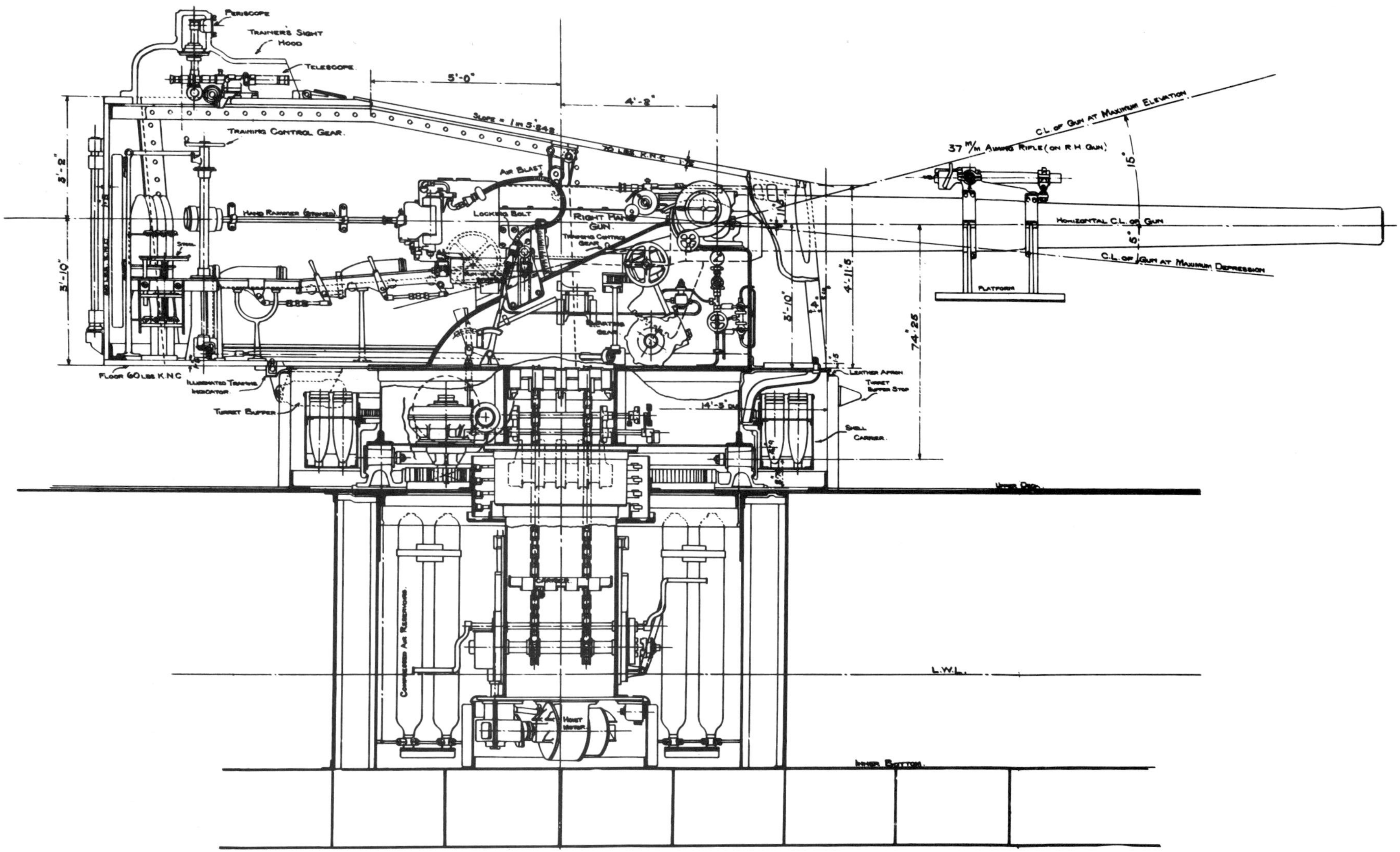

The twin 6-inch mounting fitted in the three ex-Brazilian monitors, as reproduced from the Vickers handbook. The electrically powered mounting was very similar to that fitted in the British Monmouth *class cruisers. The turret had to be removed from* Severn *and* Mersey *after their guns had been worn out off the Belgian Coast in October 1914, as there were no spare Mark XIV or XV guns. (K.N.C. = Krupp non-cemented armour).*

Africa, 70 miles south of Dar es Salaam. There she was blockaded in by a superior force of British cruisers which, because of their comparatively deep draft, could not reach close enough to shell her nine miles upstream. Stalemate had developed, which could only be broken either by the German breaking out or the British sending in well armed and protected shallow draft vessels up one of the river entrances. The ex-Brazilian river monitors were the only suitable vessels, so Fisher ordered two of them out to East Africa. As *Humber*'s armament now made her the odd man out, *Severn* and *Mersey* left Malta on 28 April under tow together with *Trent* and a collier.

After a difficult voyage, fully described in *Severn's Saga* by E. Keble Chatterton, the convoy arrived at Mafia Island on 3 June, ten miles off the Rufiji delta. The island had been captured from the Germans in January 1915 and formed an advanced base for blockading vessels, which included the cruisers *Weymouth, Hyacinth, Pioneer* and *Pyramus.* It took three weeks to get the monitors operational again, removing the temporary strengthening, patching up leaks, re-storing and ammunitioning, adding further protection in the form of $^1/_2$-inch steel plates and sandbags and filling below-deck spaces with about 9000 empty petrol cans to provide buoyancy should the hull be damaged. The monitors were then painted green to blend better with the tropical jungle backgrounds. After the crews had rejoined, trials were needed to exercise co-operation with the R.N.A.S. spotting aeroplanes. Several of these precious machines had recently arrived from England and they would provide the only means of directing gunfire onto the hidden cruiser.

Vice-Admiral H. G. King-Hall's plan called for them to enter the northernmost channel on the flood tide at daybreak, in order to surprise the shore defences, and then steam up to a position about $5^1/_2$ miles from *Königsberg,* while one plane bombed her and another spotted gunfire onto her, invisible from sea level behind the thick jungle. The two monitors entered the Kikunya mouth at 05.40 on 6 July and ran a gauntlet of fire from light guns ashore, replying with their 3-pdr. Both vessels anchored undamaged in the firing position about halfway between *Königsberg* and the river mouth, opening fire at 06.48 with their 6-inch at a range of about 11,000 yards. The cruiser soon returned fire from her 105-mm (4.1-inch), although only her five starboard guns out of her total of ten could be brought to bear. Her fire soon became uncomfortably accurate, as it was being directed by German observers hiding on the river bank near the monitors and on a hill to the northward. Her shells fell close all around the British ships but they remained unharmed until 07.30 when *Mersey* received two hits, one on her forward 6-inch putting it out of action and another aft at the waterline, which also sank her motor-boat. Six men were killed; the monitor had to retire to repair the damage. At 07.51 *Severn* scored her first hit on *Königsberg* near her foremost gun, the spotting aircraft no longer being confused by the shell bursts of both monitors. Two more hits were made before *Severn* also was forced to shift her berth by return fire.

Mersey was back in action by 08.10 and firing continued from both monitors on and off for several hours whenever there was one of the two aircraft available in a position to spot, during which time the cruiser's fire slackened, as she was conserving ammunition. The monitors had to withdraw at 15.30 with the falling tide but, although *Königsberg* had received three hits, she was still capable of fighting and steaming. 633 rounds of 6-inch had been fired but only 78 had been spotted and others failed to burst, so that it was clear that a repeat attempt would have to be made. The monitors had been severely shaken up by the repeated strain of prolonged firing and their guns were rather the worse for wear, so the next four days were spent patching them up at Mafia Island.

The river was entered again at 11.40 on 11 July. This time *Severn* anchored further up river, to be met by several salvoes from *Königsberg* which landed uncomfortably close and showered her with shrapnel. Although *Mersey* opened fire at 12.15, her sister took over shortly after, quickly finding the 9500-yard range. The Henri Farman spotting aircraft reported a hit with *Severn*'s eighth salvo at 12.39 and thereafter hits were registered continuously, severely damaging the German cruiser. A serious fire broke out aft, necessitating flooding of the magazines. At about 14.00 a heavy explosion was heard, followed by others, the Germans having abandoned ship and deliberately exploded two torpedo warheads amidships to disable the ship beyond repair. The monitors moved in closer, continuing to fire on the enemy cruiser until 14.20, making absolutely sure

With no proper drydocks in East Africa, one way of getting at the monitors' underwater hull was simply to beach and wait for low tide. Shown here at Zanzibar in August 1915 after the Königsberg *operation,* Severn *has had some leaks repaired and is getting repainted. The tunnel in which the propellers run and the hinged flap to assist astern manoeuvring can be seen. Two of the 3-pdr can be seen at boat deck level, with a machine gun above the starboard one.*

of her destruction. A total of 204 further rounds of 6-inch had been fired that day to complete the mission.

The monitors' successful action enabled the blockading force to be dispersed to other duties, although they themselves needed considerable attention. They had to be beached at Zanzibar to patch up their leaking hulls to get them back into action against other German forces in East Africa. Their shallow draft, relatively heavy guns and reasonable protection made them ideal for operations against the many small towns and harbours up and down the coast of what is now Tanzania. On 19 August, *Severn* shot up the port of Tanga, railhead to the interior. For the next six months, patrols and reconnaissances were made by both monitors until in March 1916 *Mersey* was despatched in tow of *Trent* to Durban for a badly needed refit. The same month saw the start of serious land operations by British forces against the Germans, during which the monitors again proved their worth in company with a motley collection of other vessels. Bombardments were made, landings carried out and the Army forces supported as required, while the coast was gradually cleared from Tanga in the north to Lindi in the south. Dar es Salaam itself surrendered on 3 September 1916, although German forces remained active until after the Armistice. *Severn* returned from a refit at Durban in April 1917 for a year of further patrols and minor skirmishes in company with *Mersey*. Following a decline in German activity, *Mersey* was towed back to the Mediterranean by *Trent*, leaving Zanzibar on 22 March 1918, followed by *Severn* in April. Both monitors reached Alexandria during May, where they started lengthy overhauls.

Humber had also been busy during the previous three years. She had remained at Malta during May 1915, when news came of the torpedoing of the pre-dreadnoughts *Triumph* and *Majestic* off the Dardanelles. Monitors and bulged cruisers were required as soon as possible to fill the gap caused by the withdrawal of the larger ships for fear of U-boats. She left Malta on 1 June for Mudros, arriving off Gaba Tepe on the 8th and was in action that same day. The following day she fired on the village of Biyuk Anafarta, three miles inland, but after 15 rounds a premature damaged her right gun. Her after 6-inch then took over, completing an expenditure of 13 common and 7 H.E. Artillery ammunition had been running low ashore, so naval gunfire was used whenever possible. *Humber*'s usual position for the next few months was off the Anzac beaches, firing when requested on the many Turkish batteries, particularly those sited on the olive groves to the south, as these troublesome guns enfiladed the beaches used for unloading men and supplies. Her 4.7-inch howitzers proved a useful supplement to her 6-inch, while she cruised close offshore, often fired at but never seriously damaged. In December she helped to cover the withdrawal from Suvla and Anzac.

After her forward 6-inch turret guns were replaced at Alexandria by two relined pieces which had been originally fitted in *Severn* and *Mersey*, she was sent 150 miles west to the small harbour of Mersa Matruh. *Humber* arrived on 30 January 1916, to support British forces in the area, suppressing the Senussi sect's threat to Egypt's western frontier. Late in March, she withdrew to Alexandria, leaving *M.31* to continue providing support. *Humber* then steamed through the Suez Canal to Port Tewfik at the southern end, where she formed part of the strong defences established against any possible Turkish attacks. There she remained for 16 months, her only diversions being brief visits to Alexandria or firing at the occasional enemy aircraft. She left Port Tewfik on 4 August 1917 in tow of the cruiser *Euryalus* for Akaba at the head of that gulf, where she remained as guardship until February 1918. She then returned to Alexandria in tow of *Grafton*, who had just brought her relief *M.31*, where she was soon joined by *Severn* and *Mersey* from East Africa. In October, all three monitors were sent to Mudros to assist operations against Bulgaria and Turkey, but Armistices had been signed before they could see any action.

§3 After the War

The three monitors had come through the war far better than might have been expected for former river gunboats. Although unsuitable for operation in open waters with their already low freeboard aft reduced to only two feet after modifications and their GM of 26ft, they were able to deploy a comparatively powerful gun capability from a reasonably protected platform whenever called upon. Like all the monitors, their beamy shallow draft hulls were very unmanoeuvrable. Sideways drift was always a major problem; in a Force 6 beam wind the course made good was estimated to be 45° off the original heading, while above Force 6 it was wiser to stay in harbour.

Following the Armistice, the three monitors were sent through the Dardanelles to Constantinople. *Humber* remained there for three months but the other two steamed into the Black Sea and up the River Danube. They arrived at Galati on 11 December 1918, spending the winter as part of the force supervising the Armistice with Austria-Hungary. All three were ordered back to Britain in March 1919 for service with the White Sea Squadron, as operations up the River Dvina called for powerful vessels of the shallowest draft. *Humber* was the first to arrive in England on 10 April, followed by *Mersey* on 9 May and *Severn* on 23 May. It was intended to refit them all at Devonport with triple 4-inch mountings similar to *M.27*, but before they could be installed the

(Right) *In this view taken aboard* Severn *in 1917, the Vickers' 4.7-inch port howitzer is seen sited on the boat deck, leaving the quarterdeck clear for the after 6-inch. The howitzer is shown at its maximum elevation of 70° with its shield removed. One of the four original 3-pdr Vickers can be seen with its shield at the after end of the boat deck, with on the platform above one of the 7-mm Hotchkiss machine guns and a 24-inch searchlight. Part of the high angle mounting for the 3-pdr Hotchkiss gun can just be seen on the platform at the top left.*

(Far right) Severn*'s forward 6-inch B.L. VII being prepared for the* Königsberg *operation in July 1915. Additional protection plates have been arranged at the rear of the shield. The 100-lb shells at the rear of the gun with a band painted round the head are C.P.C., the others H.E. not yet fitted with nose fuzes. Camouflage painting in the form of palm trees can be seen on the breastwork. Sailors' washing is strung up to dry.*

Severn's *forecastle in October 1915. On the bridge, the officer of the watch can be seen in tepee, with the machine guns in the wings. On the boat deck, the conning tower is visible behind the forward 6-inch, while two of the 3-pdr can just be seen behind their shields.*

A close-up of Humber *(outboard),* Severn *and* Mersey *at Malta in April 1915. Only* Mersey *has her 3-pdr H.A. gun actually mounted, and much equipment has yet to be replaced following the tow from England.*

(Above) *Monitor or submarine? The low freeboard and unsuitability of the river monitors for open sea operation are clearly demonstrated in this view of* Severn's *quarterdeck in 1916.*

(Above) *This close-up shows* Severn *(nearest camera) and* Humber *after their 18-day tow to Malta.* Humber *still retained her turret, now camouflaged, but* Severn *(and* Mersey*) has had her turret replaced by a single 6-inch, with another on the quarterdeck.*

G

Humber *is shown here at Mudros still with her original turret, but with the barrel of her extra 6-inch just visible on the quarterdeck. A 3-pdr H.A. is now sited on her after searchlight platform. The strengthening added after gun trials can be seen running along the boat deck and down to the forecastle.*

decision was made to send only the first ship as quickly as possible. So *Humber* left Devonport on 20 May under tow for Murmansk, still carrying her normal armament except that her single 3-pdr H.A. abaft the funnel had been replaced by a 3-inch H.A. Her operations in North Russia are more conveniently described with the other small monitors in Chapter VII, §5.

Severn and *Mersey* paid off into C. & M. and were moved to Queenstown (now Cobh) in July 1919. Both were sold to T. W. Ward in May 1921 as part of the huge block purchase described on p.38. *Humber* had returned to Chatham after her service in Russia, paying off on 24 October 1919. She was sold eleven months later to the Dutch salvage firm of F. Rijsdijk for £5510 and converted into a crane barge. She was resold in 1925 to the Upnor Shipbreaking Company and was employed on the dispersal of the wreck of the pre-dreadnought *Bulwark*, which had blown up and sunk in the Medway in November 1914. In the early 1930s she assisted demolition work on the 21,000-ton White Star liner *Celtic* stranded off Queenstown in 1928. Taken over by Dover Industries, she continued work on *Bulwark* from 1935-38. She was sold to French interests before WW2 but her ultimate fate is uncertain — probably a breaker's yard post-war.

Stripped to her boat deck and fitted with equipment from scrapped warships, Humber *was used as a salvage and crane ship for some 20 years after WW1. She is seen here in the Medway in August 1925 lifting material from the sunken* Bulwark.

SEVERN, HUMBER and MERSEY — TECHNICAL PARTICULARS

Displacement and Dimensions 1260 tons Navy List, 1520 tons deep. Length 266′-9″ o.a., breadth 49′-0″, draft 5′-7½″ deep.

Weight Distribution Armament 116 tons, ammunition 20, protection 308, hull 574, equipment 61, machinery and R.F.W. 131, coal (nominal) 50. Designed total 1260 tons.

Complement 9 officers, 131 men.

Armament 2—6″(twin) (50 C.P.C. + 100 H.E. r.p.g.), 2—120mm (4.72″) howitzers (150 r.p.g.), 4—3pdr Vickers (300 r.p.g.), 6—7mm (0.28″) Hotchkiss machine guns (5000 r.p.g.).

Protection Upper deck 1″ nickel steel amidships, ¾″ at ends; (1915) 2″ over 6-inch magazine; side belt 3″ C. amidships, 1½″ N.C. at ends; bulkheads at end of belt 1½″ N.C. forward, 1″ aft; machinery casings 1″ to 2″ N.C.; barbette 3½″ C.; gunhouse 4″ C. front, 3″ N.C. sides, 1¾″ N.C. roof, 1½″ N.C. rear and floor; conning tower 4″ sides, 2½″ roof.

Machinery Twin screw triple-expansion. 1450 I.H.P. at 250 r.p.m. Coal 187 tons, oil fuel 90. Endurance 2800 miles at 8 knots.

Speed 12 knots designed, 9½ service. Trials: *Javary* 11.86, *Humber* 9.67 knots.

Construction Vickers, Barrow: *Severn* laid down 24 Aug 1912/launched 19 Aug 1913/completed Jan 1914; *Humber* 24 Aug 1912/17 Jun 1913/Nov 1913; *Mersey* 24 Aug 1912/30 Sept 1913/Feb 1914.

Disposal *Severn* scrapped Ward, Preston 23 Mar 1923; *Humber* sold Rijsdijk 17 Sept 1920; *Mersey* scrapped Ward, Morecambe 1922.

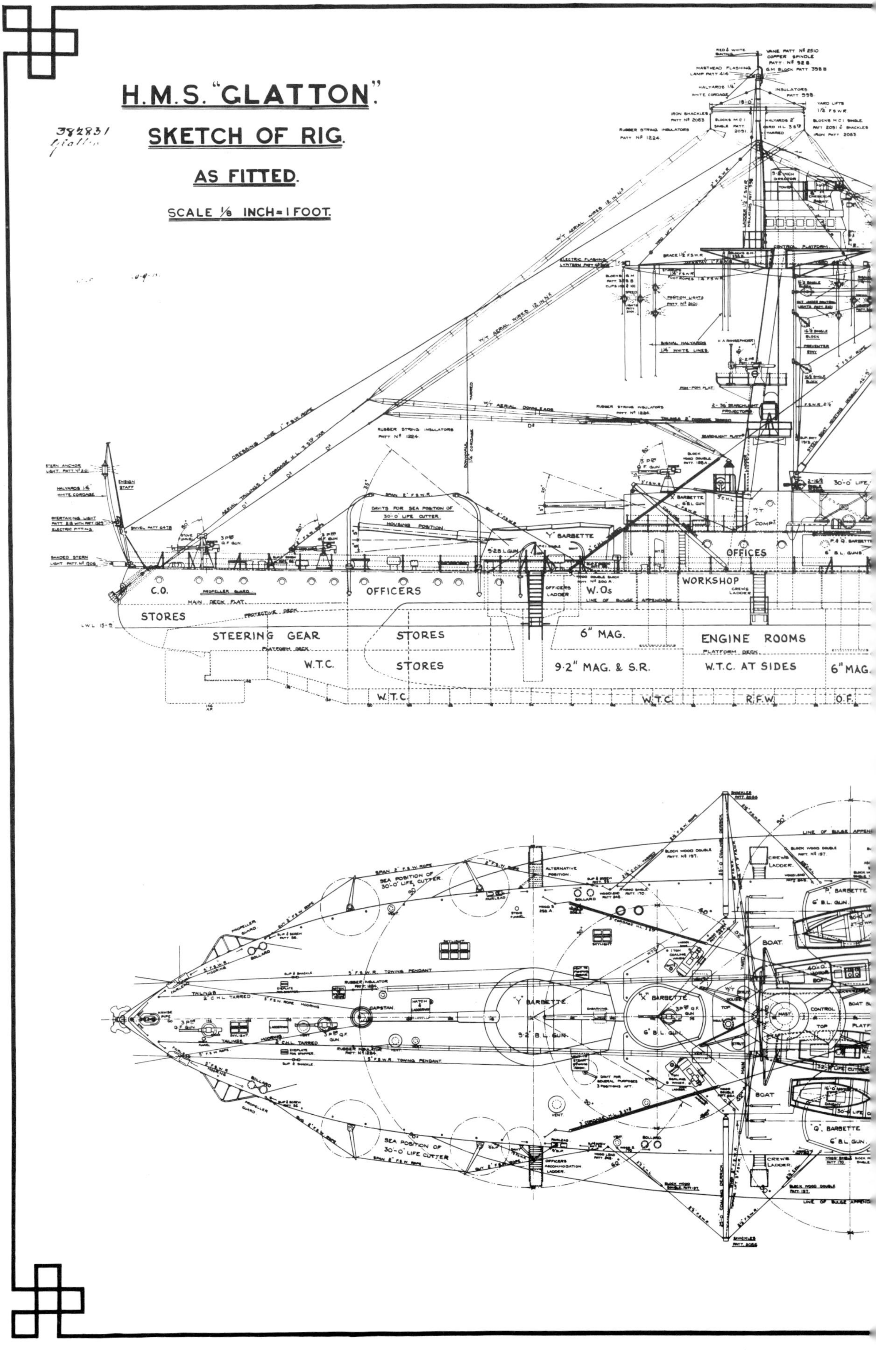
H.M.S. "GLATTON".
SKETCH OF RIG.
AS FITTED.
SCALE 1/8 INCH=1 FOOT.
C.O.
OFFICERS
W.Os
WORKSHOP
OFFICES
STORES
STEERING GEAR
6" MAG.
ENGINE ROOMS
W.T.C.
9·2" MAG. & S.R.
W.T.C. AT SIDES
R.F.W.
"Y" BARBETTE
"X" BARBETTE
9·2" B.L. GUN
6" B.L. GUN
CAPSTAN
BOAT
CONTROL
SEA POSITION OF 30'-0" LIFE CUTTER

Glatton's outboard profile and deck plan is a good example of an 'as fitted' Sketch of Rig, supplied to the Admiralty by Armstrong's — after the ship had already been lost. Names of principal compartments and the scale have been added. Gorgon *was almost identical except for a shorter funnel and different H.A. armament.*

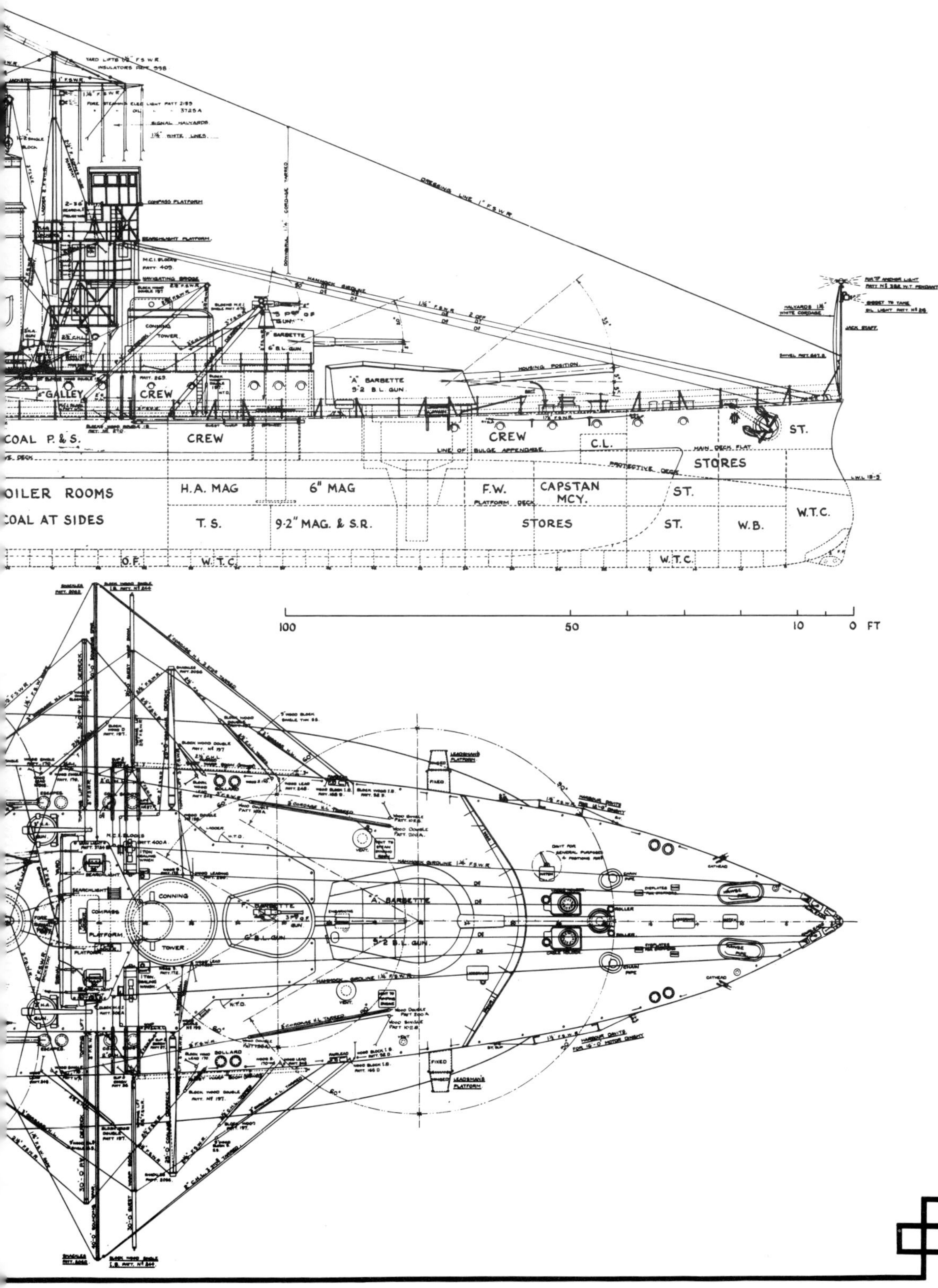

CHAPTER VI

THE EX-NORWEGIAN COAST DEFENCE BATTLESHIPS

H.M.S. GLATTON and GORGON

§1 Design and Construction

Although they were not in the mainstream of British monitor development, two coast defence battleships intended for Norway were converted into bombardment vessels during WW1 for the R.N. In 1912, the Norwegian Government envisaged a large expansion programme, which included two further vessels to add to their existing fleet of four coast defence ships as well as destroyers and submarines. In January 1913, the design and construction of the first two ships authorised in the new programme were entrusted to Armstrong, Whitworth,[1] who had built two earlier vessels, for delivery in 24 months. The hull dimensions were restricted by the only drydock at the Horten naval dockyard, near Oslo, to 290ft B.P. and 55ft breadth. On their designed displacement of 4807 tons, it was possible to carry two Elswick 240-mm 50-calibre guns (9.45-inch) mounted in single turrets forward and aft. The secondary armament consisted of four 150-mm 50-calibre (5.9-inch) also mounted in single turrets, two superfiring over the 240-mm and one on each beam amidships, plus six 100-mm (3.9-inch). Two submerged 450-mm (17.7-inch) torpedo tubes completed the powerful armament of these miniature battleships. In addition the well protected citadel with a 7-inch belt, there was also a 2-inch protective deck the full length of the hull.

The specified trial speed of 15 knots was to be obtained from 4000-I.H.P. twin screw steam reciprocating machinery, ordered from Hawthorn, Leslie's Newcastle engine works. The general arrangement was well laid out on three continuous decks, although the accommodation was a trifle cramped by British standards, owing to the space taken up by the armament. The only place for the midship 150-mm magazine was sandwiched between the engine and boiler rooms, an arrangement used in British battleships although in conjunction with insulating air spaces.

Contruction proceeded to schedule at the Elswick yard, the first ship being launched on 9 June 1914. She was named *Nidaros*, the Viking name for Trondheim, while her sister was named *Björgvin*, the Viking name for Bergen. By the time of the latter's launch on 8 August, war had broken out and work was slowed down on both ships. In November 1914, Churchill and Fisher appreciated that *Nidaros* and *Björgvin* could be readily adapted for coast bombardment. Arrangements were made with Norway to transfer the ships and for Britain to refund the instalments already paid. Two-thirds of the contract price of £370,000 each had so far been paid, the total being made up as follows:—

	£
Armament	131,000
Armour	60,000
Machinery	48,000
Hull and equipment	131,000
Total	370,000

On 9 January 1915, orders went to Armstrong's to complete the two ships for the Royal Navy at the earliest possible date. A number of modifications were needed, especially as neither 240-mm nor 150-mm guns were standard British calibres. It would not be difficult to reline the guns to 9.2-inch (234-mm) and 6-inch (152-mm) respectively, enabling existing service ammunition to be used. Twelve double bottom tanks were modified to carry oil fuel to increase the endurance and the boilers converted to dual coal/oil firing. Names of previous heavy gun ships were allocated in April 1915, *Nidaros* becoming *Gorgon* after the turret ship of 1871, while *Björgvin* became *Glatton*, which had been the name of a sister to the previous *Gorgon* as well as a floating battery of 1855. The following month, when completion was estimated to be 10-12 months off, work was suspended by

Modified from the original coast defence battleship design for Norway, Glatton *receives her finishing touches in drydock at Hebburn about August 1918. The bulges and paravane chains are new additions.*

[1] Armstrong's of Elswick, Newcastle and Whitworth's of Openshaw, Manchester had merged in 1897.

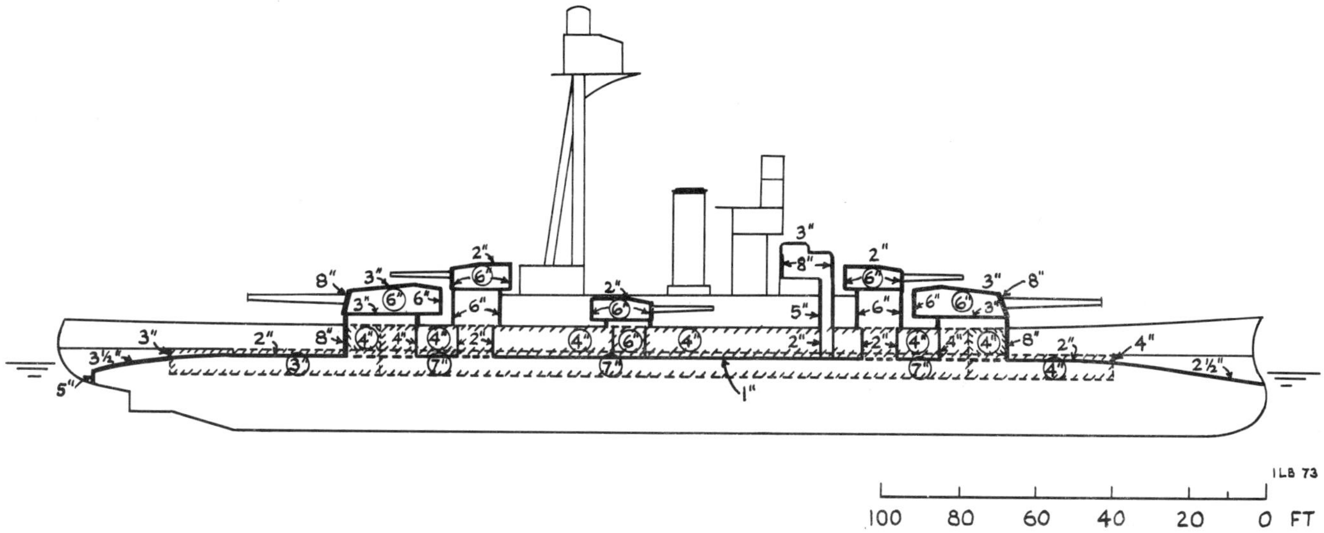

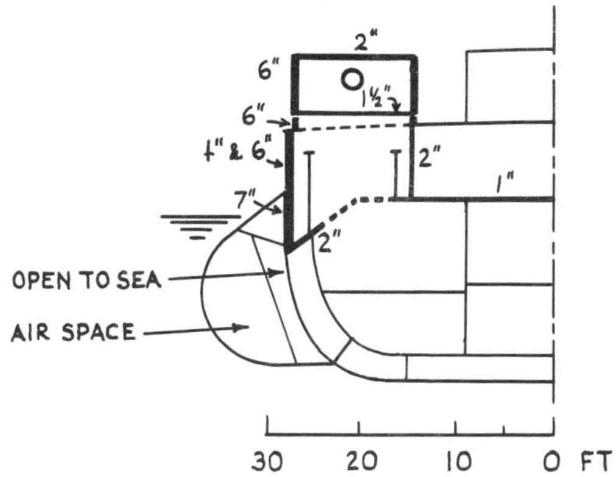

The original protection scheme of Glatton *and* Gorgon *was retained unchanged from the coast defence battleship design, except for the addition of bulges. The side protection was stronger than the other large monitors, especially in way of the wing 6-inch turrets, although the deck was weaker.*

the new Board to allow faster progress to be made at Armstrong's Naval Yard downriver on *Courageous* and *Furious*.

In September 1917 orders were sent to Armstrong's to complete the ships to a newly revised design. Anti-torpedo bulges were to be fitted covering about 75% of the length of the hull, necessitating the removal of the torpedo tubes. The elevation of the 9.2-inch guns was increased to 40°, enabling the remarkable range of 39,000 yards to be obtained with special ammunition, as described on p.189. The 100-mm gun positions in the superstructure were given over to provide more accommodation. A tripod mast was fitted abaft the funnel, with a spotting top and directors for both the 9.2-inch and the 6-inch guns; other changes included a new H.A. armament. Over two knots' speed was lost owing to the bulges, but 12 knots was still adequate for bombardment work. Deep displacement was increased to 5705 tons (*Gorgon*) but, thanks to the bulges, the designed draft of 16ft 6in remained virtually unchanged. The net result was the conversion of the two former coast defence battleships into monitors, each with two extremely powerful 9.2-inch guns, which would be a useful reinforcement to the monitor squadron off the Belgian Coast.

The modifications to the ships took some time, as there was only one graving dock on the Tyne wide enough to enable the bulges to be fitted, that at Palmer's Hebburn yard. The first ship, *Gorgon*, was commissioned on 1 May 1918 under Commander C. A. Scott. After reasonably satisfactory trials which showed that her manoeuvrability had been adversely affected by the bulges, she left for Dover on 4 June. *Glatton* commissioned at Newcastle on 31 August 1918 under Commander N. W. Diggle, who had earlier commanded *General Wolfe* and *General Craufurd* for short periods. Ammunition was taken aboard from railway wagons on 6 September and she then proceeded for trials over the next two days. She finally left her builders on the 9th, ready for action more than five years after her construction had started. One week later, her career came to an abrupt end, as described in §3.

With all the changes and the ever increasing levels of wages and material costs during the war, *Gorgon*'s final cost amounted to £777,000 and *Glatton*'s £513,000. There is no obvious reason for the considerable difference,

Glatton *leaves the Tyne for trials early in September 1918. Further changes from the original design visible include the heavy tripod mast, spotting top, lengthened funnel and 3-pdr on "F" turret, as the forward superfiring 6-inch was named.*

unless certain costs, which should have been equally divided, such as modifications to the armament, had been allocated entirely to the first ship. It is probably more representative to take the cost of each ship as about £645,000 — getting on for double that of the original design, and dearer than any of the other WW1 monitors.

§2 GORGON's Wartime Career

Gorgon's arrival at Dover on 6 June 1918 provided Keyes with a powerful addition to the monitor squadron, as he now had a vessel whose guns had a range comparable with the German long-range batteries. Her next few weeks were spent working up; she took up patrols from Dunkirk at the end of the month. Her first real test came on 26 July when she calibrated her guns on a German howitzer battery. Eight rounds were fired from 33,000 yards, provoking a few retaliatory shells from the Pommern battery, which consisted of a single 380-mm (15-inch) gun similar to Deutschland, but sited about six miles south of Ostende. Three days later, she accompanied *Marshal Soult* in a bombardment of the Tirpitz battery. August saw no firings from any of the monitors; for the next few weeks they were either out on patrol or preparing to support the big Army offensive planned for late September.

An unusual view of Gorgon, *with both her long range 9.2-inch and the director above the spotting top trained to starboard, probably taken off the Belgian Coast about September 1918.*

This attack started with a night bombardment by 12-inch and 15-inch monitors, as described on p.00. At daybreak on 28 September, these ships were joined by the two long range monitors, *Gorgon* and *General Wolfe*, which formed Division III. Anchored about seven miles off La Panne, *Gorgon* opened fire at 07.15 at Snaeskerke bridge, using supercharges as the range was about 36,000 yards. Conditions were not too good with a beam wind and tide; before long, her stern anchor cable had parted, swinging her round so that "Y" turret was left to do most of the firing. No worthwhile air spots were received, so only a general spraying of the area was possible. The monitors remained under sporadic fire from air attack and shore batteries all day, but not many shells landed close, as the M.L.'s smokescreen proved reasonably effective. Although *Gorgon* fired only 11 rounds of 9.2-inch, a repeat performance with 13 rounds was made the next day. One hit was reported, but later observation showed that Snaeskerke bridge itself had not been damaged.

When the Allied advance resumed on 14 October, *Gorgon* put in some concentrated shooting. Arrangements for all the monitors remained virtually identical to a fortnight earlier, except that *Lord Clive* now joined *General Wolfe* in firing at Snaeskerke, releasing *Gorgon* for action against the Middelkerke batteries. Her early morning bombardment put 41 rounds of H.E. into the target area from 26,000 yards. In the afternoon, *Gorgon* accompanied Keyes in the destroyer *Termagant* on a reconnaissance into the West Deep to ascertain whether the enemy was still holding the coast in strength, firing as she advanced. They were soon in no doubt; whilst *Gorgon* was off Westende, Tirpitz and the Raversyde batteries opened up. At comparatively short range, they soon straddled her, landing shell splinters aboard and severely shaking the ship. She quickly turned away and worked up to 14 knots to get out of range — faster than she had managed on trials — returning fire with her after guns. With her non-monitor appearance she must have confused the enemy spotters steaming at twice the usual speed of monitors, as she was not hit. The next day only *Gorgon* went out, and in 20 minutes' rapid firing landed 30 shells near her bridge target. Thus to the newest monitor fell the distinction of firing the last rounds of the war at the enemy-occupied Belgian Coast, after exactly four years of almost continuous bombardments. With the German withdrawal, there was nothing more for her to do, so she was sent round to Portsmouth to await a decision about her future, appropriately enough arriving on Armistice Day.

§3 The Loss of GLATTON

Glatton arrived at Dover on 11 September 1918 where she prepared for the big offensive planned for later that month. Keyes and Diggle were out for a walk on the evening of the 16th on the cliffs above Dover, when at 18.15 they heard a great explosion and saw a huge mushroom of smoke coming from a ship in the harbour.

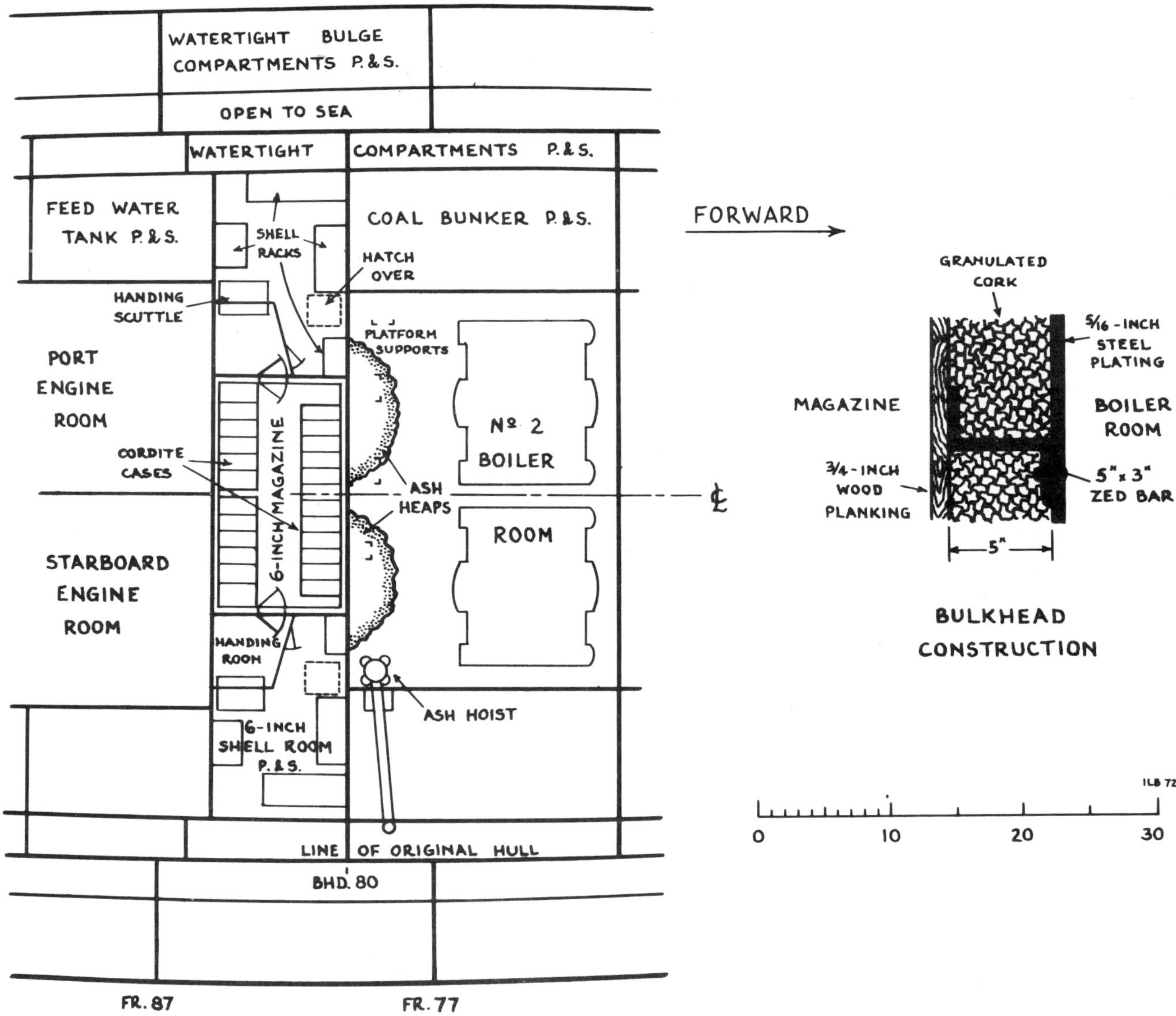

Glatton*'s midship magazine arrangement. The stokers were not aware of the position of the 6-inch magazine sandwiched between boiler and engine rooms when they piled the red-hot ashes against the bulkhead at Frame 80 to cool before sending them up the ash hoist. If properly constructed, the bulkhead should have protected the magazine, but gaps in the cork and missing rivets probably allowed the heat to penetrate and ignite the cordite.*

They saw at once that it was *Glatton* who had exploded and was now burning furiously amidships. By the time they had rushed down to the harbour, the salvage tugs including *Lady Brassey* were already pouring their water jets onto the monitor. Lying in the next berth only 150 yards away was the ammunition ship *Gransha*. Other tugs were beginning to move her, but there was still a considerable risk of her blowing up and devastating the town of Dover. Huge yellow flames from *Glatton*'s midship 6-inch magazine continued to shoot up through the roof of "Q" turret (starboard midship) and reach up to the masthead amongst clouds of white smoke. The smoke turned to black as the fire reached the oil and coal bunkers surrounding the magazine and boiler rooms, and then began to spread aft.

Keyes and Diggle clambered aboard *Glatton*'s forecastle and were able to get the forward magazines flooded, but it was impossible to flood the after spaces owing to flames on the main deck where the magazine flooding controls were situated. Attempts to sink the ship by opening seacocks were unsuccessful, as those controlling the after compartments and the bulge buoyancy spaces could not be reached. As it was only a question of time before the after magazine exploded, Keyes reluctantly decided that his only course was to sink *Glatton* by torpedo, so he boarded the destroyer *Cossack* who had just arrived from Hull. Her first 18-inch torpedo hit the bulge amidships, but embedded itself in the plating without exploding, as it had not travelled far enough to run off its safety device. At 19.40 her second and last torpedo was more successful as it blew a hole in *Glatton*'s starboard side. But 200 pounds of explosive were not enough to defeat her anti-torpedo bulge and she remained obstinately afloat, still burning furiously.

Keyes then transferred to the destroyer *Myngs* and ordered her captain to torpedo *Glatton.* Two 21-inch torpedoes were fired from close range into the existing hole in *Glatton*'s side at 20.15, and under this onslaught, she heeled over slowly to starboard until she came to rest at 148° to the vertical, with her masts and superstructure resting on the bottom and part of her port bulge showing above the water. The fire was quickly extinguished and the danger of further explosion averted.

Casualties had been heavy, involving over half the crew of 346; one officer and 59 men were missing, and a further 124 were injured, 19 of whom died later from their burns. A Court of Enquiry was set up immediately to determine the cause of the original explosion. Witnesses soon confirmed the basic facts, establishing that a fire had started in the midship 6-inch magazine. As shown in the plan, the latter was sited in the hold between the boiler rooms and engine rooms, and flanked the 6-inch shell rooms. The cause of the explosion was less easy to determine and a number of theories were examined: sabotage; spontaneous ignition of the cordite; mal-operation of the oil fuel and coal bunkers; overheating of the magazine. There was no reason why the last should have occurred as not only had insulation been provided all round the magazine, but special cooling equipment was installed. During wartime, sabotage was often suspected, but was soon ruled out, particularly as the ship had not been in contact with the shore since leaving Newcastle a week earlier. Spontaneous ignition of the cordite was also unlikely, as tests on other charges from the same batch showed that it had not deteriorated significantly in storage. However, one alarming fact was established: the stokers were in the habit of piling red-hot ashes and clinker from the boilers against the magazine bulkhead, before periodically clearing them up the ash ejector in the starboard after corner of the boiler room. The stoker P.O.s thought that the engine room was on the other side of the bulkhead and that there was no danger in the practice. Here was a promising line of investigation but, as most of the personnel working in that part of the ship had been killed, it would be necessary to examine her sister ship *Gorgon* closely and conduct experiments to see whether this might indeed have been the cause of the explosion.

Gorgon was carefully examined at Dover; her 6-inch ammunition was removed and the midship 6-inch magazine insulation partially stripped. The construction of the bulkhead adjoining the boiler room consisted of riveted $^5/_{16}$-inch steel plates, with 5 inches of granulated cork covered by $^3/_4$-inch wood planking fitted on the magazine side. It was found that the red lead paint on the bulkhead had been blistered beneath the lagging directly behind the place where, like her sister ship, ashes had been piled. Recorded air temperatures in the magazine were not particularly high, a maximum of 83° F having been noted. It was decided to undertake trials in *Gorgon* during which red-hot ashes were to be deliberately piled up against the bulkhead, while the temperatures in the magazine and in the lagging were to be recorded. The results were inconclusive; the average temperature in the

Gorgon *remained in commission after the war, partly to assist in trials to determine the cause of* Glatton*'s loss. She is seen here leaving Portsmouth early in 1919.*

lagging was only about 70° F, while even the hottest spot behind the ash-heaps was no more than 134° F. Such temperatures were nowhere near high enough to have ignited either the cork or the wood. It was then thought that oil might have seeped into the lagging from the double bottom tanks beneath, but experiments with the cork soaked in oil showed that however high the fires were stoked, the cork did not ignite. Tests did show however, that the cork could give off flammable gases in the presence of high temperatures and a supply of air under pressure. Various trials dragged on into 1919, but no really conclusive evidence appeared. Eventually in April 1919, the Court gave its verdict, concluding that:[1]

> "The slow combustion of the cork lagging of the 6-inch midship magazine of the *Glatton* led to the ignition of the magazine and then to the ignition of the cordite in it and so caused the explosion."

When shown the Court's findings, both the Engineer-in-Chief, Vice-Admiral G. G. Goodwin, and the D.N.C., d'Eyncourt, did not accept that the cork had actually burnt. Nevertheless, the insulation in *Gorgon* was replaced by silicate cotton to be on the safe side. On stripping out the rest of her old insulation, a much more likely cause of the ignition was revealed. Behind some parts of the wood panelling was found, not granulated cork, but empty spaces and folded newspapers. The latter were Newcastle journals such as the *Evening Chronicle* bearing dates in 1916 and 1917, which must have been stuffed there by men at the Elswick shipyard. Examination of the bulkhead had already shown the existence of a number of $^1/_2$-inch diameter holes in the plating, where rivets had been omitted. These two discoveries point clearly to the most likely cause of the fire, although no such conclusion was ever drawn officially. The red-hot ashes could well have raised the bulkhead temperature sufficiently to have ignited any newspapers which may well have been present in *Glatton* also, with air being supplied by the forced draught pressure in the boiler room through open rivet holes. Under these conditions, the cork would have given off flammable gases, charred the wood panelling and eventually ignited the cordite charges.

The monitor's wreck remained a hazard to navigation in Dover Harbour, as it gradually silted up with time. Enquiries amongst salvage firms to undertake its removal produced either blank refusals or estimates of about £45,000. Finally Captain John Iron was asked if he could do the job. The Dover Harbourmaster had tackled many tricky jobs during the war (see p.128) but *Glatton* would be the most difficult, lying upside down at an awkward angle. He thought that it might be possible to do the job for around £5,000, with the use of the salvage craft at Dover. The Harbour Board jumped at his offer and work started in May 1925. With the aid of the salvage vessel *Dapper* and the Dover tugs, 12,000 tons of silt were cleared from under the wreck. Its mainmast and parts of the superstructure were blasted away with explosives and then sixteen 9-inch (2. 9-inch diameter) wire ropes were passed under the hull. Four Admiralty lifting lighters, each capable of raising 1000 tons when pumped dry of water, were hired and connected to the wires on each side of the wreck. But with the silt trapped inside the wreck, 4000 tons of lifting capacity were not sufficient to lift the 6000-ton vessel. It was also necessary to seal all holes on the port (uppermost) side, as well as those across part of the deck and bottom. The additional buoyancy could then be obtained by making air connections to most of the watertight compartments and then pumping air at 70,000 cubic feet a minute into them.

[1] ADM 138/600

Sunk after a magazine explosion on 16 September 1918, Glatton *lay on the bottom of Dover Harbour for over seven years. The beacon on her bulge showed the angle at which she had been lying — 148° to the vertical. She was raised in March 1926, the view showing her after her final lift.*

By 2 December 1925, all was ready for the first lifting attempt. Just before low tide, the lifting lighters were ballasted down and the wires tightened. The tide turned, the lighters were pumped out and the air compressors put on full power. The anxious watchers waited as the tide slowly rose, then suddenly the wreck began to move. Success was in sight but the major lifting operation was deliberately held over until the following day. The wreck was again made buoyant and then moved slowly towards the shore until the ebbing tide prevented further movement. With spring tides and better weather on 16 March 1926, she was lifted again and moved to lie alongside the western pier of the submarine harbour, nestling under the cliffs at the north-eastern end of the harbour, where demolition was completed the following year. Although the final cost of the operation turned out larger than Iron had anticipated, the total sum was no more than £12,000.

§4 GORGON Post-War

There was very little that the R.N. could do after the war with a former foreign coast defence battleship, mounting an armament of unique pattern. After the experiments to discover the cause of *Glatton*'s loss were completed, *Gorgon* moved to Devonport in April 1919 to become a temporary tender to *Vivid*, paying off on 31 August after barely a year in service. In September 1919, she joined the Devonport Reserve Fleet under the flagship *Colossus*. She was offered back to Norway, but she was no longer suitable for their requirements, especially now that she was too broad to be docked at Horten. Her name was added to the Sale List, as several South American countries had expressed interest in buying a monitor. Nothing came of Argentinian or Peruvian enquiries, but in 1920, Roumania negotiated to buy *Gorgon* and six M-class destroyers. A total price of £200,000 was discussed implying about £60,000 for *Gorgon*, but the deal fell through. The following year, her armament was removed and she was made available for further trials. She was towed back to Portsmouth in June 1922, where she was used as a guinea pig to determine the effects of heavy charges or bombs bursting underwater close to the ship, and the effects of 6-inch shell fire. Her relatively modern hull construction, including bulges, made her a good choice. These and other trials continued for some time and yielded useful information for future designs. She remained available for experiments until 1928, when she was sold to Ward's and broken up at the former naval dockyard at Pembroke.

GLATTON and GORGON — TECHNICAL PARTICULARS

Displacement and Dimensions (As modified) 5700 tons nominal, 5746 tons deep (*Glatton*). Length 310′-0″ o.a., breadth 73′-7″, draft 16′-4″ deep.

Weight Distribution Armament 706 tons, ammunition 151, protection 1082, hull 2538, equipment 289, machinery and R.F.W. 445, fuel 535. Completed total 5746 tons.

Complement (*Gorgon*) 22 officers, 283 men.

Armament 2—9.2″ single (130 H.E. r.p.g.), 4—6″ (100 C.P.C. + 100 H.E. r.p.g.), 2—3″ H.A. (300 r.p.g.), 4—3pdr Vickers H.A. (*Glatton*) (300 r.p.g.), 4 (*Gorgon*)/2 (*Glatton*)—2pdr H.A. (1000 r.p.g.).

Protection Protective deck: 2″ H.T. on slope, 1″ horizontal, 2″-2½″ forward and aft; side belt: upper strake 4″ C. (6″ abreast wing 6-inch turrets), lower strake 7″ C. amidships, 4″ forward, 3″ aft; bulkheads at end of belt 3″-4″; steering gear 3½″-5″; barbettes 8″ C. (9.2-inch), 6″ C. (6-inch); gunhouses 8″ C. front, 6″ C. sides and rear, 3″ N.C. roof and floor (9.2-inch); 6″ C. front, sides and rear, 2″ N.C. roof, 1½″ floor (6-inch); conning tower 8″ sides, 3″ roof.

Machinery Twin screw triple-expansion. 4000 I.H.P. at 150 r.p.m. Coal 364 tons, oil fuel 171. Endurance 2700 miles at 11 knots.

Speed 15 knots designed, 12 service. Trials: *Gorgon* 13, *Glatton* 12½ knots.

Construction Armstrong Whitworth, Elswick: *Glatton* laid down 26 May 1913/launched 8 Aug 1914/completed 8 Sep 1918; *Gorgon* 11 Jun 1913/9 Jun 1914/4 Jun 1918.

Disposal *Glatton* blown up 16 Sep 1918; *Gorgon* scrapped Ward, Pembroke Dock Oct 1928.

CHAPTER VII

THE SMALL MONITORS

H.M.S. M.15 - M.33

§1 Design of the Small 9.2-inch Gun Monitors
With the construction of the 15-inch, 14-inch and 12-inch gun monitor classes well under way by early 1915, Fisher turned his attention to the possibility of obtaining further heavily armed vessels. The next largest calibre service gun was the 9.2-inch, fitted in a wide range of pre-dreadnoughts and cruisers. As it was usually installed in single mountings, the much smaller weight, compared with heavy battleship twin mountings, offered the chance of arming a number of small shallow draft monitors. A hasty search was instituted for available 9.2-inch mountings, as heavy mountings were always scarcer than guns. The 9.2-inch B.L. Mk X gun on a Mk V single mounting was an obvious candidate. Two single mountings had been fitted in each of five ships of the *Cressy* and *Drake* classes of armoured cruiser of 1901, but already three of the ships had been lost during the war, *Aboukir* and *Cressy* torpedoed in the North Sea in September 1914, and *Good Hope* sunk at Coronel in November. Only two ships remained fitted with the Elswick Mk V mounting, *Drake* and *Leviathan*; all other ships of the classes had the Vickers Mk VI mounting. One spare mounting had been supplied for each ship, so four could be earmarked for new monitors and still leave one spare between the two remaining ships.

The other source of 9.2-inch armament was the *Edgar* class of protected cruiser of 1893. These old ships had constituted the major part of the 10th Cruiser Squadron used for blockade work on the Northern Patrol since the outbreak of war. However they proved quite unsuited for sustained operations in those stormy waters and were replaced by converted Armed Merchant Cruisers as soon as possible. The cruisers paid off at the end of 1914, some being converted for use at the Dardanelles. These ships were armed with two single 9.2-inch Mk VI on C.P. III mountings in addition to ten 6-inch. It was decided to replace the 9.2-inch guns with 6-inch in all the now remaining five ships of the class, *Edgar, Endymion, Gibraltar, Grafton* and *Theseus* — *Hawke* having been torpedoed in October 1914. It was thus possible to arm a further ten small monitors with these old guns.

There was a considerable difference between the two types of 9.2-inch gun[1]. The Mk VI was a low velocity 31-calibre design of hoop construction dating from 1888, with a maximum range of only 11,000 yards at 15° elevation using cordite Mk I. The mounting was of the old hand-worked Vavasseur type on which the gun recoiled up an inclined slide, which was visible at the rear of the open gun shield. The Mk X was a great improvement, a high velocity steel and wire gun 46 calibres long, capable of ranging 15,400 yards at its maximum elevation of 15° using the improved cordite MD [2]. Its powered mounting and superior breech mechanism allowed it to fire about four times as fast as the Mk VI — $3^1/_2$ rounds per minute. The Mk V mounting was totally enclosed in an armoured shield, with 6-inch front and 3-inch sides. As in the case of the 12-inch monitors, any possible increase in elevation above 15° would provide a valuable extension in range; Elswick confirmed that it would be possible to convert both types of mounting to 30° elevation. The corresponding increase in range was about 45%, resulting in 16,300 yards for the Mk VI gun and 22,000 yards for the Mk X — 25,000 yards was possible with 4 c.r.h. projectiles in place of the normal 2 c.r.h. The guns were intended to be operated in local control from the mounting, so no fire control equipment was provided in the monitor design.

After the armament had been selected, detailed design work could go ahead on hull and machinery. The only requirements were a draft of about 6 feet, a speed of about 12 knots and the simplest possible construction. The weight of the Mk VI gun and mounting was about 45 tons, with the Mk X considerably heavier at about 115 tons. Substitution of light steel plate in place of the 50-ton armoured shield would bring the latter's weight down, as would the omission of the usual hydraulic machinery for working the mounting and ammunition hoists. All operations were to be by hand to keep the installation as simple as possible and to save weight, so the rear of the Mk X shield had to be left open. Ammunition supply was to be by davit and whip from hatches over the magazine on to the platform at the rear of the mounting, a method which called for considerable manual effort to handle the 380-lb projectiles. The weight of the 9.2-inch Mk X installation was thus reduced to about 70 tons, plus a further 30 tons for the 120 rounds of ammunition.

The hull was designed 170ft long with a breadth of 31ft to provide the stability needed for the heavy armament, with a legend displacement of 540 tons. It was not practicable to fit bulges or any protection in such a small hull. The hull was only a single deck deep except forward under the raised forecastle, which housed most of the crew in very spartan conditions. The gun was sited just aft of the break of the forecastle. Abaft the gun, the

[1] Further details of the guns are given in the Table on p.192
[2] See p.173 for types of cordite

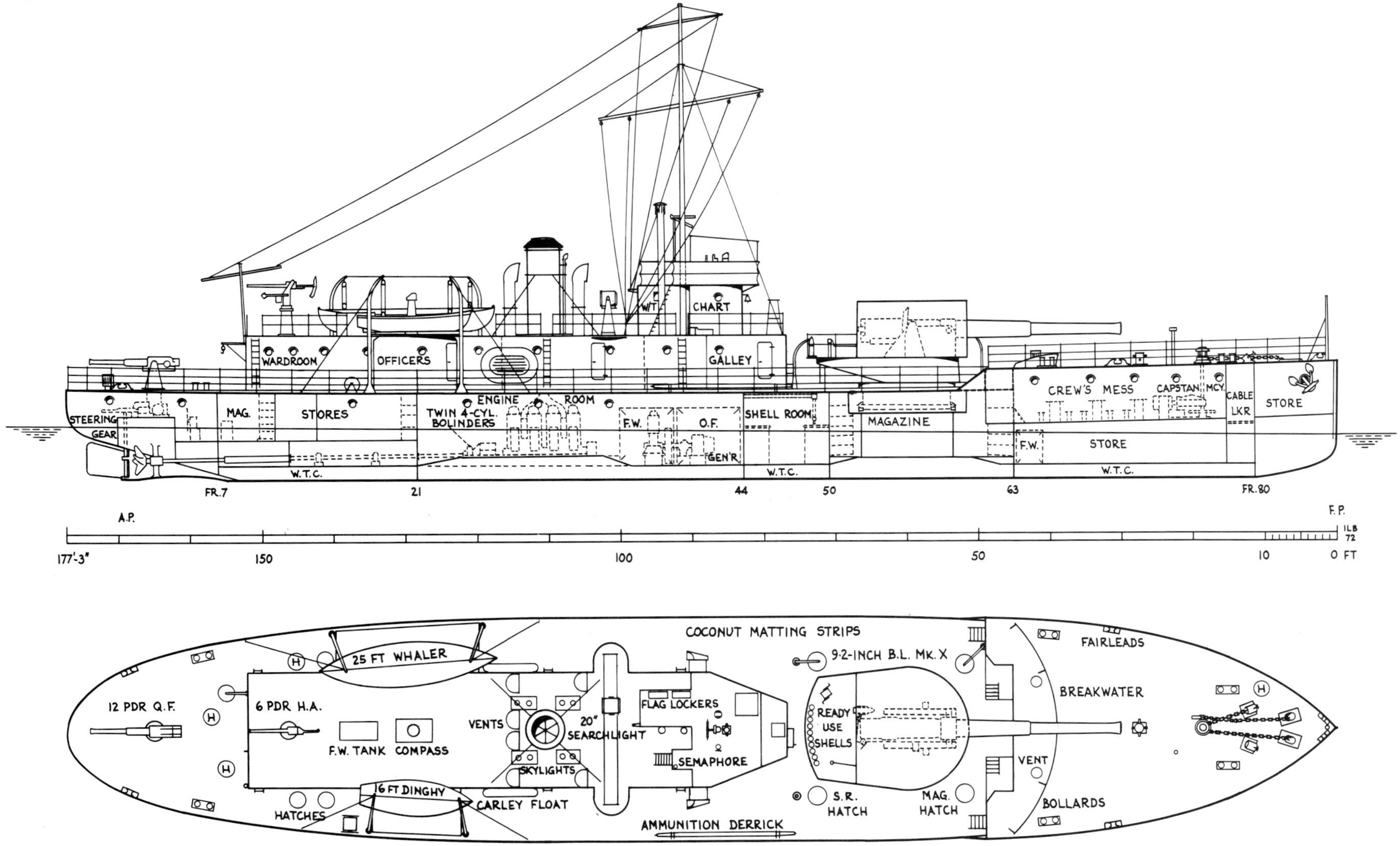

The drawing shows M.18, *the only one of the 9.2-inch Mark X monitors with diesel engines. The machinery space in the steamships was the same length, but divided into engine and boiler room by a bulkhead at Frame 31. Frame spacing was 24in throughout. The deck covering was painted steel with coconut matting walkways. The 9.2-inch Mk VI monitors were generally similar except for the gun mounting.*

A clear view of one of the short 9.2-inch gun monitors, M.21, *leaving for trials in July 1915. The aftermost gun is a 12-pdr 18-cwt as also fitted in the large monitors, but the H.A. gun is a 6-pdr Hotchkiss on a makeshift mounting. The davit abaft the 9.2-inch was used to hoist ammunition from the magazine hatches in the deck to the working platform.*

superstructure housed the officers, a few ratings and the galley, with the bridge, mast and 6-pdr H.A. gun being the only erections thereon. A single 12-pdr was sited on the quarterdeck, below which was its magazine plus various store-rooms. The main magazine, 9.2-inch gun support and machinery occupied the midship 50% of the main hull. Estimating the horsepower required was nothing like as difficult as for the large bulged monitors, as the hull shape was well within existing experience. Machinery of around 700 I.H.P. would be required, which could easily be provided by steam or diesel machinery, whichever was most readily available. There was virtually no difference in the basic design for the Mk VI gun monitors as compared with the Mk X. Their overall appearance was that of a gunboat, in some respects similar to early vessels of the true monitor type, with their large gun and low-lying hull. From the start, it was decided that the monitors would be identified by number only, continuing the series originally begun for the large monitors. The four Mk X monitors were thus numbered from *M.15* to *M.18* and the ten Mk VI from *M.19* to *M.28*.

Inquiries were made in mid-February 1915 amongst merchant shipbuilders for tenders to build the fourteen hulls. Two large companies on the North East Coast of England had not shared any of the recently allocated sloop orders, Gray's of Hartlepool and Sir Raylton Dixon's of Middlesbrough. Gray's were one of the biggest British shipbuilders in terms of annual tonnage built, so they certainly had the capacity to produce such relatively small vessels quickly, and were awarded contracts for four monitors, *M.15* to *M.18*. Their subsidiary company, Central Marine Engine Works, were allocated the machinery contracts. Dixon's were allocated the remaining ten, *M.19* to *M.28*. As they had no associated engine works, the supply of machinery had to be separately arranged.

Fisher was still keen on using internal combustion engines wherever possible and at this same time large orders had been placed for X-lighters (landing barges), mostly having Bolinder engines. James Pollock & Company had been given responsibility both for the lighters' design and for the provision of their machinery, being both consulting engineers and British representatives of the Swedish Bolinder company. Here was a ready-made source of supply of diesel engines, so arrangements were made to obtain as many of these popular engines as possible to power the monitors. The most suitable standard Bolinder engine was the four-cylinder, two-stroke M-type, developing 320 B.H.P. Two were planned to be fitted in each monitor, 640 B.H.P. being the equivalent of about 800 I.H.P. As there were only enough of the 22-ton engines readily available to power six monitors (*M.18, 19, 20, 23, 25, 28*), it was arranged that four two-cylinder units would be fitted in *M.26* and *M.27*.

The Bolinder engine was already in widespread use in small vessels for coastal and inland waterway service as well as auxiliary propulsion for sailing vessels. It worked on the hot-bulb or semi-diesel principle, which was basically similar to a normal diesel engine except that the temperature within the cylinders was insufficient to ignite the fuel due to the lower compression ratio. The necessary heat was provided by a hot bulb connecting with the cylinder into which the fuel was sprayed to initiate combustion. The low temperatures and pressures produced a solid reliable engine with remarkable powers of longevity. The arrangement was that the engines would be supplied by Bolinder's of Stockholm and installed by Pollock's. As the fourth Gray monitor, *M.18*, was also to have these engines, there were still three other vessels requiring machinery. *M.24* was given four paraffin engines by the Campbell Gas Company of Halifax, Yorkshire, and the remaining two, *M.21* and *M.22*, steam engines, by McKie & Baxter and Shields Engineering respectively.

Construction started in March 1915 and work progressed rapidly, the first vessel, *M.15*, being launched on 28 April. Fitting out took about two months, during which time the first Dixon vessel, *M.19*, overtook *M.15* and was ready for trials on 3 June, a week ahead of her near-sister and only a fortnight behind the first 14-inch monitor. There had been no problems installing the Mk VI guns, which had been removed from the cruisers and sent to Elswick for modification before being re-erected on the ships at Middlesbrough, ready for their gun trials.

M.21 *on her gun trials off the Tees in mid-July 1915, with her short 9.2-inch Mk VI at its increased elevation of 30°. Guard rails are lowered to reduce blast damage. The painted bow wave was soon removed.*

The actual allocation of the cruisers' mountings was: *Edgar*'s two into *M.19* and *M.26, Theseus'* into *M.21* and *M.27, Grafton*'s into *M.23* and *M.28, Endymion*'s into *M.24* and *M.25* and *Gibraltar*'s into *M.20* and *M.22*. The heavier Mk X were more of a problem. One of the spare mountings allocated was at Malta, whilst another had been sent out there in case it might be required for service ashore at Gallipoli. So *M.15* and *M.16* were completed without their main armament, which they would have to pick up at Malta. The other two mountings were at Portsmouth and had to be transported to Hartlepool by road, as it was considered too risky to send them by ship owing to U-boat activity and they exceeded the railway loading gauge.

Each group of monitors commissioned at roughly fortnightly intervals from June to November 1915, generally under the command of a Lieutenant-Commander. Gun and speed trials were carried out as quickly as possible, sometimes the same day. No major problems arose, although speed fell short of the expected 12 knots by up to one knot in the lower powered vessels. Deep displacement was rather greater than designed, averaging about 610 tons for the diesel Mk VI and 630 tons for the steam Mk X, increasing the mean draft by about 12 inches and giving a trim of about 2 feet by the stern. The probable expenditure on each vessel was around £35-40,000, the diesel boats being the more expensive. The true cost would have been about £50-55,000 if the armament had not already been available. The monitors left their builders' yards as soon as they were ready, those destined for overseas service spending a week or two at one of the home dockyards to be fully equipped for such operations.

§2 Design of the Small 6-inch Gun Monitors

While plans were going ahead for the fourteen 9.2-inch gun monitors, another possible source of guns presented itself. The battleship *Queen Elizabeth* had been rushed to completion in January 1915 and was immediately sent out to the Dardanelles. It soon became clear that the four 6-inch guns of her secondary armament sited on the main deck abreast "Y" turret were unworkable at sea, as their casemates were only five feet above the deep waterline. It was therefore decided to remove the guns from this position and resite them, but space could be found to remount only two of them, amidships on the forecastle deck. Thus there were two surplus guns and mountings from each of the five ships.

So early in March 1915, Lillicrap was called upon to design yet another class of monitor, which was to mount two single 6-inch. The guns were of a new pattern, B.L. Mk XII, intended to form the secondary armament of new capital ships and the main armament of light cruisers. The 7-ton steel and wire gun was 45 calibres long and could range 14,700 yards at its maximum elevation of $17^1/_2$°, although normally restricted in casemates to 14°. The mounting was transferable, i.e. merely bolted to the deck, and as the entire installation weighed less than 18 tons, there appeared to be no difficulty in mounting two in vessels of shallower draft than those carrying the heavier 9.2-inch. The estimated total weight of armament and ammunition came to 62 tons compared with an estimated 100 tons in the 9.2-inch gun vessels. As the ratio of component weights to total displacement is generally close for similar classes of ship, it was considered possible to reduce both the displacement and draft of the 6-inch monitors roughly in proportion to the reduced armament load. This load formed 18% of the legend displacement of 540 tons in the 9.2-inch monitors. A similar percentage applied to the 6-inch monitors would give a displacement of about 340 tons and a draft of about 4 feet. The design for a 10-knot vessel went ahead on this basis, the legend displacement which went up to Their Lordships for approval being estimated at 355 tons.

There was however a fundamental error in the assumption of equal ratios. The percentages of component load are only similar for ships which are weight-limited, i.e. those whose dimensions are determined by the need for buoyancy required to carry the total loads. They do not necessarily apply to ships which are space-limited, i.e. those whose dimensions are determined by the need to provide a certain area of deck or a certain internal volume. In the very hurried design phase, neither Lillicrap nor his superiors appreciated

A fine view of M.30 *(nearest camera) and* M.31 *on 22 June 1915, the day before the former was launched at Belfast. Both are well advanced and ran their trials only ten days later. The keel is that of the suspended P. & O. liner* Narkunda; M.29 *had been launched from the south side of the same Abercorn Yard berth a month earlier.*

that, although the 9.2-inch monitors fell into the former category, the 6-inch monitors fell into the latter. The decision to mount two separate guns, one forward and one aft, meant that a deck area as large as the 9.2-inch monitors was required. The hull dimensions could not therefore be reduced, so virtually no reduction in actual hull weight was possible. As hull weight constituted about half the total displacement, the final displacement would fall not far short of the 9.2-inch monitors and the draft would be increased to nearly 6 feet. By the time the error was realised, the 6-inch monitors were committed. They continued to be listed in official documents as 355-ton ships with 4 feet draft but never in their lives would they float in such a condition.

It was not difficult to find suitable builders for the five monitors. Harland & Wolff were progressing well with the 14-inch monitors and would soon have some spare capacity, so orders for all five were placed with them on 15 March 1915 as Numbers 485 to 489. When H. & W. came to plan out exactly how they would build the ships in the specified three months, a difficulty arose. Although the forthcoming launch of the two 14-inch monitors at Belfast would free a slipway on which all five could have been built, it was now needed for *Glorious.* All their other seven berths were occupied either by monitors or suspended merchant ships. However, the keel of the 16,000-ton P. & O. liner *Narkunda* had only just been laid on Berth 5, so it would be possible to construct two small monitors on either side of the small amount of steel erected to date. Pirrie therefore inquired of the neighbouring shipyard of Workman, Clark & Co. if they could build one or two of the monitors. Although pre-

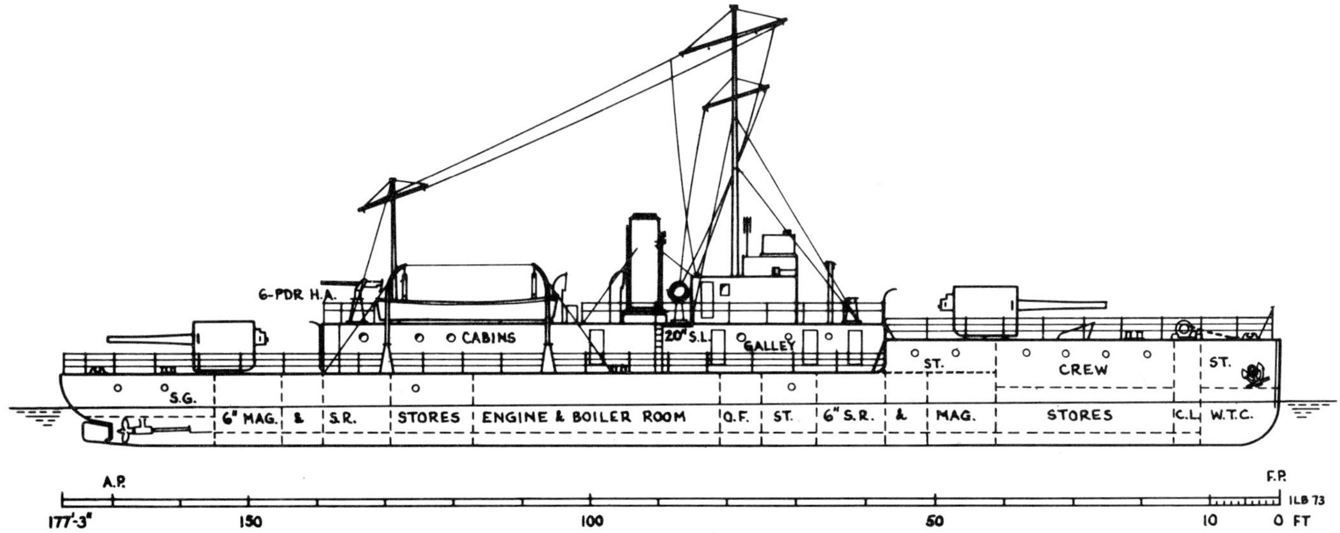

The five small monitors, M.29 *to* M.33, *had a neat and workmanlike appearance with their two 6-inch guns, and performed well despite their excess weight and draft.*

war it had been Workman Clark's policy not to build warships, they had in hand the conversion of *Theseus* and *Endymion.* They therefore agreed to build two of the monitors under sub-contract and were given *M.32* and *M.33*; *M.29, M.30* and *M.31* remained with H. & W.

Construction proceeded very rapidly, the first keels being laid only eight days after the order was placed. *M.29, M.32* and *M.33* were all launched on the same day, 22 May, the other two a month later with armament and machinery aboard. All five vessels commissioned in June and just about managed to scrape their designed 10 knots on trials. An inclining experiment confirmed that they greatly exceeded their designed displacement and, although fortunately the extra weight did not seriously affect their stability, an undesirable trim by the head resulted. The trim caused unsatisfactory steering but was easily cured by six tons of permanent ballast aft. The final deep displacement came out at 580 tons as, apart from the original error over hull weight, most of the other loads were well up on the estimate, for example oil fuel up from 20 to 45 tons and ammunition up from 25 to 40 tons, due to an increase in the number of rounds stowed.

The erroneous legend displacement of 355 tons was perpetuated in nearly every official description of the monitors. The Admiralty and naval officers showed little interest in accurate figures for the displacement of their ships, despite the vital importance of realistic figures for assessing limits of draft, stability, speed, ability to withstand flooding or the margin available for future modifications. At that period, nearly every British warship's actual displacement greatly exceeded the nominal figures, which were indeed truly 'legendary'! The corresponding poor feedback of data from completed ships into new designs, so necessary with a basically evolutionary science like naval architecture that cannot afford to build prototypes, meant that under-estimates were perpetuated. Quite possibly a few people realised the danger but in general it was easier not to question the system, thereby avoiding inquisitions by higher authorities, political and financial, who might query why ship sizes appeared to be jumping up without a corresponding gain in military performance. The small monitors are certainly one of the worst examples in this respect and, in their case, the official 355-ton figure was so conspicuously unrealistic that it was usually assumed wrongly to be a misprint for 535 tons.

H. &. W. and Workman Clark tied for the completion of the first 6-inch monitor. Both *M.29* and *M.32* left Belfast together on 20 June for Pembroke Dockyard, where their single 6-pdr H.A. guns were to be mounted. The pedestals had been fitted by the builders, one forward of the bridge, one aft, but only one gun was to be supplied. The 6-inch vessels turned out to be the cheapest of all the monitors at about £25,000 apiece, although the cost would have been about £8,000 higher if the cost of their armament had not already been allocated. Contrary to general belief, the actual 6-inch used were not those removed from the battleships, but were newly constructed mountings fresh from the production line at C.O.W., with most of the guns straight from Vickers.

§3 Mediterranean Operations

Just before his resignation in May 1915, Churchill had arranged to send the first six 9.2-inch monitors out to the Dardanelles (see p.28). By the time the first vessels had been completed, the newly formed Dardanelles Committee confirmed the arrangement and added all five of the new 6-inch monitors as well as a further four 9.2-inch. The first ship, *M.19*, actually left British waters on 22 June, two days before the first of the large monitors but, despite an occasional tow by the sloop *Aster, Abercrombie* overtook her at Malta. Then followed the two 6-inch monitors, *M.29* and *M.32,* and throughout July and August, a steady procession of small monitors left Devonport: *M.33, M.15, M.16, M.20, M.30, M.31, M.17, M.21, M.22, M.23, M.28, M.18.* All were given some towing assistance, usually by colliers also bound for Mudros, taking three to four weeks to reach the

Dardanelles. Some were held up for various reasons. *M.15* and *M.16* had to stop to pick up their 9.2-inch guns and mountings at Malta at the end of July. *M.18* was delayed leaving England by a fire in her engine room, the crew having to flood the magazine and shell-room before bringing the fire under control. *M.23* was also delayed at Malta in September when a fire broke out in her funnel and spread to the bridge. Thus started a long saga of machinery-induced fires which persisted throughout the lives of the diesel monitors, causing minor damage to most of the vessels at one time or another.

As the first small monitor to arrive at Mudros on 23 July, *M.19* was sent four days later to join *Roberts* in her berth south of Rabbit Island. From here she could help keep down the fire of the Turkish batteries on the Asiatic shore of the Dardanelles, which were harassing the British and French position at Helles on the European shore. *M.19* was replaced by *M.17* in mid-August and thereafter two or three small monitors shared the berth with one of the large monitors for the next five months. The 9.2-inch Mk X proved to be a powerful and accurate weapon for this work, despite the small gun platform, usually landing its shells within 50 yards of the target. Direct hits were obtained on enemy guns at ranges up to 24,000 yards, although all that could reasonably have been expected of the monitors would have been the temporary silencing of enemy fire.

The Suvla landings starting on the night of 6/7 August were supported by all the available small monitors. Three of the 6-inch monitors were stationed off Suvla, whilst most of the others were supporting the 14-inch monitors further to the south. The fleet of bombarding vessels, monitors, cruisers and destroyers, poured an immense volume of fire onto their targets — entrenchments, field guns, supply roads and villages. Between 7 and 10 August over 8,000 rounds were fired, including about 700 from the 6-inch and 100 from the 9.2-inch monitors. Such a rate of expenditure could not be maintained for long; thereafter considerable economy of fire was enforced. A small monitor was usually stationed off Anzac, firing a dozen rounds a day at any enemy batteries that revealed themselves, while others were off the left flank at Helles. An occasional longer range bombardment was made several times during August; *M.15* fired at ships in the Narrows at Ak Bashi Liman, once setting a steamer on fire. Their small gun platforms proved rather lively for accurate shooting in unsheltered waters, as a broadside almost rolled the deck edge under water.

A 9.2-inch monitor, probably M.20, *firing off Anzac during August 1915.*

Patrols were also maintained in the Gulf of Xeros carrying out bombardments during October and November on Turkish supply lines running down the Gallipoli peninsula. Typical targets were roads and bridges, although any likely looking strongpoints or batteries were attacked to induce the Turks to think that a landing might be planned in the area. For this type of work, the monitors with the more modern and accurate guns were preferred, usually *M.15, M.16* and *M.31*. Their 9.2-inch and 6-inch were used against the bigger targets,

The pre-dreadnought Magnificent *had already surrendered her two 12-inch turrets to* Lord Clive *and* General Craufurd *before she was sent out to the Dardanelles as a troopship. This view taken at Mudros about August 1915 shows* M.28 *alongside with her original shorter funnel and splinter protection around the bridge.*

M.30 *at Mudros about October 1915. The forward 6-pdr pedestal appears to be used for a small rangefinder.*

their 12-pdr and 6-pdr being reserved for wagons or boats. The flour mills at the town of Gallipoli on the other side of the peninsula were also a popular target, *M.16* scoring four hits out of 22 rounds from her long range 9.2-inch during 70 minutes on the afternoon of 8 November.

After Bulgaria had declared war, a further stretch of coastline presented opportunities for bombardment. The railway between Constantinople and Salonika was a tempting target near Dedeagatch. The inland junction at Bodoma was selected so, on the morning of 21 October, a British squadron consisting of the cruisers *Doris* and *Theseus* plus destroyers was in position close offshore protected by drifter-laid anti-submarine nets, although their accompanying monitors, *M.16, M.19* and *M.29,* had been delayed by a strong head wind. Visibility was too bad for *Ben-my-Chree*'s seaplanes to spot fire onto the junction so, from 13.00, the bombarding ships poured a heavy fire from close range into Dedeagatch itself, the barracks, railway station, rolling stock, warehouses, fuel stocks, bridges, shipping and harbour works, joined by the monitors as soon as they arrived. By 16.00 a good bit of damage had been done, the Bulgarians being seriously alarmed that a landing by Allied troops might be heralded. A repeat operation was made five days later with *Theseus, M.15* and *M.28.*

The small monitors continued to support the 14-inch monitors off the Gallipoli peninsula, either covering them against shore batteries or firing themselves, especially during the periods when 14-inch ammunition was limited. *M.19* was undertaking one such operation moored alongside *Abercrombie* off the left flank at Helles on the morning of 4 December when, after her second salvo, splashes were seen all round about. At first it was thought that a shell had burst prematurely outside the gun but, after the smoke cleared, it could be seen that *M.19*'s 9.2-inch gun had almost disappeared. The barrel had in fact burst 18 inches forward of the trunnions, from a premature inside the bore, set off by a choke (see p.183). The 9.2-inch magazine caught fire, but *M.19*'s crew promptly flooded it, cast her off safely from *Abercrombie* and soon got the fire under control. Over two tons of fragments were found aboard *Abercrombie*, the largest weighing about 300lb. One 6-lb chunk was found to have entered one of the slits of her conning tower, severing two fingers from her helmsman's hand. Two of *M.19*'s crew were killed, six badly burned and her deck buckled by fire. The destroyer *Colne* assisted her to Mudros, where the repair ship *Reliance* patched her up for the voyage to Malta, where full repairs were undertaken.

Meantime, some of the small monitors had been operating on the Mitylene-based patrols blockading Smyrna. *M.22* had been assigned to this squadron, which included two destroyers, from her arrival in the Aegean on 14 September, being joined three days later by *M.30* from Mudros. Long Island (Chustan Island) at the mouth of the Gulf of Smyrna had just been occupied to maintain a close blockade and cover the British minefields. The monitors' duties were manifold: shooting up shore batteries and strongpoints, wagons and camel caravans, windmills and houses, soldiers and snipers, railways and bridges, searchlights and stores, shipping and boats. They also landed spies, cut telegraph wires, reconnoitred remote islands and examined suspicious steamers.

Following the evacuation from Gallipoli, the squadron was strengthened to include generally one large and four small monitors, while an airfield was built on Long Island to assist reconnaissance. The enemy did not remain passive in the face of this close blockade, and under German guidance, heavy artillery was brought up and installed on the mainland to harass Long Island. By early May 1916, these heavy guns were able to shell the island and the British patrol vessels. On the night of 14 May, *M.30* approached the island carrying stores, anchoring close inshore at about 22.00. Soon afterwards, enemy shells began to fall around her, so she moved away to try to locate the battery. No sign of its flashes could be seen, although its shells continued to land close by. Eventually a heavy shell, probably 150-mm (5.9-inch) calibre, penetrated her machinery space, damaging one boiler and her fuel bunker and holing her bottom, killing two of her crew and wounding two others. The escaping oil

M.30 *still on fire on 14 May 1916 off Long Island in the Gulf of Smyrna after being shelled and sunk during the night. Later her guns were salvaged – perhaps also the washing drying on the guard rails.*

caught fire, water flooded in and her engines stopped. A destroyer and motor gunboat arrived to help *M.30*, now burning fiercely amidships, but they could do little except take off most of her crew. She continued to drift inshore, her magazines having been flooded, and she grounded about 200 yards offshore. Lieutenant-Commander E. L. B. Lockyer and the remaining crew took to her skiff and pulled ashore, where they were rescued by *M.32* in the morning. Over the next few weeks, an attempt was made to salvage as much useful equipment from *M.30* as possible, including her 6-inch guns, after which a 100-lb charge of guncotton was set off to destroy her hull.[1]

While *M.22* and *M.30* had been busy off Smyrna, most of the other small monitors (*M.15, M.16, M. 17, M.18, M.29, M.31, M.32, M.33*) had been concentrated off the Dardanelles to cover the withdrawals, first from Suvla and Anzac in mid-December, then finally Helles in early January 1916, as described in Chapter II. Generally three were at Rabbit Island, three in close support off the peninsula, and the other two fuelling or repairing at Mudros. The remaining four active monitors of the original fifteen in the Mediterranean had already been redeployed in support of operations elsewhere. *M.20* had been the first small monitor to arrive at Salonika on 6 November, following the landing of Allied forces. She was used as a guardship, patrolling the boom, so beginning a duty which occupied one or other of the small monitors for the rest of the war. *M.28* arrived shortly afterwards, enabling one vessel to remain at Salonika and the other to move east of the Chalkis peninsula to the small port of Stavros. The remaining two, *M.21* and *M.23*, had been towed from Mudros to Port Said at the end of November to join the East Indies Squadron, so that they could be stationed in the Suez Canal to guard against any Turkish attacks from Sinai.

With the final withdrawal from Gallipoli, only *M.17* and *M.29* remained with *Abercrombie* and two pre-dreadnoughts at Kephalo on the *Goeben* watch, which was occasionally enlivened by bombardment of Turkish positions on the mainland. *M.16* and *M.32* had gone to join the Mitylene patrol, while *M.18, M.19* and *M.33* went north to Stavros and Salonika. *M.15* and *M.31* were sent to Port Said for a quick docking, then joined *M.21* and *M.23* as Canal guardships.

The role of the Royal Navy in the Eastern Mediterranean from 1916 could be summarised as:—

(i) Blockade of the Dardanelles and harassing the Turkish coastline
(ii) Supporting the Allied Salonika Army and blockading the Bulgarian Aegean coastline
(iii) Protection of the Aegean bases and retaining Greek support
(iv) Protection of the Suez Canal
(v) Protection of Allied shipping.

Apart from the last, these duties determined the employment of the small monitors for the rest of the war. Generally four monitors were deployed on the Mitylene patrol (4th Detached Squadron), one or two at Imbros close to the Dardanelles (2nd D.S.), one at Salonika (3rd D.S.), four at Stavros (6th D.S.) and four in the Suez Canal area (East Indies Squadron). One monitor was occasionally at Syra in the Central Aegean with the 5th D.S., although there were none with the 1st D.S. based on Crete. One of the large monitors was frequently included in the main Detached Squadrons. The Table summarises the usual allocation of each of the small monitors, although occasional switches occurred between the Squadrons, which were closest to one another, so Salonika duties are included under Stavros. Gaps of a month of two between Squadrons usually indicate refits at Malta or Mudros.

During August 1916, *M.22* and *M.33* were temporarily

[1] Two photographs of her wreck are included in *Seas of Adventure* by E. Keble Chatterton. The salvaged 6-inch were put to good use subsequently:
No. 2590: *Raglan* (1916-17), *Cairo* (1918-32), *Valiant* (1934-37), *Revenge* (1939-46), scrap 1948.
No. 2628: *M.33* (1916-19), *Enterprise* (1925-40), *Ranpura* (1941-44), scrap 1947.

DEPLOYMENT OF THE SMALL MONITORS IN THE MEDITERRANEAN

M.15	Imbros Aug 1915-Jan 1916, Egypt Jan 1916-Nov 1917 (Sunk).
M.16	Imbros Aug 1915-Jan 1916, Mitylene Jan 1916-Nov 1917, Stavros Feb-Oct 1918.
M.17	Imbros Aug 1915-May 1916, Stavros May-Nov 1916, Imbros Feb 1917-Jan 1918, Stavros Jan-Oct 1918.
M.18	Imbros Oct 1915-Jan 1916, Stavros Jan 1916-Oct 1918.
M.19	Imbros Jul 1915-Feb 1916, Stavros Feb 1916-Jul 1918, Mitylene Jul-Dec 1918.
M.20	Imbros Aug-Nov 1915, Stavros Nov 1915-Apr 1918, Syra Jun-Dec 1918.
M.21	Imbros Sept-Nov 1915, Egypt Dec 1915-Jul 1917 (Dover).
M.22	Mitylene Sep 1915-Jun 1918, Stavros Jul-Dec 1918.
M.23	Imbros Oct-Dec 1915, Egypt Dec 1915-Apr 1917 (Dover).
M.28	Imbros Sept-Nov 1915, Stavros Nov 1915-Sep 1917, Imbros Oct 1917-Jan 1918 (Sunk).
M.29	Imbros Jul 1915-Jul 1916, Mitylene Jul 1916-Jan 1917, Stavros Feb-Apr 1917, Mitylene Apr-Sep 1917, Egypt Sep 1917-Mar 1918, Mitylene Mar-Dec 1918.
M.30	Imbros Aug-Sep 1915, Mitylene Sep 1915-May 1916 (Sunk).
M.31	Imbros Aug 1915-Jan 1916, Egypt Jan 1916-Mar 1919.
M.32	Imbros Jul 1915-Jan 1916, Mitylene Jan-Jul 1916, Stavros Jul 1916-Sep 1917, Egypt Sep 1917-Jan 1918, Stavros Feb-Dec 1918.
M.33	Imbros Jul 1915-Jan 1916, Stavros Jan-May 1916, Mitylene May 1916-Jan 1917, Syra Jan-Apr 1917, Stavros May-Jul 1917, Mitylene Jul 1917-May 1918, Syra May-Jul 1918, Stavros Jul-Nov 1918.

detached from the Mitylene patrols to assist French bombardments at Makri and Phineka on the southern coast of Turkey. Salonika guardship duties were dull, although enlivened in the early hours of 5 May 1916, when a Zeppelin was sighted overhead. Searchlights were burnt as all H.A. guns on ships in the harbour opened up, including *M.19* and *M.33*, although it was *Agamemnon* who hit *LZ.85* and set her on fire. The wounded Zeppelin drifted slowly eastwards before finally crashing in marshes an hour later. Several days later *M.17* found part of the wreck in the sea and towed it ashore. The Stavros squadron had a more active time, especially during the months following the Allied offensive of September 1916 and the Bulgarian occupation of Greek-held territory around Kavalla and Provista. *M.18, M.19, M.20, M.28* and *M.32* were usually off Chai Aghizi on the Allies' right flank, firing on Bulgarian defences and generally trying to keep the enemy troops tied down.

Some idea of the range of the daily activities of the small monitors can be obtained from the following extracts from the diary of Stoker Petty Officer Bass of *M.17*, covering his period in the Aegean during 1915-16 in the original spelling. (Parts in square brackets are author's notes).

10 July 1915 Commissioned at West Hartlepool. Prepared to embark ammunition.

2 August At sea. Lost O.S. [Ordinary Seaman] overboard 1 p.m. Funeral service 6 p.m.

20 August At Marvo [Mavro or Rabbit Island]. Opened fire 10.30 a.m. Cease fire 11.5 a.m. at Fort 154. Opened fire 5.9 p.m. Cease fire 6.20 p.m. at Fort 160. 14 rounds. French aeroplane fell into sea near ship both avaitors drowned.

6 October At Marvo. Went out surveying [in steam cutter] between Marvo and the entrance to the Dards. At 10.15 a.m. sighted two of the enemies Taubes [aircraft] coming from Constantinople making for Marvo and then one started droping bombs and returned then the other flew over the monitors and started dropping bombs. We returned to Marvo to see what damage was done and has [as] soon has [as] we got back they started dropping more bombs but they done no damage only killed a few fish but bombs which where [were] dropped where [were] not far off the mark. No. 21 [*M.21*] opened fire with her 9.2 and that cleared them after some good firing from the other monitors.

31 October M.17, Roberts and M.20 all opened fire on the batteries. The enemy replied and one shell hit the Roberts and made a big hole in the football ground. My boat had all her bows busted open and all the after part all smashed up. Just got her hoisted in time to stop her from sinking. Raglan went out during the forenoon. One shell just missed the steam cutter has [as] we where [were] coming along side of the Roberts. Weather blowing very bad here. Already for leaving on account of the weather. M.17 done some very good firing here today.

17 November All the lighters broke away during the night. Towed two lighters off the rocks and had to let them go on account of the bad weather and had to proceed to sea. Went at the back of Marvo for shelter. H.M.S. Roberts went ashore at Marvo. The collier come around to coal the Roberts but had to leave again on account of the gale.

25 November Watered ship already for leaving [Mudros] in the morning for Rabbit Island. Served out spuds [potatoes] first time for five months.

10 December Roberts played officers from monitors. [Football] Match started at 1.30 and everyone got recalled. We opened fire on 168 Fort and after firing the match was finished and the officers won 1-0.

28 December We opened fire on 168 Fort during forenoon and then opened on 171 Fort. After dinner we opened fire again on 168 Fort but could not reach her on account of gun being worn. Up till today we had fired 200 rounds out of our 9.2 gun.

8 January 1916 6 a.m. guns crews close up. Opened fire. S.T. Picton firing M.18 & 31 and us firing all day long. Other M [monitor] the other side of the island firing all day. A lot of horses and muels [mules] got smashed up on a small island here. Four indians in charge got killed. A very nice hour sport driving them from one island to another.

20 February 7 a.m. left for Gulf of Saros [Xeros] to bombard aerial station. M.29 come out after us. 10.25

M.15 *at Mudros in 1915, her ammunition derrick rigged and her 12-pdr aft fitted with a simple shield. The tall narrow funnel indicates that she is steam-engined.*

Seen at Stavros on the Salonika front are (left to right) M.19, M.33, M.16, M.20 *and* M.17. *Spread awnings hide much of the deck detail, but* M.33*'s gunshield can be seen on her forecastle, probably to allow her forward 6-inch to be replaced. The view was probably taken early in 1918.*

Aliki, forcing a move to Kusu, which had recently been netted. *M.17* returned fire whenever possible, generally firing about ten rounds over a period of half an hour from about 22,000 yards. The 6-inch monitors then moved north to Kavalla, 40 miles east of Stavros. In the early hours of 20 May, *Raglan* covered *M.19, M.28, M.29, M.32* and *M.33* while they opened fire on and destroyed the Custom House, which had been reported as being used to assemble submarines and motor-boats. The Post Office, barracks and fort were also bombarded for $2^1/_2$ hours, during which time each 6-inch monitor got off about 100 rounds and each 9.2-inch monitor about 15, from 8,000 yards.

A large and a small monitor remained based at Imbros on the *Goeben* watch, also guarding the British minefields off the entrance to the Dardanelles. On 20 January 1918, the long awaited sortie by *Goeben* and *Breslau* took place. The result was disaster for the two monitors, *Raglan* and *M.28* being annihilated as described in Chapter II, §8. By this time, there were only ten of the original fifteen small monitors left in the Mediterranean, mostly at Stavros or on the Mitylene patrol, continuing their regular duties until the Armistices, first with Bulgaria, then with Turkey. *M.16, M.17* and *M.18* were included in the Allied Fleet which steamed triumphantly, yet three and a half years late, through the Dardanelles to anchor off Constantinople on 13 November 1918. The other monitors were sent to various Turkish ports to supervise the Armistice and dismantle the defences. Most of the monitors paid off at Mudros early in 1919, and were then laid up at Malta.

§4 The Small Monitors at Dover

The last four small monitors to be completed were sent to join their big sisters at Dover. *M.25* was the first to arrive on 6 September 1915, captained by Lieutenant-Commander B. H. Ramsay, who was later to command these same waters for part of WW2. She was sent into action the very next day at the bombardment of Ostende, described on p.49, but the monitors were driven off by the Tirpitz battery before *M.25*'s short 9.2-inch could get within range. She was then sent round to patrol the Thames Estuary, where she soon demonstrated the lively motion of the small monitors. Bacon had serious doubts as to whether the small monitors would be effective bombarding vessels under Belgian Coast conditions. Their slow firing guns' maximum range was 5,000 yards less than the 12-inch monitors', which were already out-ranged by the German shore batteries. Their small gun platform meant that it was almost impossible to lay the 9.2-inch gun accurately in the open sea, so little more than a general strafing of large areas was possible. Gun trials had already demonstrated that the blast from firing over the bow was liable to buckle the forecastle deck, while broadside firing rolled the ship severely. Even before *M.24, M.26* and *M.27* had arrived, Bacon arranged to remove their 9.2-inch guns and mount them ashore in France, where there was a shortage of heavy artillery in the coastal sector. *M.25*'s gun was lifted out by floating crane at Dunkirk on 1 October, but the others had theirs removed at Middlesbrough before completion, for separate despatch to France.

Bacon included the small monitors as support to the large monitors in his plans for various operations described in Chapter III: bombardments of Westende, anti-Zeppelin patrols and projected landings at Zeebrugge and Ostende. In the spring of 1916, all four were sent round to Portsmouth to receive a new main armament: one 7.5-inch for *M.24* and *M.25* and one 6-inch for *M.26* and *M.27*, although *M.26*'s gun was soon replaced by a 7.5-inch as detailed on p.117. The guns were sited on top of a full width deckhouse built abaft the break of the forecastle, which provided room for a sick-bay. When the small monitors returned to Dover, their activities were manifold, although their principal duty was patrol work, for which they were better suited with their new armament. They were able to screen the larger monitors from enemy destroyer sorties, thus relieving the burden on the more valuable British destroyers. The 7.5-inch gun outranged the German destroyers' guns and its 200-lb projectile was capable of inflicting appreciable damage, while it could fire much more rapidly than the large monitors' 12-inch. The minesweepers and miscellaneous vessels supporting the barrage off the Belgian Coast in 1916 were also glad of their presence on several occasions during the summer when *M.25* and *M.26* helped drive off marauding German destroyers. Other activities included towing disabled M.L.s, rescuing ditched aircraft and sinking drifting mines. After 1916, they were often used as aiming marks for the large monitors. They would anchor about three miles further out to sea, out of range of the shore batteries, to provide a fixed reference point for the 12-inch and 15-inch directors. *M.23* joined the squadron from Egypt on 6 June 1917, followed by *M.21* four months later, each having had their 9.2-inch replaced by a 7.5-inch.

After Keyes took over the Dover Command at the end of 1917, the small monitors had rather more varied activities. Patrol work continued, especially over the

M.26 *is seen entering Portsmouth, probably after her return from North Russia in October 1919. Her 7.5-inch was mounted in 1916, replacing her earlier 6-inch — she never actually mounted her 9.2-inch which was sent to France. The range-finder can be seen ahead of the bridge and the tall galley funnel. Two 3-inch H.A. are now fitted aft in place of the original 12-pdr and 6-pdr, but the two pom-poms fitted abaft the boats have been removed. What appears to be a 3-pdr H.A. is abreast the mast. The bridge was increased one deck in height before leaving for Russia.*

deep anti-submarine minefields in the Dover Straits, depth charges being added to their normal armament. The mine barrage soon took its toll of U-boats, as strong patrol forces kept them submerged. On 23 January 1918, German destroyers attacked the drifters on the old barrage patrol line off Zeebrugge. *M.26* was in support and returned fire with her 7.5-inch but the enemy were difficult to locate in the smoke and were only forced to retire after two British destroyers put in an appearance. A more serious raid took place on the night of 14/15 February, this time on the Straits barrage, *M.26* again being the main defence of the patrol, as none of the regular large monitors was available on that date. *M.26* heard gunfire to the south and saw emergency signal rockets from the drifters, but a limited investigation revealed nothing and her few messages to Keyes at Dover gave no hint as the the severity of the German raid. In fact, two half-flotillas had attacked the patrol line, sinking eight drifters and damaging six more, returning safely to Zeebrugge without being counterattacked by the patrolling British destroyers which had observed them without realising that they were German. When belated full reports were finally received several hours later, Keyes was furious that the Germans had got away unchallenged, unreported and unscathed. The destroyers took much of the blame, but *M.26* was criticised for not investigating fully the extensive gunfire, the signal rockets and the blazing wrecks, and for not reporting any useful information until it was too late for Keyes to redeploy his remaining forces to catch the returning German ships. Her C.O., Commander A. A. Mellin, was replaced a month later. The organisation of the barrage patrols was tightened up but, as Bacon had pointed out before his supersession, such hit-and-run raids would always be very difficult to counter.

Three of the small monitors were in attendance at the Zeebrugge Raid, allocated to the diversionary forces bombarding Ostende. *M.21, M.24* and *M.26* acted as aiming marks for the large monitors. Their consorts *M.23, M.25* and *M.27* undertook similar duties at the second attempt to block Ostende on 10 May. As a small recompense for their faithful service, *M.23, M.26* and *M.27* were allowed to make a night bombardment of the German batteries at Westende. On the night of 14/15 May, they landed 51 rounds near their target, supported by French artillery ashore. A repeat performance was made two nights later with a further 62 rounds. Two months later, *M.23* and *M.25* were withdrawn from the Squadron to be prepared for service with the White Sea Squadron as described in §5.

The small monitors continued to accompany the large ones on their bombardments, but it was four months before they were given another chance to use their main guns during the preliminaries to the Allies' September offensive. In the early hours of the 28th, *M.26* and *M.27* opened fire with the 12-inch monitors on the coastal batteries around Westende. This was the last offensive operation carried out by the small monitors off the Belgian Coast, which was evacuated by the Germans shortly afterwards. The latter had left a strong minefield off the approaches to Ostende, which ensnared *M.21* on 20 October, two explosions occurring at 17.35. Her whole fore end was wrecked but she could still steam, so she was brought further inshore before finally sinking in 20 feet of water a mile from the West Pier. Five of her crew were missing, the remainder taking to the boats to be picked up by *Terror* and *M.27.* The three remaining monitors, *M.24, M.26* and *M.27,* were temporarily stationed at Ostende and Zeebrugge for the next few weeks, before returning to Dover in December. *M.27* then steamed round to Chatham, the other two to Portsmouth, where they were refitted for service in the White Sea.

§5 The Small Monitors in Russia

There had been a small number of British ships in North Russian waters since 1915, protecting the main supply route to the ally Russia through Archangel. After the

Revolution in 1917, the main concern of the British forces was to safeguard the accumulated military stores, to stiffen resistance against any German advance from Finland and to prevent German troops being transferred to the Western Front, as well as to give help to refugees. Troops were sent to Archangel to protect the monitors and to secure the two main transport routes south — the railway to Vologda, and the River Dvina to its limit of navigation at the railhead of Kotlas. For such operations, shallow draft vessels would be needed, so at the end of June 1918, *M.23* and *M.25* were ordered to prepare for service with the White Sea Squadron. They departed from Chatham on 26 July after a quick docking and arrived at Murmansk on 9 August.

Archangel had already been occupied a few days earlier by a small British and French force under Captain Altham, fresh from the Belgian Coast, so *M.23* could be sent on to Kem on the south-west shore of the White Sea to assist the modest forces holding the railway south from Murmansk against possible attacks from the Bolsheviks, from whom the Murmansk region had dissociated. *M.25* was sent up the Dvina from Archangel to back up with her heavy artillery the British, American and Canadian troops, as there was a possibility of their being able to link up with the Czech Legion, formed from troops released from prisoner-of-war camps in Siberia. The Bolsheviks had withdrawn to the south-east up river, taking several armed river steamers with them. The wide but shallow river was the only worthwhile means of communication in the area, the normally frozen ground thawing to almost impassable bog during the short summer. The Bolsheviks held the river banks down to Beresnik, at the junction with the River Vaga, some 160 miles above Archangel. Their well armed gunboats had been able to hamper seriously any advance of the Allied forces, but the arrival of *M.25* with her 7.5-inch gun changed the situation completely. She engaged the gunboats on 26 and 28 August as well as enemy batteries on the banks near Tulgas, about 20 miles above Beresnik. Her relatively powerful armament was able to drive the gunboats off and silence the batteries, although she did suffer one hit in her captain's cabin, which caused casualties of four killed and seven wounded, mostly amongst the 12-pdr crew on the quarterdeck. A further operation on 14 September took place to strengthen the Allied position for the approaching winter, in the course of which *M.25* sank the large gunboat *Moguchi* with two well-directed 7.5-inch shells. Thereafter, the other Bolshevik vessels used their superior speed and shallower draft to keep well out of the range of the monitor's guns. With the imminent icing up of the river, it was necessary to withdraw all ships to Archangel on 7 October, leaving the force of Allies and White Russians (anti-Bolsheviks) to hold the Tulgas-Beresnik position until the following spring, much harassed by the Bolsheviks.

By the time of the Armistice with Germany, the Allied intervention had gradually developed into outright support of the White Russians against the Bolsheviks, not only in North Russia, but in the south and east as well. However, early in 1919, the Allies decided to withdraw their active forces from Russia but, in order to extricate them without loss from any Bolshevik spring offensive, reinforcements would be needed to cover the withdrawal. Churchill, now Secretary for War, organised the despatch of volunteer troops and ships, to be sent to Russia as soon as possible. Naval forces included the remaining three ex-Dover monitors, *M.24, M.26* and *M.27,* the latter now carrying a triple 4-inch in place of her 6-inch, plus *M.31, M.33* and *Humber* from the Mediterranean, as well as four China gunboats. All six monitors left Britain in mid-May ready for the break-up of the ice in the White Sea and in the Dvina.

The campaign the previous year had shown that the 7.5-inch monitors were really of too deep draft for satisfactory operations up the Dvina drawing over 8 feet aft so, on arrival in North Russia, *M.24* and *M.26* were left behind at Archangel. As soon as the river ice showed signs of breaking up, *M.23* forced her way up above Beresnik, dynamiting the ice as she went, in case the Bolsheviks and their gunboats should overwhelm the scanty Allied forces before military reinforcements could arrive. She was in action the next day, 6 May, bombarding Tulgas, now held by the Bolsheviks; the four China gunboats arriving to help soon after. The flotilla was under the command of Commander S. W. B. Green in *M.23*, as his own ship *M.25* was still refitting at Archangel. The latter ship joined up on 17 May, taking part in many of the minor skirmishes with the Bolshevik gunboats that took place over the next few weeks. Altham arrived in the river steamer *Borodino*, now converted into a headquarters ship, to take command of the Archangel River Flotilla on 3 June. The intention had been to withdraw the Allied forces as soon as they could be safely extricated but, just at this time, one of the White Russian leaders, Admiral Kolchak, was having some success with his forces from Siberia away to the south-east. At Churchill's insistence, offensive operations were continued to try to reach Kotlas and to link up with Kolchak. *Humber, M.27* and *M.33* arrived on 14 June, *M.31* the following day, together with shallow draft minesweepers to combat the troublesome drifting Bolshevik mines. These reinforcements permitted the deeper draft *M.23* to return to Archangel on 23 June.

Steaming off Dover about October 1918, M.24 *shows her final armament — a 7.5-inch (ex-*Triumph*) on the deckhouse forward, two 2-pdr and a 3-inch H.A. abaft the boats and a 12-pdr on the quarterdeck. Her funnel has been lengthened.*

A major offensive was undertaken shortly afterwards to consolidate the Allied position by capturing the villages of Troitsa and Seltso, some 30 miles above Beresnik. *Humber, M.27* and *M.33* were all heavily engaged, not only firing on enemy batteries on the banks but also warding off any gunboats or armed barges that appeared round the bends in the river. *M.27*'s triple 4-inch proved a potent weapon with a rate of fire approaching 50 rounds of H.E. per minute. The monitors also made good use of their lighter guns, their 3-inch H.A. generally being used for low angle work. Owing to the relatively low maximum elevation of their main armament, the British monitors and gunboats were outranged by 2,000 yards or more by the Bolshevik vessels. They did, however, have the advantage of air spotting, as kite balloons and seaplanes could operate almost unmolested and so direct fire from the anchored ships onto their targets, which were usually invisible from ground level.

The Allied situation changed on 7 July, when White Russians fighting alongside the British mutinied, killing both their own and British officers. News was also received of setbacks to Kolchak, so with the imminent withdrawal of the Allies, disaffection spread quickly among the White Russians, fearful of their fate at the hands of the Bolsheviks. The naval forces soon came under heavy Bolshevik attack, *M.33* being hit in the wardroom but without suffering casualties. She returned a heavy fire, some 200 rounds of 6-inch in two days, supported by *M.27, M.31, Humber, Cricket* and *Cicala*. By 9 July, the situation had stabilised, withdrawal now being only a question of suitable opportunity. It would be several weeks before the rains would raise the river sufficiently to allow the ships to clear the sandbars, so it was necessary to obtain some freedom of manoeuvre until that time. A bombardment of Seltso on the south bank above Troitsa was made on 10 August as a preliminary to a powerful offensive by British and White Russian troops. After capture of the village with heavy enemy losses, both banks were secured with some assistance from parties of armed seamen landed from the ships.

After supporting the White Russians against the Bolsheviks, M.27 *was unable to get down the shallow River Dvina to Archangel. She was blown up on 16 September 1919 to prevent her falling into enemy hands, after her triple 4-inch and all useful equipment had been removed.*

Now that the Bolshevik forces were in no position to harass the Allies, detailed preparations for the withdrawal were put in hand. Every effort was made to lighten the ships sufficiently to get them down river, transferring into barges all removable equipment and stores. *Humber* shed her 3-inch side armour plating as well as her after 6-inch, 3-inch H.A. and 3-pdr guns; most of the vessels got their drafts down to about 5ft 3in, except *M.25* and *M.27*. By 30 August, all the major vessels had managed to get back to Archangel with the exception of these two. Attempts were made to blast channels for them through the sandbars but it was a losing battle as the river level had already begun to fall again. After the last troops had been withdrawn, *M.25* and *M.27* were abandoned and blown up with guncotton charges on 16 September.

During the summer, *M.24* and *M.26* had remained at Archangel, ready to answer any calls for assistance, later being joined by *M.23* from up river. Their first action came after the mutiny of Russian troops around Onega at the southern end of the White Sea, which fell to the Bolsheviks on 22 July. *M.23* was sent to Onega on the 23rd to rescue the small British contingent and to assist 350 White Russian troops in their attempt to recapture the town, being followed by *M.26*. While *M.23* evacuated the wounded to Archangel, she was replaced by *M.24*. Heavy fighting took place on 1 August, with the two monitors firing at enemy guns on the river banks. The Bolsheviks proved to be too strong to be dislodged, so *M.24* and *M.26* returned to Archangel on the 3rd. *M.23* was sent to Kem on 27 July to cover the withdrawal of the British force which had advanced down the Murmansk railway to Lake Onega. All the remaining monitors gathered at Archangel during September to be prepared for the voyage to Britain under tow, *Humber* and *M.24* leaving first, followed by *M.26, M.31* and *M.33* on 27 September 1919. *M.23* was the last monitor to leave North Russia, as she had been sent to Kandalaksha at the north-west corner of the White Sea on 24 September to evacuate Allied troops, finally departing ten days later for Murmansk and arriving at Sheerness on 4 November.

Meantime British naval forces had also been engaged in South Russia. They had entered the Black Sea after the armistice with Turkey and by early 1919 were supporting General Denikin against the Bolsheviks. With the withdrawal of German forces, the Bolsheviks had taken over most of South Russia, including nearly all of the Crimea, but White Russians were still holding out in the extreme eastern corner of the peninsula in April 1919, as well as to the south-east on the mainland. Two of the

From right to left, M.27, M.31 *and probably* M.33 *up the River Dvina at Shestakovo in July 1919.* M.27 *has a triple 4-inch in place of her previous 6-inch.*

small monitors were transferred from their guardship duties at Constantinople to give assistance, *M.17* arriving off Sevastopol on 24 March. She was soon in action, firing on Bolshevik-manned shore batteries at Bakal north of Sevastopol on 7 and 8 April. *M.18* arrived two days later so both monitors were sent round into the Sea of Azov in mid-April to provide support at the ends of the White Russian lines stretching across the narrow Kertch Peninsula. While Allied battleships, cruisers and destroyers guarded the southern flank from Kaffe Bay, the monitors were anchored with two cruisers off Akhmanai in Arabat Bay on the northern flank. Their powerful 9.2-inch were in action right away, helping repulse Bolshevik attacks and firing on railway junctions behind the lines. *M.29* joined the force on 3 May, her two 6-inch being particularly useful with their solid punch and reasonable rate of fire. The 9.2-inch gun was much less handy than the 6-inch, with only about one-sixth the rate of fire, but none-the-less some 100 rounds were fired by *M.17* and *M.18* during April and May, although not without some blast damage to their hulls. *M.17* particularly felt the strain and had to be towed back to Mudros, where she handed over to her replacement *M.22.*

By the time *M.22* reached the Crimea on 15 June, the Bolsheviks were being driven back, so she was sent to Genichesk at the north end of the Sea of Azov. In company with *M.18*, she fired on Bolshevik positions and cavalry, as well as railway lines, helping the White Russians assert control of the Crimea and Lower Don area. As Denikin advanced northwards, the monitors were withdrawn, *M.18* and *M.22* to Yalta, *M.29* to Constantinople for refit. Early in August, *M.18* was sent to pay off at Malta, leaving *M.22* and *M.29* to assist forthcoming operations in the north-west Black Sea, which included plans to capture Nikolaiev. In order to get armed barges up the Rivers Bug and Dnieper for Denikin's offensive, it was necessary to reduce the forts at Ochakov and Kinburn. *M.22* had made a brief bombardment on 3 August, which was followed on the 12th and 13th by heavy fire on the 6-inch batteries by *M.29,* the cruiser *Caradoc* and the destroyer *Steadfast.* Nikolaiev was taken shortly afterwards, so plans were made to support the attack on Odessa, but that city fell without the British ships needing to fire. By September, most of South Russia was in the hands of the White Russians, so the two remaining monitors were withdrawn. *M.22* and *M.29* left Yalta on 23 September under tow, arriving at Malta on 2 October. A number of other R.N. ships remained in the Black Sea into 1920, a year which was to see Denikin's defeat and total triumph for the Bolsheviks.

§6 Armament Changes

All of the 9.2-inch monitors based at Dover underwent considerable armament changes. After Bacon had ordered the removal of their 9.2-inch guns, a makeshift armament of five 6-pdr H.A. was provided for *M.25,* an additional three being sited in place of the 9.2-inch and one abaft the funnel, as well as the existing gun. The provision of a new main armament was not too easy, as most spare guns of suitable calibre, such as 6-inch, were required for armed merchant cruisers. However the loss of *Triumph* in May 1915 meant that her two spare 7.5-inch guns became available, as she had been the only ship in the R.N. with the Vickers-designed 50-calibre Mk IV gun, because she had originally been built for Chile. The spares were dispatched from Malta to Portsmouth where they were installed one each in *M.24* and *M.25* in May 1916. Both *M.26* and *M.27* were each allocated one 6-inch Q.F. removed from *Redoubtable,* which were fitted at Portsmouth in March 1916. By then, *Triumph*'s near-sister *Swiftsure* had left the Dardanelles and was carrying out patrols in the Atlantic. As she was unlikely to require both her spare 7.5-inch Mk III, one was dispatched to Portsmouth where it replaced *M.26*'s 6-inch in September 1916. *M.27*'s 6-inch Q.F. was also replaced, but by a longer range 6-inch B.L. VII. When *M.21* and *M.23* arrived back in England in the summer of 1917, *Swiftsure* had been paid off at Chatham. Her fourteen-gun secondary battery could thus be raided, so both monitors got one of the Elswick-designed 50-calibre 7.5-inch Mk III, while their 9.2-inch were sent to France. Unlike the earlier 7.5-inch which had been fitted with full

M.16 *steams through the busy harbour of Mudros in 1915. The breech of the 9.2-inch Mk X can be seen at the open rear of the shield.*

gunshields in the monitors, only the original small semi-circular casemate shield protected these last two 7.5-inch. The Mediterranean vessels had no changes made to their main armament apart from the routine shifts of worn-out gun barrels.

Changes were also made to the H.A. armament, first of all replacing the makeshift converted 6-pdr H.A. IC mounting by the new H.A. IV mounting illustrated which could elevate right up to 90°. As 3-inch H.A. guns became more widely available, they replaced the 6-pdr in the Dover monitors while, later in the war, the Mediterranean monitors shipped them in place of their 12-pdr. Towards the end of the war, 2-pdr pom-poms were being added to supplement the Dover vessels' light armament, two being mounted on platforms next to the boats where they could be used against aircraft, D.C.B.s or floating mines. The following table shows the armaments of the small monitors in 1918 as far as they can now be ascertained:—

M.16	1—9.2″, 1—3″
M.17	1—9.2″, 1—12pdr, 1—6pdr
M.18, M.19, M.20, M.22	1—9.2″, 1—3″, 1—6pdr
M.21, M.25	1—7.5″, 1—3″, 1—12pdr
M.23, M.24, M.26	1—7.5″, 1—3″, 1—12pdr, 2—2pdr
M.27	1—6″, 1—3″, 1—12pdr, 2—2pdr
M.29, M.31, M.32, M.33	2—6″, 1—6pdr
M.15, M.28, M.30	All lost whilst still mounting original armament.

Before service in the White Sea, *M.27* had her 6-inch replaced by three 4-inch B.L. IX on a triple mounting, similar to *Renown* and *Repulse*, while a 3-inch H.A. replaced the 12-pdr in *M.24, M.26* and *M.27*, and the 6-pdr in *M.31* and *M.33*. Two 3-pdr H.A. were fitted in *M.23* to *M.26*, their 2-pdrs being removed.

§7 Performance

The small monitors exhibited one feature which was not present in the large monitors — a tendency to roll excessively, due to their having been built without bilge keels, plus a relatively high GM of about 6ft. Several cases were recorded of very large rolls, *M.25* claiming 45° from the vertical when at anchor in the Thames Estuary and *M.23* 57° in the Mediterranean — both probably a little exaggerated. Bilge keels were fitted at the first convenient opportunity but, although they provided some damping, the monitors' roll period remained uncomfortably short. The general handling characteristics of the shallow draft hulls were also poor, although slightly better than the large vessels. The 6-inch monitors were worse than the 9.2-inch as the 10 sq ft rudder area and steering gear proved inadequate, having been designed for 4 feet draft. Astern steering was bad, while occasional breakdowns of the steering gear did nothing to enhance the monitors' popularity when manoeuvring in confined waters and harbours.

The machinery of the diesel ships never lived up to expectations. Designed for merchant ship conditions of steady steaming, the engines often proved unequal to the demands of naval service, with frequent speed changes, stops and starts. A recurrent problem was fires in the funnels of Bolinder-engined ships. Unburnt fuel in the exhaust could collect inside the uptakes and either produce showers of sparks or catch fire as the temperature rose after a spell at full power, or when reversing. The problem was never completely overcome, despite frequent funnel cleanings and adding 6-foot extensions to their length for larger silencers. In theory, the diesel monitors had an endurance of about 2200 miles, but in practice the unreliability of their engines resulted in their being towed on most of their longer voyages. The steamers were also towed, not because of any unreliability, but owing to their very short endurance of only about three days. Despite a specific fuel consumption nearly four times that of the diesel vessels, their bunker capacities were just about the same.

The hulls proved somewhat on the light side for the relatively heavy guns mounted and all required some stiffening, especially the decks of the 6-inch vessels. Various painted camouflage schemes on the hulls were tried at the whim of individual officers, *M.18* sporting green for a while, *M.19* dazzle painting, *M.21* khaki, *M.23* pale blue and *M.29* a false bow wave.

§8 After the War

With the paying-off of the remaining small monitors from the White and Black Seas towards the end of 1919, thirteen were left of the original nineteen ships. There was little use for such vessels in the slimmed down post-war Royal Navy, although a few could be converted for other duties. All of the diesel boats except *M.23* were put on the Sale List late in 1919 plus three of the steamers. With the post-war boom in merchant shipbuilding, there was a brisk demand for surplus naval vessels which were suitable for conversion to mercantile use, thus overcoming the long delivery times being quoted by the shipyards for new construction. Early in 1920, Anglo-Saxon Petroleum Company (now Shell) snapped up *M.16* to *M.20, M.24, M.26* and *M.32* on behalf of the Dutch associate Curaçaosche Scheepvaart Maatschappij, with the intention of converting them into

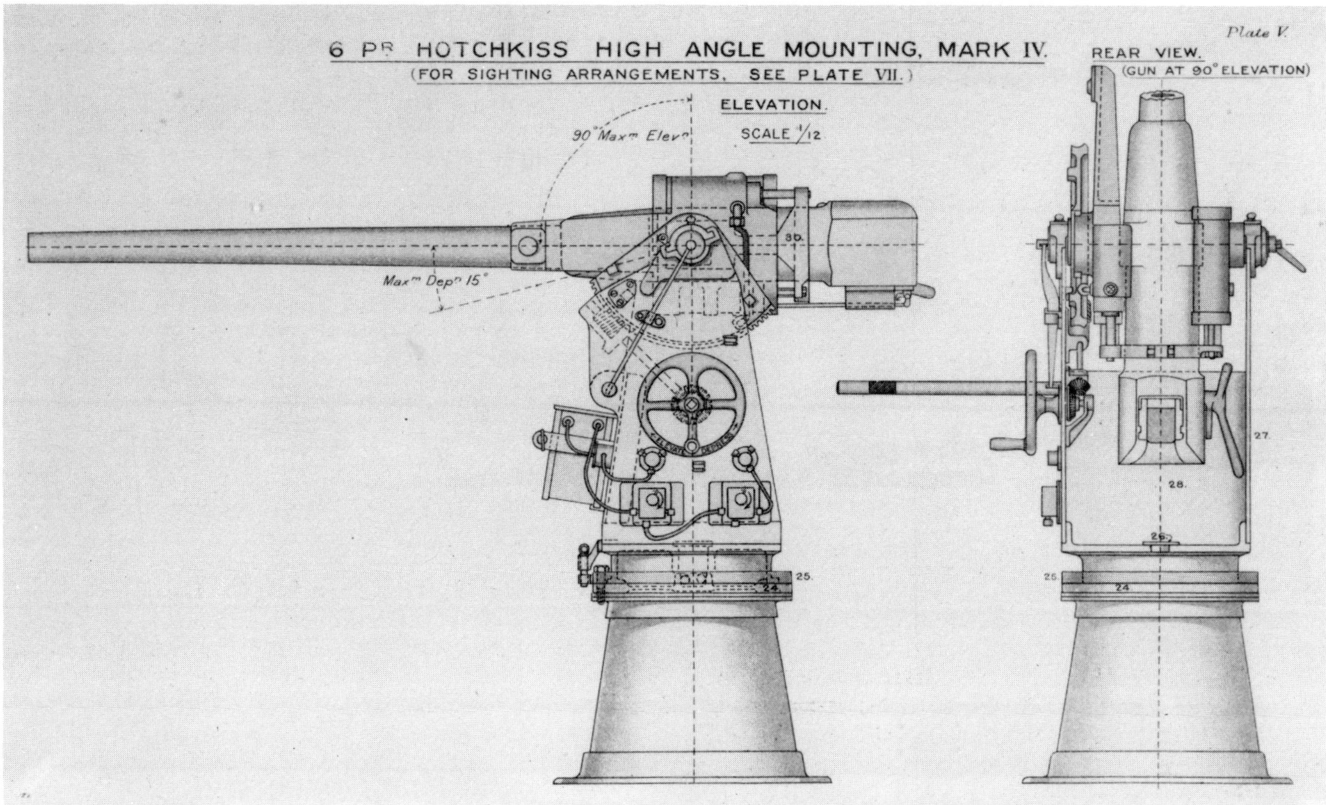

This illustration from the official handbook shows the standard 40-calibre 6-pdr Hotchkiss quick-firing gun on the Mk IV high angle mounting. This improved design replaced the earlier converted H.A. IC mounting in most of the small monitors around 1917.

small tankers. Each was sold for £7500, a good price about four times scrap value. *M.20, M.24* and *M.26* were converted in Britain, the others in Holland during 1920, their armament being removed and four cargo oil tanks replacing the magazines forward and aft. As converted, the ships had a gross registered tonnage of about 510 tons and could carry about 500 tons of oil. With their shallow 10ft 3in draft, they were mostly engaged shuttling oil from the Lake Maracaibo wells to the refineries at Curaçao. Over the next two decades, many of the vessels were transferred to various Shell companies overseas, as summarised in the Table.

Ship	*Name*	*Date and Port of Registry*
M.16	*Tiga*	1920 Willemstad, Curaçao;
		1923 Kingston, Jamaica;
		1924 Sydney
M.17	*Toedjoe*	1920 Willemstad;
		1922 Montreal;
	Nanaimolite	1927 Nanaimo, Canada
M.18	*Anam*	1921 Willemstad;
		1924 London for service at Hamburg;
	Alcione C.	1932 Genoa
M.19	*Delapan*	1921 Willemstad (service at Hamburg from 1925)
M.20	*Lima*	1920 Willemstad;
		1924 Genoa; 1932 Dakar;
	Marie des Fleurs	1948 Dakar, French West Africa (wine tanker);
	Maria Augusta	1954 Rio Martin, Morocco;
	Alvin	1960 Panama
M.24	*Satoe*	1920 Willemstad
M.26	*Doewa*	1920 Willemstad;
		1924 London for service at Suez
M.32	*Ampat*	1920 Willemstad
	Delta	1924 Marseilles;
	Colette Richard	1946 Marseilles (wine tanker)

Each first name represents a Malayan number, respectively 3, 7, 6, 8, 5, 1, 2, 4. The final fates of the vessels are shown in the Technical Particulars as far as they can now be ascertained.

The five remaining small monitors were retained by the R.N. for further service. *M.23* was converted into a stationary drill ship for service with the R.N.V.R. After conversion at Sheerness, she was towed to Leith in August 1922, where she remained as H.M.S. *Claverhouse* for the next 37 years. The other four were earmarked for conversion into coastal and instructional minelayers for service with Torpedo Schools. After the war, large scale mining experiments were planned, to take account of wartime experiences. *M.22* was the first to be converted early in 1920 at Portsmouth; she took part in experiments at the Kyles of Bute and Loch Crinan from August 1920. *M.31* followed soon afterwards, completing her conversion at Portsmouth in January 1921. Their

M.29 *was converted to a coastal minelayer in 1925 and renamed* Medusa. *She is seen here at Malta in June 1937, with a load of moored mines on the rails each side.*

armament was stripped out and narrow gauge mine rails added on the upper deck on either side of the superstructure while the necessary derricks, winches and mine handling gear were fitted. *M.31* was assigned to H.M.S. *Defiance,* the Torpedo School at Devonport, where she remained in commission for minelaying instruction until 1937; *M.22* was based at Portsmouth for similar duties.

M.29 and *M.33* had also been earmarked for conversion but, with the shortage of defence funds, the former lingered at Devonport until September 1923 when she was taken in hand by Pembroke Dockyard, while *M.33* did not arrive at Pembroke from the Nore until May 1924. The conversion work was completed in January and February 1925 respectively at a cost of about £21,000 each, being two of the last major refits undertaken before the Dockyard closed down the following year. As converted, the ex-monitors were capable of laying either 52 H-type moored mines (44 in *M.22*) or 8 (later increased to 16) L-type loop mines, the latter laid to protect harbours and controlled by cables from observation stations on shore. Carrying moored mines, their deep displacement was virtually unchanged at 576 tons, although with loop mines and the heavy associated cables, it rose to 614 tons. The crew was reduced to 26 for peacetime instructional duties but would be doubled in time of war to 3 officers and 49 men.

All four minelayers were given the distinction of names in December 1925, *M.22* being named *Medea, M.29 Medusa, M.31 Melpomene* and *M.33 Minerva.* The latter was based at Portsmouth as a relief ship for *Medea,* in reserve except when the latter was refitting. *Melpomene* remained at Devonport, while *Medusa* was sent out to Malta, commissioning in May 1925 as a tender to *Egmont* to act as an instructional minelayer. For the next ten years, no changes occurred in this pattern, until they were replaced by new purpose-built coastal minelayers which began to join the Fleet from 1937. *Medea* was the first to be discarded, being towed away from Portsmouth in January 1939 for scrapping at Newport, Monmouthshire. There was a heavy gale on the night of the 22nd when she broke her tow, running on to the rocks near Trevose Head on the north Cornish coast. One of the towing crew was lost overboard but the others were taken off safely by breeches buoy. Salvage was impossible as she was firmly wedged on the rocks, so she was eventually broken up in situ.

The other three vessels had not been sold by the time war broke out, so they were restored to naval service. *Melpomene* served the whole war at Devonport as a torpedo instruction vessel, having been fitted with a single 21-inch tube on her forecastle. When the small destroyer *La Melpomène* joined the Free French forces in

Minerva *(ex-*M.33*) in August 1971 as a floating workshop (*C.23*) for auxiliary craft at Gosport — and still in service in 1978.*

September 1940, the ex-monitor was renamed *Menelaus* to avoid confusion. She was finally scrapped in 1948 with the great post-war clear-out of surplus naval vessels. *Medusa* had a more varied life in the Mediterranean. She was fitted in May 1941 with the main winch from the badly damaged minesweeper *Fermoy* and used for lifting the sterns of M.T.B.s to permit changing their propellers without the need for slipway hauling or drydocking. In September 1941, she was renamed *Talbot* and became the depot ship for the newly formed Tenth Submarine Flotilla, based in Lazaretto Creek with workshops ashore. She was damaged in the heavy Luftwaffe bombing of March 1942, which culminated in the temporary withdrawal of the Flotilla. She took up her duties again when the Flotilla returned in July, until it departed for Sardinia in December 1943. When the First Submarine Flotilla arrived in February 1944, she adopted the name of its depot ship which had been sunk in June 1942, *Medway II*, and continued her service as a mini-depot ship. After the war, she was towed back to Britain and scrapped in 1947.

Minerva's early war years were spent as a fuelling hulk at Portsmouth but in November 1943, she was taken in hand at Southampton for conversion into a Boom Defence Workshop. Her machinery was removed and the whole space from the original oil fuel bunkers forward of the boilers to the store abaft the engines was fitted out with workshop equipment. She was towed to the Clyde in December 1944, where she helped service the extensive boom system. She returned to Portsmouth in 1946, based at the Royal Clarence Yard at Gosport as a floating workshop and office servicing local auxiliary craft. Her official title is now Royal Maritime Auxiliary Ship *Minerva — Hulk C.23,* but her monitor origins can still be discerned in her hull form and superstructure shape. She has continued in this service to the present day, her hull still in remarkably good condition after over 60 years — the longest lived of any of the 42 British monitors.

Medea *(ex-*M.22*) broke her tow on the way to the shipbreakers on 22 January 1939 and was driven on to the rocks near Trevose Head, where she was eventually broken up.*

THE SMALL MONITORS — TECHNICAL PARTICULARS

M.15 - M.28

Displacement and Dimensions 540 tons legend, 650 tons deep (*M.15-M.18*), 610 tons deep (*M.19-M.28*). Length 177′-3″ o.a., breadth 31′-0″, draft 7′-0″ (*M.15-M.18*), 6′-7½″ (*M.19-M.28*) deep.

Weight Distribution (*M.17*) Armament 75 tons, ammunition 35, hull 340, equipment 50, machinery and R.F.W. 118, oil fuel 32. Completed total 650 tons.

Complement 5 officers, 64 men.

Armament 1—9.2″ single (*M.15-M.18*: Mk X; *M.19-M.28*: Mk VI) (60 C.P. + 60 H.E. r.p.g.), 1—12pdr (200 r.p.g.), 1—6pdr Hotchkiss H.A. (500 r.p.g.), 2—0.303″ Maxim (8000 r.p.g.).

Protection Hull nil. 9.2-inch gunshield (*M.19-M.28*) 4″ front, 1¼″ sides.

Machinery Twin screw triple-expansion: *M.15-M.17* 800 I.H.P. at 210 r.p.m.; *M.21* 600 I.H.P. at 270 r.p.m.; *M.22* 650 I.H.P. at 210 r.p.m. Twin screw Bolinder 4-cyl semi-diesels: *M.18-M.20, M.23, M.25, M.28* 640 B.H.P. at 225 r.p.m. Quadruple screw Bolinder 2-cyl semi-diesels: *M.26* 480 B.H.P. at 275 r.p.m., *M.27* 560 B.H.P. at 275 r.p.m. Quadruple screw Campbell 4-cyl paraffin engines: *M.24* 640 B.H.P. at 300 r.p.m. Oil fuel: *M.15-M.17* 32 tons; *M.18, M.25, M.26* 25 tons; rest 28 tons. Endurance at 9½ knots: 660 miles (steam ships), 2200 miles (diesel ships).

Speed 12 knots designed, 11 service. Trials: *M.21* 11.5 knots.

Construction Wm Gray, Hartlepool: *M.15* launched 28 Apr 1915/completed 12 Jun 1915; *M.16* 3 May/24 Jun; *M.17* 12 May/14 Jul; *M.18* 15 May/31 Jul. Sir R. Dixon, Middlesbrough: *M.19* 4 May/11 Jun; *M.20* 11 May/3 Jul; *M.21* 27 May/20 Jul; *M.22* 10 Jun/7 Aug; *M.23* 17 Jun/28 Jul; *M.24* 9 Aug/4 Oct; *M.25* 24 Jul/5 Sep; *M.26* 24 Aug/18 Oct; *M.27* 8 Sep/3 Nov; *M.28* 28 Jun 1915/17 Aug 1915.

Disposal *M.15* torpedoed 11 Nov 1917; *M.16* disposed Sydney 1953; *M.17* disposed Nanaimo 1939; *M.18* sunk off Corsica 14 Apr 1943; *M.19* stranded near Danzig 14 Apr 1945; *M.20* scrapped Italy 1968; *M.21* mined 20 Oct 1918; *M.22* wrecked 22 Jan 1939; *M.23* scrapped Shipbreaking Industries, Charlestown, Fife 21 Apr 1959; *M.24* expended as target West Indies 29 Sep 1936; *M.25* blown up 16 Sep 1919; *M.26* disposed Suez 1934; *M.27* blown up 16 Sep 1919; *M.28* sunk 20 Jan 1918.

M.29 - M.33

Displacement and Dimensions 355 tons legend, 580 tons deep. Length 177′-3″ o.a., breadth 31′-0″, draft 5′11″ deep.

Weight Distribution (As designed/as completed) Armament 35/40 tons, ammunition 25/40, hull 180/325, equipment 25/50, machinery and R.F.W. 70/80, oil fuel 20/45. Total 355/580 tons.

Complement 5 officers, 67 men.

Armament 2—6″ single (100 C.P.C. + 125 H.E. + 25 shrapnel r.p.g.), 1—6pdr Hotchkiss H.A. (500 r.p.g.), 2—0.303″ Maxim (8000 r.p.g.).

Protection Hull nil. 6-inch gunshield 3″front.

Machinery Twin screw triple-expansion. 400 I.H.P. at 250 r.p.m. Oil fuel 45 tons. Endurance 1440 miles at 8 knots.

Speed 10 knots designed, 9 service. Trials: *M.29* 10.0, *M.30* 9.98, *M.31* 10.13, *M.32* 9.95, *M.33* 9.61 knots.

Construction Harland & Wolff, Belfast: *M.29* launched 22 May 1915/completed 20 Jun 1915; *M.30* 23 Jun/8 Jul; *M.31* 24 Jun/9 Jul. Workman Clark, Belfast: *M.32* 22 May/20 Jun; *M.33* 22 May 1915/24 Jun 1915.

Disposal *M.29* scrapped Dover Industries, Dover 1947; *M.30* sunk 13 May 1916; *M.31* scrapped Rees, Llanelly 1948; *M.32* scrapped France 1951; *M.33* still afloat Portsmouth 1978.

CHAPTER VIII

THE SECOND 15-INCH GUN MONITORS

H.M.S. EREBUS and TERROR

§1 The Cancelled Monitors

The protests of the Army at the decision to bring home the *Queen Elizabeth* from the Dardanelles underlined the importance of having bombardment ships carrying the heaviest guns. Although there could be no question of sending modern battleships out to the Dardanelles, *Marshal Ney* with her 15-inch guns was allocated on 14 May 1915 together with eight other large monitors (see p.28). On that same day, the decision was taken to build four more monitors carrying 15-inch guns. Tudor minuted:[1]

> "It has been decided to place orders for four more 15″ monitors to be propelled by steam, as follows:—
> 2 Harland & Wolff, 1 Hamilton, 1 Swan Hunter. These vessels to be completed in 6 months but not to be allowed to interfere with progress on work already in hand. The gun mountings are being ordered separately, so alternative trunks, shell-room gear etc, in order that if so desired at a later stage, it would be possible to transfer mountings from *Royal Oak* to these four vessels.
> The necessary action should be taken forthwith as it is desired to place the orders for the hulls and machinery as soon as possible."

It was already known from A.E.W.'s tests that none of the large monitors would be capable of their designed 10 knots, as was confirmed by *Abercrombie*'s first trial the very next day. A.E.W. had already shown how it was possible to improve the monitors' hull form to get the designed speed, so a new set of lines was drafted out which were sent to Haslar for testing. With this new form and more powerful steam reciprocating machinery of 3600 I.H.P., there would be little difficulty in attaining the required speed of 10 knots. The basic ship design was similar to the earlier monitors, although the hull was slightly larger than the Marshals, 350ft B.P., 89ft 3in broad and 10ft draft, with a legend displacement of 6780 tons.

Orders for the four ships, provisionally named *M.34* to *M.37*, went to the builders on 18 May, all of whom were now finishing off their first monitors. Harland & Wolff allocated their two, *M.34* and *M.35*, the hull numbers 492 and 493, Swan Hunter's *M.36* No. 1009 and Hamilton's *M.37* No. 313. But when the new Balfour/Jackson Board met on 4 June, the question of continuing the new monitors' construction was reconsidered. It was appreciated that the only way of getting delivery in the specified six months would be to commandeer all of *Royal Oak*'s turrets, which would delay her completion until 1917. The new Board was not prepared to accept such a delay in the battleship programme, so on 10 June the four monitors were cancelled.

[1] Lillicrap Workbook 188/1, Ministry of Defence, Bath

§2 A New Design

Two months later came the disappointing news of *Marshal Ney*'s machinery trials, as described on p.71. As an ex-D.N.O., Tudor was well able to assess the possible ways of making better use of the *Marshals*' valuable 15-inch guns. One of the possibilities considered was their transfer to two brand new monitor hulls. So once again, Lillicrap was called on to work up a detailed design; he started on 6 September 1915. The new design was particularly significant as it was the only one during WW1 which incorporated from the keel up any feedback of experience from completed ships — the normal process of evolution in naval architecture. The overriding consideration was the need to achieve the specified ten knots and if possible to get twelve. On the basis of the earlier monitors' trials and new model tests, it was estimated that about 6000 I.H.P. would be required, over double the power of the previous vessels.

The hull was appreciably longer than the other monitors at 380ft B.P., but this was necessary to obtain a relatively fine entrance and run. The angle of entrance at the waterline was reduced to about 50° compared with about 120° in the earlier monitors. The better flow of water aft would improve propulsive efficiency, assist steering and permit the use of a single centre-line rudder. The main hull breadth was kept at 62ft as in the *Marshals* but the bulge was reduced in width. Experiments with new forms of bulge construction for battleships had been carried out during 1915. As a result, the bulge consisted of an outer and an inner watertight compartment, the outer being empty and the inner, instead of being open to the sea, filled with steel tubes sealed at their ends. The idea was that much of the force of the explosion would be dissipated in crushing the tubes. Thus the new monitors had a bulge only 13ft wide — an air space of 9ft and a tube space of 4ft, filled with about 70 tubes nine inches in diameter lying fore and aft in each bulge compartment. Inboard, 1½ inches of H.T. steel protected the hull proper. The overall breadth was thus reduced to 88ft, but there was no chance of keeping the draft as low as 10 feet. The extra weight of the larger hull and the more powerful machinery meant that nearly 8000 tons of

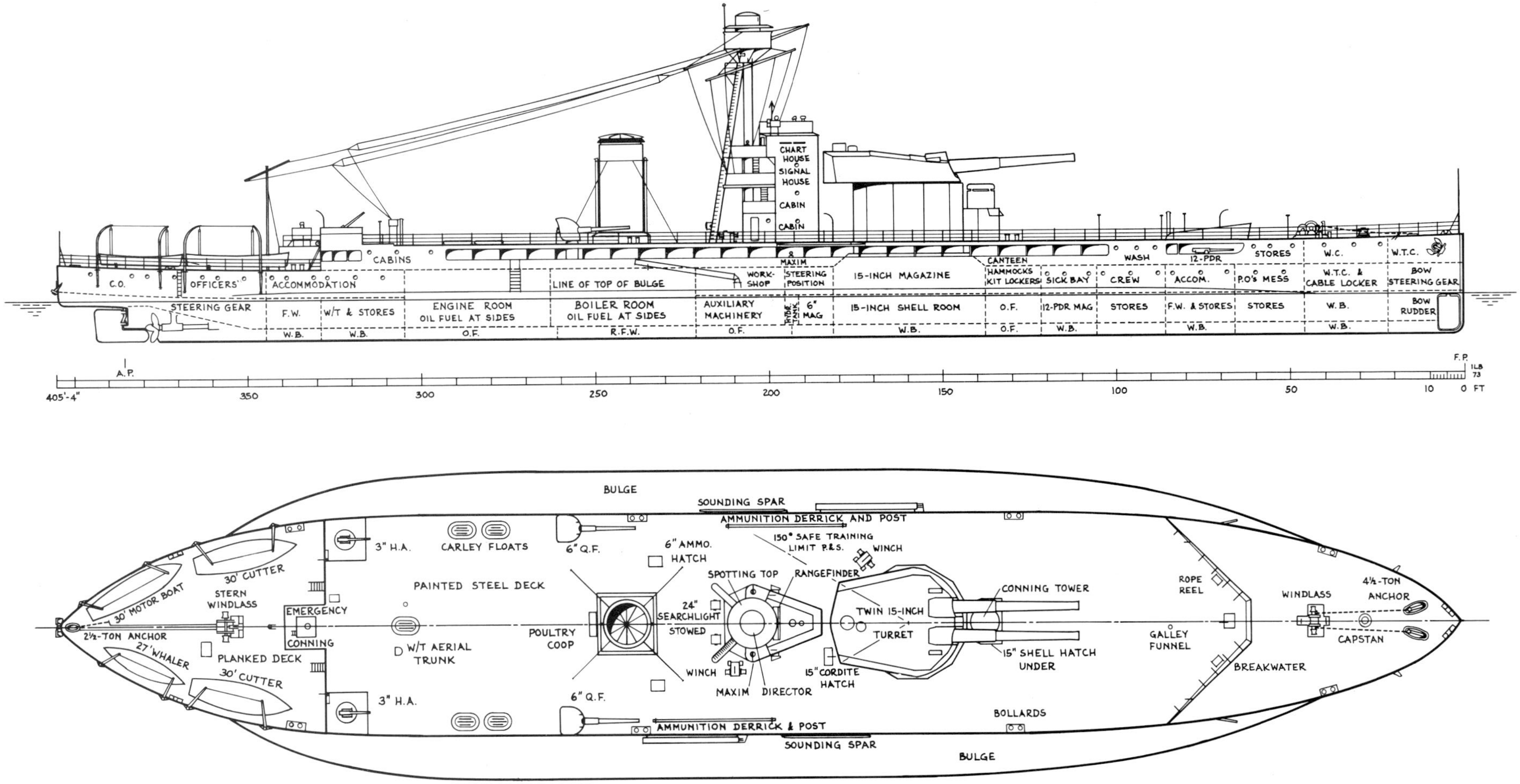

Erebus *as completed. She and* Terror *were the first monitors to profit from service experience of the earlier designs. With a reasonable 12-knot speed and 30° elevation 15-inch, they were the most effective of all the* ***WW1*** *designs. Secondary armament was increased from two 6-inch to four; these were then replaced by four 4-inch, later increased to eight.*

buoyancy had to be provided, which required a draft of 11 feet.

For the first time, a proper bridge structure was provided, four decks high. Associated with a funnel large enough to keep the smoke away from the bridge, the design took on a distinctly more ship-like appearance than the earlier monitors, although the straight stem and lack of sheer forward did not enhance their looks. When it came to settling detailed design features, Bacon put forward several suggestions from Dover. His experience in *Lord Clive* on 7 September showed that maximum gun range was essential. It was therefore arranged that the 15-inch mountings would be modified to give 30° elevation, resulting in an extra 6000 yards' range. He also considered that it would be useful to be able to back off an enemy coastline while keeping the turret trained on target. Consequently a bow rudder was fitted, which necessitated a vertical stem in place of a curved profile. A further request was for a properly fitted stern anchor and windlass to make mooring head and stern easier when bombarding. The bow anchors were increased from 4 tons each in the earlier monitors to $4^1/_2$ tons, with 750ft of $2^1/_4$-inch diameter cable. The *Marshals* had found that the mass of the turret affected their magnetic compass, so one of the newly introduced gyro compasses was fitted below the armoured deck.

The barely submerged bulge had proved a nuisance in the earlier monitors, neither deep enough to avoid being an underwater obstruction to boats, nor high enough to form a really dry platform for access to the ship's side. The top surface was therefore raised so as to be about 18 inches above the waterline, so also providing great initial stability. The spartan standards applied in the earlier monitors to outfitting were improved above the bare necessities, although not to full peacetime standards. Armour protection remained much as before: four inches on the belt slope and over the magazines, two inches on the upper deck and one inch on the forecastle deck. The turret armouring was the same as in the 15-inch battleships. The legend displacement put up to the Board was calculated as 7960 tons, made up as shown in the Technical Particulars. A comparison with the 14-inch design of a year earlier shows the following differences in percentage weight distribution:

	14-inch	*15-inch*
Armament and ammunition	13.7	13.7
Armour and protection	30.1	30.0
Machinery and fuel	12.3	17.2
Hull and equipment	43.9	39.1
Total percentage	100.0	100.0
Designed deep displacement, tons	6157	8460

The percentages allocated to offence and defence were identical, but the faster ship required a greater proportion devoted to propulsion and a correspondingly lesser amount to the hull.

An approximate breakdown of the estimated total cost

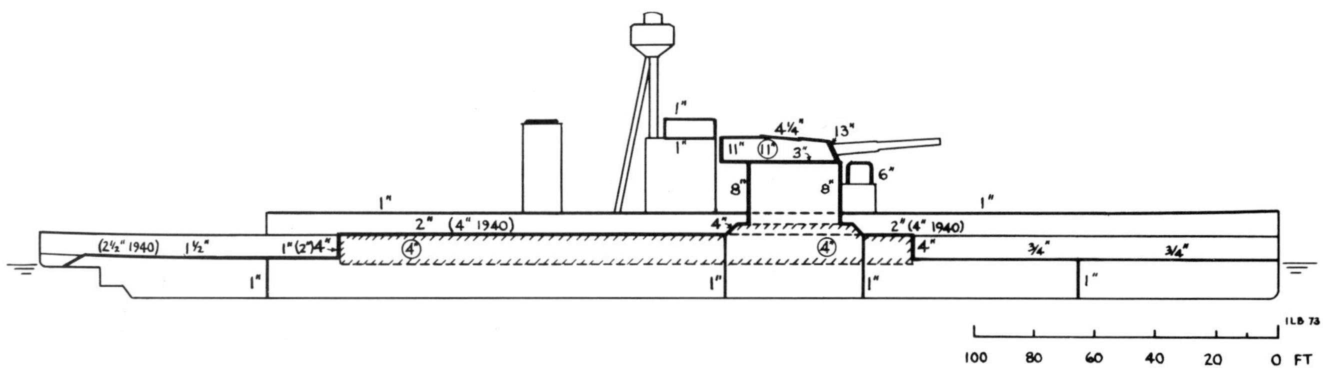

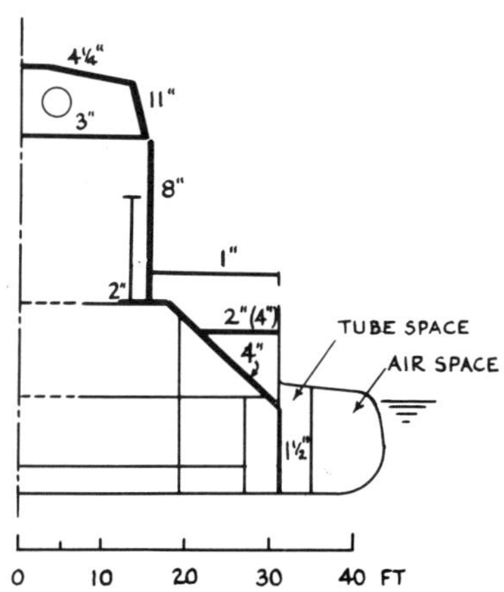

Erebus *and* Terror *had the 'standard' WW1 monitor protection, except for the water space in the bulge being replaced by steel tubes. Splinter protection was provided for the bridge. Figures in brackets show thicknesses after 1940 re-armouring — two inches were added on the upper deck over the 15-inch magazine, and one inch on the main deck aft.*

Terror *leaves Harland & Wolff's yard on 31 July 1916 for speed and gunnery trials. The upper surface of the bulge can clearly be seen. Her 6-inch secondary armament was not installed until November.*

is given below but, as the cost of the 15-inch turrets and one set of barbette armour had already been charged to other ships in the Admiralty accounts, there was a difference between the apparent 'as built' cost and a realistic 'if new' cost.

	'If new' cost, £	*'As built' cost,* £
Armament	155,000	15,000
Armour	70,000	50,000
Machinery	85,000	85,000
Hull	230,000	230,000
Total	540,000	380,000

§3 Construction

Harland & Wolff had already laid down the keel of one of the cancelled monitors, which had remained on the slipway at Govan. They were thus the obvious choice of builders for the two new monitors to take over *Marshal Ney*'s and *Marshal Soult*'s turrets, orders being placed on 29 September 1915. The previous hull numbers 492 and 493 were revived, the former for the Govan hull, the latter for the Belfast hull; machinery for both being built at Belfast. Material which had already been ordered for the cancelled ships was utilised, not only to speed construction but to reduce costs. Although shipbuilding steel plate only cost about £11 per ton at that time (having risen from £7 pre-war), 4-inch armour plate cost about £90 per ton and could not lightly be discarded. Names were allocated on 13 October: 492 becoming *Erebus* and 493 *Terror*. Gone were the generals' names; in their place two famous names of previous bomb vessels were revived, the first *Terror* having been lost at the Siege of Gibraltar in 1704. The names had also been borne by two of the Crimean War floating batteries. Completion in six months had been specified but with the increasing shortage of labour and the larger more complex design, such a short period was not realistic. *Marshal Ney* only arrived at Elswick at the end of January 1916 and the work of converting her mounting to 30° elevation would take several months, before it could be shipped to Belfast for installation in *Terror*. Furthermore, *Soult* had proved more satisfactory than *Ney*, so her turret was no longer available. It was therefore necessary to hurry on for *Erebus* one of the two turrets ordered for spares for *Furious* should her 18-inch prove unsatisfactory.

No official figures of displacement as completed were recorded, although the ships' drafts suggest that it was about 8450 tons in the deep condition, very close to the designed figure. Although the raised turret, high bridge and tall tripod mast produced a top-heavy appearance, in fact the very broad beam provided ample stability. At 32 feet, the metacentric height GM[1] was one of the highest for any British warship; typical figures for battleships of the WW1 period being 4-8 feet and destroyers 1-3 feet.

Terror was the first to be commissioned on 22 July under Captain C. W. Bruton. Speed trials were carried out on 1 August which, after all the disappointments of the earlier monitors, were a great success. The four hours' full power trial went off without a hitch and, in place of the expected 12 knots, she made 13.09. She left Belfast on 6 August 1916 to join the Monitor Squadron at Dover. *Erebus* followed a month later, which gave her time to have two 6-inch Q.F. guns mounted abreast the funnel on the forecastle deck to augment the meagre secondary armament of two 12-pdr. Her trials went even better than *Terror*'s as she averaged 14.1 knots. In place of the

[1] Vertical distance between the centre of gravity, G, and the metacentre, M. The metacentre can be considered as an imaginary point of suspension used to determine a ship's stability at small angles of heel. As long as G remains below M, the ship will be in stable equilibrium. The height of the metacentre above the keel, KM, is largely dependent on the ship's breadth at the waterline which, in the case of *Erebus* and *Terror*, included the width of the bulges, while the height of the centre of gravity, KG, is of course much affected by top weight. Then GM = KM − KG.

leisurely ten-minute cruises between the mile-posts of some of the earlier monitors, she covered the distance in just over four minutes, amidst clouds of spray thrown up off the bulges. The next day, 2 September, she was able to leave for Dover with Captain C. S. Wills in command.

§4 Service in the First World War

The arrival of *Terror* at Dover on 8 August 1916 marked the appearance of the first monitor carrying big guns and having a reasonable turn of speed. After steaming across to Dunkirk, she was soon in action on the 16th, firing at a canal bridge near Middelkerke. Her three rounds at maximum elevation were more in the nature of a gun trial than a serious attempt to hit the target. *Erebus* arrived at Dover on 5 September, just in time to join the other monitors supporting Haig's offensive described on p.52. *Erebus* and *Terror* were out on several days, but were not allowed to fire as many rounds as the 12-inch monitors, to avoid wearing out their guns prematurely on non-essential targets. Firing on 12, 13 and 15 September was carried out at anchor from behind a smokescreen, gnerally using the 12-inch monitors as back aiming marks in conjunction with shore spotting. About 70 rounds of H.E. were fired between the two ships, with no great attempt at accuracy, as only a general harassment was required. A more careful bombardment was made of Zeebrugge on 24 September by *Terror* from 27,400 yards, using two seaplanes to spot. The weather proved to be too hazy for accurate observation, so firing was abandoned after 12 rounds. This turned out to be the last bombardment by any of the Dover monitors for seven months, as winter and increasingly strengthened German defences restricted operations.

At the end of January 1917, Bacon took *Erebus* and *Terror* out to bombard the German torpedo boats which usually berthed inside the mole at Zeebrugge, but the operation had to be called off at Dunkirk owing to heavy snow. The early months of 1917 had seen a number of German destroyer raids on shipping anchored in the Downs, so all 15-inch monitors took their turns as guardships at night. Although there were several raids in their vicinity, they never had a proper chance to fire their main guns, but such powerful defences did have a deterrent effect. Preparations had also been going ahead for the bombardment of the lock gates at Zeebrugge, as related in detail on p.74. When the Zeebrugge bombardment finally took place on 12 May, both *Erebus* and *Terror* put in some concentrated shooting, contributing 63 and 61 rounds respectively.

Bacon had intended to follow up this bombardment with one of Ostende Dockyard almost immediately but, as on so many occasions, several attempts had to be abandoned before conditions were finally suitable. Although the dockyard was a much bigger target than the lock gates, great care had still to be taken in restricting the spread of shot, as the area was surrounded by civilian houses. At last all was ready on the evening of 4 June, when *Erebus* and *Terror* set out accompanied by a fleet of 22 destroyers and smoke-producing M.L.s. The monitors anchored 13 miles N.N.W. of Ostende in the early hours of the 5th. At 03.20, ranging shots were dropped deliberately short into the sea so that the splashes would check for direction; after eight rounds, fire was lifted straight into the dockyard area. Aircraft spotting corrections were obtained as dawn was not far off; good results were reported. Enemy retaliatory fire from Deutschland and Tirpitz batteries soon began and became uncomfortably hot until the spotting balloon was shot down by a Sopwith Pup. Both sides were using smokescreens; after 15 minutes the German one obscured the target. Firing was continued using estimated corrections until 04.00 when the monitors weighed anchor. A good morning's work had been done; 20 hits out of 115 rounds, sinking the submarine *UC.70*,[1] a dredger and two barges, and inflicting damage on other vessels and various buildings. The bombardment worried the Germans considerably, as an effective repeat performance would prohibit regular use of the dockyard.

Unfortunately neither of the two floating docks had been damaged, so Bacon was anxious to take advantage of any further favourable opportunities of bombarding the dockyard. When the B.O. Patrol (see p.75) was instituted, there was generally a 15-inch monitor available to open fire whenever conditions were favourable. Although a few rounds were fired during August, it was September before any really suitable opportunities came, first for *Soult* on the 4th, then *Terror* on the 22nd (35 rounds with *M.23* as aiming mark) and again on the 25th (31 rounds with *M.25*). Considerable damage was done to the dockyard installations and, in particular, one of the floating docks holding two torpedo boats was sunk, although both vessels were later salved. The lock gate was also hit, causing the basin to drain at low water.[2] With such continual harassments from sea and land bombardments, the Germans decided to transfer most of the dockyard equipment to Bruges, and thereafter Ostende was little used.

The three 15-inch monitors were then sent in succession to the Tyne floating dock, returning in mid-October to resume patrols. But it was not to remain so for long; both *Erebus* and *Terror* were very soon put out of

[1] Later raised, repaired and returned to service, but sunk again in the North Sea August 1918.

[2] *The Dover Patrol* includes two aerial photographs showing the dockyard after these bombardments.

Erebus *moored in Dover Harbour in April 1917. Apart from the chequer painting on her mast and the shield added to the 6-inch (just visible abaft the funnel pointing at the camera), she is as completed. Her single motor-boat is lying at the quarter-boom — it was more useful than her three pulling boats put together.*

action by German counterattacks, albeit temporarily. Since before the war, the Germans had been experimenting with distance-controlled explosive motor-boats (D.C.B.), but such craft only became fully operational during 1916. The 6-ton Fernlenkboote were 43 feet long and could reach 30 knots. They could be steered by means of a 30-mile trailing cable from shore in accordance with instructions signalled from an accompanying seaplane. As they were unmanned, the intention was to crash them into the side of a monitor, when it was hoped that the 700-kg (1540-lb) charge would sink it. The first D.C.B. used against the Allies in the west blew up when it hit Nieuport pier in March 1917, but later attacks on ships on patrol were more troublesome. It was thought unwise to attempt to cut the wire cable or to shoot down the guiding plane, as the boat would remain highly dangerous circling out of control. The method adopted to combat them was great vigilance by the patrol crews and considerable skill in using the ships' lighter armaments. On 6 September, *M.23* was successful in shooting up *FL.8* with her 3-inch at 400 yards.

Another attack shortly after midday on 28 October was not so easily repelled. Amidst a hail of shells from escorting vessels ranging from 2-pdr to 6-inch, *FL.12* was seen to approach *Erebus* as she was steaming west away from the coast about 20 miles off Ostende, cross under her stern and turn 180° to hit her squarely on the starboard bulge amidships. A huge explosion severely shook the ship, sending debris over a wide area, killing two and wounding fifteen of her crew. The monitor was not however badly damaged, as the bulge took the main force of the blast. She got back safely to Dover and was then sent round to Portsmouth for repairs. In drydock, it was found that about 50 feet of the outer bulge had been destroyed, but that the main hull was almost unscathed apart from a minor dent in the main longitudinal protective bulkhead and a few scratches above water. She was soon back in service at Dunkirk on 21 November. A few more attacks were made by D.C.B.s but without further success. They were abandoned by the end of the year, owing to the lack of suitable targets within easy range, the small number of boats available and technical difficulties such as the breaking of the cables on the net barrages.

Terror was out of action for a slightly longer period. She was lying at anchor off Dunkirk about midnight on 18/19 October when heavy explosions were felt on the port side forward. Three torpedoes from raiding German torpedo boats had struck her in quick succession, two right forward, the third about 80 feet abaft the stem at the start of the full bulge protection. The boats, *A.59, A.60* and *A.61,* had approached unseen and, after discharging one 450-mm (17.7-inch) torpedo each, opened fire with their guns from close range. Although considerably damaged, with the fore part of the ship opened to the sea, *Terror* was able to beach herself with tug assistance in about 15 feet of water.

Captain Iron, whom Bacon had appointed as Chief Salvage Officer, was roused from bed and brought across from Dover in the tug *Lady Brassey* in the early hours of the 19th. His survey showed that the main deck, normally level with the sea, was flooded to a depth of several feet from forward of the 15-inch magazine. The hold below was severely damaged nearer the bows but, owing to the close subdivision, most of the compartments further aft seemed to be watertight. By now a second tug, *Lady Crundall,* had arrived, so together the two tugs brought *Terror* round to Dunkirk. With the monitor beached at low tide, the damage could clearly be seen. The foremost 50 feet below the main deck had been largely blown away and damage also extended up to the forecastle deck. The hit further aft had been mostly cushioned by the bulge and the tubes, so damage was limited. As in *Erebus*' case, the bulge had proved its worth, and these two episodes reinforced in d'Eyncourt's mind the value of including bulges in new designs where practicable.

Iron and *Terror*'s shipwright and their men attempted to build cement boxes over the holes, but were frustrated by the rising tide. Instead they shored up leaking bulkheads and pumped out compartments only slightly damaged, repeatedly interrupted by German air raids. By Sunday the 21st, *Terror* was ready to proceed to England for full repairs. The passage to Dover was safely made going ahead at 7 knots, but Iron recommended to Bruton that the longer voyage to Portsmouth should be made stern first to reduce the strain on the damaged bulkheads and to ease steering problems resulting from the trim by the head. When *Terror* set off for Portsmouth on the evening of 23 October, it was clear that the bluff-spoken Iron's advice and services were not welcomed by the prickly Bruton. Her departure was made just as the weather began to deteriorate, being towed head first by *Lady Brassey* assisted by *Lady Crundall.* At about midnight off Hastings, the strong wind began to whip up the seas and wash them along the upper deck, being open at the sides. She became difficult to steer and, when the temporary salvage pumps broke down, water began to accumulate on the upper deck. Too late, Bruton tried to turn her 180° stern on to the sea but she lay wallowing broadside in the trough of the seas, becoming deeper and more sluggish in the water as the waves washed over her. Although there was no sign of water below decks, Bruton gave the order to abandon ship when the head rope parted at about 03.30. *Lady Crundall* was left holding her by a single line. About 08.00, the weather moderated, *Terror* was reboarded and found to be sound, so *Lady Brassey* was again secured and towed her safely back to Dover. She was readied for a second attempt to reach Portsmouth on 27 October, this time with Iron in control. The tow was made stern first, much to Bruton's annoyance, but on arrival at Spithead the next morning, the Dover tugs cast off and dockyard tugs turned her bows first for the final entry into Portsmouth.

At the Court of Inquiry into *Terror*'s abandonment, evidence centred on the breakdown of the salvage pumps, rather than how she was ever allowed to get into her dangerous situation in the first place. Bacon supported Bruton's decision to abandon; Iron was not called to state what recommendations he had made for the voyage. Bruton and his fellow officers could count themselves fortunate indeed in receiving a favourable verdict, as they were officially absolved of any blame.

Terror *early in 1918 after her torpedo damage had been repaired. At this stage, she only had four 4-inch in place of her four 6-inch. Her wash always gave the impression of greater speed — she is probably doing about 11 knots here.*

Terror's repairs took ten weeks; she returned to Dover on 5 January 1918. *Erebus* and *Terror* continued to make the occasional bombardment of Ostende Dockyard on B.O. Patrols as the opportunity offered during the early months of 1918 after Keyes had taken over. German defences were continually being strengthened; sound-ranging was developed for their coastal batteries, wireless jamming and smokescreens became more effective, while dummy shell bursts were rigged, which could be set off during a bombardment to mislead British spotting. British bombardment techniques were also steadily improving, especially the accuracy of position-finding assisted by sound-ranging and other features described in Chapter X.

The big German land offensive started on 21 March 1918. That night a minor diversion was made by three groups of German destroyers bombarding the railway between Dunkirk and Nieuport. As usual, a force of monitors and destroyers was anchored offshore to frustrate such operations, the enemy vessels being spotted in the early hours of the 21st. As the latter opened fire from seaward, *Terror* fired star-shell and followed up with her 6-inch. British and French destroyers from Dunkirk had slipped and were approaching fast, so the German forces retired to Ostende, hotly pursued. *Terror* and her patrol consort, *M.25,* were of course too slow for such an engagement, but when Keyes heard of the action, he ordered *Terror* to bombard the enemy ships, now holed up in Ostende. In the afternoon, she anchored offshore and from 26,500 yards put 39 rounds into the dockyard, before enemy return fire and smokescreens prevented further bombardment. Considerable damage was done in the Gare Maritime area, although none of the destroyers was hit; inevitably there were also casualties to Belgian civilians and houses.

In the plan for the blockading of Zeebrugge, *Erebus* and *Terror* were assigned as part of the covering force. They took up their position 14 miles north of the port at about 23.30 on 22 April. Having been slightly delayed en route they were unable to bombard the locks as planned, but opened fire directly onto the Kaiser Wilhelm battery. In poor weather conditions, there was no attempt to spot, but a steady fire was kept up for two hours whilst the main assault took place. On the second attempt to block Ostende on 10 May, *Erebus* and *Terror* were both used to keep down return fire from the Tirpitz and other heavy batteries, firing off a total of 92 rounds with *M.23* and *M.25* acting as aiming marks.

Air raids and long range artillery bombardments of Dunkirk continued throughout the summer. On 7 July *Erebus* was hit by two bombs on the starboard bulge — only the second monitor to be damaged by aircraft at Dunkirk during the whole war, despite innumerable attacks. Damage was slight so she was soon repaired at Portsmouth. She also received two new 15-inch guns in readiness for the forthcoming Allied offensive, while at the same time Moreton transferred from *General Wolfe* to take command. *Terror* received her new guns two weeks before the September offensive. *Erebus* and *Terror* carried out a 40-minute night bombardment of the Zeebrugge area in the early hours of the 28th to keep enemy forces occupied in this sector. Enemy return fire was uncomfortably accurate — *Erebus* counted 56 rounds landing nearby from which she received many shell fragments, but fortunately nothing heavier. By 07.00 they had both taken up new positions six miles N.E. of Dunkirk, whence they fired at German howitzers at Slype, about five miles S.W. of Ostende. Some 120 rounds of C.P.C. and H.E. were got off over a period of eight hours.

Very little firing was possible over the next two weeks, but on 14 October the monitors were out again in force for another similar operation. Two hours' intensive bombardment of Slype was carried out from 05.30 at a rate of one round per ship every two minutes. In the afternoon both ships steamed up the coast to Zeebrugge, accompanied by three small monitors and 34 supporting vessels, to encourage the Germans to continue retaining troops in that sector, but in fact the Germans were busy evacuating the coast. Following the Armistice, both ships

Erebus' *turret and forecastle as seen after her 1918 refit, showing her 12-sided barbette armour — quicker to make than the usual circular. Armament changes visible include the 12-pdr H.A. under the guns, 4-inch on the beam and 3-inch H.A. aft. The port ammunition derrick is rigged.*

A view of Erebus' *port side looking forward showing four 4-inch B.L. IX low angle guns. The base of one of the 36-inch searchlight platforms can also be seen. A sailor is painting the bulge, which also provided useful access to the ship's side. This and the forecastle view were probably both taken early in 1919 at Sheerness.*

returned to Dover to await a decision as to their future. The role that *Erebus* and *Terror* had played in strengthening the Dover Patrol was fully recognised. Their modern armament, reasonable speed and generally more satisfactory design than the earlier monitors, all pointed towards their being retained in peacetime, even if only for training duties.

§5 Between the Wars

Of all the World War 1 monitors, *Erebus* and *Terror* had the most interesting post-war careers. Although *Erebus* was attached as a tender to the Chatham Gunnery School from January 1919, she remained in full commission. She was thus readily available to reinforce the British White Sea Squadron when a request came in July for a cruiser or other well armed vessel to support the forces in the Murmansk area. Orders were sent to *Erebus* on 30 July to complete to full complement, stores and ammunition. She left Sheerness three days later under Captain Moreton for the voyage to Murmansk, where she arrived on 13 August by way of the Norwegian leads. After a week at Kem, she moved to Onega, 100 miles to the south-east. Onega had been taken by the Bolsheviks some weeks earlier, as mentioned on p.116; attempts to recapture it had failed. A heavy bombardment was ordered for 28 August by *Erebus* and *M.23* in collaboration with seaplanes from *Nairana.* Anchoring 18,000 yards from the town, *Erebus* used her 15-inch and two of her 4-inch to fire on such varied targets as steamers, enemy headquarters, A.A. gun batteries, ammunition dumps and troop concentrations. *M.23* also opened fire at noon from 10,500 yards adding 28 rounds of 7.5-inch to *Erebus'* 28 15-inch H.E. and 20 4-inch. A similar bombardment took place next day but without dislodging the Bolsheviks. *Erebus* moved on to Archangel on the 30th, *M.23* joining her after two more days firing on Onega. Both monitors returned to Kem in September to cover withdrawals on the Murmansk front.

Following the final evacuation of British forces from Murmansk on 12 October, *Erebus* was on her way home when she received orders to divert to Copenhagen. A British squadron had been in the Baltic since the Armistice: helping the smaller Baltic states resist Bolshevik pressures, ensuring that German forces in the area kept to the terms of the Armistice and preventing Bolshevik naval forces from taking any offensive action. With a modest force of light cruisers, destroyers, submarines, coastal motor boats and minesweepers, Rear-Admiral Walter Cowan had been particularly successful in the latter role by blockading the Gulf of Finland and attacking the naval base at Kronstadt in August 1919. Cowan had already requested the assistance of monitors for support but had been refused on the grounds that they would be useless against forts in the area. In August, he again asked for two monitors to help the Estonians deal with the Bolshevik-held forts barring the way to Petrograd (now Leningrad). Eventually the Admiralty agreed to release *Erebus* and on 23 October she arrived at Cowan's advanced base at Biorko, on Finland's southern shore some 50 miles west of Petrograd. She was in action early on the 27th, bombarding Krasnaya Gorka Fort in company with the cruisers *Delhi* and *Dunedin.* Some return fire from the Bolsheviks was experienced but no hits received. Damage to the fort was not great, some shells failing to explode, but the Estonians were certainly heartened by the demonstration. Bombardment continued intermittently for the next three days, but the advance of the Estonians and White Russians against Petrograd had already begun to falter and the ships could do little to help in the circumstances.

By now *Erebus* was out of ammunition so she was sent to Libau (now Liepaja) on the Latvian coast, where the British were assisting the Letts in their fight for independence against both the Bolsheviks in the east and the Germans in the south. On 4 November, the Germans had advanced right up to Libau, where British cruisers and destroyers were able to give some fire support. *Erebus* arrived on the 7th, ammunitioned from *Querida* and fuelled from *Mixol* on the 8th, and was in action on the 9th. She was able to counter German shelling of the port area over the next few days.

After receiving reinforcements, the German Iron Division attacked more strongly on the morning of the 14th, taking part of the town. A fierce Lettish counter-attack was supported by a lifting shrapnel barrage from *Erebus*, the cruisers and destroyers. The range was very short, barely over a mile, so the ships fired over open sights using half-charges. The barrage was devastating and, by early afternoon, the Germans had been driven out of range of the guns. *Erebus* had fired over 100 rounds of 15-inch and over 400 4-inch that day between 05.50 and 13.40, expending nearly all the ammunition available. Although the Germans did not attack again, *Erebus* remained at Libau until mid-December when the Baltic began to freeze over. The Baltic states having been effectively freed, she finally withdrew at the end of the year with the remaining British forces returning to Chatham on 31 December 1919.

Meantime, *Terror* had relieved *Marshal Soult* as Director and Fire Control Ship at Portsmouth, where she had arrived on 3 January 1919. In addition to these duties, she was also used as a firing ship in gunnery trials with ceded German warships as targets. Her first trial took place off Portsmouth in July 1919, when she fired a series of test projectiles against 100-mm (3.9-inch) armour plates which had been mounted on board *Swiftsure*. The plates had been removed from the German battleship *Baden*, which had been scuttled at Scapa Flow on 21 June but had been beached and subsequently salvaged. The trials were to determine the best type of projectile to use against moderately armoured vessels such as cruisers. Performance had to be assessed at the anticipated future battle range of about 16,000 yards. As there was no guarantee that *Terror* could hit the target consistently from eight miles, special reduced charges of 172lb were prepared, which would give the projectiles the same striking velocity of 1500 ft/sec from 500 yards as the full 428lb charge from 16,000 yards. *Terror* could hardly miss from 500 yards, but the striking angle would not be correct unless the target ship was heeled 13½° towards the firing ship to simulate the correct angle of descent. A whole series of 15-inch projectiles of the latest types was fired to compare their performance and the extent of the damage.

Several other trials were undertaken over the next two years, testing the effects of a whole range of guns from 2-pdr to 15-inch, to determine the most suitable gun and projectile to use against different ship types. The targets were again German ships which, apart from the submarines, had been salvaged from Scapa Flow. The guns were all mounted aboard *Terror*, firing from about 300 yards simulating ranges from 7000 to 16,000 yards, the trials taking place off Portsmouth, as summarised in the table below. The guns temporarily mounted in *Terror* were: 7.5-inch Mk I, 6-inch B.L. XII and 4.7-inch B.L. I, the others being part of her normal armament.

The sinking of *Baden* sounds very impressive but was not the objective of the trial. Because she had to be heeled for the trials, she flooded easily through damage holes when rolling in a moderate sea. Being in a neglected state below decks, the flooding through shell holes spread rapidly and she sank after 17 hits. Fortunately the water was shallow and she was easily salved. Later in 1921, the trials were continued against *Baden*. This time, it was *Erebus* who was used to simulate firing from 22,000 yards with the latest designs of projectile, which proved to be much more satisfactory than those used in the war, especially in terms of penetration and detonation. *Baden* was badly mauled by 14 hits from *Erebus* on 10 August off the Isle of Wight, so was towed away and was scuttled in deep water off the Casquet Rocks in the Channel Islands six days later. Two important conclusions were derived from the trials: that an outfit of 100% A.P.C. for battleships would prove adequate against all likely targets, and that semi-armour-piercing projectiles should be introduced for medium calibre guns such as those carried by cruisers.

Erebus also participated at this time in trials of H.A. control equipment using targets towed from kite balloons. She paid off into C. & M. at Chatham on 31 August 1921 but continued to be used as Turret Drill Ship there until March 1926 when she changed places with *Marshal Soult* at Devonport. After a refit, she recommissioned in September 1926 as combined Turret Drill Ship, Training Ship for Special Entry Cadets and Senior Officer Devonport Reserve Fleet. Her profile remained familiar to all naval personnel because, after seven years at Devonport out in the stream, she transferred to Portsmouth in October 1933 replacing *Terror* as Turret Drill Ship and Harbour Training Ship.

It had been originally intended to dispose of *Terror*

TRIAL FIRINGS BY *TERROR* AGAINST GERMAN SHIP TARGETS

Date	Target	Guns Used	Result
30 Sep 1920	Submarine *UB.21*	4.7″, 4″, 12pdr	Target sunk
7 Oct 1920	Submarine *U.141*	4.7″, 4″, 12pdr	Severely damaged
13 & 15 Oct 1920	Destroyer *V.82*	4.7″	Damaged and beached
5 & 8 Nov 1920	Cruiser *Nürnberg*	7.5″, 6″	Damaged
8 Dec 1920	Destroyer *V.44*	6″, 4.7″, 4″, 2pdr	Damaged
2 Feb 1921	Battleship *Baden*	15″	Target sunk

Erebus *off Whale Island at Portsmouth as Turret Drill Ship in June 1938, disfigured by the huge recreation hall and gymnasium. The bulge is serving as a useful platform for repairing the ship's boats.*

after her 1921 trials, but fortunately this economy measure was rescinded so that the R.N. retained three monitors capable of operational use. In May 1922, she was again used for trial firings, this time against armour plates mounted on *Superb*, in connection with the design of new capital ships. *Terror* formally recommissioned at Portsmouth in May 1924 as Turret Drill Ship in place of the battlecruiser *Tiger*, with a complement of 55. She remained there until 1933, when plans were made to send her out to Singapore. A huge naval base had been under construction for several years as part of the defence of British Far Eastern interests against possible Japanese expansion. A monitor would form a useful base and guardship while the dockyard and fixed defences were being completed.

After a long refit at Devonport, *Terror* left on 9 October 1933 on the three-month voyage. Her complement of 13 officers and 202 men was not enough for both her 15-inch and 4-inch L.A. armament to be manned simultaneously but was sufficient for her general duties. Her gunnery role envisaged anti-ship operations rather than shore bombardment, so practice firings against surface targets were carried out. Her ammunition outfit now included only 10 rounds of H.E. to 100 A.P.C. In April 1937, a joint shoot by *Terror* and some of the new coast defence batteries was carried out against a high speed target towed by the cruiser *Berwick*. *Terror* fired nearly 60 rounds of 15-inch at a rate of almost two per minute to provide information for spotting and fall of shot trials. She remained based at Singapore with only the occasional jaunt up the Malayan coast until the outbreak of WW2. Her war station was planned between the sandbanks south-east of the naval base, connected up with the fortress plot, and with a Walrus amphibian aircraft attached for spotting duties.

During the 1930s, the South Africans were also worried about possible Japanese threats, fearing that warships might bombard Cape Town and other major ports which were not heavily defended. The existing shore defences at Cape Town consisted of 15° elevation 9.2-inch guns mounted around Table Bay, with a range of only about 17,000 yards. It was therefore suggested by Oswald Pirow, the South African Minister of Defence, that 15-inch guns be mounted on Robben Island, a few miles north of Cape Town. The Admiralty were asked if they would provide the guns, but they considered 15-inch ordnance to be an over-insurance. Even if Singapore were in Japanese hands, bombardment was judged unlikely and certainly by nothing larger than a cruiser. Instead, the Admiralty suggested additional 35° elevation 9.2-inch and 6-inch guns, pointing out that the mounting of even a single 15-inch ashore would cost over £250,000 with all the associated works and ammunition, compared with about £40,000 for a 9.2-inch installation and about £15,000 for a 6-inch.

Pirow was not easily dissuaded from getting his 15-inch guns for the ports, being also Minister for Railways and Harbours, so discussions about loans of equipment dragged on during 1935-36. Eventually a compromise was reached: a 15-inch monitor, *Erebus,* would be loaned for the defence of Cape Town, with South Africa paying the running costs. She would be manned by a fighting crew from the South African Artillery, with deck and engine room crews from local harbour craft, plus a nucleus of experienced R.N. men. It was intended that she should operate as a self-contained unit in action, going to sea to meet any threat, relying on her own fire control equipment and whatever air spotting could be provided from shore. In 1938, steps were taken to put the plan into effect but only as an interim measure while the fixed shore defences were being modernised, first at Cape Town, then at Durban. *Erebus* was taken in hand at Southampton for a refit in January 1939, returning to Portsmouth on 15 August. But war broke out before she could sail and she was not destined to reach South Africa until 1942.

§6 TERROR in the Second World War

With the progress that had been made on Singapore's permanent shore defences, the question of *Terror*'s future employment was considered during 1938. A number of other British overseas bases were also awaiting the installation of up-to-date coastal defences, so it was planned to station *Terror* at one of them, either Aden or Trincomalee. The latter was considered the best place for *Terror*, situated so that she could move either east or west as any threats developed. War broke out while she was undergoing a refit at Singapore, which included the fitting of six 4-inch H.A. guns. In November she was ordered home to prepare for service off the Channel coast. She left Singapore on 29 January 1940, but by the time she reached Suez, a more urgent need arose to use her in the Mediterranean, as many of the ships there on the outbreak of war had been withdrawn to home waters when it was realised that Italy was not likely to follow Germany immediately into declaring war on Britain. She arrived at Alexandria on 11 March, which had become the main Fleet base owing to the weakness of the defences at Malta. *Terror* arrived at Malta on 4 April to supplement the island's scanty defences. She was fully integrated into the fortress plot as her main armament far outranged the island's old 9.2-inch. Her 4-inch also formed a welcome addition, as there were only 34 heavy A.A. guns on the entire island at this time.

Italy declared war on Britain on 10 June, following the collapse of France; air attacks commenced on Malta the very next day. A total of about 150 high-level bombers attacked in the morning and in the evening, *Terror* opening fire with all her A.A. guns and getting off 212 rounds of 4-inch in 75 minutes. From then on, air attacks from Sicilian bases were virtually a daily occurrence. *Terror* was able to put up a good A.A. barrage from her berth in Lazaretto Creek; she claimed to have damaged several aircraft, without having been hit herself. She was able to start a re-armouring refit on 4 September, as new supplies of anti-aircraft guns had just arrived in Malta by sea.

The Italians invaded Greece on 28 October, which gave Britain the opportunity of using Suda Bay in Crete as an advanced Fleet base. As there were no defences of any kind there, *Terror* was sent as guardship on completion of her refit, air attacks on Malta having slackened off meantime. From 13 to 30 November, she provided a useful service while shore defences were being hastily improvised. She was then ordered to Alexandria, where she arrived on 2 December, to prepare to give assistance to the forthcoming British offensive against the Italians, who had advanced from Libya into Egypt, thus reverting after a lapse of 22 years to her originally designed role of coastal bombardment.

The Army were to attack on the morning of 9 December, so it was arranged that *Terror*, in company with the China gunboats *Aphis* and *Ladybird*, would bombard Italian positions at Maktila and Sidi Barrani, 200 miles west of Alexandria, to discourage reinforcements being sent further inland. Just before midnight on the 8th/9th, *Terror* and *Aphis* opened fire on strongpoints and motor transport at Maktila from ten miles offshore, meeting a little return fire from Italian batteries. In 73 minutes, she put down 100 rounds of C.P.C., assisted by Fleet Air Arm Swordfish for spotting and flare-dropping duties. A repeat performance took place on the 11th at the small harbour of Sollum, 60 miles further west. Italian forces retreating along the exposed coastal road formed excellent targets, so firing continued during the night and day, *Terror* emptying her 15-inch magazine of the remaining 124 rounds.

She returned to Alexandria on the afternoon of 11 December to replenish and was back at the front on the 14th, this time to soften up the heavily defended town of Bardia, 13 miles north of Sollum. For three days, she pounded the area around the town, especially the road leading west to Tobruk, being well supported by the gunboats and the Australian destroyers *Vendetta* and *Voyager*. On the 17th, she engaged shore batteries while *Aphis* shot up Bardia and its harbour. The enemy's retaliation was strong: coastal batteries, torpedo bombers and torpedo boats, but *Terror* emerged unscathed. During the three days, she had fired 193 rounds of 15-inch. Wherever the range permitted, ¾-charges were used in order to reduce bore wear as, although her guns had been replaced the previous year, they were half-worn pieces which had already spent 12 years in the battleship *Revenge* from 1916-28, without having been relined subsequently. For the rest of the month, she carried out a variety of other duties, as part of the newly formed Inshore Squadron. She ferried stores

Erebus *entering Portsmouth in August 1939 after refitting as a guardship for South Africa. All the extra forecastle deck accommodation has been stripped off, the upper deck re-opened at the sides and secondary armament reduced to only two 3-inch. The stern anchor and the platform on which the anti-D.C.B. 2-pdr were mounted can be seen.*

and fresh water from Alexandria to Sollum; she undertook repairs on the smaller vessels and most importantly she acted as A.A. guardship.

The army were preparing to capture Bardia with an attack starting on 3 January 1941. On the previous day, *Terror, Aphis, Ladybird* and *Gnat* moved up in support, keeping up a heavy fire on the enemy defences in company with *Voyager* and *Dainty*, despite air attacks. The next morning, the three Mediterranean Fleet battleships *Warspite, Valiant* and *Barham* also brought their 15-inch to bear, with the carrier *Illustrious* providing air cover and spotting aircraft. *Terror* bore the brunt of the ensuing Italian air attack, during which she shot down a Savoia bomber. After the huge dust clouds ashore had settled, she continued an intermittent harassing fire for the rest of the 3rd, bringing her contribution over the two days to 135 rounds. After a powerful land offensive, Bardia surrendered on 5 January.

The Army pressed on to Tobruk where *Terror* was again called upon to soften up the defences on the night of 20/21 January just before the attack was to commence, supported by *Gnat, Stuart, Vampire* and *Voyager*. This time she fired off 96 rounds, but by now her guns were so worn that the driving bands on the projectiles were not being properly gripped in the rifling, with the result that insufficient spin stabilisation was obtained and the projectiles somersaulted their way to the targets, where they usually burst after performing a few cartwheels. The effectiveness of these heavy barrages was diminished by the shortage of aircraft for spotting duties, but nevertheless they had an extremely demoralising effect on the Italians who could not feel safe even when sheltering in deep wadis. In six weeks, *Terror*'s two 15-inch had fired a total of 660 rounds, more than she had fired during the whole of WW1, as well as about 1300 rounds of 4-inch and 4700 of 0.5-inch. Including those fired whist in *Revenge*, each gun had fired over 600 rounds, probably a world record for a gun of such calibre at the time.

Terror *shows off her lines at her annual drydocking in AFD 9 at Singapore about 1937. Her anchors and cables are laid out on the bottom of the 50,000-ton floating dock. The bow can be seen plated over where the rudder used to be before it was blown away in October 1917.*

Tobruk was to be the last occasion on which her big guns were fired. After three weeks as air and sea defence guardship at that port, subjected to heavy air attacks from the end of January, she escorted a convoy to Benghazi on 16 February, which had been captured ten days earlier. Conditions in the port were very bad, especially as it was well within range of German air bases, the Luftwaffe having arrived the previous month to assist the Italians. British air cover and A.A. defences were almost non-existent so far to the west, particularly as forces were already being withdrawn to help in Greece. Although *Terror* was able to augment her A.A. armament with seven captured Italian 20-mm guns, she lacked early warning radar. She sustained damage from three near-miss bombs at dawn on 22 February, which caused flooding in some bulge compartments and started leaks into the magazines, but fortunately no casualties. That same day C-in-C Mediterranean, Admiral Sir Andrew Cunningham, ordered her return to Tobruk, as her C.O., Commander H. J. Haynes, had reported, "I consider it only a matter of time before the ship receives a direct hit".

On leaving Benghazi at dusk with the new corvette *Salvia* and the old minesweeper *Fareham* as anti-submarine escorts, she exploded two acoustic mines nearby, which severely shook the ship and caused further flooding. She was caught the next day by five German dive-bombers and three fighters, a few minutes after her lone Hurricane escort had departed. The bombers came in from the starboard quarter, where only the two aftermost 4-inch and two 20-mm would bear. These guns managed to put most of the bombers off their aim, but at about 18.25 *Terror* received three very near-misses amidships, two to starboard and one to port. The already weakened hull began to buckle and split between the turret and the bridge, and a list to starboard developed. An oil fuel fire broke out in the boiler room, which was only extinguished by the rising water level which also cut off the steam to the engines, pumps and generators. An attempt to tow by *Fareham* failed as *Terror* gradually settled by the bows. At 20.00, all the crew except those manning the A.A. armament were evacuated to *Salvia* and, three hours later, she began to settle more rapidly. With her seacocks opened and depth charges exploded to hasten her sinking, *Terror* finally succumbed but without any casualties, at 04.20 on 24 February 1941, 20 miles north-west of Derna. She had given a fine demonstration of the value of monitor-type vessels in close support of military operations, which she was still able to perform efficiently after a quarter of a century of service.

Terror *leaves Malta in November 1933 on her way to Singapore, with someone's motor car stowed abreast the after deckhouse. The battleship in the background is* Resolution.

§7 EREBUS in the Second World War

It had been planned that *Erebus* would sail for South Africa on 7 September 1939 and arrive at Cape Town eight weeks later. Her crew of 151 was already aboard when Britain declared war on 3 September. 58 of them were South Africans, while most of the rest were the R.N. steaming crew who would return home after she had reached the Cape. In view of the possibility of South Africa remaining neutral, her departure was immediately postponed. On the 20th, Churchill, First Lord of the Admiralty again, telegraphed General Smuts:[1]

> "Monitor *Erebus* is ready to sail for Cape Town. As you know, we have never considered 15-inch guns necessary for defence of Cape Town, but to please Pirow agreed to loan *Erebus* until those defences were modernised in view of his fear of attack by Japan. We realise the defences of Cape Town remain weak but the Germans have no battleships, and the only two battlecruisers they possess, the *Scharnhorst* and *Gneisenau*, would be very unlikely to try to reach South African waters, or if they did so to risk damage far from a friendly dockyard from even weak defences. Should they break out a major naval operation would ensue, and we shall pursue them wherever they go with our most powerful vessels until they are hunted down. Therefore it seems to me you are unlikely to have need of this ship. On the other hand, she would be most useful for various purposes in the shallows of the Belgian Coast, especially if Holland were attacked. She was indeed built by Fisher and me for this very purpose in 1914 (sic). The question is therefore mainly political. Rather than do anything to embarrass you we would do without the ship. But if you can let us have her either by re-loan or re-transfer, Admiralty will be most grateful, and would of course reimburse Union. All good wishes."

Smuts readily agreed to Churchill's request, so *Erebus* remained under full R.N. control. However in the weeks since the outbreak of war, pro-German elements amongst the South African artillerymen had been causing unrest, and the detachment demanded to return to South Africa, but not in *Erebus* who might be a target for a U-boat. Their truculent attitude was compounded by weak officers, in particular a major who had expected to be given command of *Erebus* and who became totally unco-operative when, not unreasonably, a R.N. officer was appointed to command her on her voyage to the Cape, Commander I. W. Whitehorn, who had served in *Terror* in WW1. The situation was reported to Churchill, who minuted on 24 September: [2]

> "Now that General Smuts has agreed to release *Erebus* for imperial uses, the sooner these sulky South African artillerymen, twenty-six in number, are sent home the better."

The South African detachment was therefore removed to the Royal Marine barracks at Eastney and sent home as soon as passages could be arranged. Meantime *Erebus* remained based at Portsmouth for the next five months for gunnery instruction and occasional trial firings.

She returned to Thornycroft's at Southampton on 17 February 1940 to begin another refit, during which her A.A. armament and deck protection were considerably strengthened, as detailed later. She recommissioned under Captain H. F. Nalder on 10 July, by which time the Germans had overrun the Channel coast of France, Belgium and the Netherlands. Churchill, now Prime Minister, was anxious for her to repeat her WW1 performance against German-held territory; he visited her at Portsmouth on 17 July in company with Lord Beaverbrook. With an inexperienced crew, she had to do an extensive work-up before she could begin bombarding the Channel Coast, so she was sent west-about to Scapa Flow where she arrived on 12 August. Churchill was

[1] ADM 1/9876
[2] ADM 1/10543

anxious for her as soon as possible to bombard the heavy battery positions, which the Germans were constructing around Cap Gris Nez, before the guns were actually installed. But mechanical defects plagued her work-up — it was over 20 years since she had done any serious steaming. Finally, after several full-calibre bombardments around Stack Skerry, she was ready to depart for Sheerness, which was intended to be her new base for bombarding the Channel Coast. The passage without escorts was uneventful until she was off Lowestoft in the early hours of 25 September, when she was attacked by E-boats. The four torpedoes fired passed just a few yards ahead of her bows, the Germans evidently thinking that *Erebus* was doing much more than her nine knots, on account of the extensive wash set up by her bulge.

Vice-Admiral Ramsay, C-in-C Dover, had planned that *Erebus* should make her first target the barges that were gathering at Calais for the projected invasion of

Erebus *in September 1941 after modernisation. Among the new features visible are the three 4-inch H.A. in pits each side, the H.A. rangefinder/director with Type 285 radar, one of the 20-barrelled U.P. (rocket) projectors abaft the funnel, two quadruple 0.5-inch machine guns abaft the stumpy mainmast, and beneath on the quarterdeck platform one of the 3-inch U.P. launchers. The topmast has been struck. A degaussing cable runs round the hull just below deck level, the side now being all plated in. Skids are fitted to enable the Carley floats to clear the bulge when launched.*

Britain but that, if this proved impracticable, the target should be the new batteries being built nearby to command the Straits of Dover. *Erebus* had set out on the afternoon of the 28th but was attacked while still in the Thames Estuary by a single German aircraft which dropped four bombs just ahead of her. Her subsequent progress down the narrow swept channels proved very difficult owing to her lack of manoeuvrability in the prevailing weather conditions, so she had to abandon the operation.

She set out again the next day with a tug to help her. Escorted by the destroyers *Garth* and *Vesper*, she reached the firing position shortly after midnight, a specially-laid buoy eight miles east of the South Goodwin lightship. Fire was opened at 01.50 on 30 September on Calais docks but had to be stopped 15 minutes later after 17 rounds, owing to loading difficulties and the lack of spotting reports from the two Swordfish aircraft, so *Erebus* returned to Sheerness. Another bombardment of the Gris Nez batteries was planned for the following week but had to be postponed until minefields off the Goodwins had been swept. The target was then switched to Dunkirk, *Erebus*' old WW1 base, so she left the Thames again on 11 October with her WW1 consort *Lady Brassey* assisting. The operation was postponed before she could reach the firing position, owing to mechanical difficulties and the grounding of the spotting aircraft by fog. It was successfully carried out on the early hours of the 16th when, from 25,000 yards, she landed 50 rounds of C.P.C. within the area of Dunkirk docks, although causing no serious damage as the harbour was almost empty at the time.

It was now fully apparent that she was nowhere as effective a bombarding unit as she had been during WW1. Apart from the severe operational limitations engendered by the presence of powerful enemy air forces, *Erebus*' general performance and mechanical condition had deteriorated appreciably. She was sent for overhaul, firstly to Chatham, then to Tilbury for drydocking. She returned to service at Christmas, fitted with a larger rudder and sporting additional A.A. weapons, including rocket projectors, as described in p.141. During the early months of 1941, she was stationed off Southend as part of the A.A. defences against minelaying aircraft. A bombardment of Ostende took place on the night of 10/11 February. Assisted by spotting Swordfish, she put 54 rounds into the dock area. Six hits on submarine pens were observed out of 24 shells which landed in the target area.

Erebus left Sheerness on 30 July for another working-up period at Scapa. Orders for her to sail to the Eastern Mediterranean came in mid-September, as she was urgently required to support the forthcoming British offensive against the Germans under General Rommel in Cyrenaica, *Terror* having served so well in this role earlier in the year. But she had yet to attain her full complement of 400, as well as her outfit of the newly available 20-mm Oerlikons, so she returned to Sheerness on 22 September. Two months later, she was ready for her long voyage round the Cape; sailing north-about with an escort of two destroyers to Lough Foyle, where she was joined by the new monitor *Roberts*, likewise bound for the Mediterranean. The small convoy sailed on 1 December, consisting of *Erebus, Roberts,* the sloop *Scarborough* and the corvette *Fritillary*. By the time she reached South Africa, Japan had entered the war and was striking a series of devastating blows at British possessions in the Far East. It was therefore decided to divert her to strengthen British defences in the Indian Ocean, so she sailed from Durban on 31 January 1942 for Ceylon.

Erebus arrived at Trincomalee on 2 March to take up guardship duties. Early in April, a powerful Japanese fleet struck at Ceylon and British ships in the surrounding waters. Trincomalee was attacked by carrier-based aircraft on the 9th about 07.30. *Erebus* opened fire as the enemy attacked the harbour, but considerable damage was done to shore installations, while *Erebus* suffered casualties from six near-miss bombs on the port side. Seven of her crew were killed and twenty wounded, while her hull was well peppered by splinter damage. As a result of the Japanese attack on Ceylon which caused the loss of several ships, the British Eastern Fleet was withdrawn to Kilindini (Mombasa). A proposal that *Erebus* be used to defend the entrance to the Persian Gulf was turned down, so she was sent to Kilindini where she arrived on 16 May to become part of the defences at the new Fleet base.

There was nothing for *Erebus* to do until early September when she joined the force that was to land in Madagascar (now Malagasy). Diego Suarez at the north end of the island had been captured from the Vichy French in May 1942 to secure British lines of communication in the Indian Ocean, but it was later decided to occupy the whole island. A landing was therefore made at Majunga on the north-west coast on 10 September supported by *Erebus* but she did no shooting, as there was little opposition. She remained as guardship in Madagascar for six weeks, before sailing for Durban where she arrived on 2 November. Here she had a general overhaul before taking up duties as Turret Drill Ship, taking classes to sea for firing exercises. After a refit, she left Durban on 9 April 1943 for the Mediterranean to prepare for the forthcoming assault on Southern Europe from North Africa. After a stop at Kilindini, passage of the Suez Canal was attempted on 27 May without tugs, a rather unwise course of action in view of her known poor manoeuvrability. After she had touched both banks and damaged her rudder, one tug was secured ahead and another astern. On arrival at Alexandria on 1 June, she had to go into the large floating dock (AFD 5) for repairs.

She had been allocated to the bombardment force covering the Sicilian landings, so sailed from Alexandria on 3 July. Her detailed operations in support of Operation "Husky" are more conveniently described with *Roberts* and *Abercrombie* in the next chapter (p.159). After Sicily had been cleared of the Germans, *Erebus* also supported the Allied landings on the Italian mainland near Reggio early in September. As her guns were by now worn out, she did not take part in the Salerno landing but returned to Malta before sailing for the U.K. for overhaul. She departed on 18 September with the 7-knot convoy MKS.25, arriving at Devonport on 6 October 1943 for a four-month refit.

Erebus left Plymouth on 10 February 1944 for the Clyde to work-up under the command of Captain J. S. P. Colquhoun. She had been allocated as one of the bombarding ships for Opertion "Neptune", the naval part of the Normandy landings, due to take place in June. Practice bombardments were made of targets on the Kintyre peninsula, using both aircraft and ground spotting, both by day and by night. As defects had begun to reappear, she was sent to Glasgow for repairs in March, a tricky passage for such an unwieldy vessel. More bombardment practices followed at the end of April, in company with the battleships *Rodney*, *Ramillies* and U.S.S. *Texas*, which were all earmarked for "Neptune". *Roberts* joined company on 5 May so for three more weeks all the heavy gunfire support ships exercised in the Clyde, practising especially the newly developed technique of using fighter aircraft for spotting, as described in greater detail in Chapters IX and X.

Erebus departed from Greenock at midnight on 24 May to take her place in Bombarding Force "A" of the Western Task Force which was to cover the two American landings on the Normandy beaches. After brief stops in Belfast Lough and Torbay, she anchored off Weymouth on the 28th. She sailed at 16.30 on 5 June, taking station astern of convoy UA.1, part of the force destined for "Utah" beach, escorted by the U.S. destroyer *Gherardi*. After an uneventful passage through the swept channels, she dropped anchor 12 miles north-east of "Utah" beach at 04.20 on the 6th, ready to fire on any German coastal batteries which showed signs of interfering with the landings. Allied air force bombers had already attacked the batteries, while the other ships of the bombarding fleet carried out neutralising bombardments from their positions closer inshore from

Erebus *in Scapa Flow on 8 August 1941, showing among her new A.A. armament a 3-inch U.P. launcher with its rectangular shield on the forecastle.*

05.50 to H-hour at 06.30. *Erebus*' first bombardment took place five minutes after H-hour with four rounds at a battery north of the beaches. Unfortunately the blast broke the port anchor cable; it was over an hour before she next opened fire with 26 rounds at the Pernelle battery with its three 170-mm (6.7-inch) on the north-east corner of the Cherbourg peninsula. During the morning of D-day, she remained on patrol with the U.S. battleship *Nevada* and cruisers *Black Prince*, U.S.S. *Tuscaloosa* and U.S.S. *Quincy*, ready to open fire on any targets requested by the Shore Fire Control Parties. Ten rounds were fired at St. Marcouf battery in the early afternoon, *Erebus* scoring a direct hit on No. 2 gun. By the end of the day, all three of its 210-mm (8.3-inch) guns had been knocked out by naval and air bombardment.

About 16.40, *Erebus* received a request to fire on a radar station controlling the fire of the shore batteries. Just as her left gun was fired, the Marine officer commanding the turret, Captain D. A. Farquharson-Roberts, felt a thud followed by another one. On looking out of his vision slit, he saw splashes in the water ahead and reported to the bridge that the turret had been hit. When he went into the gunhouse proper, he found the guns' crews reeling about, the left gun run in at near maximum elevation and a strong smell of cordite. He then realised that the projectile in the left gun had exploded as it passed up the barrel, bursting off the jacket, splitting the gun open, distorting the cradle and trunnion supports. The breech had held, so there were no serious casualties, but the turret was unfit for further use owing to ruptured hydraulic piping. Closer examination showed that repair of the mounting would be a major dockyard job, but she had to remain at anchor off "Utah" beach for two days while arrangements were made for her return passage and repair. She sailed on the 8th as Commodore of a convoy of twelve L.S.T.s returning to Portland, having on board some 150 American glider pilots for passage. The 28 British officers simply evacuated their cabins and the wardroom in the face of such numbers, and slept at their action stations. They had their reward however: the pilots were aboard 25 hours, two days by American reckoning, and the generous subsistence allowance paid to the ship covered the wardroom mess bills for quite two months.

After a few days in Stokes Bay off Gosport, *Erebus* berthed at Devonport on 14 June. The next day she moved under the big 160-ton hammerhead crane at No. 5 Basin. The gunhouse roof was removed, the damaged gun cut halfway along its length, and both halves lifted out, followed by the cradle. The cause of the burst was traced to a faulty fuze in the American-made 15-inch H.E. projectile. As it would take some time to prepare a new cradle and gun, the turret was re-assembled with only the right gun operational. She remained anchored in Plymouth Sound for the next fortnight, available for emergency use if required. She returned to the dockyard on 8 July, where a new left gun was fitted. Gun trials were satisfactorily completed on the 22nd, so she departed for the Normandy beaches again, escorted by the destroyer *Brissenden.*

By this time, the Normandy front-line had moved out of reach of naval gunfire everywhere except on the eastern flank, where the German batteries between the Rivers Orne and Seine continued to harass Allied shipping in Seine Bay. *Erebus* was the only big gun bombardment ship now deployed off Normandy, though there were still a number of cruisers, destroyers and support vessels such as L.C.G.s (Landing Craft, Gun). Her fire was therefore reserved for the longest range targets and the well protected coast defence batteries. Between 25 July and 14 August, she fired some 150 rounds at these targets, generally from an anchored position about three miles north of Courseulles. Enemy retaliation was varied: coast defence and mobile batteries, night bombing attacks, human torpedoes (Marder), pressure mines, midget submarines (Biber), long-running torpedoes (Dackel) and explosive motor boats (Linsen). The constant vigilance by naval and air patrols, the defensive smokescreens and the counter-measures like balloons and 'window' to spoil German fire control radar prevented *Erebus* from suffering any damage.

After the collapse of the stubborn German defence around Caen and Falaise, the whole front moved rapidly eastwards during mid-August. The British I Corps was able to push along the coast towards the mouth of the Seine, so *Erebus* was called upon to help subdue the troublesome mobile batteries around Houlgate. Fire was not possible on the first day of the advance, 18 August, owing to the confused situation ashore, but on the evenings of the 19th and 20th, she fired 64 rounds at the batteries. The latter were finally overrun shortly afterwards and, although *Erebus* replenished her ammunition from the coaster *Errol* to avoid wasting time returning to Portsmouth, no more targets remained within range for her on the Normandy coastline.

Le Havre still held out north of the Seine mouth, with a dozen batteries covering the seaward approaches, ranging from 75-mm (2.95-inch) to 170-mm (6.7-inch), which had been harassing Allied shipping in Seine Bay for the past three months. An even larger battery had

Erebus *in February 1944 with much reduced freeboard aft. A new topmast has been shipped for the Type 79B air warning radar aerial and the Type 272 surface warning, while a lattice mainmast supports the Type 276 combined surface/air warning. Compare* Erebus' *final appearance with* Terror *as built on p.126.*

Erebus *in Plymouth Sound on 4 February 1944 after her final refit, showing her camouflage. The bulge has been completely submerged. Quadruple pom-poms and Oerlikons have replaced the ineffective 0.5-inch machine guns and U.P.s.*

been under construction at Octeville north of Le Havre, planned to mount three 380-mm (15-inch). Construction had however been seriously hampered by air bombing and the only gun to be installed had been knocked out by a direct hit in May 1944. Following a week at Portsmouth, *Erebus* was ordered across to bombard Le Havre at the same time as I Corps closed in, the latter's artillery being insufficient to reduce the defences. She positioned herself close to a buoy 12 miles north-west of the port, opening fire at 11.32 on 5 September. After seven rounds, the Germans returned fire, shell splashes being observed nearby. At 11.55 she was hit on the port bulge forward of the turret, taking a list of 3°. The shell was from the enemy's 170-mm battery which had three modern guns covering the seaward sector with a range as great as *Erebus*' guns — 32,000 yards. As the enemy firing continued, *Erebus* made smoke and moved farther out of range, and then returned to Portsmouth for repairs.

She was temporarily patched up and returned to bombard Le Havre on the 8th. She opened fire at 13.00 firing ten rounds before the enemy retaliated. Despite firing 'window', *Erebus* was hit with the second 170-mm salvo in the port bulge abreast the engine room. Fortunately the hole was only about 15in × 18in as the shell did not explode; there was only a slight list, so she carried on firing. Very accurate return fire was encountered, but she was not actually hit again. On the 10th, R.A.F. bombers attacked the Le Havre batteries, as they had been doing for several days, then *Erebus* opened an accurate fire from a position 12 miles south-west, followed by *Warspite* from further north. 'Window' and smokescreens were put up to confuse the enemy fire control. From 10.15 onwards, *Erebus* put 112 rounds into her targets, the spotting fighters reporting about 30 as hits. *Erebus* remained unmolested by the shore batteries as she was outside their principal training sector, although *Warspite* was given some attention. In the late afternoon, I Corps launched its attack on the German defences, which had been thoroughly demoralised by the combined sea and air onslaught. Le Havre surrendered on the 12th, the British Corps Commander signalling his thanks to the bombarding ships for their support.

On returning to Portsmouth on 11 September, she was taken in hand by the dockyard to complete the damage repairs and to change her guns. The unexploded 170-mm shell was found in the bulge by dockyard workers but it was a young sailor who had to remove it. *Erebus* was ordered to Dover early in October in company with *Roberts* to support operations against the Belgian and Dutch ports and their coastal defences. The two ships formed part of the bombarding squadron for the assault on the island of Walcheren on 1 November, described in detail in the next chapter (p.167). Thereafter both monitors remained based at Portsmouth, one being at 48 hours' notice anchored out in Spithead on call for any further bombardments. Although several were planned, none took place; for example, Operation "Nestegg", the re-occupation of the Channel Islands planned for mid-March with *Roberts*, was deferred until after the surrender of Germany.

After five years' arduous war service, *Erebus* was in no condition to join her two more modern sisters allocated to the East Indies Fleet to continue the war against Japan. She was therefore sent round to the Nore, arriving on 3 July 1945, where she bacame Turret Drill Ship at Chatham again after a lapse of 19 years, also providing accommodation for Stoker Mechanics under training. She was approved to scrap a year later, so left Chatham under tow for Rosyth on 13 July 1946, where her guns could be removed. She made her final four-mile voyage to Inverkeithing for breaking up on 29 January 1947.

§8 Modifications

Such was the benefit of a design that could incorporate most of the lessons learned in the earlier monitors that few modifications were made to *Erebus* and *Terror* during WW1, and these confined mostly to secondary armament. *Terror* was quickly fitted with two 6-inch Q.F. II like *Erebus*, while both ships soon got a second 3-inch H.A. and late in 1917 both got two more 6-inch, making a total of four guns each. During the repairs to *Terror*'s bow at this time, her bow rudder was removed or, rather, not replaced. Two 2-pdr pom-poms were added on sponsons at the stern, while the two 12-pdr were resited amidships, the origninal embrasures being plated up to keep the upper deck drier. As in *Marshal Soult*, first four then eight single 4-inch B.L. IX were fitted in both ships in the summer of 1918. At the same time, the little used conning tower was removed and replaced by a platform carrying the two 12-pdr, now converted to H.A. firing. The two 3-inch H.A. remained at the after end of the forecastle deck, so that by the end of WW1, both ships carried:—

2—15″, 8—4″, 2—12pdr H.A., 2—3″, 2—2pdr.

A secondary control position was added abaft the funnel, while the two 24-inch searchlights at the base of the mast were replaced by two 36-inch on towers close to the funnel. A normal battleship-type 15-foot rangefinder was fitted in the turret, as already existed in *Marshal Soult*.

Between the wars, the ships were modified as required for their variety of duties. During 1924, three of *Terror*'s 4-inch were temporarily removed to provide more space on the forecastle deck. Although her major refit prior to going out to Singapore cost £72,000, most of the changes were not apparent, being largely internal. Improvements were made to accommodation and ventilation, while refrigerated stores were fitted for the first time in a British ship designed as a monitor. A Dreyer fire control table was installed in the lower steering position on the main deck to improve her anti-ship gunnery capability, necessary for service at Singapore. As her 12-pdr and 2-pdr guns were removed, changes were made to the secondary magazines, including extensions into spaces previously occupied by oil fuel tanks and kit lockers. Much of the extra space was fitted out to carry over a thousand rounds of 8-inch and 6-inch ammunition as reserves for cruisers in the Far East. Thus, apart from a coat of white paint, *Terror*'s external appearance was little changed from 1918. Deep displacement was now

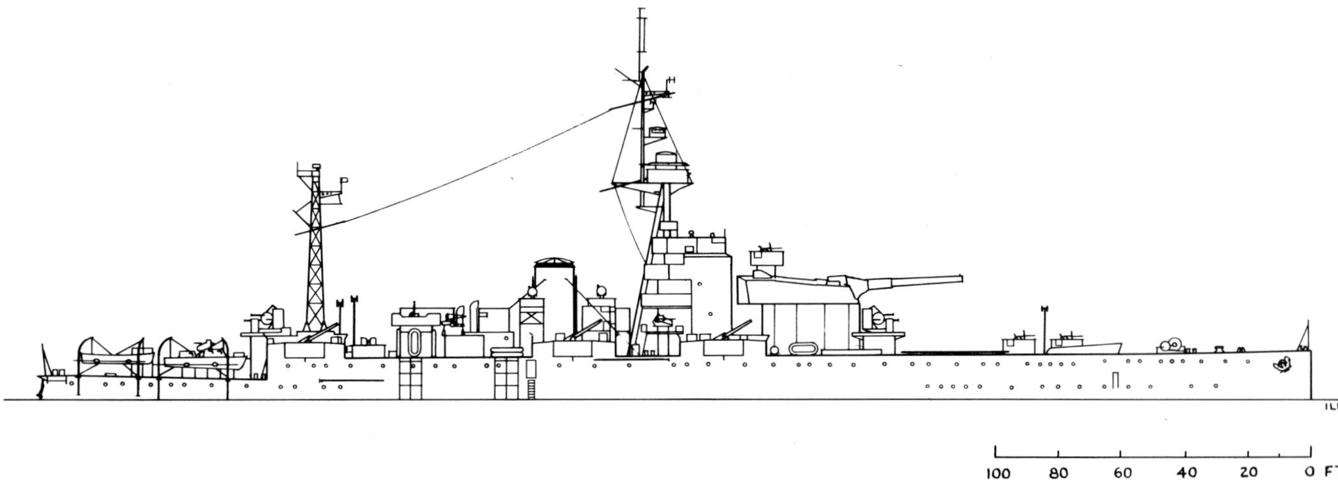

By 1944, Erebus' *profile had changed considerably compared with her original appearance — superstructure extensions, additional A.A. armament, radar, lattice mainmast, closing in of the sides of the upper deck, submergence of the bulge (and boot-topping).*

8600 tons, so her true standard displacement[1] was about 7830 tons. Officially her standard displacement was listed as only 7200 tons, but this was a mistake which stemmed from the lack of recorded data on the ship as completed.

With the threat of war in 1939, *Terror* commenced a refit at Singapore in April to improve her H.A. armament and to replace her 15-inch barrels. The eight low angle 4-inch were replaced by six single H.A./L.A. 4-inch Q.F. V. The two 3-inch were removed and replaced by two quadruple 0.5-inch Mk III machine guns, basically similar to the gun fitted in tanks and aircraft. No changes were made to her armament at Malta in 1940, but she did get additional armour plating on the upper deck, similar to *Erebus* (see below) and her sides were fully plated. Fresh water capacity was trebled, this and the other changes increasing her deep displacement to a final figure before her loss of about 9400 tons.

The modifications made to *Erebus* were considerable, especially during WW2. Her conversion to Turret Drill Ship and Cadet Training Ship in 1926 necessitated the provision of additional accommodation and class-rooms. The space was obtained partly by glazing in the sides of the upper deck and partly by fitting cabins on the sides of the forecastle deck in place of six of the 4-inch guns, leaving only two. Two years later, she was disfigured by the erection of a huge deckhouse on the forecastle, used as a recreation room and gymnasium by the cadets.

Her £85,000 refit in 1939 by Thornycroft for guardship duties in South Africa restored her almost to the basic simplicity of the original design. All the deckhouses were removed except for a small one abaft the funnel, while the upper deck was opened up again at the sides. New 15-inch guns were installed but her secondary armament was reduced to only the two 3-inch H.A., the 4-inch being considered unnecessary for her duties. In this condition, *Erebus* was no longer suitable for war in European waters so, after war broke out, she was soon back in shipyard hands. The original 2-inch upper deck was reckoned proof against 250-lb S.A.P. bombs dropped from up to 2000 feet but inadequate against the sort of attacks that were now anticipated from high-level and dive-bombers. A number of re-armouring proposals were put forward late in 1939, generally incorporating two or three inches of armour added to the existing upper and main deck plating. That finally adopted provided an extra two inches of N.C. armour on the upper deck over a length of 220 feet amidships, making a total of four inches over the magazines and machinery spaces, and an extra inch on the main deck — see drawing on p.125. The same plans were also approved for *Terror* and the manufacture of the necessary 366 tons of armour plate for each ship was put in hand.

The armour was fitted at *Erebus*' 1940 refit, when the upper deck was plated up at the sides for good. Three single 4-inch H.A./L.A. were fitted in zarebas on each side of the forecastle deck as in *Terror*, with associated H.A.C.P. (High Angle Calculating Position) port and starboard. Four quadruple 0.5-inch guns were also fitted, two mountings forward and two aft. In addition, a brand new A.A. weapon favoured by Churchill was provided: the rocket launcher. Two 20-barrel U.P. (unrotated projectile) mountings were fitted on a platform abaft the funnel, capable of firing a cloud of 7-inch parachute and cable projectiles into the path of an attacking dive-bomber. Each rocket released a parachute carrying a small aerial mine on a cable which was intended to catch on the aircraft's wing and explode. A normal 3-inch rocket motor was used, filled out to 7-inch diameter by the mine canister.

Other modifications included removal of the topmast, fitting of degaussing cables on the hull externally and provision of Carley life-rafts and their launching skids, but radar was not yet fitted. All these changes considerably increased her deep displacement to 9100 tons, with serious effects on her handling, as discussed in the next section. A substantially increased crew was

[1] Standard displacement was introduced by the Washington Treaty of 1922, broadly defined as full load displacement minus fuel and reserve feed water.

required to man all the extra equipment, her authorised wartime complement being raised to 308. The usual wartime disruptive camouflage scheme was adopted, which did not include the display of the ship's pendant number. Apart from the small monitors showing their M. numbers, which coincided with their pendant numbers during WW1, such numbers were never displayed on any monitor. Further improvements were made to *Erebus*' armament throughout the war, as shown in the table.

Vickers 2-pdr was an impressive-looking weapon in operation, delivering nearly 400 rounds per minute, but its effective range was less than a mile and its accuracy and mechanical reliability could have been better. Until the Swiss-designed 20-mm Oerlikon became available from British production in 1941, the 2-pdr was the only British close range weapon with any reasonable chance of downing enemy aircraft. Late in 1941, seven single Oerlikons were installed around the forecastle deck and

SECONDARY ARMAMENT FITTED IN *EREBUS*

Mounting	1938	1939	1940	1941	1942-3	1944-5
Single 4-inch C.P.I	2	—	—	—	—	—
Single 4-inch H.A.III	—	—	6	6	6	6
Single 3-inch H.A.II	2	2	—	—	—	—
Quadruple 2-pdr Mk VII	—	—	—	—	3	3
Single 2-pdr Mk VIII	—	—	—	—	1	1
Single 40-mm Mk III	—	—	—	1	1	1
Twin 20-mm Mk V	—	—	—	—	—	4
Single 20-mm Mk II	—	—	—	—	7	7
Quadruple 0.5-inch Mk III	—	—	4	4	—	—
20-barrel 7-inch U.P.	—	—	2	2	—	—
Single 3-inch U.P.	—	—	—	3	—	—

Normal outfits of ammunition per barrel, excluding practice rounds were:

15-inch	60 C.P.C., 40 H.E.
4-inch	250 H.E.T.F., 150 S.A.P. + star (50 per ship)
3-inch	150 + star (50 per ship)
2-pdr	1800
40-mm	1440
20-mm	2400
0.5-inch	2500
7-inch U.P.	3

By the time *Erebus* left for the Indian Ocean at the end of 1941, the 20-barrel U.P. mountings had been removed, as well as the three single U.P. mountings for 3-inch rockets. The latter had been mounted late in 1940, two on the forecastle and one on the quarterdeck, differing from the 7-inch U.P. in that they carried a normal time fuze and explosive charge. This 'Harvey Projector' had been developed from a weapon originally designed for the Army; particulars are given on p.193. In practice the 7-inch U.P.s had proved ineffective at downing enemy aircraft. It was found that the wire barrage took so long to establish itself that it could easily be dodged by enemy aircraft, while the weapons were too slow to reload to allow a second salvo. They were also dangerous to the ships carrying them, owing to the mines tending to drift back on to the firing ship and the risk of fires from the cordite propellant in the ammunition lockers. The 3-inch was not accurate enough to score a direct hit and trials with an early design of proximity fuze were unsuccessful.

In place of these weapons, three quadruple pom-poms had been installed, two sided abreast the turret and one on the quarterdeck, plus a single 2-pdr abaft the funnel flanked by a solitary 40-mm Bofors. The multiple pom-pom developed between the wars from the pre-WW1 on the turret, providing a useful defence against dive-bombers and low-flying aircraft — C-in-C Home Fleet had commented a year earlier that he would prefer one Oerlikon to four U.P.s.

The demands of war service and the increasing crew numbers necessitated continuous extensions to accommodation, electrical generating capacity, fresh water storage, evaporating capacity and store-rooms. By the end of *Erebus*' 1944 refit at Devonport, she carried five radar sets: two Type 285 A.A. gunnery sets dating from 1941 — one for each of the H.A. rangefinder/directors for the 4-inch; one Type 79B air warning set with aerial on the fore-topmast in place of the previous Type 286 combined surface/air warning; one Type 272 surface warning with its 'lantern' just above the spotting top, and one Type 276 combined warning with aerial on the new lattice mainmast aft, together with associated interrogators. With all the extra equipment, her bulge was now completely submerged, as she drew 13ft 6in forward and 14ft aft, with a deep displacement of 9800 tons — some 15% above the original figure — each extra 60 tons adding one inch to her draft. The metacentric height had now been reduced from the original 32ft to about 6ft, due to a rise of 2ft in the centre of gravity and a drop of 24ft in the height of the metacentre following the submergence of the bulge.

§9 Performance

By comparison with the earlier large monitors, *Erebus* and *Terror* were relatively fast and handy vessels, although still poor when viewed against ships of normal form. In the waters around Dover, they did all that was asked of them, their reliability making them the backbone of the Monitor Squadron during WW1. With a clean hull, they could make a maximum of 13 knots but lost about one knot when several months out of drydock, as shown in the curves of horsepower, r.p.m., fuel consumption and endurance against speed.

During WW2, so many alterations were made that performance deteriorated considerably. The erections added at the aft end of *Erebus*' forecastle deck in 1940, plus her increased draft made her difficult to control. With wind or sea on the beam or quarter, she required full rudder just to maintain course while, if conditions worsened, even working the engines was of no avail. Her centre of pressure had been moved so far aft by the modifications that her stern was blown round, with her bows pointing upwind. In such conditions, there were only two actions possible: heave to or go astern. The latter was not a popular manoeuvre as, with the reduced freeboard aft, the quarterdeck was easily swamped and the boats damaged. In pilotage waters, it was not really safe to handle her without tugs, so navigation in swept channels through minefields was always risky. Only in a head wind could a course be held, but at the expense of a fair drop in speed. Often the simplest way of altering course upwind was to turn almost full circle downwind to reach the desired course.

In 1940, Nalder made urgent representations to the Admiralty about the ship's lack of control, requesting that the now plated-over bow rudder be put back into operation, as he considered that handling would be improved thereby. D.N.C.'s Department were not keen on his suggestion as the bow steering gear had been removed at the last refit and scrapped. Instead, a larger stern rudder was suggested, in conjunction with rigging a temporary canvas screen forward, which would balance the windage profile. A 30% larger rudder of 130 sq ft was fitted, trials in December 1940 showing that conditions were improved without having to fit the screen forward. But the margin of improvement was modest; with beam winds of Force 6 to 7, 25° to 30° of weather helm still had to be carried.

The weights continually being added to *Erebus* during WW2 seriously reduced her freeboard aft by about $2^1/_2$ feet. Parts of the quarterdeck were thus only about 5ft above the waterline so that, with the submergence of the bulge, she became a very wet ship in quite moderate sea conditions. A further consequence of these alterations was a drop in speed and endurance. Although she managed a creditable 12.53 knots on the measured mile in the Clyde in February 1944, her best speed normally during WW2 was about $11^1/_2$ knots. This could drop well below ten under adverse conditions of weather and hull fouling — indeed when rounding the Cape in January 1942, she could make no headway against the strong current and was reputedly carried backwards at two knots!

Fuel consumption at cruising speed was around 92 tons of oil per day at sea; in harbour about 9 tons. Her original endurance was reduced, not only by her lower speed, but also by her bunker capacity being cut back by 90 tons in 1940 to provide additional space internally. By the end of the war, her endurance at maximum speed was down to about 1700 miles but, by this time, her days of long distance voyages were over. In practice, she would

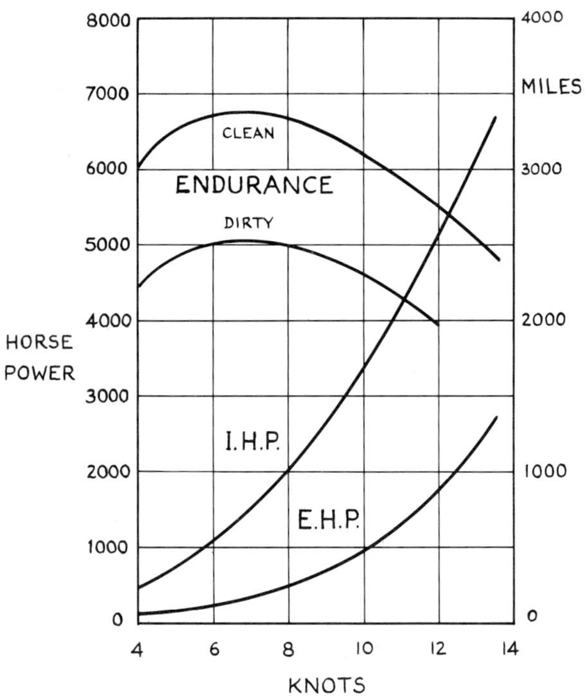

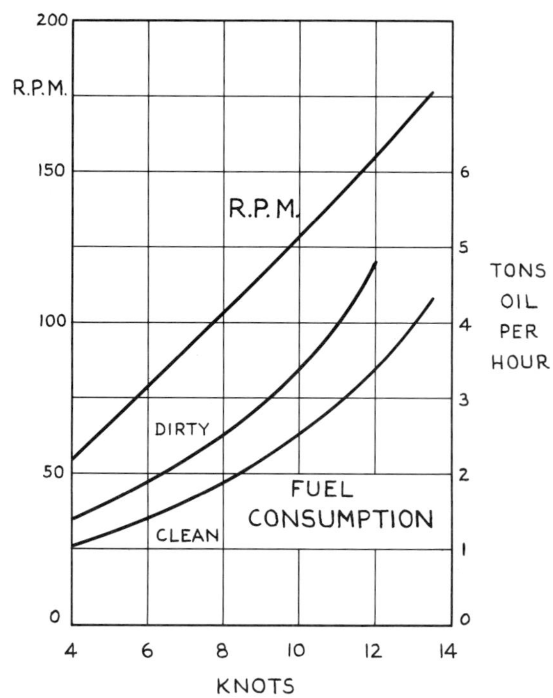

The performance curves for Erebus *and* Terror *show the indicated horsepower developed by the engines in service, and the effective horsepower required to tow the ship estimated from model experiments. E.H.P./I.H.P. is a measure of propulsive efficiency — about 40% at top speed. The endurance curves are based on 780 tons of oil fuel, and show economical speed as about seven knots. The 'dirty' condition corresponds to about six months out of dock, resulting in a loss of about $1^1/_2$ knots in maximum speed compared with clean out of dock, and a decrease of endurance of about 25%.*

'coast-hop' between frequent refuelling bases on long voyages in a manner reminiscent of the WW1 coal-burners. Less strain was put on the engines this way and the overworked engineers given a chance to put right the enless minor breakdowns that occurred in the old ship.

A rare view of Erebus *in Spithead early in 1945, showing her now in standard light grey camouflage with blue band. The Type 272 radar has been removed. Single Oerlikons can be seen in their pits, twin abreast the bridge and on the quarterdeck. Ready-use lockers surround the 4-inch guns.*

EREBUS and TERROR — TECHNICAL PARTICULARS

Displacement and Dimensions 8000 tons nominal, 8450 tons deep. Length 405′-0″ o.a., breadth 88′-2″, draft 11′-8″ deep.

Weight Distribution Armament 860 tons, ammunition 300, protection 2530, hull 2970, equipment 350, machinery and R.F.W. 700, oil fuel (nominal) 250. Designed totai 7960 tons.

Complement 13 officers, 191 men.

Armament 2—15″ (twin) (100 H.E. r.p.g.), 2—6″ Q.F. (200 r.p.g.), 2—12pdr (200 r.p.g.), 1—3″ H.A. (300 r.p.g.), 4—0.303″ Maxim (5000 r.p.g.).

Protection As 14-inch monitors except: upper deck over 15-inch magazine 4″ N.C.; gunhouse 13″ C. front, 11″ C. sides and rear, 5″ N.C. roof (4¼″ *Erebus*), 3″ H.T. floor.

Machinery Twin screw 4-cyl triple-expansion. Four Babcock & Wilcox boilers. 6000 I.H.P. at 170 r.p.m. Oil fuel 784 tons. Endurance 2480 miles at 12 knots.

Speed 12 knots designed and service. Trials: *Erebus* 14.1, *Terror* 13.09 knots.

Construction *Erebus* Harland & Wolff, Govan laid down 12 Oct 1915/launched 19 Jun 1916/completed 2 Sep 1916. *Terror* H. & W. Belfast 26 Oct 1915/18 May 1916/6 Aug 1916.

Disposal *Erebus* scrapped Ward, Inverkeithing 29 Jan 1947; *Terror* sunk 24 Feb 1941.

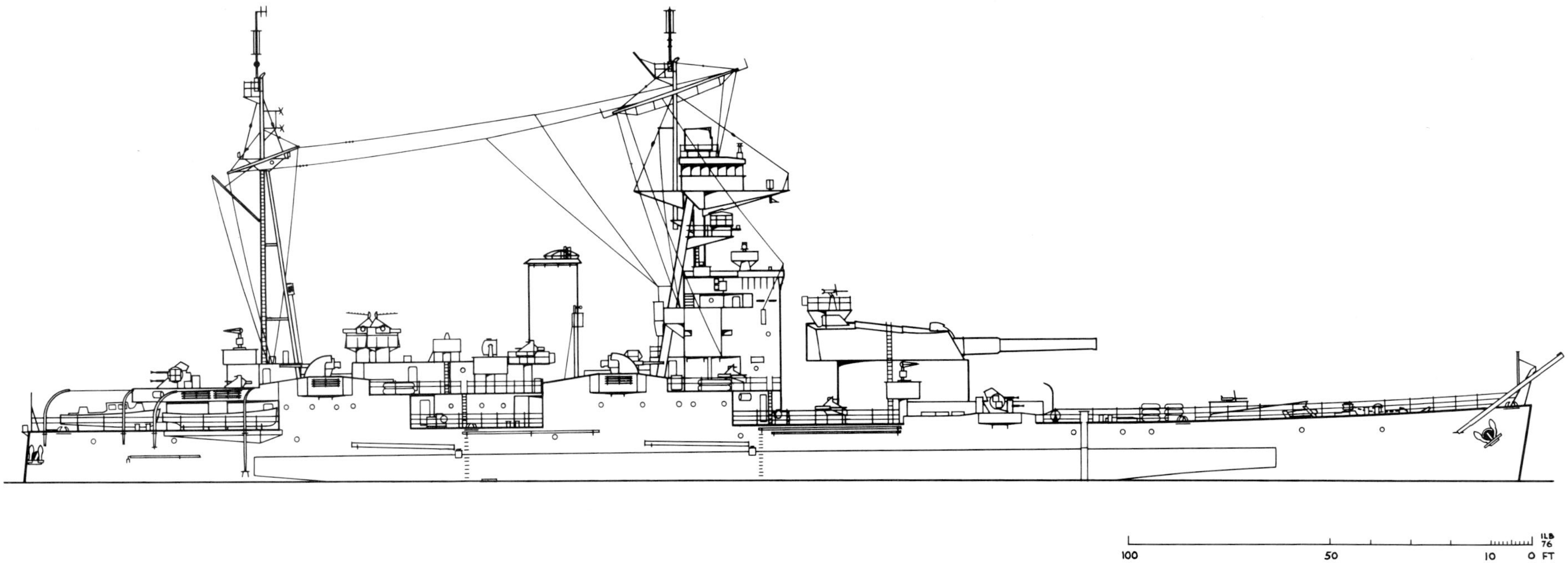

Abercrombie *as completed. The final monitor design — in principle the same basic layout as her namesake of three decades earlier, but much refined in detail for WW2 operations.* Roberts *was completed with a shorter funnel, 4-inch guns one deck lower and no Oerlikons on the turret.*

CHAPTER IX

THE LAST 15-INCH GUN MONITORS

H.M.S. ROBERTS and ABERCROMBIE

§1 Design

Winston Churchill returned to the Government as First Lord of the Admiralty on the day that Britain declared war on Germany for the second time, 3 September 1939. He lost no time re-familiarising himself with the Royal Navy, making visits to ships and naval establishments. Both at Portsmouth and Chatham, he found monitors dating from WW1 — *Erebus* earmarked for South Africa and *Marshal Soult* as Turret Drill Ship at the Nore. Including *Terror* at Singapore, there were but three monitors left in anything resembling their original state out of the fleet of 40 that he had authorised during 1914-15. *Marshal Ney* and a few of the small monitors still existed but converted to support roles. No new monitors had been proposed between the wars; not only would they have been of limited value, but they would have been regarded as battleships under treaty tonnage quotas if they mounted guns of greater calibre than 8-inch.

With Germany likely to strike France again through the Low Countries, Churchill realised that coast bombardment vessels could again play a useful role in any new conflict off the shallow waters of the southern North Sea or even in the Baltic. Anxious to make the monitors fully effective again, he minuted on 4 November:[1]

> "We really must get the monitors into working order. The *Erebus* is already in good condition, but her deck must be armoured against air attack. Pray let me have at our next meeting a definite plan for putting a strong armoured deck upon *Erebus* and *Marshal Soult*. How long would it take? *Soult* requires new engines. Let me have estimates in time and money for bringing her up to the mark."

A detailed survey of *Soult* showed that it would not be worth reconstructing her but, as her turret was still in reasonable condition, her twin 15-inch guns could be transferred to a new hull with more powerful machinery.

Preliminary design work was put in hand right away, including model tests at A.E.W. on hull lines derived from *Erebus* who had the best of the WW1 forms. As it was estimated that 12 knots could be obtained on trials with about 3500 H.P., this more modest power introduced the possibility of installing diesel machinery instead of steam. Twin Atlas diesels were suggested, which would be very economical in fuel consumption. However diesels would take longer to build than steam turbines so, as delivery was required in twelve months, it was decided to use the latter. As with the WW1 ships, a bulged form was adopted which would provide good protection against torpedoes and mines for the 54-foot wide main hull. With machinery spaces about 32ft shorter than *Erebus*, the hull length could be reduced below the latter's 385ft B.P.; the final figure selected was 354ft B.P. In association with a moulded breadth of 88ft and a draft of 12ft, the preliminary estimate of deep displacement was about 8380 tons — about the same as *Erebus* when new.

The protection of the hull took particular account of the threat of air attack, but otherwise followed broadly the lines of the WW1 ships. The vertical protection was designed to resist 6-inch naval gun or 9-inch howitzer projectiles striking normally at 90° to the surface of the armour. The side armour was disposed at an angle of about 35° to the horizontal, corresponding to the angle of descent of long range projectiles. The side protection system below water was designed on the pattern adopted in the new *King George V* class battleships and Fleet carriers then under construction. A 17-foot wide sandwich layer was arranged in the bulge abreast the vitals of the ship, consisting of an outer air space, a jacket space partly filled with water and an inner air space, giving protection against torpedoes carrying a 1000-lb warhead. The theory was that detonation should take place as far as possible from the main hull proper. The outer air space served to reduce the pressure pulse set up in the sea by the explosion. The middle water space or jacket absorbed, distributed and dissipated the energy of the explosion over a wide area and reduced the momentum of splinters. The inner air space prevented the pressure waves in the water jacket from being transmitted to the protective bulkhead. The plating of this bulkhead formed the side of the hull proper in way of the bulge, consisting of a double thickness of $^3/_4$-inch D.1 quality steel,[2] supported by heavy stiffeners. Yet further protection was provided by watertight compartments inboard of this protective bulkhead in way of machinery spaces and main magazine to limit flooding. The side sloping armour belt, consisting of 5-inch N.C. plates abreast the magazine and 4-inch elsewhere, was laid on top of the two inboard bulge compartments for ease of construction, unlike the WW1 ships where it was fitted internally. A water ballast ring main, served by four 550-ton per hour pumps, connected all these watertight

[1] *Roberts* Ship's Cover, N.M.M.

[2] D and D.1 quality steels were improved high-tensile steels introduced by the Admiralty in the 1920s.

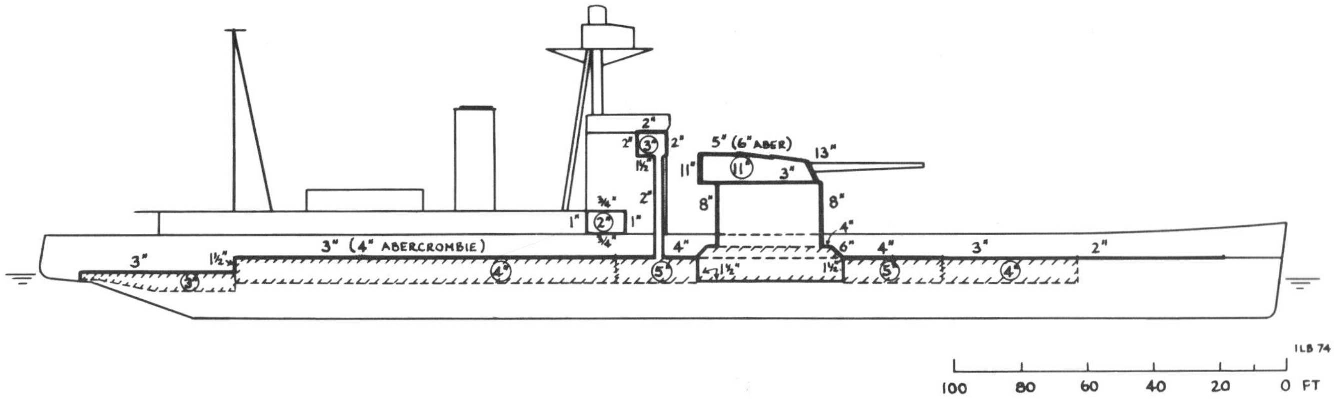

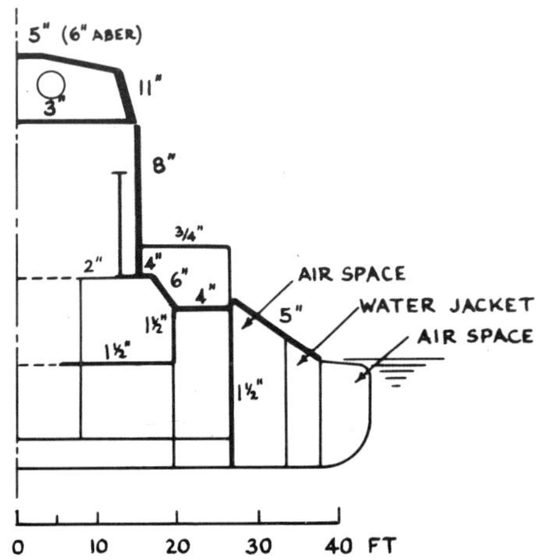

Roberts *and* Abercrombie *had a well balanced protective scheme, especially the latter with her thicker main deck, capable of resisting a wide range of air, surface and underwater attacks.*

compartments. The system could be used to pump out damaged spaces or to flood magazines above the waterline or to fill tanks to correct heel or trim.

The horizontal deck protection was intended to resist a 500-lb bomb dropped from a height of 12,000ft, necessitating 3-inch N.C. plating. The protection was fitted on the main deck rather than the upper deck to reduce the height of the side armour. As the forecastle deck extended right to the stern, unlike the WW1 ships, this level was now described as the upper deck, the old upper deck level now becoming the main deck. The cramped circular conning tower of the WW1 designs was dropped in favour of an armoured compartment built into the bridge structure below the compass platform, as in the new battleships. Plating varied from 3-inch to 1½-inch, proof against medium projectiles and splinters.

§2 Armament

Although the main armament was 25 years' old, the 15-inch was still a very effective and accurate weapon. Apart from a general overhaul, the only important change needed was modification to handle the new longer 6 c.r.h. projectile, just coming into service as the standard 15-inch ammunition. More modern fire control equipment was to be installed, including a Dreyer table which would enable the corrections for firing underway to be easily calculated. As with the earlier monitors, a director was sited at the tripod masthead above the spotting top. The transmitting station with the Dreyer table was on the lower deck beneath the bridge under armour, receiving information from aloft, then calculating and transmitting bearing and elevation to the receivers in the turret. The conspicuous spotting top was much more comfortable than in the WW1 ships, as it was glassed in and heated.

In view of the monitors' likely operations off hostile shores, the selection of anti-aircraft armament was given special attention. The original suggestion of six single 4-inch as in *Erebus* and *Terror* was not regarded as adequate for a new construction monitor. Two twin 4.5-inch between deck mountings were proposed, similar to those being fitted in the reconstructed capital ships and in the new Fleet carriers, but there were not enough available. The only remaining suitable H.A. equipment worthy of such a ship was the standard twin 4-inch H.A./L.A., which formed the secondary armament of cruisers and the main armament for A.A. sloops. The Mk XVI* gun was already proving a useful weapon, with an A.A. ceiling of 39,000 feet and a rate of fire of 15-20 rounds per minute. In conjunction with a combined rangefinder/director, the H.A.C.P. could calculate and pass to the guns the appropriate bearing, elevation and

(Opposite) *The upper drawing shows* Abercrombie*'s inboard profile, where frames are spaced 4ft apart. The lower cross-sections are from* Roberts' *as fitted general arrangement.*

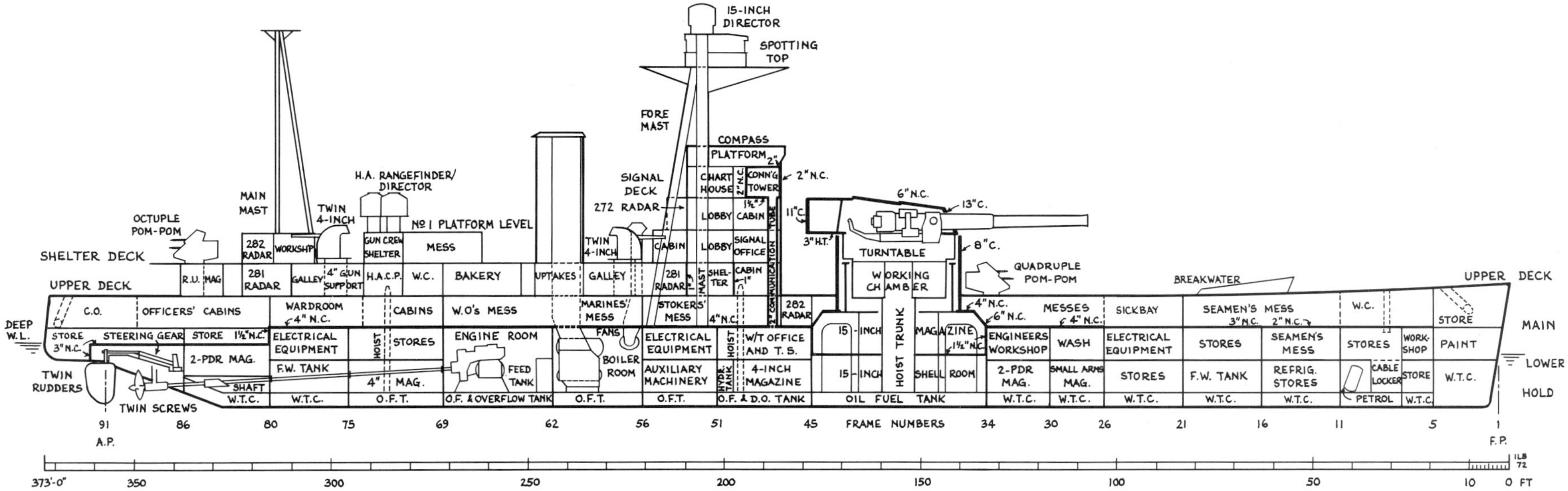

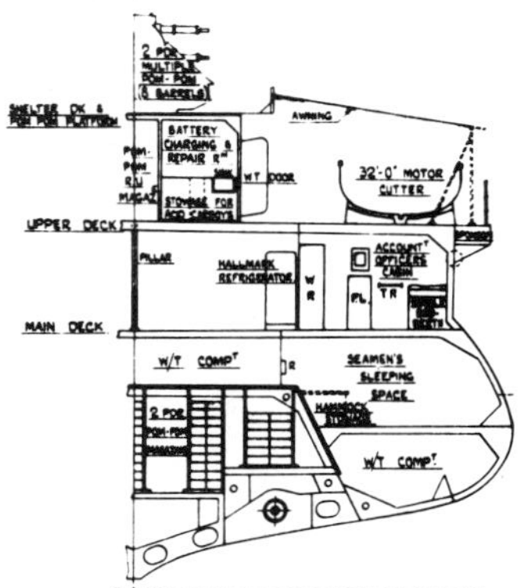

SECTION AT FR. 84.

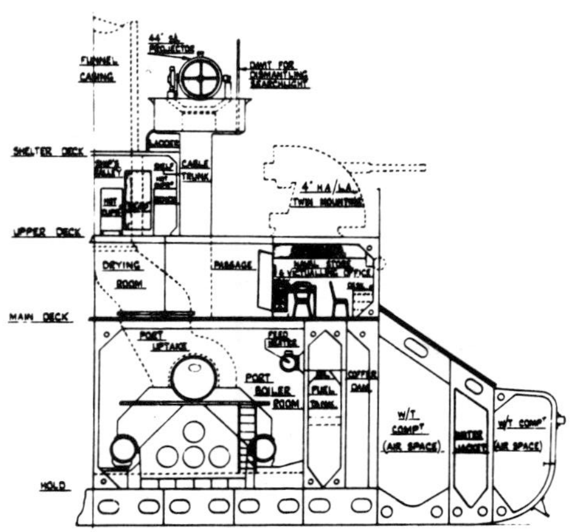

SECTION AT FR. 59.

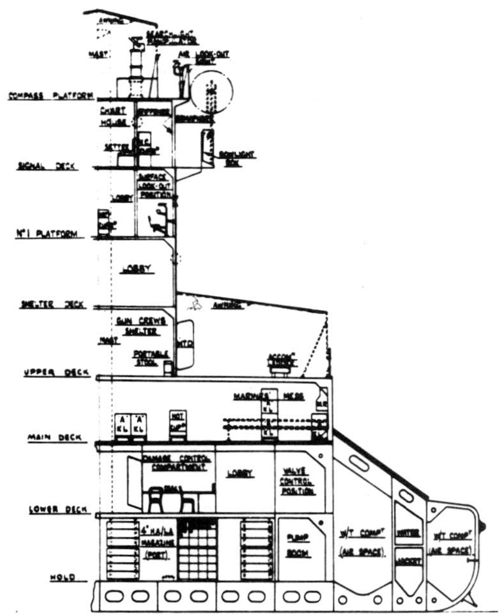

SECTION AT FR. 50.

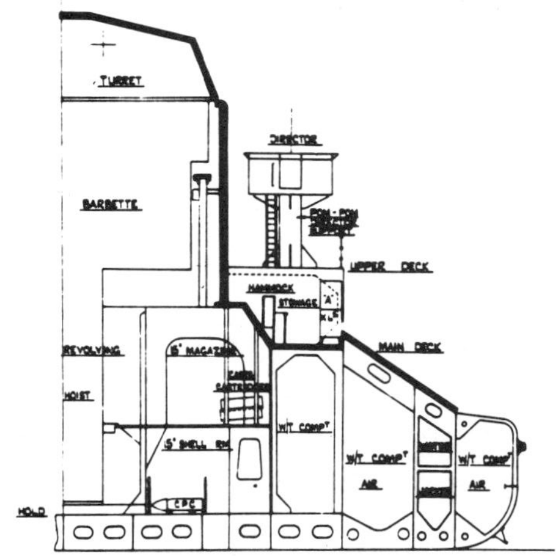

SECTION AT FR. 39½.

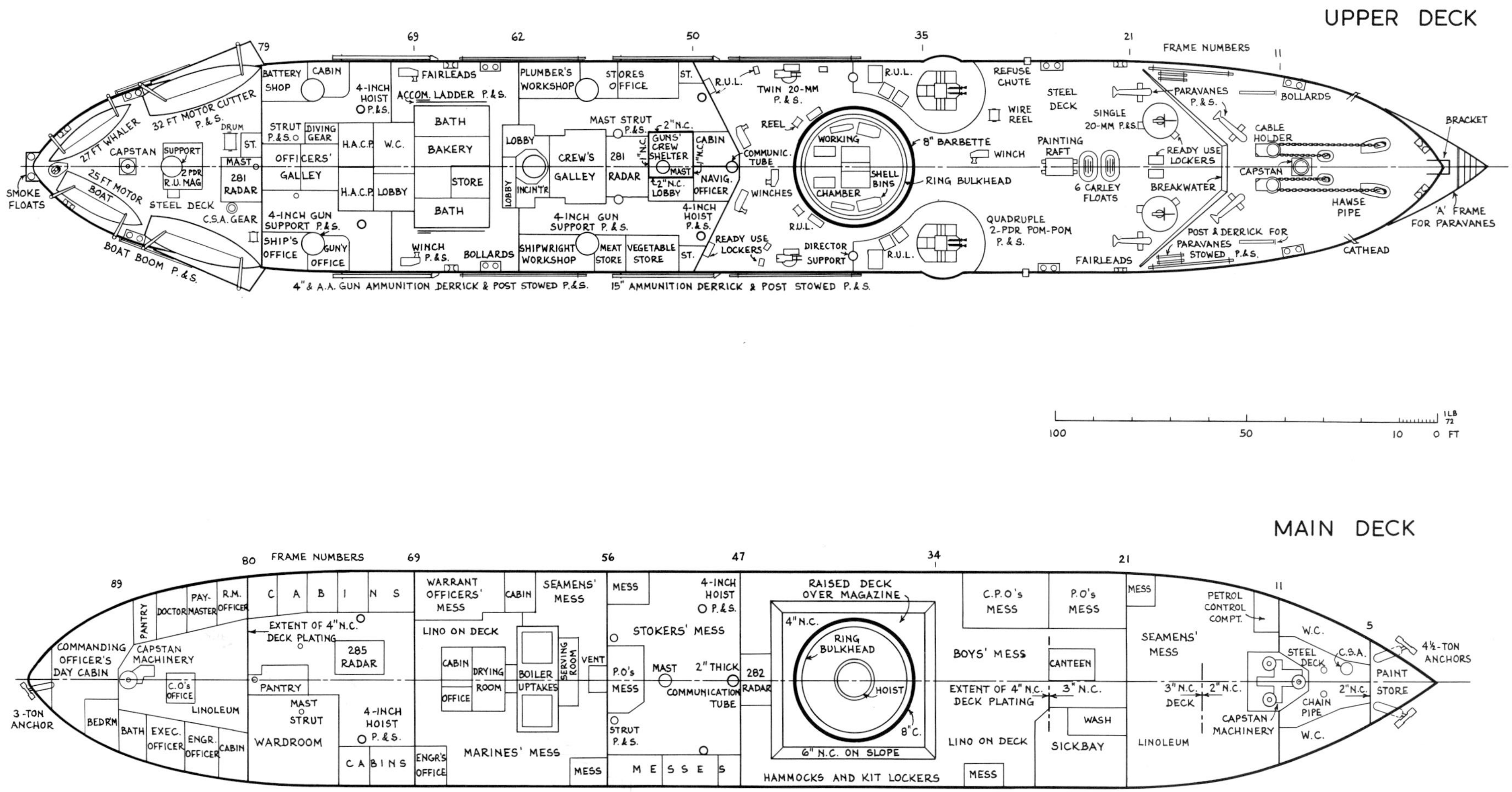

Abercrombie's *upper and main deck. With a crew more than double the WW1 monitors, the main deck was completely enclosed to provide maximum accommodation. The cramped arrangement of boats and after mooring arrangements resulted from the design error of siting the turret too far aft. With her 4-inch guns sited on the upper deck,* Roberts' *superstructure did not extend out to the ship's side, and her accommodation was less extensive.*

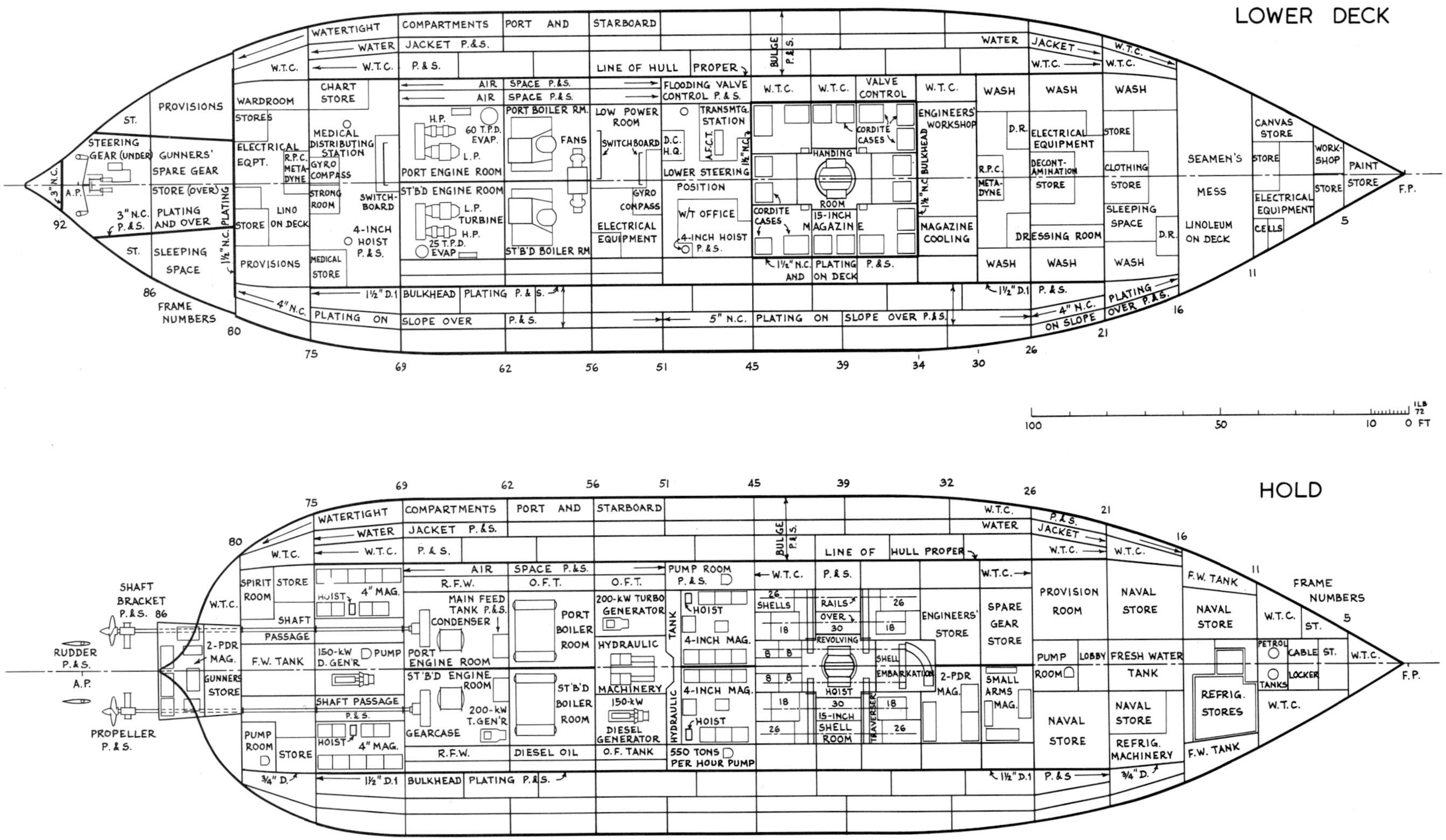

Abercrombie's *lower deck and hold. The side protection abreast the turret and machinery spaces took up half the breadth. The forward lines were finer than in the first monitors — compare with the 14-inch ships on p.19.*

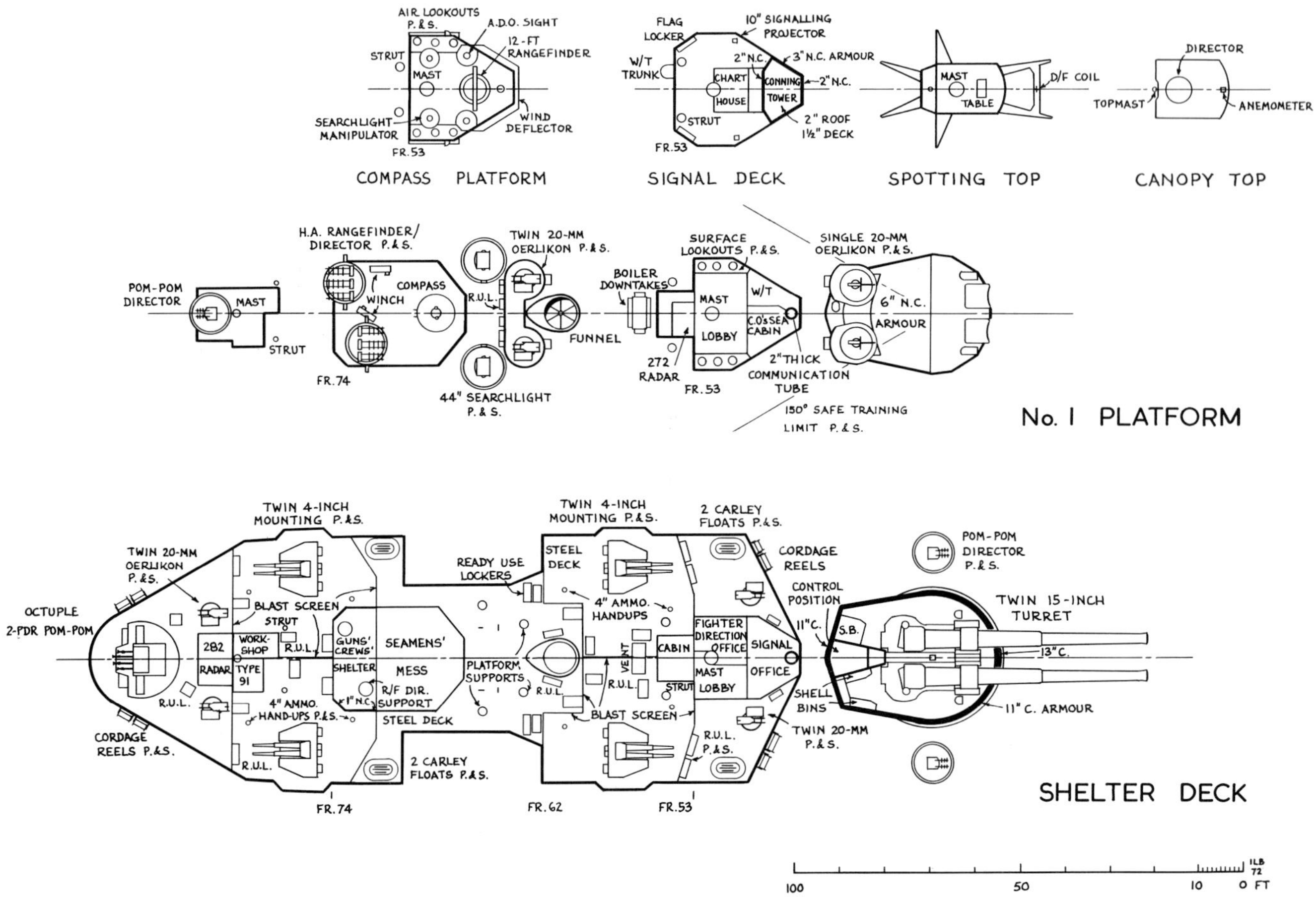

Abercrombie's superstructure decks. Decks were generally painted steel, although the compass platform and roof of the seamen's mess were planked. Roberts' *deckhouses were less extensive, and she only mounted eight Oerlikons as completed.*

fuze-setting. The latter determined the time interval between firing the shell and its detonation — direct hits on a fast-moving aircraft were unlikely but a near-miss burst could be lethal. Multiple 2-pdr pom-poms were to be the principal close range weapons, 0.5-inch machine guns being rejected, but the newly designed U.P. mounting for firing 7-inch rockets was included as a stopgap while pom-poms were in short supply. The proposal originally adopted was for two quadruple Mk VII pom-poms and three 20-barrel U.P. mountings.

The siting of the 4-inch guns was straightforward: two twin mountings port and starboard abreast the funnel, surrounded by $^3/_4$-inch bullet-proof screens. Each mounting was served by an endless-chain ammunition hoist, one each side from the forward 4-inch magazine immediately abaft the 15-inch shell-room to the upper deck, and another pair to the after mountings from their magazine abaft the engine room. Siting of the pom-poms was more difficult. A centre-line location would give the best arc of fire, but a forecastle mounting would suffer from blast whenever the 15-inch guns fired on bearings within 65° of the bow. If the mountings were sited on each side of the turret, one would always be usable, except when the 15-inch were firing within 10° of the bow. The latter arrangement was the one finally adopted, plus one U.P. mounting on the centre-line aft and one on each side of the bridge on the upper deck. The end result was an A.A. armament as good as a new cruiser's, and much more powerful than *Erebus* or *Terror* even after their latest refits.

§3 Construction

While design work was going ahead, preliminary arrangements for construction were being made. Building of the *Lion* class battleships had been suspended for one year in October 1939 to speed up work on ships which could be completed more quickly. John Brown's of Clydebank had been allocated the third ship of the class, *Conqueror,* so had intended to lay her keel immediately after the launch of the battleship *Duke of York*. With *Conqueror* postponed, it was anticipated that they could lay down and launch a monitor on their battleship berth before construction was due to be resumed. John Brown were therefore involved in discussions about design and construction from November 1939 onwards. Although the original intention had been to transfer as much equipment and auxiliary machinery as possible from *Soult,* it was found that all her electrical equipment was designed for 105 volts d.c., compared with the current R.N. standard of 220. Deck and internal fittings were not in very good condition, so it was decided to transfer nothing other than the turret, the barbette armour and the hydraulic pumping machinery. The plan was for the turret to be refitted in the ship at Portsmouth by Vickers-Armstrong and then shipped in pieces to Clydebank for installation in the new hull.

The preliminary design work had been carried out under the title "Replacement *Marshal Soult,* 1939 Monitor Design" but, as the final design characteristics were not approved until 6 February 1940, the ship actually became part of the 1940 New Construction Programme. Her official identification was J.1573 — her Admiralty Job Number; later she was given the name *Roberts,* the same as one of the first monitors.

As the design progressed, the estimated deep displacement crept up to 8675 tons, with a corresponding standard displacement of 7505 tons. Some objections had been raised to building a monitor at all, on the grounds that large quantities of armour plate would be required which could be better used in tank production. In fact, little over half of the total weight of protection was new armour quality plate, the remainder coming from *Soult* or being D quality material, so this objection was overruled. Although preparatory work on the new monitor had already started, the formal order for hull and machinery was not sent to John Brown until 16 March, with delivery scheduled for April 1941.

In common with contemporary British warships, the design of the steam turbines was carried out by the Parsons Marine Steam Turbine Company of Wallsend, for building under licence at Clydebank. Parsons based the 4800-S.H.P. design on the twin screw river gunboat *Scorpion*'s machinery of 4500 S.H.P. The boilers were however similar to the Admiralty 3-drum type fitted in the *Black Swan* class sloops, although slightly modified for the lower headroom in the monitor.

Special tests were made by A.E.W. to determine turning characteristics, as a monitor had to be as manoeuvrable as possible in view of air attacks and shore battery fire. Twin rudders, each sited in the wake of a propeller, gave the best results. As *Erebus* had always been a wet ship forward, model experiments were made to check whether the spray coming over the bows and off the bulge would be a serious problem; the increased sheer and freeboard showed an improvement in this respect.

In addition to the armour and protective plating, the hull itself was strongly built. The bottom plating was generally $^5/_8$-inch thick and the upper deck $^3/_4$-inch, both D quality steel. The longitudinal stresses in the main hull were moderate at about 4 tons per sq in, except at the most highly stressed region in way of the barbette opening, where it rose to 5.8 tons per sq in compression at the deck. All of the main strength structure was riveted, although a number of less important items like bulkhead stiffeners were welded.

The new monitor's keel was laid on 30 April 1940 on the slipway in the East Yard at Clydebank from which *Duke of York* had been launched two months earlier. In order to hasten progress, the normal procedure of submitting working drawings for official approval was not followed. Instead, most decisions were made and details settled at fortnightly meetings between Admiralty and builder's representatives. The work of refitting

Construction at John Brown's is well under way in this view of Roberts, *then known as No. 573, in about September 1940. Framing has reached the main deck — the armoured deck level with the top of the bulge. The double cruciform bulkheads in the magazine supporting the ring bulkhead and turret have been erected. The compartments nearest the camera are the port and starboard boiler and engine rooms.*

Soult's turret took longer than anticipated, so in September 1940 the feasibility was examined of substituting one of the twin 13.5-inch turrets which had been removed from the battlecruiser *Tiger* before she was scrapped in 1932. This plan was found to be practicable, although the work of conversion and overhaul would take just as long, while there would be the additional complication of ammunition supply, as the 13.5-inch was no longer in seagoing service. By this time, sufficient A.A. guns were available to substitute an octuple pom-pom for the after U.P. mounting.

Although wartime costs were not recorded in much detail, *Roberts*' estimated cost was made up as follows:

	£
Gun mountings and armament items	192,000
Armour plating	143,000
Machinery	168,000
Hull and equipment	600,000
Total	1,103,000

This did not include any Vote 8 items from the Estimates like gun barrels (about £70,000 total) or ammunition or stores. If the 15-inch armament had not already existed, the total would have been about £400,000 more — at a time when the purchasing power of the pound was about 7 to 8 times greater than the late 1970s.

A number of discussions took place on the best way of shipping the turret. Towing *Roberts* to Portsmouth was considered too lengthy a process, while towing *Soult* to Clydebank would interfere with her base ship role. Most of the turret components far exceeded the road or rail loading gauges, so there was no alternative left but to send the turret by sea and accept the risk of the ship being lost. The only two coasters likely to be available which were capable of carrying such large loads were also needed for transporting *Duke of York*'s 14-inch turrets. It was therefore planned to make use of one of the coasters for the shortest possible time during February 1941. The intention was that *Roberts* would be launched on 1 February, the twelve 8-inch thick barbette armour plates fitted by the 5th and the roller path and training rack completed by the 19th, ready to receive the turret. The coaster would arrive the next day and would unload the lighter components onto the quay. After the ammunition trunk and working chamber had been lifted into *Roberts* by the 200-ton crane, the 155-ton turntable would be lifted from the coaster and suspended from the crane hook while *Roberts* was manoeuvred underneath to receive it. On the third day, the gun slides and guns would be erected and, on the fourth day, the gunhouse shield and roof plates transferred from coaster to monitor.

Unfortunately the whole operation turned out quite differently in practice. The newly built 2800-ton coaster *Goodwood* arrived at Portsmouth on 30 January to load the turret components. The intention had been to put all the readily dismantlable parts into No. 1 Hold, leaving the large indivisible turntable to go into No. 2 Hold. But over the previous quarter of a century, the gunhouse armour plates and locking keys had become firmly welded together and could not be separated. It was therefore necessary to stow the 168-ton gunhouse in one piece in the bottom of No. 2 Hold and to position the turntable above it, with its roller path sitting on the hatch coamings, all wedged up with timber shores. When *Goodwood* finally departed from Portsmouth on 6 March with her precariously stowed load, the weather was fine but during the night a heavy gale blew up in the Channel. The violent motion of the ship dislodged the shores allowing the turntable to slip, damaging both itself and the ship to such an extent that the crew thought she was sinking and abandoned ship. By the morning however, the weather had moderated and *Goodwood* was found to have survived with her precious cargo still aboard. The crew reboarded and brought her safely into Dartmouth, where the damage was surveyed. The damaged turntable would have to be repaired at Devonport, while *Goodwood* delivered the remaining undamaged parts to the Clyde.

The problem of storage then arose. There were only three cranes on the Clyde capable of lifting the gunhouse: John Brown's, Fairfield's 250-ton fitting-out crane and Glasgow Corporation's 175-ton Stobcross Quay crane. None of these three parties wished to have several hundred tons of assorted 15-inch turret components lying about on their quaysides for several weeks, so a meeting took place at the Naval Headquarters in St Enoch's Hotel to settle the matter. At the end of the day, it was the Lord Provost of Glasgow who found himself the reluctant temporary custodian of a 15-inch turret, which was delivered by *Goodwood* on 4 April. The turntable was not ready to leave Devonport until 9 May, so *Roberts*' turret was not finally erected until the end of May, three months later than planned. Completion of the ship was further delayed by the air-raid of 7 May, when a landmine fell on the quay alongside *Roberts*,

Roberts *is seen here in March 1941 in the fitting-out basin at Clydebank awaiting her turret, which had been damaged on the voyage from Portsmouth. The 12-sided 8-inch thick barbette armour surrounds the ring bulkhead, with its 48 rollers covered by canvas ready to take the 760-ton turret.*

This view taken on 30 May 1941 shows Roberts *with her turret now in place, together with the 4-inch mountings and pom-poms. The minor damage to equipment from the air-raid earlier in the month is not apparent apart from one of the broken searchlights. The battleship in the background is* Duke of York.

severely damaging boats, searchlights and H.A. directors.

The delay did permit a number of worthwhile modifications to be incorporated. Eight single 20-mm Oerlikon guns in small pits on the upper deck and superstructure were substituted for the two remaining planned U.P. mountings. The Mk II gun (Mk I was the Swiss-made version) was a useful close-range weapon which the R.N. badly needed at that time — and reasonably cheap at £320. Manually operated with a rate of fire of eight rounds a second, it could open fire on and follow a target very quickly and, although it lacked killing power compared with the heavier 2-pdr, its explosive projectile proved much more effective than the bullets of the puny 0.5-inch machine gun. The multiple pom-poms were originally fitted only for eye-shooting but, by mid-1941, a director with radar ranging had been developed. Although the early Type 282 was not very reliable and needed coaxing, it did provide some assistance by measuring the range of a fast-moving target, a difficult problem using optical means. Type 285 radar had also been developed for medium range H.A. fire and was fitted to the two rangefinder/directors before completion.

Moored, acoustic and magnetic mines were presenting increasingly serious threats, so *Roberts* was fitted with additional defensive equipment besides the passive bulges. Bow protection gear was installed to reduce the risk from moored mines, a modified type of paravane being streamed from a hinged A-frame lowered over the bows. Acoustic sweep gear was fitted below water forward to detonate acoustic mines at a safe distance, while internal degaussing cables guarded against magnetic mines.

The modifications during construction aggravated an already serious overcrowding problem in the crew accommodation. From the original complement estimate of 308, the number crept up until *Roberts*' official complement when she went off to war was 442, made up as follows:—

	Officers	*Ratings*	*Total*
Seamen and gunners	11	237	248
Engineers	2	64	66
Royal Marines	1	40	41
Radar operators	—	22	22
Signallers	—	11	11
Shipwrights and artificers	1	16	17
Supply	2	29	31
Medical	2	4	6
Total	19	423	442

Few of the officers or ratings were regular R.N. being mostly reservists or, like the operators of the top secret radar equipment, specially recruited and trained young men.

§4 ROBERTS As Completed

Although the layout of *Roberts* was basically similar to *Erebus*, there was no mistaking the final appearance of the two ships. The profile of the WW1 monitor as built was bare, virtually the only erections above the deck being the turret, bridge, mast and funnel, although subsequently extended during WW2. Contrast *Roberts*, with her extensive superstructure, her two masts and her radar aerials, her considerable A.A. armament, her flush upper deck and her external sloping armour belt on top of the bulge. *Roberts* had more additions during construction than normal, totalling 475 tons or over 5% of her displacement, raising her deep load to 9150 tons as built. The main components of weight are listed in the Technical Particulars, showing that Hull and Equipment increased the most between design and completion. The percentages of the deep displacement allocated to armament and protection were remarkably similar to those of the *King George V* battleships, but in the latter, a much higher percentage was taken up by machinery and fuel, with a corresponding reduction in hull. Compared with the first *Roberts*, the savings from using oil-fired steam turbines as against coal-fired steam reciprocators permitted a heavier armament load to be carried:

	Roberts (1915)	*Roberts (1941)*	*K.G.V.*
Armament and ammunition	13.7	16.6	16.5
Armour and water protection	30.1	30.6	30.5
Machinery, fuel and R.F.W.	12.3	9.4	16.4
Hull and equipment	43.9	43.4	36.6
Total percentage	100.0	100.0	100.0
Deep displacement, tons	6157	9150	41,000

Roberts finally commissioned six months late on 6 October 1941 under Captain J. G. Y. Loveband. She left Clydebank three days later for the Gareloch, where she was drydocked in the floating dock AFD 4, the only dock on the Clyde wide enough to take her. Official trials started on 26 October with full power ahead and astern trials. As the Clyde measured miles were not available on that day, her speed had to be estimated from bearings as about 13½ knots. Gunnery trials took place the following day, with the usual four rounds from each 15-inch at various bearings and elevations. Ten rounds from each 4-inch and about 30 from each close range weapon rounded

Roberts *is launched on 1 February 1941 flying John Brown's house flag, with slope armour, bulge fender and ring bulkhead in place. The guys support the slipway derrick cranes.*

Roberts *leaves Clydebank for trials on 9 October 1941, sporting her camouflage. The censor has blanked out the air warning radar aerials, but left the Type 285 on the H.A. rangefinder/director. Oerlikon mountings have been fitted but not the actual guns, which were still in short supply.*

off a generally satisfactory trials programme. After final adjustments at the shipyard, particularly to the turret hydraulic pump, she left Clydebank on 13 November to prepare for the long voyage out to the Mediterranean via the Cape to replace *Terror*, lost nine months earlier.

§5 ABERCROMBIE's Design and Construction

Terror had given such a good account of herself off North Africa that no time was wasted ordering a replacement, *Erebus* then being the only operational monitor. To speed delivery, the new monitor was to be a near-replica of *Roberts*, with such minor modifications as could be incorporated without too much trouble. In June 1941, *Terror*'s last C.O. submitted a number of suggestions for improving the design of monitors, especially those features affecting the Guard Ship and Advanced Base Ship roles which had been undertaken in the Mediterranean. Haynes' main suggestions affecting the bombardment role were:

(i) A speed of 18 knots to enable the ship to move with the Fleet
(ii) Longer range guns, about 48,000 yards
(iii) Carriage of own aircraft in view of the shortage of spotting aircraft off North Africa.

Such major changes would need a totally new design of ship considerably bigger than *Roberts*, while no existing British naval gun could range even 40,000 yards. Some of Haynes' more modest suggestions could readily be incorporated in the new ship, including larger store-room and fresh water capacity, better W/T facilities, heavier stern anchor, more motor boats, and better repair and workshop facilities. With delivery planned for September 1942, only the following differences from *Roberts* were finally permitted:—

(i) 15-inch gun mountings brought up to latest Mk I/N standard
(ii) Deck armour over machinery spaces increased from 3 to 4 inches; circular and slightly shorter barbette armour
(iii) More close range weapons, and remote power control (R.P.C.) fitted to 4-inch and 2-pdr mountings
(iv) Shelter deck extended to full breadth of main hull to provide more accommodation and better arcs of fire for 4-inch guns mounted thereon
(v) Extra stowage for ammunition, stores and fresh water
(vi) Additional generating capacity necessitated by R.P.C. and other additions, by substituting two 150-kW diesel generators for the two 60-kW, but retaining the two 200-kW turbo-generators
(vii) Three instead of two motor boats, with only one pulling boat (a change which cramped the boat stowage even further, restricted as it was by the bulge to the extreme aft end)
(viii) Accommodation designed for up to 500 men
(ix) Various minor changes in layout and equipment, including taller funnel.

No 15-inch turrets had been manufactured for over 20 years but there was still in existence at Chatham the second spare which had been built for *Furious*. As it had been designed for a WW1 battlecruiser, fairly extensive modifications were required to make it suitable for a WW2 monitor, as detailed on p.177.

In view of the continued suspension of construction of the battleship *Lion*, Vickers-Armstrong's Naval Yard at Newcastle was given the contract for the new monitor's hull on 4 April 1941, the machinery contract going to Parsons. With copies of *Roberts*' drawings sent from John Brown, construction proceeded well up to the launch on 31 March 1942. The new ship was christened *Abercrombie*, reviving a WW1 name complete with mis-spelling. Delays then arose, particularly with the turbines and generators, which held up completion of the structure over the engine room until September. Refitting the turret took longer than expected so it was not ready to leave the erection pit at Elswick until January 1943. Labour troubles at the shipyard added further delays, so it was 22 April before *Abercrombie* finally left the shipyard under the command of Captain G. V. B. Faulkner. She carried out gunnery and speed trials on the way to Rosyth for drydocking but, having been lying in the Tyne for over a year, she could only manage an estimated 12 knots with her fouled bottom.

The effect of all the minor modifications was to add 567 tons to the deep displacement compared with *Roberts*, largely hull and armour. Most of the additions were aft of the turret, accentuating the trim by the stern to the extent that *Abercrombie* drew 15ft 8in aft and 12ft 11in forward — a big change from the 13ft 1in and 12ft 4in for which *Roberts* had originally been designed. The position of the turret was relatively further aft than *Erebus* at 41½% of the length from the bow, which not only worsened the trim but severely cramped the deck, superstructure and A.A. gun arrangement. A shift forward of the turret of about 10 feet would have been very beneficial, but *Abercrombie* had been committed before *Roberts*' large 22-inch trim as completed became apparent. Standard displacement worked out at 8536 tons, although official records continued to show the figure at its preliminary estimate of 7850 tons, an error which was never corrected, implying that *Abercrombie* was smaller than the 7973-ton *Roberts*. Her metacentric height, GM, was 14ft deep, 4ft less than her sister's. *Abercrombie* cost appreciably more than *Roberts* at £1,563,000 as not only was more extensive equipment fitted but much more work had to be done modifying the 15-inch turret, as well as supplying additional armour.

Abercrombie's electronic and control outfit was of the most up-to-date pattern. In place of the obsolescent Dreyer table, a new cruiser-style Admiralty Fire Control Table Mark VI was fitted in the transmitting station. Her 4-inch armament was one of the first installations to receive R.P.C., whereby mountings were controlled directly by the H.A.C.P.s with their associated rangefinder/directors and improved Type 285 radar. The octuple and two quadruple pom-poms were each controlled via R.P.C. by their own Mk IV director and Type 282 radar. The eight twin power-operated Mk V 20-mm mountings were at first fitted only for eye-shooting, later receiving gyro gunsights which considerably improved performance. The four manually-operated single Oerlikons retained their normal cartwheel-like eye-shooting sights, once described as having the appearance and durability of spiders' webs. Type 281 air warning radar at the mastheads and Type 272M surface warning in its 'lantern' below the spotting top plus the usual interrogators rounded off the radar outfit.

Abercrombie was completed on 5 May 1943, just in time to take part in the Sicilian landings, the newest, the best equipped and the last to be built of all Britain's big gun monitors.

This stern view of Abercrombie *before her launch in March 1942 shows her bluff afterbody lines and the twin propellers with the rudders in their wake. The sloping armour has yet to be shipped, but some of the 1½-inch plating around the steering gear is visible above the propellers. The 250-ton hammerhead crane in the background was used to lift the turret components from their barges after their trip from Elswick up-river, for installation in Ship No. 42.*

§6 Wartime Service Overseas

When *Roberts* was allocated to the Mediterranean in October 1941 together with *Erebus*, it was hoped that she would be able to emulate *Terror* in supporting the Eighth Army's offensive against Axis forces in North Africa. Owing to enemy air superiority in the Central Mediterranean, the two monitors would have to steam to Egypt via the Cape. *Roberts* and *Erebus* left Lough Foyle on 1 December, stopping at the Azores, Freetown and Pointe Noire for fuel before arriving at Simonstown on 11 January. C-in-C Mediterranean then requested *Roberts*' presence as soon as possible, to assist forth-coming operations in Tripolitania. Delayed by boiler repairs at Durban, she did not arrive at Suez until 26 February, by which time Rommel had succeeded in pushing the Eighth Army back towards Egypt again. As the Luftwaffe had been making bombing and mining attacks on the Suez Canal, *Roberts* remained stationed at Suez as A.A. guardship. She was anchored about three miles south of the canal entrance, whence she could cover the approaches to the anchorages where the merchant ships supplying the Eighth Army lay. Although she closed up pom-pom crews on many nights, there were few air raids whilst she was there. Hot and uneventful months passed until July, when she moved down the Red Sea for a few weeks, which included some target practice at some old oil drums ashore. In August, she was ordered to prepare to sail for an unspecified operation, so she departed from Suez on the 17th for drydocking at Durban, as she had lost two knots' speed lying at anchor. After leaving Durban on 20 September for Freetown, she learned that she was to support the Allied landings in North Africa, Operation "Torch", due to take place on 8 November.

Roberts arrived at Gibraltar on 2 November, where most of the Allied covering naval and air forces were gathering. She left just after midnight on the 6th and took station with convoy KMS(A).1, which formed part of the force which was to land at Algiers. She carried the largest guns that would be available to suppress any opposition from the French forts guarding Algiers; the battleships of the main covering force were further to seaward to intercept any sortie by the Italian battle fleet. The landings were made from 01.00 on 8 November in three sectors, two to the west and one to the east of Algiers. *Roberts* stopped about seven miles offshore, ready to open fire if required. Little opposition was encountered; Fort Sidi Ferruch in *Roberts*' sector did not resist the Allied troops, formally surrendering in the morning. *Roberts* could therefore anchor safely in the afternoon of the 8th to act as radar guardship, warning of the approach of any German aircraft from the direction of Tunisia. The next day, she anchored in Algiers Bay and opened fire with her 4-inch at Ju.88s which were attacking the Allied ships. The air attacks were sustained, necessitating a continuous stand-by by the crews of her A.A. weapons.

A further landing had been planned at Bougie (now Bejaia) 130 miles east of Algiers, to take place on the morning of the 11th. *Roberts* sailed on the evening of the 10th as part of the covering force, but again no bombardment was required, the landing being unopposed by the French. The airfield at Djidjelli, 40 miles east, was also occupied, but swell prevented the troopship *Awatea* from landing petrol and air stores there. The Spitfires which were to provide air cover for the ships and troops were therefore unable to operate for two days, while the nearest airfield in Allied hands was 120 miles west of Bougie. With no carrier support, the result was that there was no fighter cover when German aircraft attacked Bougie later on the 11th, and they caused severe damage.

The nearly completed Roberts *enters Admiralty Floating Dock 4 in the Gareloch on 13 October 1941. The dock had been towed from Devonport early in the war; it was the same one as used by the monitors drydocking in the Tyne in WW1.*

Roberts helped beat off the first attack by Ju.88s early in the afternoon, claiming one shot down. She continued her patrolling; at dusk another heavy attack took place. Despite concentrated A.A. fire from all the ships, the troopships *Cathay* and *Awatea* were bombed and sunk, while *Roberts* was attacked by three Ju.88 dive-bombers at 17.15. One came in from the bow and two from the stern in 30° dives, releasing their 500-kg (1102-lb) bombs at about 1000 feet. One bomb was a near-miss about 30 feet to port but the other two were direct hits. Casualties were heavy, although her good protection saved her from fatal damage. One bomb hit her sloping bulge armour on the port side abreast the funnel, dishing the 4-inch thick plating about ten inches and flooding two of the inner bulge compartments. A hole about 7ft × 6ft was blown in the ship's side, starting a fire on the main deck. The second hit was more serious: the bomb landed just abaft the funnel and penetrated as far as the armoured main deck. The explosion wrecked compartments above the main deck and started several fires. Although the damage did not appear at first to be severe, the hole in the upper deck being about 12ft × 8ft, the engine room ventilation fans had been destroyed. Despite steam being shut off, the engine room, hot at the best of times, soon became unbearable and one man died of heat exhaustion before the jammed hatches could be opened.

Considerable secondary damage was caused below decks: both turbo-generators out of action, piping and electrical systems destroyed, feed and fresh water contaminated. Above decks, the funnel was crumpled, one Oerlikon destroyed and much of the superstructure amidships damaged, although the bullet holes in the bridge were attributed to 'friendly' close range fire. Radar sets, rangefinders and degaussing equipment were also put out of action for some time. Total casualties were 17 killed and 35 wounded. *Roberts* was effectively immobilised for two days until new engine room fans could be improvised from mess-deck fans, so she did not take part in the assault on Bône as had been intended. Air attacks continued, with *Roberts* still able to put up a formidable A.A. barrage. About midnight on the 12th she replenished with A.A. ammunition from the sloop *Pelican*, as she had fired off some 30,000 rounds in less than a week. Spitfires began patrolling from Djidjelli on the 13th, so thereafter the air attacks on the ships at Bougie became less intense. On the 16th, two torpedo bombers attacked *Roberts*; fortunately both torpedoes missed, exploding harmlessly against the harbour breakwater. *Roberts* was able to repair some of the less serious damage herself; she left Bougie on 1 December for Algiers and Gibraltar for temporary repairs. She berthed in Gladstone Dock, Liverpool on 6 January, where Cammell Laird took her in hand for permanent repairs, lasting until the end of May 1943.

Abercrombie arrived in the Clyde from Rosyth on 9 May 1943 for working up; *Roberts* arrived there on 1

June, now under the command of Captain R. E. C. Dunbar, who had been *Lord Clive*'s navigating officer at the end of WW1. The two monitors engaged in lengthy bombardment practices, exercising in particular the spotting of gunfire by shore observers. The British practice was to have a small team ashore consisting of an artillery officer called a Forward Observation Officer (F.O.O.) to spot the fall of shot and to estimate corrections, and a naval telegraphist to signal to the bombarding ship. On the ship, the Gunnery Officer was assisted by another artillery officer called a Bombardment Liaison Officer (B.L.O.) in carrying out the shoot as required by the troops ashore. *Abercrombie* carried out some of her exercises with U.S. Shore Fire Control Parties (S.F.C.P.), as she would be supporting American forces in forthcoming operations.

Both monitors had been allocated, together with *Erebus*, to provide gunfire support for the next phase of Mediterranean combined operations. With North Africa now cleared of the enemy, the next step was to land in Europe itself, first Sicily, then the Italian mainland. The British Eighth Army and the American Seventh Army were to make the assault early in July on the southern coast of Sicily. The three monitors would be the only heavy gun ships in direct support, as the battleships assigned to Operation "Husky" were required to stand off to intercept any ships of the Italian fleet that approached.

Roberts and *Abercrombie* sailed from the Clyde on 18 June 1943 as part of convoy KMS.17. On passage, *Roberts* suffered the misfortune of damage to one of her turbo-generators. The turbine blading was found to be stripped; Gibraltar dockyard could do nothing but request urgent spares from the U.K. So she had to sail on her most important operation to date, knowing that if the other turbo-generator failed, she would have to withdraw as her diesel generators had insufficient capacity. She arrived at Algiers on 2 July where many of the invasion ships were gathering, while *Abercrombie* went on to Tunis arriving on the 4th, after embarking the U.S.N. liaison officer and signallers who had trained with her in the Clyde. *Roberts* would join up with convoy KMS.18B coming from U.K. which included the store and other ships destined for "Bark West", the British landing beaches to the west of Cape Passero, the south-east tip of Sicily. *Abercrombie* would sail with convoy TJM.1, most of whose L.S.T.s had been assembling at Tunis, to cover the landings on the easternmost of the American beaches, "Cent", about 40 miles west of Cape Passero. Meantime *Erebus* had been approaching from the east with convoy MWS.36 which had left Alexandria on 3 July; she would cover the northernmost British landings at "Acid North" about 15 miles north of Cape Passero.

The two newer monitors sailed for the invasion of Sicily on 8 July, their convoys making for the rendezvous positions south of Malta. *Abercrombie* arrived in position off Scoglitti at 02.30 on D-day, 10 July. No pre-H-hour bombardments had been planned, in order to obtain tactical surprise. The landing craft went in soon after she arrived; conditions were not easy although there was little opposition. Her first call for fire came at 07.15 when she was asked to fire on inland targets including

Anchored south of the entrance to the Suez Canal, Roberts *served as A.A. guardship during the summer of 1942.*

Comiso airfield. Following counterattacks by enemy tanks, *Abercrombie* was ordered up to help on the 11th. She opened fire on the town of Niscemi eight miles inland and managed to knock out the enemy headquarters from a range of 30,000 yards. The supporting American cruisers and destroyers returned a huge volume of fire from their 6-inch and 5-inch guns on the less distant targets. *Abercrombie* used her big guns to good effect also, but British records tend to be less comprehensive than American and details of her targets and ammunition expenditure are not available, although she claimed a 5-gun enemy battery destroyed with five rounds.

Most of the spotting had been done by the S.F.C.P.s as, although the cruisers carried observation seaplanes, the latter were vulnerable to enemy fighters during the initial period when Allied fighter cover was poor. As the Americans pressed inland on the 13th and 14th, there were fewer calls for fire as the front advanced out of range. On the 14th, *Abercrombie* was called on to bombard Porto Empedocle and Agrigento on the Seventh Army's west flank, in company with the U.S. cruisers *Birmingham* and *Philadelphia.* Spotting conditions were not suitable until the next morning, when *Abercrombie* engaged ten separate targets including an Italian railway battery, with the help of *Philadelphia*'s spotting aircraft. Some return fire was experienced but the shells from the shore batteries fell well short. By the evening, she had expended nearly all her H.E. ammunition, so was sent to Malta to replenish, where she arrived on the morning of the 16th.

Meantime, the British and Canadian landings had also been successfully carried out. *Roberts* had opened fire at 05.10 on the 10th on the only battery to fire on the landing craft, the five 149-mm (5.9-inch) guns near Pachino, inland from Cape Passero. The battery was silenced by 14 rounds from *Roberts* anchored 9000 yards away, and was captured soon after. *Roberts* was then requested to bombard Pachino airfield, but cancellation quickly followed; the airfield was taken shortly afterwards and put into service by the R.A.F. In the afternoon, R.M. Commandos came under heavy mortar fire near the town of Spaccaforno. Fourteen rounds from *Roberts* induced

(Above) *An impressive photograph of* Abercrombie *steaming down the Tyne on 20 April 1943. The circular barbette armour shows the change of camouflage pattern on the centre-line.*
(Below) Abercrombie *passing South Shields on her way down the Tyne. Clearly visible are her many radar aerials, largely directed towards A.A. defence. Transmitting and receiving aerials for the Type 281 air warning are at the mastheads, Type 285 on the two rangefinder/directors, Type 282 on the pom-pom directors. The only surface warning set is the Type 272 in its lantern under the spotting top.*

the Italians to surrender, protesting that it was unfair to be bombarded by shells of such calibre. The next morning, an enemy troop concentration near Rosolini was broken up by 30 rounds from 18,000 yards, the Italian defenders quickly surrendering. No calls for fire were received by her on the 12th.

Erebus had been ready to support an airborne brigade at her bombardment position about ten miles south-east of Syracuse since 07.00 on D-day but her first call for fire did not come until 14.15. With 12 rounds, she destroyed a strongpoint east of Ponte Grande. Shortly afterwards, shipping in the "Acid" sector was subjected to heavy air attacks from Ju.88s and Me.109s. *Erebus* suffered eight near-misses but without incurring any damage, so was able to respond to an F.O.O's call for fire on another strongpoint at about 20.00. Eight rounds from 19,000 yards sufficed to destroy it. Owing to the speed of advance and the ineffective coastal defences, she received no calls for fire on D+1, but spent D+2 in almost continuous bombardment. At 05.40 she began firing at a coast defence battery on Cape San Croce near Augusta. This and other batteries received attention during the morning in seven separate shoots to cover the advance on the important naval base of Augusta, which would permit the entry of Allied ships. The first attempt by destroyers to enter was repulsed so, after noon, *Erebus* and the cruisers *Mauritius, Uganda* and *Orion* switched their fire to the town of Melilli about five miles from Augusta. *Erebus*' total fire for the day amounted to about 130 rounds, over half her ammunition outfit.

Roberts transferred from "Bark" to "Acid" sector on 13 July to supplement the A.A. defences around the port of Syracuse, which had been captured on the 11th. *Erebus* moved north for bombardments of the strongly defended Catania area. Catania airfield was fired on from maximum range at 11.05 and other bombardments were made in company with *Mauritius, Uganda, Orion* and *Newfoundland* of batteries harassing Allied ships offshore. Enemy air attacks continued, both monitors being shaken by near-misses. Smokescreens provided some cover as continuous fighter protection was not yet available.

Roberts took over off Catania on 14 July after *Erebus* had sailed for Malta to replenish with fuel and ammunition. Despite ideal firing conditions, her F.O.O. was not in an area from which he could direct any useful fire nor was the exact position of the Allied troops known, so *Roberts* had to return after a fruitless day to her buoy in Augusta harbour. The next day was much more successful; in the afternoon and evening, she fired some 90 rounds at Catania, its batteries, docks and the roads leading into the town. The longest range shoots were from 25,000 yards at the town of Misterbianco. During one of the shoots at a road full of German military traffic, a factory chimney was selected as the point of aim. The very first shot hit the base of the chimney, collapsing it into a heap of bricks and dust. A minor gunfire accident due to a faulty 15-inch projectile damaged one of her 4-inch and an Oerlikon, so she returned to Malta where she joined the other two monitors on the 16th.

Abercrombie returned to Gela on 18 July but the Americans were now advancing steadily and there was little for her to do which could not be equally well undertaken by the Army's artillery or the U.S. cruisers and destroyers. After a period as radar guardship, she therefore returned to Malta on 23 July before sailing to Bizerta to prepare for the invasion of Italy itself.

Erebus and *Roberts* were back at Augusta on the 18th and 19th respectively. An Inshore Squadron was formed to provide gunfire support to the Army on the east coast of Sicily, consisting of these two monitors, the Dutch gunboats *Flores* and *Soemba*, plus minesweepers and M.L.s. Nightly bombing and torpedo raids were frequent over Augusta, often necessitating several hundred A.A. rounds from each ship in the harbour, the sky being lit by scores of tracer and searchlight beams. *Erebus* was straddled by two bombs on the night of 20 July which killed six of her crew and wounded 26. *Roberts* sent her shipwrights over to help patch the damage. *Erebus*' next bombardment was on the evening of the 21st when she put 16 rounds into the Catania area. A shore battery returned fire, but its range was too short to reach the monitor. Thereafter virtually no calls for fire were received by either monitor for quite some time while on patrol.

Although the Germans were stubbornly defending the north-east corner of Sicily, it was clear that before long they would have to withdraw from Catania to Messina and then to the mainland. *Roberts* was therefore ordered to bombard the coastal road and railway line between the two towns at Taormina. On a cliffside, the road ran directly above a railway tunnel, so it appeared possible to block both lines of retreat. Two Army Air Co-operation Squadron Spitfires were briefed to spot for the bombardment, so initiating a technique of spotting from fighter aircraft that was to become standard method. Sailing in company with the destroyers *Brocklesby* and *Tynedale*, *Roberts* commenced her bombardment at 11.40 on 4 August from a range of 19,000 yards. The range was found using A.P.C. spotted by the Spitfires, then *Roberts* switched to H.E. After the ship had closed to 16,000 yards, the fall of shot could be directly observed by those on board. Fire was kept up for just under an hour until dust blotted out the target and the aircraft had to return to base. A small battery ashore opened up towards the end of the shoot, so *Roberts* made smoke and opened the range. Most of her 32 shots fell in the target area and large amounts of debris could be seen blocking the road and railway. Over the next four days, destroyers continued to bombard the area to hamper repair work. Although the road had not been fully cleared when the Eighth Army took Taormina eleven days later, the Germans claimed that their withdrawal was not seriously affected by this operation.

Only two other bombardments of Sicily were carried out by the monitors: *Erebus* near Taormina on 14 August in company with *Flores, Ledbury* and *Wheatland*; and *Roberts* supporting a landing near Cape Scaletta on the early morning of the 16th. 40 R.M. Commando landed from two L.S.I.s ten miles south of Messina to blow bridges, but found that the Germans had already almost all withdrawn. A heavy battery at Cape Pellaro on the mainland opened fire at *Roberts* at 07.00 so she increased the range and returned fire from 23,000 yards when the battery began firing on the landing beaches. Neither the battery nor its gun-flashes could be seen and low-lying mist hampered spotting, so she ceased fire after four rounds. An hour later, two Spitfires arrived to spot, so another ten rounds were aimed at the battery before the ships withdrew. The following day, *Erebus* fired ten rounds at another mainland battery near San Giovanni. The nights at Augusta were now much quieter following the completion of the German evacuation of Sicily on the 16th. On 21 August, *Roberts* led an impressive flotilla consisting of *Erebus, Flores, Soemba, Ledbury, Wheatland, Aphis, Scarab* and *Cockchafer* to Malta to rest and replenish. *Abercrombie* returned from Bizerta on the 28th, so all the monitors were together again, preparing for the assault on the Italian mainland.

Naval gunfire support was not used as extensively as it might have been at Sicily. *Roberts* fired a total of 232 rounds over a six-week period, *Abercrombie* and *Erebus* approaching 200 each. No calls were made on the bombarding fleet to neutralise the coastal batteries covering the Straits of Messina, which would have allowed smaller craft to harass more effectively the vessels ferrying the Germans to the mainland.

With the Germans driven out of Sicily, the Allies planned to invade the mainland of Italy as soon as the necessary forces for a landing could be assembled. The Eighth Army were to cross the Straits of Messina and advance up the toe of Italy, while the Fifth Army were to land in the Gulf of Salerno, south of Naples. The three monitors sailed from Malta for Augusta on 30 August to support the first of these operations. Operation "Baytown" commenced with a heavy artillery barrage across the Straits from the hills surrounding Messina, followed by landings near Reggio on the morning of 3 September. Although the monitors expected a busy time, the landings were virtually unopposed and only *Erebus* was called upon for ten rounds in the early afternoon. The Germans were busy withdrawing northwards, while the war-weary Italians were on the point of surrender.

After anchoring for the night off Taormina, the three monitors were back in the assault area next morning, but no calls for fire were received. In the afternoon, *Roberts* and *Abercrombie* sailed for Bizerta to join the convoys preparing for the Salerno landings, leaving *Erebus* to undertake any bombardments required. Several calls for fire were received on the 6th and 7th in the Gioia area north of the Straits; most of her 40 rounds were directed at enemy transport on the coastal road. The next day, *Erebus* supported the landing of 231 Brigade near Pizzo, about 50 miles north-east of Reggio. The Germans were just in the process of withdrawing past this point, so gave the landing vessels a hot reception. *Erebus* fired 25 rounds at various targets and was met by replies from enemy artillery and Fw.190s, but without being hit. With her guns now nearly worn out, she was ordered to return to Malta, where she arrived on 10 September.

Meantime, *Roberts* and *Abercrombie* had departed from Bizerta on the morning of 7 September, the former to support the British landings at the northern end of the Gulf of Salerno, the latter the American landings at the southern end. News was received on passage of the armistice with Italy; the cheering optimists in the assault force who thought that the war was over were rudely reminded that stiff opposition was still to be expected from the Germans. Both monitors arrived in their firing positions soon after midnight although, as no pre-H-hour bombardment had been ordered, they would not expect calls for fire for some time until their F.O.O.s were established ashore. The Germans at Salerno were well prepared when the first troops landed at about 03.30 on the 9th. In the southern sector, *Abercrombie* received her first call for fire at 08.25: an enemy battery near the town of Capaccio about five miles inland. The spotting aircraft had some difficulty identifying the target in the morning mist, so it took 50 minutes to get off 11 rounds without any observed result. The assembled ships were under frequent air attacks; at one time, *Abercrombie* was firing on He.111s on one side of the ship and Me.109s on the other. Three more calls for fire were received during the morning, all at ranges of about 27,000 yards. Tanks were engaged with nine rounds, and it is believed that she managed to destroy two of them.

In the meantime, minesweepers had been busy clearing several channels and had exploded a number of mines. As the channels had not yet been properly buoyed, it was difficult to keep to safe areas; during the day *Abercrombie* drifted slowly out to sea under a light offshore breeze. By 17.00 she had drifted unknowingly into an area purposely left unswept, when three minutes later a large explosion occurred amidships on the starboard side. She had hit a moored contact mine in 450 feet of water, which had gone off under the starboard bulge abreast the foremast, throwing a great column of black water into the air. A hole was torn in the bulge about 20ft × 12ft and the ship quickly took on a heel of 10°. The bulge and protective bulkhead had taken the

The damage to Abercrombie *after her mining can just be seen in this view taken on 11 September. The sloped bulge armour has been pushed upwards (*arrowed*) and men are working on the light coloured area securing the armour with brackets.*

In the afternoon of 9 September 1943, Abercrombie *drifted into an unswept minefield while awaiting calls for bombardment in the Gulf of Salerno. She is seen here the following day with the U.S. salvage tug* Moreno *assisting. No damage is apparent in this view, as the mine struck the starboard bulge amidships.*

main force of the charge estimated to be 500lb, both being damaged over a length of about 100 feet. Inboard there was little structural damage and only a few compartments were flooded, resulting from buckled or leaking bulkheads. The port bulge was counterflooded to bring the ship back upright and a survey was made of the damage. The belt armour had been displaced up to $2^1/_2$ feet but operationally the more serious damage was confined to fittings and equipment. The 15-inch director had been unseated, preventing further indirect bombardment. Although the turret could be fired, it was feared that more structural damage would result. The 281 and 272 radars had been put out of action, the latter only temporarily, together with W/T sets, while piping and lighting systems and two Oerlikon mountings were damaged. Fortunately there were only two casualties. The U.S. salvage tug *Moreno* was near at hand to give assistance, so berthed alongside *Abercrombie* next morning to commence stopping leaks and securing the loose armour plating. *Abercrombie* sailed for Palermo on the 11th, her machinery being undamaged, leaving U.S. cruisers to provide heavy gunfire support in the southern sector.

Meanwhile *Roberts* had been busy in the northern sector, in company with four cruisers. Two shoots were made on the morning of D-day in the area of Faiano east of Salerno town, on both occasions the F.O.O. reporting "O.K." The next day, she was ordered to bombard the road through Cava about five miles north-west of Salerno, so 19 rounds were fired at five-minute intervals. This road to Naples was shot up twice on the 11th from ranges of eight to nine miles. The F.O.O.s had some difficulties in observing in the hilly country as well as in maintaining radio contact. *Roberts* experienced a little trouble from faulty projectiles, but three shoots were made on the 12th at places which were important road and rail junctions. Full details of all the monitors' firings at Salerno are given in the table on p.163. A heavy German counterattack with tanks was made down the River Sele dividing the British and American sectors on 12 September. At one time, the Americans were considering withdrawing from their beach-head, but the Germans were finally halted on the 14th after three days of heavy naval bombardment by cruisers and destroyers, both British and American. Surprisingly, *Roberts*' assistance was not requested and indeed for the three days 14-16 September, she did not fire a shot, although *Warspite, Valiant, Aurora* and *Penelope* were ordered from Malta to give gunfire support.

During this period, *Roberts* was either at anchor or steaming slowly about in the fire support channels. Air attacks were frequent; on the 11th she had the satisfaction of seeing her close-range guns down a Me.109 off her port side. Enemy headquarters in Cava were engaged three times on the 18th-19th. After the second shoot, *Roberts* dropped a buoy to mark her position and recorded the setting of her fire control table. She returned to this point at 23.59 on the 19th and thoroughly disturbed the Germans' rest with 12 rounds into her target of the previous day. The following day, she left the area for Augusta and Malta, having expended 215 rounds, virtually her entire outfit.

Salerno was the first combined operation in the European theatre in which naval bombardment played a crucial role. Sceptical Army officers were now convinced of the ability of the Allied Navies to put down heavy and accurate fire where the Army wanted it, especially in the early stages before their own artillery was fully deployed. A detailed analysis was made of Operation "Avalanche" to point up lessons for future landings. Over a period of twelve days at Salerno, the Allied warships had fired 22,800 rounds of 4-inch calibre and above at 322 targets, totalling about 1000 tons. The importance of pre-H-hour bombardment to soften up the enemy defences was

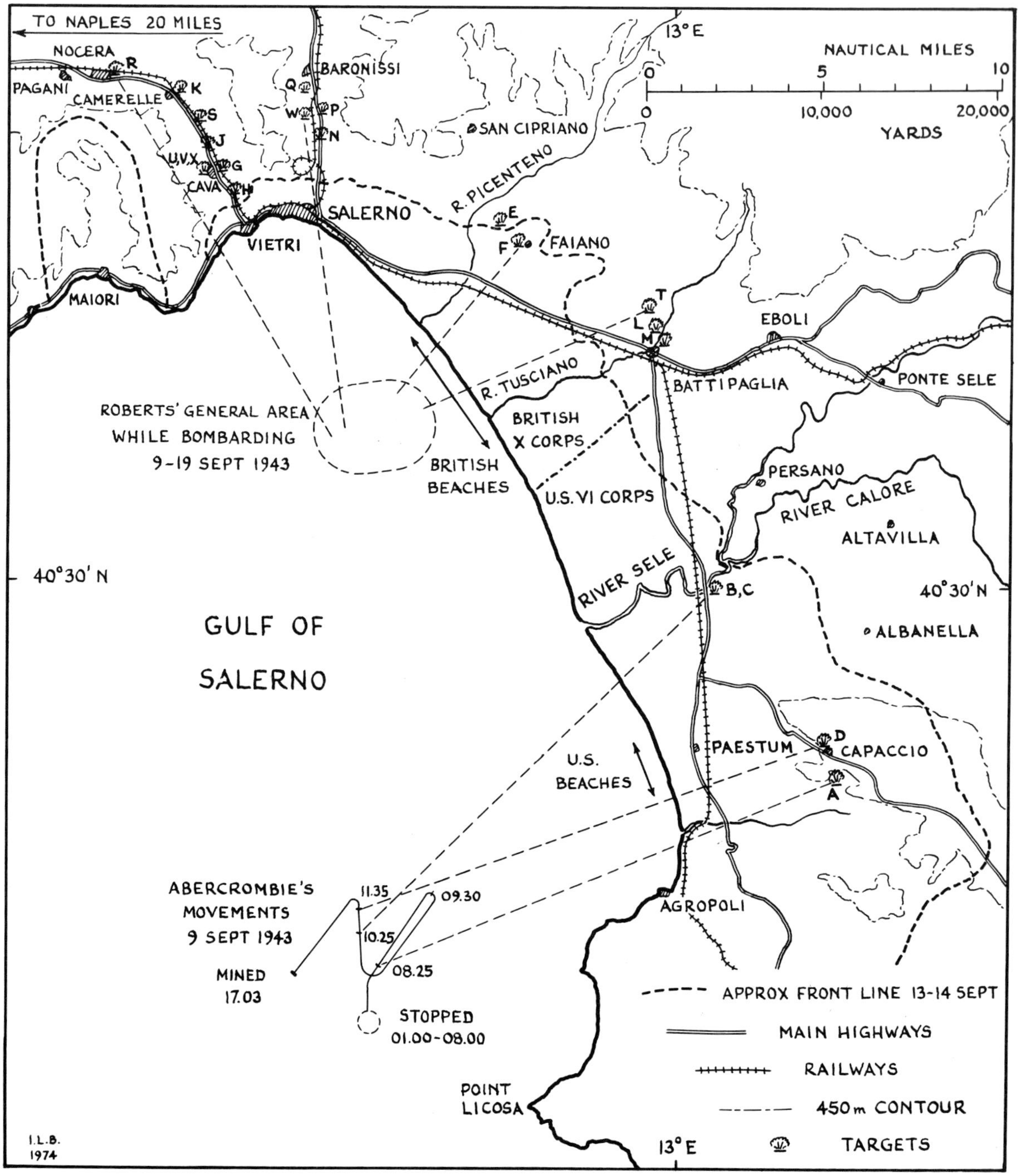

Map of the Salerno bombardments. Lettered targets are detailed opposite.

emphasised and the value of spotting by fighter aircraft recognised, together with the need for special training and equipment for sustained gunfire support.

After a few days patching up at Palermo, *Abercrombie* had steamed on to Bizerta, while a decision was made about permanent repairs. After the armistice with Italy, she was sent to Taranto dockyard, where she arrived on 7 October. Serious work did not start until January 1944, so she remained a total of ten months in dockyard hands. Her 15-inch guns were exchanged, but otherwise work was mainly confined to restoring her original condition.

Roberts also required new guns, but the nearest were at Port Said, so she was ordered to Egypt to refit, arriving on 20 October after a fortnight at Malta. Replacement turbine blades for her turbo-generator at last caught up with her, while her troublesome hydraulic pump was again patched up. None of the monitors participated in the landing at Anzio in January 1944; demands for naval gunfire were relatively modest. *Roberts*' crew thought that she might have been used in operations against German-held Aegean islands, but in fact they were able to spend nearly five months in Egypt, which included social and sporting activities, plus a bombardment practice south of Suez with 40 full calibre rounds during February.

Monitor Bombardments at Salerno 1943

Key	Time	Target	Range, yards	Rounds	Spotting
		Abercrombie			
	19 September				
A.	08.25-09.20	Guns and troops south of Capaccio	26,600	11 HE	Air
B.	10.25-10.30	Tanks near River Sele	27,300	2 HE	Unobserved
C.	11.12-11.25	Tanks near River Sele	26,500	7 HE	Air
D.	11.35-11.41	Capaccio town	27,500	4 HE	FOO
		Roberts			
	9 September				
E.	08.45-	Area bombardment Faiano	21,500	5 HE	FOO
F.	11.00-11.05	Crossroads at Faiano	11,000	5 HE	FOO
	10 September				
G.	12.35-13.15	Road through Cava	14-15,000	19 HE	Unobserved
	11 September				
H.	13.54-	Guns and troops south of Cava	14,500	7 HE	FOO
J.	17.30-19.00	Road and bridge between Cava and Nocera	16-19,000	42 HE	FOO
	12 September				
K.	09.10-09.20	Road junction at Camerelle	20,600	7 HE	Unobserved
L.	17.45-	Tanks and troops near Battipaglia	17,000	14 HE	FOO
M.	18.24-	Enemy H.Q. Battipaglia	17,000	8 HE	FOO
	13 September				
N.	06.50-07.15	Transport on road to Baronissi	17,000	10 HE	Unobserved
	17 September				
P.	10.48-	Guns on road to Baronissi	18,500	10 HE	FOO
Q.	11.10-	Buildings near Baronissi	18,300	12 APC	FOO
R.	19.17-	Nocera town	25,000	2 APC	FOO
	18 September				
S.	10.18-	Guns on road between Nocera and Cava	19,200	13 APC	FOO
T.	13.20-13.40	Guns and troops near Battipaglia	13-14,000	13 HE	FOO
U.	16.21-16.46	Enemy H.Q. Cava	16,200	11 HE	FOO
	19 September				
V.	10.00-	Enemy H.Q. Cava	16,200	10 HE	FOO
W.	15.40-	Guns near Baronissi	16,700	15 HE	FOO
X.	23.59-	Enemy H.Q. Cava	16,200	12 HE	Unobserved

Note: Letters correspond to locations on map opposite

§7 Wartime Service in Home Waters

The Allies recognised that the final defeat of Germany could only be accomplished by an invasion of north-west Europe to strike directly at the heart of the Reich. Hitler had strongly reinforced the defences of all the coastlines on which landings might be made with his Atlantic Wall, so any assault would be a much more hazardous operation than those in the Mediterranean. In particular, the well sited coast defence batteries and strongpoints would need concentrated bombardment by large numbers of warships if they were not to impede a landing. The preliminary plan for Operation "Neptune", drawn up in December 1943, envisaged a fleet of five battleships and monitors, plus some 170 other major British warships. When later the scale of the initial assault was raised from three to five divisions, Ramsay, who had been designated Allied Naval Commander Expeditionary Force (A.N.C.X.F.), encountered some difficulty in finding a sufficient number of heavy gun ships and of landing craft. The U.S. Navy were reluctant to release any ships which might be needed for operations in the Pacific, so R.N. ships had to be withdrawn from other areas, especially L.S.T.s. There was little likelihood that *Abercrombie* would be repaired, worked up and steamed home by the date of the invasion, planned for June 1944. As many battleships as possible were therefore required for bombardment purposes, but the Home Fleet at Scapa could not be denuded of its newer vessels, so four older ships were selected as the major units of the bombarding fleet — *Warspite, Rodney, Nelson* and *Ramillies* — in addition to the two monitors, *Roberts* and *Erebus*.

The proposed landing areas on the Normandy beaches were known to be strongly defended on their western extremity by the batteries on the Cherbourg peninsula and, to the east, by those around Le Havre and the mouth of the River Seine. With about one hundred guns emplaced either in pits or casemates and others still to be

Following repairs after her damage at Bougie, Roberts *is seen here working up in the Clyde in June 1943. A number of modifications have been made, including lengthening of the funnel, new radars and additional Oerlikons. The shades of camouflage on the hull are (starting from the bow): light grey, dark grey, light grey and blue grey below the bridge (not easily distinguished in this view), dark grey (mass aft), light grey.*

mounted, ranging from 105-mm (4.1-inch) up to 380-mm (15-inch), six big gun ships were not really sufficient; the guns of the more numerous cruisers, destroyers and smaller support craft earmarked had neither the range nor the punch to take on heavily protected batteries. It was a relief to Ramsay when Admiral Ernest King, Chief of U.S. Naval Operations, relented in April 1944 and allocated three old battleships — *Nevada, Texas* and *Arkansas* — together with additional cruisers and destroyers.

The strongest bombarding fleet was assigned to the easternmost of the five landing beaches, codenamed "Sword", as not only were the coast defences strongest here, but the Germans were likely to defend nearby Caen most stubbornly as it blocked the direct route to Paris. *Roberts, Warspite* and *Ramillies* plus six cruisers were allocated to this sector as Bombarding Force "D" of the Eastern Task Force, each ship being assigned one particular heavy battery as its principal target on D-day. The Mediterranean landings had shown how important it was to have a heavy bombardment to neutralise enemy defences both prior to and during the actual assault. While it was not expected to knock out batteries by direct hits on the guns themselves — except by a sheer fluke — the massive weight of fire would drive their crews into their shelters, disrupt control of return fire, damage communication links and generally keep the defenders' heads down. Such preliminary bombardment could only be accurately observed from the air, so the assault had to take place in daylight, after sufficient time had been allowed to pound the defences into a demoralised state. H-hour was therefore selected as 07.25 at "Sword" beach allowing two hours for bombardment, but owing to the earlier tide, it had to be an hour sooner than the two American beaches, "Utah" and "Omaha", allowing only a bare 40 minutes' fire before touchdown. As described on p.137, *Erebus* had been allocated to the force covering "Utah" beach. *Texas* and *Arkansas* were to be stationed off "Omaha" beach but the two other British beaches, "Gold" and "Juno", would be covered only by cruisers and destroyers. The Allies expected to have air superiority over the beaches, which would not only diminish the risk from enemy air attack but would mean that Allied spotting aircraft would be able to operate more effectively, while the enemy batteries would be denied accurate spotting. The Germans would however still have their gun control radar, so these stations would also be targets for air and sea bombardment.

Roberts departed from Port Said on 5 March 1944 for the voyage to the U.K. to work up for "Neptune". She arrived in the Clyde on 3 April to carry out practice bombardments on the Kintyre range, in company with the other ships of the five bombarding fleets. Owing to her slower speed, she had to sail several days in advance of the rest of Force "D", arriving in Spithead on 28 May to await orders for the invasion fleet to sail for France. On the evening of 5 June, she set off as part of convoy S.6, joining up with the other bombarding ships and minesweepers coming from the Clyde. During the night, over 1000 British bombers attacked the German coastal batteries, followed at daybreak by U.S. aircraft.

Roberts anchored in her firing position eleven miles west of Le Havre at 05.20 on 6 June and three minutes later opened fire from about 20,000 yards' range on Houlgate battery, which had four ex-French 155-mm (6.1-inch) guns ten miles east of "Sword" beach. Two of the guns were in casemates, two in concrete pits, but there were also two additional pits from which guns had been withdrawn. As the bombarding positions were all within range of the long range batteries around Le Havre, aircraft laid a smokescreen along the eastern flank of the fleet. Owing to the effectiveness of this screen, electronic countermeasures and damage to the German radar, there was very little interference from these heavy batteries. Three torpedo boats did however put out from Le Havre, penetrate the smokescreen and fire off 17 torpedoes into the mass of Allied shipping at 05.30. Two torpedoes were observed coming straight for *Roberts*, but one passed down one side of her and one down the other. As her 15-inch guns were busy engaging Houlgate, she could not fire at the torpedo boats which were out of range of her 4-inch, but immediately weighed anchor and continued firing whilst underway.

A heavy fire was kept up on the enemy batteries until H-hour. *Roberts* fired 27 rounds during this period, but had some difficulty spotting owing to enemy defensive smokescreens and the failure of some A.P.C. shells to explode in marshy ground. Enemy return fire from these batteries was directed mainly at the ships offshore, rather than at the more vulnerable landing craft and beaches. Periodic fire was necessary during the day to silence any batteries that showed signs of interfering with the build up of troops, vehicles and stores on the beach-head. As the Allied Armies penetrated inland a few miles, the Forward Observers Bombardment (F.O.B., as the F.O.O. was now called) deployed in positions from which they were able to report targets and call for fire, although there were some difficulties initially in communication and in spotting owing to the general fog of war over the battle area.

During the afternoon of D-day, *Roberts* made a particularly successful shoot on Houlgate; after 16 rounds, the spotting fighter reported several direct hits and two large explosions. At 21.30, she had just started to fire on a troop concentration inland from "Sword" when a crash was heard and a large chunk of metal was seen to fly up in front of the bridge. On ceasing fire, it was found that the right 15-inch had burst its jacket, an accident similar to one on board *Erebus* during that afternoon, 35 miles to the west. The jacket had split into several pieces without the whole gun bursting, so further damage was prevented by strapping it with wire rope. *Roberts* was then ordered to Portsmouth, partly to top up with ammunition, although she had fired only 75 rounds so far. *Ramillies* also returned in company with her, leaving *Warspite* as the only big gun ship off the eastern beaches until the reserve battleship *Rodney* arrived the next day. Between them, the three 15-inch gun ships had fired about 500 main battery rounds, mostly at the coastal defences.

Roberts' damaged gun was inspected at Portsmouth but it was decided to defer changing it until the left gun was worn out. She sailed again for Seine Bay in the early hours of 9 June, with only one of her two 15-inch guns operational, arriving back off "Sword" at a time when the Germans were making heavy counterattacks. On the 10th, she moved to "Gold" beach a few miles to the west to support 7 Armoured Division's thrust towards Villers-Bocage south-west of Caen, which was getting out of range of the cruisers' guns. For two and a half days from the early hours of the 11th, *Roberts* was called upon to fire on enemy concentrations, strongpoints, road junctions, mobile batteries and motor transport, in the area around Juvigny about 11 miles west of Caen.

A well known view of Roberts *bombarding Houlgate battery on 6 June 1944. The left gun has just fired: the right is being reloaded. Extra counter-measures equipment has been fitted: the X-shaped aerial abaft the funnel is for the Type 650 missile jammer, while a 'window' rocket launcher is on top of the turret (not visible here). The cruiser in the background is* Frobisher.

Shoots during daylight hours were generally spotted by fighters, given such codenames as "Eyebrow"; those at night were usually unobserved, as they were general shoots on area targets such as troops and vehicles concentrating in woods. Each of the 19 shoots lasted up to about half an hour with from 4 to 20 rounds apiece. Despite being anchored only about a mile offshore, the range was usually near the guns' maximum at about 30,000 yards. So devastating was the heavy calibre naval gunfire that the Army had to be discouraged from calling for it on targets which could be tackled as readily by the smaller guns of the other bombarding vessels. *Roberts* returned to Portsmouth on 14 June with 37 rounds remaining, to exchange both her guns and re-ammunition. Special arrangements had been made to supply ammunition to the bombarding ships quickly, barges being preloaded with the correct outfits for the various types of ship. Most of the 2800 15-inch shells stockpiled were the newer 6 c.r.h., but some old 4 c.r.h. were included to be used up by *Roberts* and *Ramillies*.

Roberts was again stationed on the eastern flank on her return to France on the 21st. I Corps held the ground eastwards only to the mouth of the River Orne, ten miles north-east of Caen. Further to the east, the enemy held on to the coast very determinedly, using both casemated batteries and mobile field guns to harass Allied shipping off the beaches. Although the field guns were difficult to locate in woods, their fire could usually be temporarily silenced fairly quickly, as they were unprotected. Direct hits on these or emplaced guns were very unlikely; sooner or later the guns would open up again. Enemy air activity was mostly confined to night bombing and mining raids.

Bombardments were usually carried out at anchor, as not only was accuracy improved but there was less danger of steaming over a mine, particularly one of the almost unsweepable pressure mines.

During the first three days following her return to the beach-head, *Roberts* spread some 80 rounds between defended buildings east of Caen and the batteries east of the beaches. On 26 June, she supported Operation "Epsom", the British advance across the River Odon south-west of Caen. During the morning, she was asked to fire 100 rounds at two targets near Carpiquet village west of Caen but, as she could not make proper contact with either her F.O.B. or fighter spotter, the results were largely unobserved. The situation over the next few days was quiet, so she was ordered to sail for Portsmouth on 1 July to replenish with ammunition and stores.

By the end of June, the Americans in the west had advanced out of range of naval gunfire, so the remaining bombarding vessels were concentrated on the eastern flank — the relatively static 'hinge' around Caen about which the whole Allied advance was intended to pivot. The heavy bombardment fleet could be reduced to an average of one battleship or monitor and four cruisers, while control of fire support switched from the H.Q. ship *Largs* to shore headquarters at Courseulles. *Roberts* was back again on 3 July ready to support the forthcoming attack on Caen itself. *Rodney, Belfast* and *Emerald* were also present to bombard the German defences, which ringed Caen at a distance of about three miles. Targets allocated to the ships were strongpoints around Carpiquet airfield, defended villages on the roads leading north from the city and tank concentrations. The British and Canadian attack commenced on 8 July, with naval gunfire backing the bombing and artillery barrage. When Canadian 3 Division asked for support when being heavily counterattacked, *Roberts* directed some 40 rounds on to the road junction through which the German reinforcements were moving. The target was just outside the range of her guns but, as it would take too long to flood the bulges to heel the ship, the Gunnery Officer obtained the extra elevation by using an initial salvo to get the ship rolling, then timed the firing of each subsequent round to the extremity of the roll. Caen was entered the next day, although the German defence south of the Orne remained stubborn.

Enemy batteries east of the Orne continued to fire on the shipping offshore, but the ships of the bombarding fleet received few hits, *Roberts* suffering no more than splinters through the funnel from a near-miss. Although eventually four gun sites at Houlgate — one casemate and three pits — were knocked out, including one by *Roberts* on D-day, replacement guns in this battery continued their harassment, together with mobile batteries in the area. By the time Houlgate was finally overrun in mid-August, it had taken 218 rounds of 15-inch and 16-inch from the battleships and monitors plus 928 6-inch from the former's secondary armament, in addition to frequent bombing raids.

The final operation in which naval gunfire could still assist active front-line engagements was "Goodwood", the British and Canadian offensive south-east of Caen on 18 July. This time *Roberts* was supported by *Mauritius* and *Enterprise*. Most of the targets were field artillery, so both F.O.B.s and aircraft spotting could be used. Here again, the naval bombardment followed R.A.F. bombing; in concentration, accuracy and continuity of fire, the former complemented the sheer volume of explosive dropped in a short period by the latter. This was *Roberts*' last big shoot off Normandy as she was relieved by *Erebus* who arrived on 23 July. *Roberts* returned to Portsmouth for the next ten weeks to change her guns again, give leave and repair the wear and tear of six weeks' almost continual bombardment in which she fired a total of 692 rounds of 15-inch.

The lessons from the Mediterranean landings had been well learned; fire support in Operation "Neptune" fulfilled all that was required with a lesser expenditure of ammunition than expected. German reports indicated that they found naval bombardment an extremely powerful, accurate and inhibiting weapon. Indeed Field-Marshal von Rundstedt counted it as one of the three principal factors which determined the outcome of Operation "Overlord" (the other two were Allied air superiority and their abundance of supplies). Troop and vehicle movement and concentration during daylight rapidly brought either air attack or naval gunfire or both; the sheer weight demoralised troops whether or not direct hit were obtained.

Between them, the four British battleships and two monitors fired 3371 main battery rounds in 137 shoots. The monitors were on call for 70 ship-days, the battleships 45, as shown in the deployment diagram. 26% of the shoots were against coastal batteries, 23% against other artillery, 26% against towns, buildings and strongpoints, and 25% against tanks, vehicles, troop concentrations and miscellaneous. In all some 141,000 rounds of 4-inch calibre and above were expended by the Allied ships against targets at Normandy, including aircraft, the majority being 6-inch and below. H.E. projectiles were used most frequently although they were sometimes in short supply, A.P.C. being used mainly against fortifications or buildings. The well trained fighter spotters were especially effective, so they were employed as the principal means of spotting for the big ships (52% of shoots) although they had originally been intended to be used only until the F.O.B.s got established. The F.O.B.s spotted only 14% as they were restricted by the close nature of the Normandy countryside. Ship observation (4%) and Air Observation Post (2%) — slow and vulnerable Austers — were used a little, the remaining 28% being unobserved blind shoots, often at night.

Meantime, *Abercrombie* had completed repairs at Taranto, arriving at Malta on 15 August 1944. She was exercising off the Delimara Light, south-east of the island, on the 21st when she had the bad luck to strike not one but two mines in 420 feet of water. She hit one on her starboard side forward, which blew a hole about 16ft × 4ft, flooding part of the lower deck. The second hit was on the bottom abaft the mainmast and did considerable damage. Although the hole was only about 10ft × 4ft,

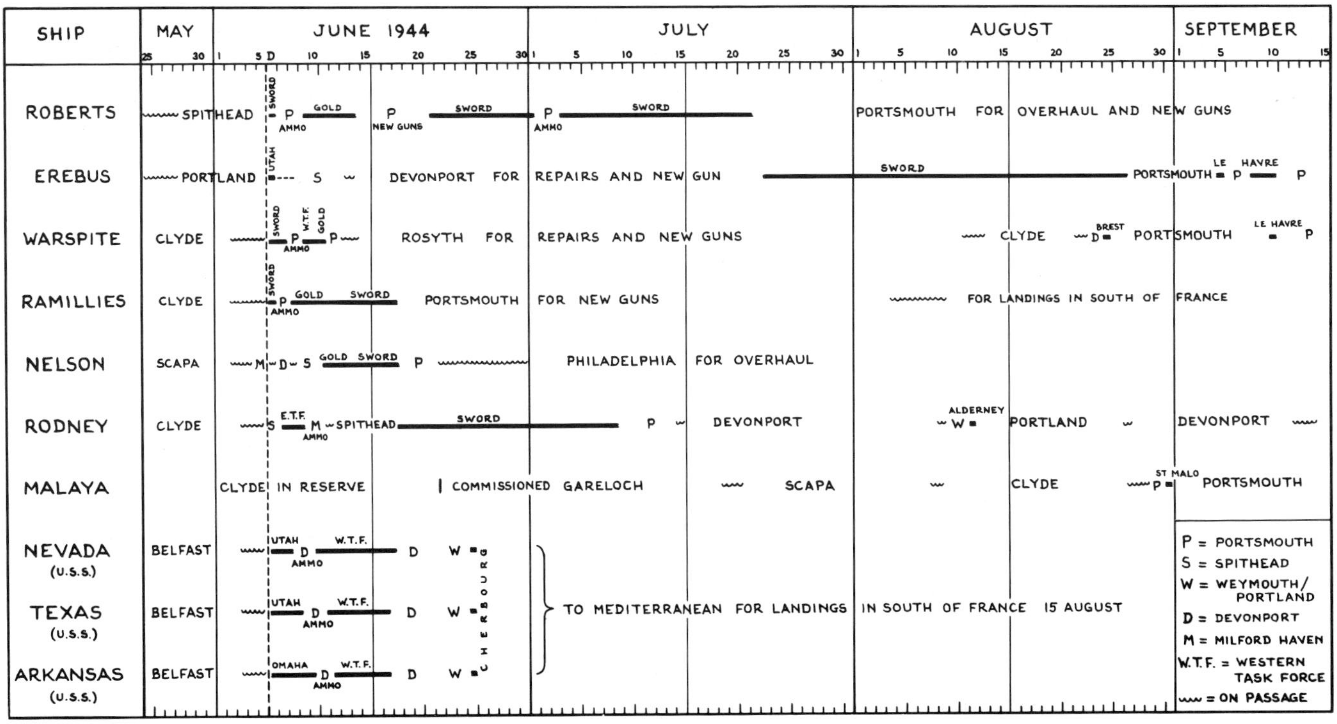

The chart shows the deployment of monitors and battleships off the Channel coast of France from just before D-day to the fall of Le Havre. The thick lines show the periods when the individual heavy gun ships were on station. After concentration of four to six ships on the firing line during the first two weeks of Operation "Neptune", only one or two ships were required on call for fire support for the remaining three months. As well as direct support of Allied forces ashore on the Normandy beachheads, bombardments were made of individual fortified targets such as Brest. Malaya *was recommissioned following the withdrawal of* Warspite *and* Nelson *in mid-June for overhaul, which included damage repairs after mining.*

both shafts were bent and the starboard A-bracket broken, the lower deck aft flooded and radar and gyro-compasses damaged. The $4^1/_2°$ starboard heel was quickly reduced, while the ship dropped anchor to avoid hitting any more mines. The trawlers *Cava* and *Juliet* swept around her, finding four more German moored mines, then tugs towed her into Grand Harbour. She spent the next eleven months in Malta Dockyard repairing the damage.

After the fall of Le Havre, the remaining French channel ports were either captured by the Canadian Army without the need for naval bombardment or simply surrounded until the war ended. Although Antwerp had been captured as early as 4 September, this valuable port could not be used for supplying the Allied Armies until both banks of the River Scheldt had been cleared of Germans. After a hard struggle, the south bank up to the river mouth had been taken by the end of October 1944, but the Germans still held out on the strongly fortified island of Walcheren commanding the river entrance. As only a narrow and easily defended causeway connected the island with the mainland, plans were made for a seaborne assault. A bombarding force consisting of *Warspite, Roberts* and *Erebus* was organised, in addition to the heavily armed converted landing craft of the Support Squadron, massed artillery on the shore opposite Flushing and bomber aircraft. *Roberts* and *Erebus* had left Portsmouth for Dover on 5 October to prepare for the operation, which included bombardment of any batteries around Zeebrugge that might still be holding out.

The ships remained at 48 hours' notice throughout October, either off Ramsgate or in the Thames Estuary. After the order had been given to land a R.M. Commando force at Westkapelle on the western corner of the island and another force at Flushing, the bombardment force gathered at the Downs on 31 October. *Warspite, Roberts* and *Erebus* set sail at 23.00 at 8 knots escorted by the destroyers *Garth* and *Cottesmore,* in company with minesweepers and M.L.s, with the tug *Growler* in attendance in case the monitors should need help in the tricky waters.

The bombardment fleet arrived in position 11 miles west of Westkapelle at dawn on 1 November, unable to get closer owing to the minefields and sandbanks (see map on p.46). Before fire was opened, news was received that the spotting Spitfires were grounded by fog at Manston airfield. Fire had therefore to be spotted using direct observation from the ships, when *Warspite* and *Roberts* opened up at 08.15. *Warspite* took on the heavy Domburg battery north-east of Westkapelle with its four 220-mm (8.7-inch) guns. *Roberts*' first target was a radar station, whose destruction would handicap the German gunnery. After five rounds, she switched to the W.15 coastal battery at Westkapelle, which had six ex-British 3.7-inch and 3-inch guns. This battery had been allocated to *Erebus* but she was unable to open fire until 09.26 as her turret training machinery had broken down.

Roberts *leaves Malta on 8 November 1945 to pay off after returning from her intended deployment against the Japanese in Malaya. Her eight single Bofors are clearly seen.*

Roberts and *Erebus* then kept up a steady fire until just before the Commandos touched down at 09.45. Fire was switched to W.13 battery at Zoutelande south-east of Westkapelle with its six guns, four casemated 152-mm (6-inch) and two 75-mm (2.95-inch). Accurate direct observation at ranges of about 24,000 yards proved very difficult for such low-lying targets, often shrouded in smoke from shell-bursts or smokescreens, so firing was stopped for three hours.

The fog over Manston lifted during the morning, so fighter spotting was available from 13.40. With the F.O.B.s well in position, *Warspite, Roberts* and *Erebus* were able to pour a heavy fire onto the remaining batteries and strongpoints until darkness fell about 17.30. W.15 and W.13 had been captured after fierce fighting, followed by Domburg at dusk. Although the bombarding ships had not been directly responsible for putting them permanently out of action, they and the fighter-bombers had contributed largely to reducing their effectiveness. The Germans had not fired on the bombarding fleet at all, reserving their ammunition for the landing craft. The fleet retired to lie off the Belgian Coast for the night to avoid possible E-boat attack, while *Warspite* returned to England, her guns worn out.

Roberts and *Erebus* were back in position at 08.20 on the 2nd, the latter opening fire on a strongpoint almost immediately. *Roberts* turned her attention to an A.A. battery that had been firing at the spotting aircraft. Both monitors then switched to the troublesome W.11 battery with its four casemated 152-mm and two 75-mm guns sited at Duinrand between Westkapelle and Flushing. Sometimes using F.O.B.s and sometimes fighter spotters, fire was kept up for the rest of the day on W.11. Despite continuous troubles with her working chamber frequently flooded with water to a depth of over a foot, *Erebus* put in some very good shooting at this battery. She fired 99 rounds at it over four different periods of the day, 27 being reported hits and a further 33 within 100 yards. When the battery was finally captured the next day, it was found that there had been direct hits on the casemates themselves. *Erebus* generally found the target with about the fifth round, thereafter firing for effect about 20 rounds at a rate of one a minute. Over the two days, *Erebus* fired a total of 179 rounds, *Roberts* 104 and *Warspite* 353.

As there was no further need of bombardment, *Roberts* and *Erebus* departed the next morning, the latter direct to Portsmouth, the former to Sheerness for ammunition before returning to Spithead. The two monitors then took it in turns to remain on call for any further bombardments that might be required as the Allied Armies advanced into Germany but, although two operations were planned for *Roberts* in the early months of 1945, neither came off. The last operation in Europe for which she and *Erebus* were put at four hours' notice was a possible bombardment of Heligoland if its batteries should show signs of firing on the Allied minesweepers opening up the Elbe to Hamburg following the final German collapse in early May. Much to the relief of the crews of both monitors, there was no call for them to sail, so they could celebrate VE-day comfortably in harbour at Portsmouth. On 12 May, A.N.C.X.F., now Vice-Admiral H. M. Burrough following Ramsay's death in January, signalled:—

> "On your release from "Overlord" I wish to congratulate you on the results of your operations since D-day. The recent lack of targets is a measure of your former successes."

With the war in Europe over, the Allies turned to the final defeat of Japan, already reeling from the American Pacific island offensives. The war in the Indian Ocean was being progressed much less spectacularly owing to lack of resources, Burma being reoccupied only in May 1945. Plans to recapture Malaya included assaults on Port Dickson (Operation "Zipper") and Singapore (Operation "Mailfist"). In view of the strong defences at Singapore, "Mailfist" required one or two monitors for bombardment purposes, so both *Roberts* and *Abercrombie* were allocated to the East Indies Fleet. *Roberts* was despatched to the Mersey for a quick overhaul, before sailing for the Indian Ocean on 27 July. *Abercrombie* had already left Malta on 17 July, her repairs completed. She was ordered to reach Ceylon by 1 September to allow time for her crew to become acclimatised before "Mailfist" which was to follow about 50 days after "Zipper", scheduled for 9 September. On the day of the Japanese surrender following the dropping

Abercrombie *is seen here moored in the Medway in June 1946 as an accommodation ship. She is virtually unchanged from her original condition, although the C.O's sea cabin has been moved to the aft end of the compass platform and the rangefinder removed.*

of the two atomic bombs, 14 August, *Roberts* was off Port Said and *Abercrombie* was approaching Aden. Both vessels continued their eastwards passage until the formal Japanese surrender on 2 September. The decision to order them to return home and reduce to reserve was taken on the 11th, by which time *Roberts* had reached Kilindini and *Abercrombie* was approaching the Seychelles. Both ships reached their home ports in November 1945, the one after a busy and varied four years' operations, the other after barely six months' active service owing to her misfortune with mines.

§8 Performance

Although there was no time for lengthy trials on completion, *Roberts* took the opportunity at Suez to make some turning and stopping trials. These confirmed the model experiments that she had a very small turning circle about 200 yards in diameter with 35° of rudder. This was accompanied however by a great loss of speed at full helm, so that after turning through 180° in two minutes, she had slowed down from 12 to 2 knots. Stopping trials showed that by going half astern at 160 r.p.m., she could stop in 975 yards, taking five minutes but ending up slewed 60° to port. The very small tactical diameter (less than twice the ship's length) resulted from the use of twin rudders and the large cut-up (the rise aft of the keel from the base-line up to the stern) with corresponding lack of deadwood effect. As a consequence, course stability was not good and the response to the helm once turning had commenced was poor. Indeed *Roberts* was quite capable of emulating *Marshal Ney*'s and the other WW1 monitors' trick, where a moderate alteration of course could not always be checked before the ship had swung in a complete 360° circle.

When these reports reached D.N.C's department, the comment was made that, as *Erebus* did not turn fast enough, special attention had been paid to this feature in *Roberts* but it appeared to have been overdone. Approval was given to fit a deadwood in the form of a vertical fin on the centre-line below the cut-up, but in neither ship was this modification ever carried out. It was also found that in a strong beam wind, the mass of superstructure aft of midships produced a large turning moment, which required a rudder angle of up to 25° to be carried to maintain course, also resulting in considerable leeway. Experience however showed that the monitor's peculiar shiphandling qualities were actually quite predictable, so that they could perform quite versatile manoeuvres in capable hands.

Although the two WW2 monitors had a better hull form than any of their WW1 predecessors, they still exhibited the same loss of speed at sea. The bluff form, with its large underwater area on which fouling could take place, led to losses of speed of about two knots when six months out of drydock — a serious matter when 12 knots was the best cruising speed. A further $1^3/_4$ knots was lost when the bow defence gear was streamed, which made station-keeping on other ships difficult. Bad weather also produced a great loss of speed; three or four knots was the best speed that could be made heading into Force 7 winds. Such losses of speed had a marked effect on the endurance. The specified endurance of 3600 miles at 10 knots could be achieved with a clean hull, but it dropped to about 2700 miles six months out of dock. Appreciable quantities of fuel were required to keep auxiliaries such as turbo-generators and evaporators running, so that even at the lowest speeds some 30 tons of oil a day were needed. At maximum speed, consumption rose to 66 tons per day; in harbour about 8 to 10 tons were required. The corresponding specific fuel consumption was about 1.28lb per H.P. per hour, which was about 50% higher than more powerful warships using superheated steam. In *Roberts*' four years of active service, she steamed a total of 62,287 nautical miles made up as shown, burning some 15,000 tons of oil fuel:—

Year	*Miles*	*Operations*
1941	6,022	Two months' service
1942	25,333	Twice round the south of Africa
1943	9,967	Under repair; in Mediterranean
1944	6,579	Operations in north-west Europe
1945	14,386	Out to Indian Ocean and back.

§9 Modifications

Because of her well equipped start in life and her bad luck with mines such that she spent less than twelve months in active service, *Abercrombie* experienced few of the normally extensive range of wartime modifications. During her repairs at Malta, some changes were made in the internal layout, including the conversion of empty watertight compartments to carry about 180 tons of extra oil fuel. The most important modification was the installation of a full Action Information Organisation, with Operations Room, Aircraft Direction Room, Target Indicating Room and Y Office. The associated air-conditioning plant was fitted in place of one of the cabins in the shelter deck; similar plant would have been even more welcome on the mess-decks, which were very hot under the bare steel decks. Externally there was very little change, although surface warning radar was changed from Type 272M to combined surface/air warning Type 293 on the mainmasthead. The two-aerial Type 281 air warning was changed to Type 79B, with its single aerial on the foremasthead.

Roberts however underwent quite a number of modifications. Early experience had shown that smoke from the short funnel was troublesome on the bridge — the same problem as the WW1 coal-burners. At her first overhaul at Cammell Laird's early in 1943 following damage off North Africa, the funnel was raised 12 feet. Haynes' comments from *Terror* about lack of storage space for food and water were also borne out in service. The boilers required 12 tons of fresh water per day for make-up feed, while the ship's company used another 30. Since the single evaporator could supply a theoretical maximum of 60 tons per day and there was stowage for only 100 tons, the margin for breakdown and deterioration was small. Two replacement evaporators were fitted, each with an output of 40 tons per day, while stowage capacity was increased to nearly 300 tons.

The close range armament was increased, with twin

Mk V power-operated Oerlikons replacing all but the forecastle singles, making a total of fourteen 20-mm (six twin, two single), while the 4-inch and pom-poms were converted to R.P.C. The radar was also augmented: Type 279 replaced the Type 281, improved versions of the Types 285 and 282 A.A. gunnery sets were fitted (although still not accurate enough in elevation to permit full blind-fire), and surface warning Type 272P was added below the spotting top. The after 282 controlling the octuple pom-pom was removed. Improvements were also made to the W/T equipment, the electronic counter-measures (E.C.M.), and the anti-ship and night-fighting capabilities, including better searchlight control. A new design of disruptive camouflage was borne by the ship when she returned to service in May 1943, with three shades of grey plus white, as illustrated on p.164.[1]

When the monitors were earmarked for the Indian Ocean in 1944-45, improvements to the accommodation were planned. It proved impossible to undertake all that was needed during *Roberts*' two short subsequent refits, although ventilation to the 15-inch turret was improved for hot climates. The main outward change following her 1945 Liverpool refit was the addition of eight single Army-style hand-operated 40-mm Mk III Bofors and the substitution of Type 268 for the Type 272 radar. Two of the twin Oerlikons were replaced by Bofors, as well as the two forecastle singles, while the other four were straight additions — two in place of the 44-inch searchlights (now completely superseded by radar and star-shell), one on top of the turret in place of the E.C.M. rocket launcher fitted for "Neptune", and one abaft the mainmast. The Bofors had proved itself the best close-range weapon of the war, being used by both sides, with a range, rate of fire and punch that could down the larger, faster aircraft being encountered. *Roberts*' total A.A. armament then comprised:—

8—4", 16—2pdr, 8—40mm, 8—20mm

The modifications that were made during the war

[1] A coloured drawing of this pattern is given in *Royal Navy Warship Camouflage* by P. Hodges.

This view from the foremasthead shows Roberts *awaiting the shipbreaker's men in early August 1965. In the foreground is the roof of the spotting top. The mounting ring for a single Bofors can be seen on the turret, but the circular tubs for the two fitted on the forecastle have been removed.*

Another view from Roberts' *foremasthead, showing much of the preserving kooncoting stripped. De-equipping has already taken place: the 20-mm guns have been removed from the twin mountings by the funnel, the compass from the after conning position, the aerial arrays from the rangefinder/directors and the boats from the davits.*

increased her deep displacement to about 9500 tons and *Abercrombie*'s to about 9900 tons, mostly resulting from the additional fuel and water carried.

§10 Post-War Careers

After the surrender of Japan, *Abercrombie* arrived back at Sheerness on 6 November 1945 to be placed into reserve. Initially used as an accommodation ship, she replaced *Erebus* as Turret Drill Ship at Chatham in July 1946, lying at moorings in the Medway. Later her role was that of living ship for the Nore Reserve Fleet. In the spring of 1953, she was towed to Portsmouth and laid up in Fareham Creek until November 1954, when she was handed over to BISCO for scrapping. Allocated to Ward's Barrow yard, she arrived on Christmas Eve. Demolition work started almost immediately, but it was three weeks before there arrived from the Admiralty the list showing the items which were to be salvaged for return to naval stores. In addition to the usual things like electronic equipment and spare parts, the eight 4-inch guns were included but, by the time Ward's were notified, they had been mutilated beyond further use, in accordance with standing instructions for gunnery equipment. In preparing the 1955-56 Naval Appropriation Account, the Auditor-General drew attention to the resulting £25,000 loss and asked for a tightening up of Admiralty procedures concerning equipment to be returned from ships to be scrapped.

Breaking up *Abercrombie* yielded the following approximate amounts:—

Material	*Tons*	*Sale value £*
Armour quality scrap	2100	33,000
Other ferrous scrap	4500	44,000
Non-ferrous scrap	440	53,000
Re-usable equipment	50	2,000
Sundries	30	1,000
Rubbish, insulation etc.	490	—
Total recovered	7610	133,000
Cost of demolition, towage etc.		41,000
Net surplus		92,000

The £92,000 constituted the effective sale price under the BISCO system (see p.79). It corresponded to about £11 per ton: four times greater than the first *Abercrombie* but only about 7% of the second *Abercrombie*'s original cost.

Roberts survived for considerably longer. She had arrived at Devonport on 22 November 1945, where she remained for the next two decades. Initially she was used as a Turret Drill Ship with a complement of about 120, later as an accommodation ship for the Reserve Fleet base *Orion* with a crew of about 40. Various downgradings of reserve readiness occurred, so that by 1953 in Class III Reserve, she would not have been available to the Fleet until six months after mobilisation. Although she was removed from the official "Strength of the Fleet" in 1955, she continued to be useful at the Dockyard. She remained in the role of part living-ship, part fender-ship until 1963, when she was moved to lie at buoys in the stream. Her distinctive profile with the prominent spotting top and the raised turret made her a familiar sight to a generation of sailors at Devonport. To the older ones, she was a reminder of the big gun ships in which most had once served; to the younger ones who would never see a British battleship, she gave a fleeting impression of the naval might which once had dominated the seas.

By late August 1965, demolition of Roberts *at Inverkeithing is well advanced, masts and bridge stripped.*

In 1965, invitations to tender for her purchase for scrap were sent out to British shipbreakers. Ward's bid of about £150,000 was successful, so *Roberts* left Devonport on 19 July. The tow to Inverkeithing was made by the Royal Fleet Auxiliary tugs *Typhoon* and *Samsonia*, but she did not finally berth until 3 August, as Ward's yard was closed for the summer holiday. *Roberts* thus became the eleventh large monitor to be broken up by Ward's out of a total of seventeen which survived the two World Wars, the last of the big gun types whose existence had spanned exactly half a century.

ROBERTS and ABERCROMBIE — TECHNICAL PARTICULARS

Displacement and Dimensions (As completed) 7973 (*Roberts*)/8536 (*Abercrombie*) tons standard, 9150/9717 deep. Length 373′-4″ o.a., breadth 89′-9″, draft 13′-6$^1/_4$″/14′-4$^3/_4$″ deep.

Weight Distribution (*Roberts* as designed/as completed) Armament 970/1012 tons, ammunition 480/504, armour and protective plating 2130/2200, hull 3270/3445, equipment 380/537, machinery 275/275. Standard displacement 7505/7973 tons. Water protection 580/586, reserve feed water 40/42, oil fuel 550/549. Deep displacement 8675/9150 tons.

Complement (*Roberts*/*Abercrombie*) 19/20 officers, 423/440 men.

Armament (As completed) 2—15″ (twin) (30-60 A.P.C. + 80-50 H.E. + 8 practice r.p.g.), 8—4″ (twins) (80 S.A.P. + 320 H.E.T.F. + 12 star + 83 practice r.p.g.), 16—2pdr (2 quad, 1 octuple) (1800 H.E. + 114 practice r.p.g.), 8 (*Roberts* - single)/20 (*Abercrombie* - 4 single, 8 twin)—20mm (2400 H.E. + 300 practice r.p.g.).

Protection Main deck 4″ and 6 ″ N.C. over 15-inch magazine, 3″ (*Roberts*)/4″ (*Abercrombie*) machinery and aft, 2″ and 3″ N.C. forward; sloping external belt 5″ N.C. abreast 15-inch magazine, 4″ elsewhere; torpedo protective bulkhead 1$^1/_2$″ D. ($^3/_4$″ at ends); steering gear 3″ N.C.; barbette 8″ C.; gunhouse 13″ C. front, 11″ C. sides and rear, 5″ (*R*)/6″ (*A*) N.C. roof, 3″ H.T. floor; conning tower 3″ N.C. sides, 2″ front, rear and roof, 1$^1/_2$″ floor; splinter protection 1$^1/_2$″ N.C. sides and floor 15-inch magazine, $^3/_8$″ to 1″ D. superstructure positions.

Machinery Twin screw Parsons single-reduction geared steam turbines. Two Admiralty 3-drum boilers, 250lb/sq in. 4800 S.H.P. at 250 r.p.m. Fuel oil 491 tons, diesel 58. Endurance 2680 miles at 12 knots.

Speed 12$^1/_4$ knots designed and service. Trials: *Roberts* 13.5, *Abercrombie* 12.0 knots.

Construction *Roberts* John Brown laid down 30 Apr 1940/launched 1 Feb 1941/completed 27 Oct 1941. *Abercrombie* Vickers-Armstrong, Tyne 26 Apr 1941/31 Mar 1942/5 May 1943.

Scrapped *Roberts* Ward, Inverkeithing 3 Aug 1965; *Abercrombie* Ward, Barrow 24 Dec 1954.

CHAPTER X

GUNNERY IN THE MONITORS

§1 The 15-inch Mark I Gun

When Churchill authorised the development of a 15-inch gun in 1912, he provided the Royal Navy with its most successful piece of heavy ordnance, which was to remain afloat for half a century. In order to ensure a margin of superiority over any German developments in capital ship construction, a weapon larger than the exisiting 13.5-inch was needed for the British battleships of the 1912 Programme. Amidst great secrecy, development was rapidly pushed ahead, the Woolwich-designed gun and the Elswick-designed mounting being basically scaled-up 13.5-inch. The design of the Mark I gun adopted the well-tried principles of wire-wound ordnance, used for 20 years by the R.N. The 42-calibre 100-ton gun was similar in construction to that of the 18-inch illustrated on p.186; other characteristics are given in the Technical Particulars at the end of the section on p.181.

The twin mounting followed the now well established British design practice using hydraulic power. The drawing on p.174 shows the general arrangement as fitted in *Abercrombie* in 1943 which, although including many minor improvements, was basically similar to all the earlier 15-inch mountings fitted in capital ships and monitors. Each gun was mounted in a cradle, which could move in recoil on a forged steel slide. The slide was pivoted to permit elevation between trunnions which were fixed to the 3-inch thick gunhouse floor, the latter also supporting the shield armour keyed to its edge. The floor also formed the top of the main rotating turntable structure, whose diameter was about two feet less than the 30ft 6in diameter of the barbette armour. Forty-eight roller bearings beneath the edge of the turntable supported the whole turret weight, which was then transferred to the hull structure by a ring bulkhead just inside the barbette armour.

Beneath the turntable was the working chamber about 25ft in diameter. The main hoist from the magazine and shell-room below fed into the centre of this chamber via flashtight doors. After transfer to the gun loading cage, the projectile and charge were then lifted up to the breech of the gun for loading and ramming, the gun having already been brought to the loading angle of 5°. The chamber also contained the hoisting machinery as well as spare projectiles. The main hoist trunk was about 8ft in diameter and was made as long as required to reach the shell-room floor — only 23ft in a monitor but up to 43ft in a battleship. Each gun had two cages, one for projectile, one for cordite, which were loaded separately at shell-room and magazine handing room levels and then brought together and hoisted as one. In the shell-room, the projectiles were stowed horizontally in bins each holding about 20, from which they were lifted and traversed by hydraulically powered grabs suspended from overhead rails. In the magazine, two quarter-charges of cordite MD 45[1] were stowed in each airtight cylindrical case, which were arranged horizontally in layers. Ammunition was embarked by derricks on the upper deck abreast the bridge and lowered vertically to the magazine by winch and davit through hatches on the centre-line.

Typical manning of a 15-inch installation comprised:

Gunhouse: Turret officer, captain of turret, two gunlayers, trainer, four crew for each gun, four sightsetter and communication numbers	17
Working chamber	6
Magazine	12
Handing room	7
Shell-room	22
Total mounting crew	64
Control top: Gunnery officer, B.L.O., spotting and communication numbers	8
Director: Layer, trainer, sightsetter, phone man	4
Transmitting station: Officer, twelve at fire control table, four communication numbers	17
Ordnance artificers	2
Total 15-inch crew	95

The breakdown of the total revolving weight of the twin turret was approximately:

	Tons
Two guns	200
Two slides and cradles	80
Turntable and gunhouse floor	160
Working chamber	50
Hoist trunk	20
Gunhouse and shield plates	180
Roof plates	70
Total	760

[1] The 'modified' cordite introduced before WW1 to give increased gun life was designated MD, the number being the nominal diameter of the sticks in hundredths of an inch, i.e. 0.45in. Increasing the proportion of nitrocellulose from 37% in cordite Mk I (with 58% nitroglycerin and 5% mineral jelly) to 65% (with 30% nitroglycerin) approximately doubled gun life.

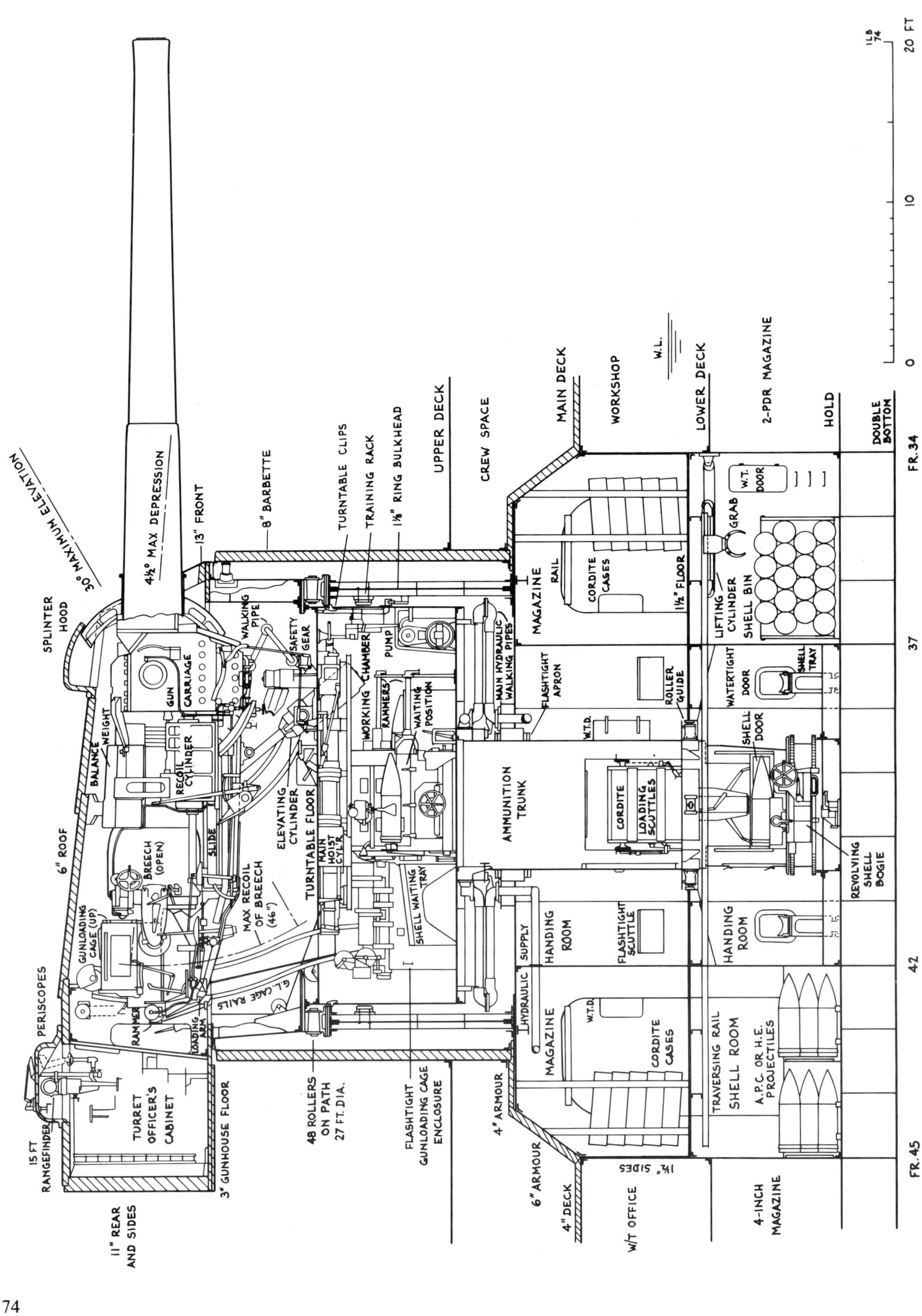
30° MAXIMUM ELEVATION
4½° MAX DEPRESSION
13" FRONT
8" BARBETTE
TURNTABLE CLIPS
TRAINING RACK
1⅛" RING BULKHEAD
UPPER DECK
CREW SPACE
MAIN DECK
WORKSHOP
W.L.
LOWER DECK
2-PDR MAGAZINE
HOLD
DOUBLE BOTTOM
FR. 34
37
42
FR. 45
0
10
20 FT
SPLINTER HOOD
WALKING PIPE
SAFETY GEAR
GUN CARRIAGE
BALANCE WEIGHT
RECOIL CYLINDER
WORKING CHAMBER
PUMP
RAMMERS
WAITING POSITION
MAIN HYDRAULIC WALKING PIPES
FLASHTIGHT APRON
MAGAZINE
RAIL
CORDITE CASES
1½" FLOOR
GRAB
LIFTING CYLINDER
SHELL BIN
W.T. DOOR
WATERTIGHT DOOR
SHELL TRAY
ROLLER GUIDE
W.T.D.
SHELL DOOR
6" ROOF
BREECH (OPEN)
SLIDE
ELEVATING CYLINDER
TURNTABLE FLOOR
MAIN HOIST CYL'R
AMMUNITION TRUNK
CORDITE
LOADING SCUTTLES
REVOLVING SHELL BOGIE
GUNLOADING CAGE (UP)
MAX RECOIL OF BREECH (46")
SHELL WAITING TRAY
SUPPLY
HANDING ROOM
FLASHTIGHT SCUTTLE
PERISCOPES
RAMMER
LOADING ARM
G.L. CAGE RAILS
HYDRAULIC
TRAVERSING RAIL
SHELL ROOM
A.P.C. OR H.E. PROJECTILES
15 FT RANGEFINDER
TURRET OFFICER'S CABINET
3" GUNHOUSE FLOOR
48 ROLLERS ON PATH 27 FT. DIA.
FLASHTIGHT GUNLOADING CAGE ENCLOSURE
4" ARMOUR
6" ARMOUR
1½" SIDES
4" DECK
W/T OFFICE
4-INCH MAGAZINE
11" REAR AND SIDES

(Above) Abercrombie's *turntable and working chamber leave Elswick on 29 January 1943. The upper roller path of the 204-ton unit is resting on the pillars at the corners of the bogie.*
(Right) Abercrombie's *ammunition trunk leaves Elswick for the down-river trip on a barge to Naval Yard on 28 January 1943. The 22-foot long trunk weighed 16 tons, but many smaller fittings have yet to be added. The shell door is just above the toothed rack, the twin cordite doors halfway up. The turntable can be seen in the background.*

The five battleships of the 1912 Programme, the *Queen Elizabeth* class, were designed to carry four 15-inch Mark I twin mountings, as were the five vessels of the *Royal Sovereign* class. The work was divided among the three main ordnance contractors: five ships by Elswick, four by Vickers and one by Coventry Ordnance Works. The contracts were of substantial value, as the armament of a battleship comprised over 25% of its cost. Typical figures for the cost of one twin 15-inch mounting at this time were:—

	£
Two slides and mountings	19,000
Turntable	13,500
Hoists	11,000
Gunhouse armour	36,500
Hydraulic machinery	11,500
Turning gear and shell-room machinery	9,000
Miscellaneous and spares	8,500
Delivery and erection	7,000
Total	116,000

(Opposite) *The drawing shows the Mk I/N mounting for the twin 15-inch 42-calibre guns installed in* Abercrombie. *The earlier Mk I mounting originally designed for 20° elevation was generally similar, although many minor details of for example loading gear and protection were different. The guns could be loaded at any angle between* $-4^1/_2°$ *and* $+20°$*, while turret safe training limits were 150° to port or starboard. Although the revolving weight was 810 tons, the centre section of the ship between frames 34 and 45 weighed 2600 tons, over a quarter of the ship's displacement.*

The guns were ordered separately under a different Vote in the annual Estimates; the cost of one 15-inch was made up approximately as follows:—

	£
Steel forgings	6,900
Gun manufacture	7,500
Breech mechanism	1,600
Total	16,000

Mountings for only two of the four ships of the 1914 Programme had been ordered before war broke out: *Repulse*'s four from Elswick and *Renown*'s four from C.O.W. Thus when these two ships were redesigned as six-gun battlecruisers in December 1914, it appeared that there would be two spare 15-inch mountings available to arm monitors. But the ships had only been ordered in May 1914 and trials of the gun mountings were not due until April 1916, whereas the monitors were to be completed in six months. The only way of obtaining the necessary turrets quickly was to take them from one of the battleships of the 1912 or 1913 Programmes. The *Queen Elizabeth* class were by now well advanced; indeed the name ship was just about to commence her gunnery trials. As these 24-knot ships were the most powerful battleships then under construction, it would have been a grave error to have delayed completion of one of them, merely to arm two strategically much less important vessels. But the 1913 *Royal Sovereigns* were quite a

A fine view of Abercrombie*'s twin 15-inch turret nearing completion at Vickers-Armstrong's Elswick Works in December 1942. The turret had been originally intended as a replacement for* Furious *should her single 18-inch prove unsatisfactory, but it had not been needed so lay for 24 years in Chatham Dockyard. The ammunition trunk projected into a pit below the turret. The two 12-ton balance weights needed on the Mk I/N mounting to permit elevation to 30° can be seen on top of each gun. In the foreground cna be seen one of the platforms for the Oerlikons which were sited above the rangefinder hood, and what looks like a 13.5-inch gun, probably one of those which were linered down to form a hyper-velocity 8-inch.*

different proposition. They were of an inferior design and only capable of 21 knots. Although originally due to complete at the end of 1915, they had already been delayed by more urgently needed new construction. To take the turrets from one of these ships and order replacements would not have such serious repercussions on the strength of the Grand Fleet vis-a-vis the High Seas Fleet. The first set of mountings due to complete were the four that Vickers were building for *Ramillies*, so the two most advanced mountings, "Y" and "X", were taken over and transferred to Elswick for modification and erection in the two *Marshals* building at Palmer's.

Apart from having to cut the trunk of "X" turret down to the same minimum length as "Y" turret, the 15-inch mounted in the *Marshals* were identical to the battleship mountings. At the designed elevation of 20°, the extreme range was 23,400 yards, but experience off the Belgian Coast soon showed that this was insufficient. The subsequent conversion of the monitor mountings to 30° elevation necessitated lifting the trunnions 25½in, so providing extra space for the breech end to recoil into the turntable when maximum elevation was being used. A price had to be paid for this increase: the gun could no longer be used at angles of depression. The firing angles were thus +2° to +30° compared with −5° to +20° originally. Other changes included the fitting of a more powerful elevating mechanism, the cutting of larger gun ports in the front armour covered by ½-inch thick bonnets, and the use of fixed-angle loading at 5° elevation; whereas all-angle loading was possible on the battleship mountings. This modified mounting was fitted in *Erebus, Terror* and *Marshal Soult*, and thus also in *Roberts* (1941) when *Soult*'s turret was transferred. *Abercrombie*'s mounting was the second spare completed for *Furious* in 1917, converted into the Mark I/N version as fitted in all 15-inch capital ships built or reconstructed from 1936 onwards. The differences between the old and the modernised mountings are best described by summarising the main points of the Admiralty order of April 1941 to Vickers-Armstrong for the reconditioning of the turret originally planned for *Furious*, then lying at Chatham Dockyard:

(i) Complete overhaul and repair, plus supply of missing parts
(ii) Elevation to be increased to 30°
(iii) Improvement in flashtightness
(iv) Modification to use both 4 c.r.h. and 6 c.r.h. projectiles
(v) Shortening of trunk by about 7ft 6in to fit into monitor hull
(vi) General modernisation of hydraulic, electrical, compressed air and ventilation systems
(vii) Improvement of ammunition supply and stowage arrangements.

The 30° elevation on the Mk I/N was achieved by moving the trunnions back 7¼in to 8ft 2¾in forward of the turret axis and raising their axis from 2ft 6½in to 3ft 3¼in above the gunhouse floor. Moving the trunnions shifted them away from the centre of gravity of the gun, so a 12-ton balance weight had to be fitted to reduce the force required to elevate the gun. Pneumatic run-out gear was fitted in place of the original hydraulic recuperator, so imposing less of a strain on the hydraulic machinery. The gun could be loaded at any elevation between 20° and the maximum depression of 4½°, permitting a slightly faster rate of fire than the previous monitors with their fixed-angle loading. The various changes increased the revolving weight to 810 tons, while the total installation weighed about 900 tons including all the associated equipment mounted on the hull proper, such as the 500-H.P. hydraulic machinery.

The additional elevation to 30° produced a useful 25% increase in range, but it was still not enough to permit the WW1 monitors to keep out of range of the heavy German batteries on the Belgian Coast. A successful design of 8 c.r.h. projectile weighing 1965lb with an added ballistic cap was developed during 1918, giving an extra 3000 yards' range compared with the standard 4 c.r.h. High-explosive projectiles were used the most frequently, as they had the largest bursting charge, 224lb lyddite (picric acid) or 11¾% of total weight. They were made of forged steel so that their thin walls, necessitated by the large volume of the bursting charge, would withstand the shock of firing. Shrapnel were also used against targets such as troop concentrations; in form they were similar to H.E. except that they were filled with 13,700 1¾-oz lead alloy balls. Common pointed capped projectiles were used against well protected targets such as coastal batteries, owing to their better penetration qualities. They were made of cast steel with a special cap to assist penetration by easing the shock of impact so allowing the point of the shell body to pierce the hard face of armour without shattering. They had a bursting charge of 129lb black powder. Armour piercing capped were made of forged steel with a hardened head and cap to improve penetration against the most heavily armoured targets, leaving a volume for the bursting charge of only about 2½% of projectile weight; they were reserved for capital ships during WW1. A typical ammunition state for the Dover monitors' magazines for one day in October 1917 showed:

Projectiles	*Erebus*	*Terror*	*Marshal Soult*
H.E.	71	56	106
C.P.C.	100	74	49
Shrapnel	34	35	44
Practice	—	—	16
Total	205	165	215
Full charges	188½	213½	215

The official outfit in 1918 was 90 H.E. and 10 C.P.C. per gun. At the outbreak of WW1, a C.P.C. projectile cost about £65, H.E. about £37 and a full charge about £40. These prices increased over the years and had nearly doubled by WW2.

The figures tabulated for range are conservative, as they are based on 2400 ft/sec muzzle velocity, corresponding to a well-worn gun. When new, a gun was capable of 2470ft/sec which gave about 4% greater range, i.e. about 1200 yards at maximum elevation. The life of the gun firing A.P.C. was shown by service experience to be about 335 equivalent full charges. Life using H.E. projectiles was usually restricted to about 250 e.f.c.,

Date shipped	Registered number	Maker	Rounds fired in action	Previous allocations	Subsequent allocations
				Marshal Ney	
Jul 1915	52	RGF	35	New	*Terror* 1916
Jul 1915	75	VSM	35	New	*Terror* 1916
				Marshal Soult	
Sep 1915	27	COW	210	New	Dover CD 1942. *Ramillies* 1944. Scrapped 1948
Sep 1915	28	COW	210	New	Removed Nov 1940. Scrapped 1957
				Lord Clive	
Dec 1920	158	COW	Trials	New	Removed Dec 1921. *Erebus* 1939
Dec 1920	159	COW	Trials	New	Gun burst Feb 1921
Dec 1920	162	RGF	Trials	New	Removed Dec 1921. *Warspite* 1941. Dover CD 1944. Scrapped 1948
May 1921	163	RGF	Trials	New	*Warspite* 1929. *Abercrombie* 1944
				Terror	
Jun 1916	52	RGF	230	*Marshal Ney* 1915	*Repulse* 1935. Lost with ship Dec 1941
Jun 1916	75	VSM	250	*Marshal Ney* 1915	Scrapped 1951
Aug 1918	149	WB	70	New	*Warspite* 1942. 14-inch experimental 1945
Aug 1918	150	WB	70	New	*Ramillies* 1941. Scrapped 1948
Jul 1939	93	WB	330	*Revenge* 1915	Lost with ship Feb 1941
Jul 1939	94	WB	330	*Revenge* 1915	Lost with ship Feb 1941
				Erebus	
Jun 1916	15	AW	60	Trials	*Repulse* 1935. Lost with ship Dec 1941
Jun 1916	36	VSM	70	Trials	*Renown* 1941. Scrapped 1948
Jul 1917	64	EOC	110	New	*Malaya* 1928. Scrapped 1948
Jul 1917	65	EOC	120	New	*Vanguard* 1945. Scrapped 1960
Jun 1918	143	EOC	180	New	Scrapped 1949
Jun 1918	144	EOC	180	New	*Warspite* 1944. Scrapped 1948
Jan 1939	72	VSM	170	Trials	Converted to 14-inch experimental 1945
Jan 1939	158	COW	30	*Lord Clive* 1920	Removed Nov 1940. Scrapped 1950
Nov 1940	60	EOC	160	*Royal Oak* 1916	Scrapped 1955
Oct 1943	190	RGF	200	New	Scrapped 1948
Oct 1943	76	VSM	20	*Royal Sovereign* 1915	Damaged Jun 1944 and scrapped
Jul 1944	173	VSM	190	*Malaya* 1928	Scrapped 1949
Sep 1944	100	RGF	90	*Repulse* 1916	Removed Jan 1947. Scrapped 1948
Sep 1944	104	VSM	90	*Revenge* 1915	Removed Jan 1947. Scrapped 1948
				Roberts	
May 1941	4	EOC	225	*Malaya* 1915	Scrapped 1955
May 1941	5	EOC	215	Trials	Scrapped 1949
Nov 1943	33	VSM	230	Trials	Scrapped 1957
Nov 1943	140	COW	40	New	Damaged Jun 1944. Scrapped 1945
Jun 1944	102	VSM	215	*Resolution* 1915	I.W.M. exhibit 1968
Jun 1944	10	EOC	210	*Malaya* 1915	Scrapped 1955
Jul 1944	14	EOC	55	*Courageous* 1916 *Warspite* 1929	Scrapped with ship 1965
Jul 1944	39	VSM	50	*Warspite* 1915 *Hood* 1936	Scrapped with ship 1965
				Abercrombie	
Jan 1943	95	WB	110	*Royal Oak* 1916	Scrapped 1948
Jan 1943	118	RGF	110	*Resolution* 1916	Scrapped 1948
Aug 1944	124	WB	Nil	*Resolution* 1916	Scrapped with ship 1954
Aug 1944	163	RGF	Nil	*Lord Clive* 1921 *Warspite* 1929	Scrapped with ship 1954

Notes
Number of rounds fired are approximate, showing only those fired while the gun was in a monitor. Practice rounds excluded. Approximate total 4900.

RGF = Royal Gun Factory, Woolwich
EOC = Elswick Ordnance Company, Newcastle (Sir W. G. Armstrong, Whitworth)
AW = Armstrong, Whitworth Co., Openshaw, Manchester
VSM = Vickers, Son and Maxim, Sheffield
WB = William Beardmore, Glasgow
COW = Coventry Ordnance Works, Coventry
CD = Coast Defences (Royal Artillery)
I.W.M. = Imperial War Museum, London

owing to a lower limit on bore wear being set, as the longer body and greater longitudinal inertia of the H.E. could result in unsteady flight if the rifling was too worn to give sufficient spin stabilisation. The life of a gun was determined by the extent of erosion in the bore, caused mainly by the burning gases of the propellant charge. Erosion depended on the size of the charge; for example, a three-quarter charge caused only one-quarter the erosion of a full charge, while proof or supercharges caused about double. Thus the wear caused by each firing could be calculated in terms of equivalent numbers of full charges. Measurements of bore wear were taken after each major firing operation and the projected remaining life assessed. A gun was generally condemned when wear reached about 0.74in at one inch from the commencement of rifling. In practice, guns were usually replaced when their remaining life fell below the ship's normal full outfit of ammunition per gun, which ensured that the entire magazine could be safely fired in action. After removal from its mounting, a gun in good condition otherwise could be relined by replacing the inner A-tube at a cost of about £5000. Guns could thus have been fitted in several ships during their overall life-span; the Table shows that most of the 15-inch guns fitted in the monitors had either already been installed in other ships, or were so transferred later. The total numbers of rounds fired whilst in the monitors would be greater than those shown in the Table as having been fired in action, as trial and practice shoot figures are not included. Although these latter were often undertaken using the special sub-calibre 6-pdr guns temporarily fitted in the bore, on occasion full charges would be used.

At the start of WW2, a switch was made from 4 c.r.h. to the more efficient 6 c.r.h. projectiles in most 15-inch gun ships, which increased range by about 10%. Only A.P.C. and H.E. were manufactured, but the monitors helped use up surplus stocks of obsolete projectiles, which included some 2000 C.P.C. and shrapnel left over from WW1. Nose and base-fuzed H.E., now filled with T.N.T., were fired most frequently being the most effective against the lighter targets such as troop concentrations and vehicles, leaving the occasional A.P.C. to cope with any heavily protected targets. After WW1, experiments with improved types of cordite had been made to overcome the problems of short storage life and variation between batches. By WW2, solventless carbamite cordite (SC)[1] had become the standard, but a 432-lb charge was needed to give the same performance as 428lb of cordite MD.

Without any doubt, the 15-inch was the most successful of the monitors' various gun armaments. Indeed it was probably the most successful tactically and strategically of any of the world's navies' large guns. It was the mainstay of the Royal Navy's battle fleet in two World Wars and it remained in active seagoing service until 1954. 58 turrets and 186 guns, all made between 1912 and 1918, were drawn on to arm 22 ships — 16 capital ships and six monitors. Although later designs were technically superior in terms of range, life or construction, the 15-inch remained a thoroughly reliable and effective piece of ordnance for 40 years. It was a consistent weapon which could regularly drop its shells onto small targets if properly controlled. A 15-inch is believed to hold the world record for maximum range of hitting another ship in action — *Warspite* firing at the Italian battleship *Giulio Cesare* from 26,200 yards in the Mediterranean in July 1940. While minor troubles occurred from time to time — leaky hydraulics, troublesome air compressors, faulty firing mechanisms and even a few guns burst from imperfect projectiles — these difficulties could be overcome. Indeed it was the

[1] The manufacturing process was 'solventless', the carbamite acted as a stabiliser to improve storage quality, constituting 9% by weight, with 41% nitroglycerine and 50% soluble nitrocellulose. SC was designated by its stick diameter in thousandths of an inch; that used for the 15-inch was SC 280, i.e. 0.28in.

A view inside Roberts' *turret when she was ready for scrapping. The hydraulic cylinder and rack for opening the breech can be seen above the left gun (No. 39). The breech is open on the right gun (No. 14) although the obturator pad is missing.*

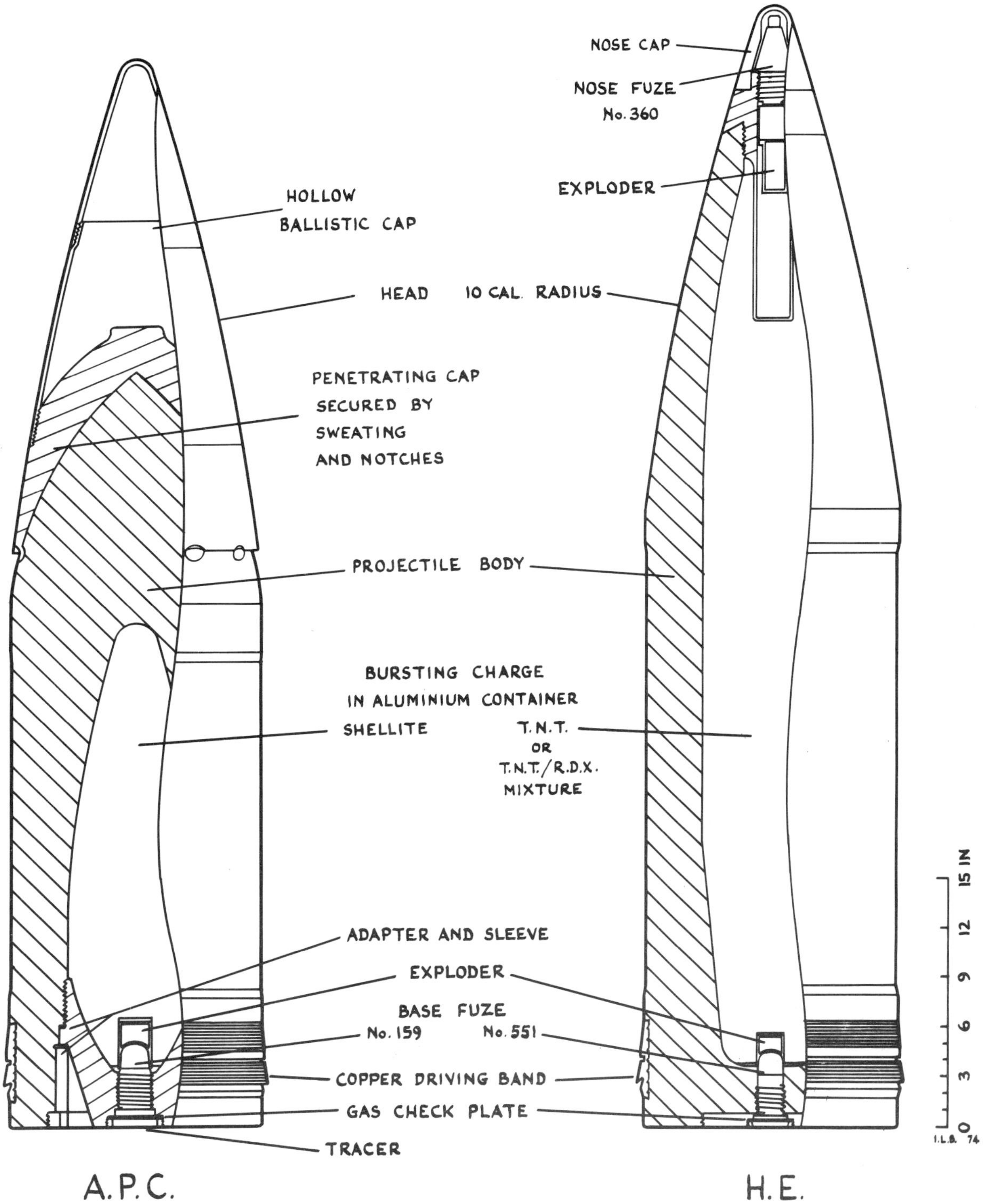

Typical 15-inch projectiles. The left hand part cut-away drawing shows a Mk XXIIB armour piercing capped projectile, the right hand a Mk VIIIB high-explosive, both used during WW2. Although usually described as 6 calibre radius of head (c.r.h.) — indicated by the B in the Mark number — the design was actually a 5/10 c.r.h., i.e. the length of the head corresponded to a 5 c.r.h. shell (about 32in) but its radius was 10 calibres (150in). The body of the H.E. was longer than the A.P.C. to keep the same overall 1938lb weight in spite of the larger volume of burster — respectively 130lb of T.N.T. and 48½lb of shellite. The A.P.C. had only a base percussion fuze with a slight delay action to defer detonation until after penetration, while the H.E. had both nose and base percussion fuzes to reduce the chance of misfire. Sensitive tetryl exploders were used to magnify the impulse of the fuze in detonating the main charge. The gas check plate prevented gases from the cordite damaging the fuze. The conical relieved adapter was designed to allow the impact of the shell on armour plate to distort the base without dislodging the fuze. Examples of 15-inch projectiles are on display at the Imperial War Museum, London.

15-INCH ORDNANCE — TECHNICAL PARTICULARS

Mark I Gun Length overall of gun body 650.4in; length of bore 42 calibres; length of rifling 516.3in; weight of gun including 2.85-ton breech mechanism 100.0 tons; recoil 46in.

Mark I / Mark I/N Twin Mounting Revolving weight 760/810 tons; maximum elevation 30°, minimum +2° / −4½°; loading angle +5° to +20° / −4½° to +20°; armour protection — see Ship Technical Particulars.

Ammunition 4 c.r.h.: weight of projectile 1920lb; length of projectile C.P.C./H.E. 63.3/63.9in; weight of bursting charge C.P.C./H.E. 129/224lb; weight of cordite MD 45 428lb. 6 c.r.h.: projectile 1938lb; length A.P.C./H.E. 65.0/67.0in; bursting charge A.P.C./H.E. 48.5/130lb; cordite SC 280 432lb. Magazine stowage — see Ship Technical Particulars.

Performance Nominal muzzle velocity 2400 ft/sec; range at 30° elevation 4 c.r.h./6 c.r.h. 29,000/32,200 yards; penetration by 6 c.r.h. A.P.C. 14" C. at 15,000 yards; maximum rate of fire 1¾ rounds per minute per gun.

intensive service in the monitors firing some 5000 rounds, rather than the big ships, which was the real proving ground, not only revealing minor shortcomings enabling them to be corrected, but also doing the most to advance the British techniques of long range naval artillery, from which the capital ships were able to benefit after the First World War.

§2 The 12-inch Mark VIII Gun

The 12-inch armament of the *Majestic* class pre-dreadnoughts of 1895 marked a major advance for the Royal Navy. Wire-wound guns were used for the first time, proving much superior to the 13.5-inch of the *Royal Sovereigns* of 1892 with their shrunk-on hoop construction. The 35-calibre 46-ton guns were designed by the Royal Gun Factory at Woolwich Arsenal, who shared manufacture with the private ordnance companies. Winding high-tensile steel wire circumferentially over the inner tubes of a gun gave considerably greater radial strength, as well as greater consistency of material, thus permitting higher stresses and the use of the new more powerful 'smokeless' propellant cordite. The Elswick-designed and built mountings were also an improvement over the open barbettes of the *Royal Sovereigns*. The guns were protected by an armoured shield which also provided space for secondary loading facilities. The normal loading position required the turret to be trained fore and aft with the guns at their maximum elevation of 13½°. Ammunition hoists and rammers in the pointed after end of the pear-shaped barbette structure were then used to supply the gun in this fixed position. Hydraulic machinery was used for training, elevating, ramming and hoisting, although manual power could be used in emergency. The turret itself and the turntable immediately below were thus the only revolving parts, weighing about 264 tons altogether, as training machinery and hoists were mounted on the fixed supporting structure. As originally built, a twin B.II

(Left) Roberts' *15-inch guns being changed at Port Said in November 1943 using a floating crane.* (Right) *Prolonged firing of the 20-year old 12-inch Mk VIII guns gave rise to rapid wear and damage to the liner. The photograph shows* Sir John Moore *exchanging her 46-ton right gun in October 1915. The work had to be done at Portsmouth rather than her home port of Chatham, as the monitors were too beamy to reach the basin at the latter yard where the heavy lift sheerlegs were situated.*

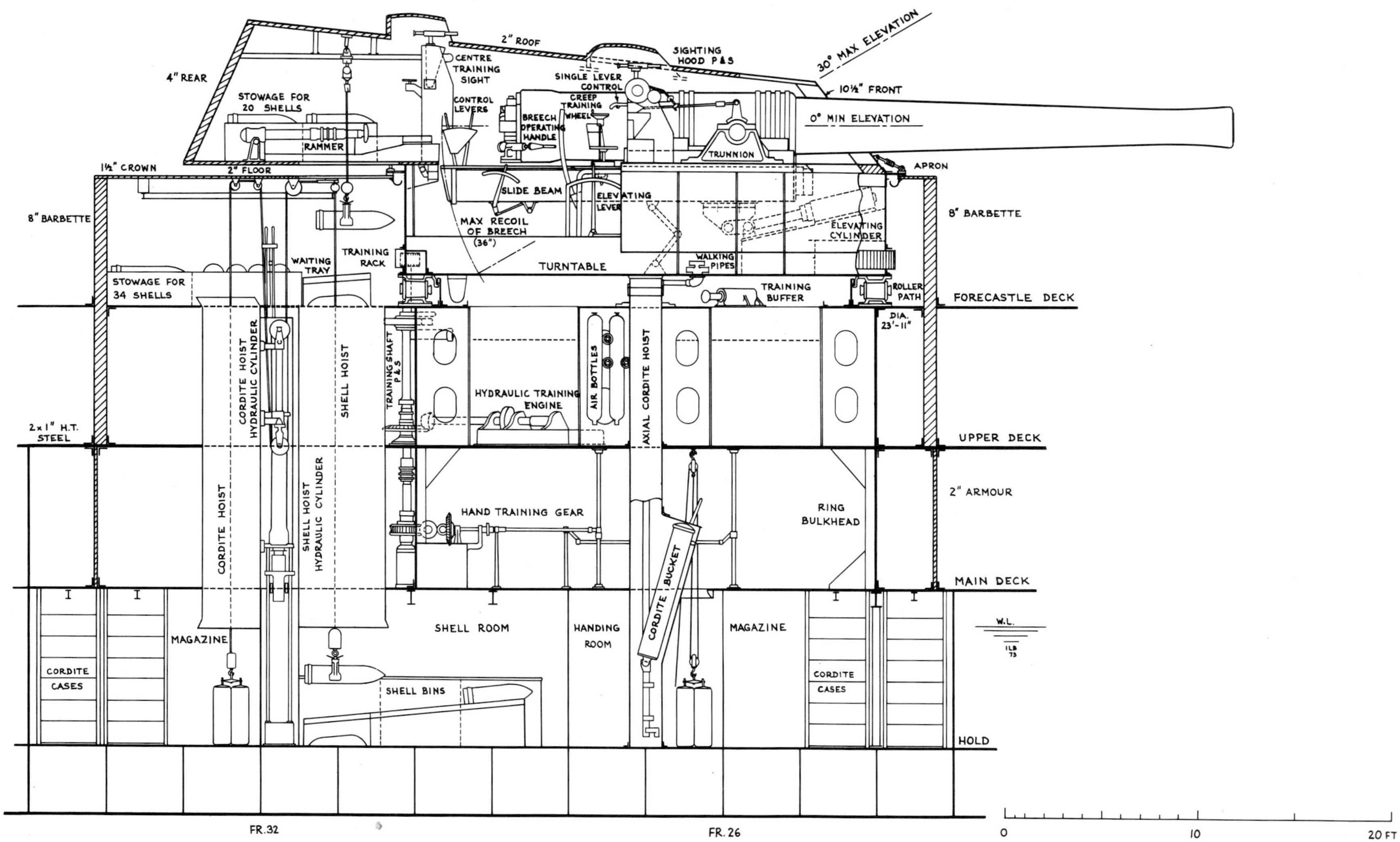

The twin 12-inch 35-calibre guns and mounting installed in the Majestic *class pre-dreadnoughts in 1895 marked a significant advance in naval ordnance. When transferred to the monitors twenty years later, it was only necessary to convert the mounting to 30° elevation from the original 13½° and modify the ammunition supply arrangements.* British Battleships *by Oscar Parkes shows on p.384 a drawing of a mounting very similar to the original design which was fitted in the Japanese pre-dreadnoughts* Yashima *and* Fuji.

12-INCH ORDNANCE — TECHNICAL PARTICULARS

Mark VIII Gun Length overall 445.6in; length of bore 35.43 calibres; length of rifling 349.4in; weight of gun 46.12 tons.

Mark B.II Twin Mounting Revolving weight 264 tons; maximum elevation 30°, minimum 0°; total crew 47 men.

Ammunition Weight of projectile, 2 and 4 c.r.h. 850lb; length of projectile, 4 c.r.h. H.E. 48.3in; weight of bursting charge, 4 c.r.h. H.E. 107lb; weight of cordite MD 45 200lb.

Performance Nominal muzzle velocity 2350ft/sec; range at 30° elevation, 2 c.r.h./4 c.r.h. 21,300/24,500 yards; penetration by A.P.C. 8½" C. at 10,000 yards.

mounting cost about £30,000 plus a further £10,000 for each Mk VIII gun.

After twenty years' service, this 12-inch ordnance had become distinctly obsolescent, as continuous advances had been made in naval gunnery, culminating in the new 15-inch. However, with two major changes, the 12-inch could be adapted for shore bombardment work. The first was to increase the elevation to 30° to secure an additional 7600 yards' range. The second was to remove the primary loading position in the barbette and use only that in the turret, thus permitting the guns to remain trained on target during reloading. The stowage of projectiles at the rear of the turret was increased from 16 to 20 rounds, while the existing small centre-line trunk was used as a cordite hoist. Thus at the normal bombardment rate of fire of one round per minute per turret, it was only necessary to replenish the turret stock every 20 minutes. Pre-war annual gunlayers' tests had showed that a faster rate could be maintained for shorter periods: one aimed round every 50 seconds. The original main combined projectile and cordite hoist was retained but converted to carry projectiles only while, in place of the original inclined rammer at the back of the barbette, stowage was arranged for 34 projectiles. To replenish the ready-use ammunition, the turret had to be trained fore and aft and the projectiles hoisted up through hatches at the top of the barbette into the bottom of the turret at the rear. The projectiles were then stowed in bins and lifted out when required onto a bogie for loading and ramming into the gun, with the four quarter-charges of cordite being transferred manually.

The eight monitor mountings were converted in early 1915 while still aboard the four pre-dreadnoughts. The conversion was carried out hurriedly; as a result the monitor mountings proved troublesome for the first few weeks in service. The 20-year old hydraulic systems were not fully able to meet the demands of the modified mountings. The greater elevation increased recoil and run-out forces, requiring higher hydraulic pressures to be maintained, which frequently burst the leather gaskets and inadequately brazed piping joints. Troubles also recurred throughout their life, but with careful maintenance, these could be minimised.

The guns themselves could also cause trouble. The substitution of 200-lb cordite MD propellant in place of the original 174-lb cordite Mk I caused problems under repeated firing, although doubling the nominal life of the gun to 500 e.f.c. Depositions of copper in the bore from the projectile driving bands needed frequent removal, but more serious were troubles with the liners. The continual drag of the driving bands caused the liner to be gradually stretched forward. The resulting projection at the muzzle could be simply cut off, but in addition the liner began to form a ridge in the bore near the shoulders of the outer A-tube (see drawing). The ridge accumulated copper from the driving bands, which could give sufficient retardation to a projectile to start the fuze, with the result that a premature detonation could occur either within the bore or soon after leaving the muzzle. While the choke could be temporarily removed by rubbing down with an emery-covered block pulled back and forth in the bore, the only

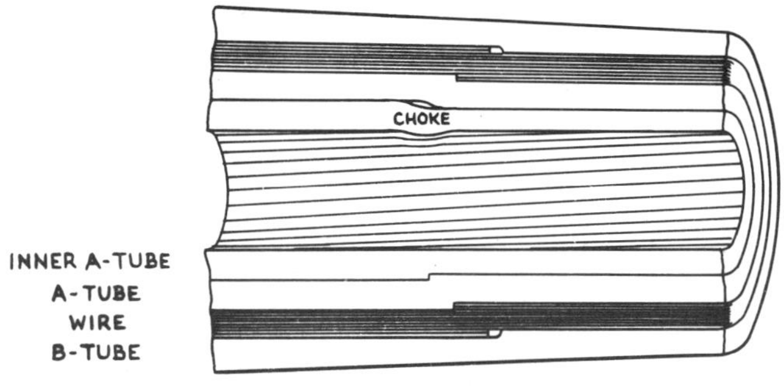

The intensive firing of the 12-inch Mk VIII in the monitors revealed a weakness in the liner design, whereby a choke was set up at one of the internal shoulders. Although exaggerated in the drawing, it could impart sufficient retardation to the projectile fuze to cause a premature detonation.

permanent cure was to fit new guns with a modified design of liner, which had a different arrangement of internal shoulders and rifling.

When the 12-inch monitors were first completed, they had no accurate information on their guns' improved performance. Range Tables for the Mk VIII only went up to 13½° elevation, so approximations had to be used to estimate the figures up to 30°. For some time only 2 c.r.h. projectiles were available from existing stocks. The need for maximum range speeded the production of the 4 c.r.h. introduced before the war, giving a 15% increase in range. In 1918, a 878-lb 8 c.r.h. also became available, capable of reaching 26,000 yards using a supercharge. The effective range of the guns in service off the Belgian Coast was considered to be about 1000 yards less than the figures quoted in the Range Tables to allow for average bore wear, cordite temperature and wind. H.E. projectiles were most often used, with C.P.C. if greater penetration was required, while shrapnel with a time fuze was occasionally used as a makeshift A.A. projectile. A 12-inch H.E. projectile cost about £14 before the war and C.P.C. about £25, both with a further £20 for the propellant.

The 12-inch Mk VIII was less accurate than the 15-inch but could perform adequately under good conditions, if care had been taken to equalise bore wear on the two guns and to keep the magazine temperature constant for 24 hours before firing to ensure consistent performance. Off the Belgian Coast, the 12-inch was mostly used for general bombardment, strafing back areas and keeping the enemy's heads down, while the 15-inch tackled the more specific targets. Taken overall, the gun and mounting performed reasonably well for their age and certainly put down some impressive barrages, especially in 1918. The eight monitors between them fired well over 2000 12-inch shells on bombardment work, while additional rounds were used to drive off enemy warships.

§3 The 18-inch Mark I Gun

The 18-inch gun was fitted in the monitors almost by accident. Fisher's enthusiasm for the heaviest guns in the fastest ships led to an extension of the *Courageous* and *Glorious* 15-inch design. In March 1915, *Furious* was designed as a 'large light cruiser' of 19,100 tons mounting two 18-inch guns in single turrets, one forward and one aft. For security reasons, the 18-inch gun was known as the "15-inch B", and indeed it was basically a scaled-up 15-inch. The 40-calibre piece was 62 feet long, weighing 149 tons, constructed as shown in the drawing, similar to the 15-inch. The gun was also regarded as a potential coast defence weapon, so that its official name later became "15-inch B C.D.". Design and construction of the three guns (one spare) and the two mountings were entrusted to Elswick, with orders for completion in 1916. Like the gun, the mounting was based on the 15-inch design; indeed the barbette structure was capable of taking a twin 15-inch turret should the 18-inch prove unsuccessful. The total revolving weight of the single mounting, including the heavily armoured gunhouse, was slightly greater than the twin 15-inch at 826 tons.

Designed performance in *Furious* was a range of about 30,000 yards firing a 3320-lb projectile using a 630-lb charge with a muzzle velocity of 2300ft/sec at 30° elevation.This range was virtually the same as the 15-inch, as manufacturing difficulties prevented the use of cordite any larger than the existing MD 45, which would have given improved ballistics. First trials of the gun at Elswick's proving ground at Ridsdale were undertaken in September 1916. Performance was not quite as good as expected, only 2260ft/sec being obtained with the standard charge. The two mountings and their guns were shipped at Armstrong's Naval Yard at Walker-on-Tyne early in 1917, just as the Admiralty were having second thoughts about *Furious*' design. In March 1917, the Board agreed to modify *Furious* into a sea-plane carrier. Her forward turret was removed and a hangar with a flying-off deck was built over the forecastle from the bow to the bridge. Gun trials were carried out in July 1917, the remaining after gun fairly shaking the lightly built hull. After three months' service, it was decided to convert her fully into an aircraft carrier by building a flying-on deck aft in place of the remaining 18-inch.

In the meantime, some thought had been given to alternative uses for the three 18-inch guns. Their existence was revealed to Bacon in the summer of 1917, when he was invited to submit proposals for using two of them. In August, he put up a plan to mount them inside the ruined shell of the Palace Hotel at Westende, whence they could bombard Bruges docks and Zeebrugge locks from a distance of about 18 miles.. It was hoped that the Army's Third Ypres offensive would have resulted in the capture of Westende by the time the guns became available. Bacon planned to ferry the guns and mountings across the Channel lashed on top of the bulges of a monitor — a full account is given in *The Dover Patrol*. He also conceived the alternative plan of mounting the guns on the monitors' decks to fire on Bruges from the sea, particularly when it became apparent that the Army's offensive was making little progress. A dual-purpose mounting was thus envisaged, capable of being used ashore or afloat. For use ashore, the mounting required only a small arc for training but 45° elevation was needed to give maximum range. Board approval to use the guns was given on 23 September, resulting in an order to Elswick to design and construct the new mountings for delivery in five months.

The mounting consisted of two massive side girders parallel to the barrel, tied together at each end, between which the gun carriage and slide was slung. At the forward end was a strong support and a pivot about which the gun could train in a limited arc. The gun would be loaded at the fixed angle of 10°, but actual firing would only be permitted between 22° and 45° in order to distribute the recoil forces fairly evenly between the forward and after supports. 10° of training on either side of the centre-line was achieved by a push-pull hydraulic cylinder, but only the mounting itself trained, the shield being fixed to the deck. Hydraulically-operated cranes, loading tray, rammer and breech mechanism were all provided to ease the physical effort by the gun's crew. The ammunition supply parties were not so fortunate as all movement had to be done by muscle power. The projectiles were to be stowed horizontally on the upper deck and moved by overhead transporter rail to the hatch in the forecastle deck through which they were to be lifted to the breech, while the cordite was to be transferred from the stowage tanks onto a small bogie running on rails, two one-sixth charges at a time. Total stowage was provided for some 60 projectiles and 72 full charges. The mounting was designed to be installed on the monitor's forecastle deck abaft the funnel, permanently trained over the starboard beam. By cutting out the armoured gunhouse and all the elaborate ammunition working arrangements associated with the

After her conversion to a seaplane carrier, Furious' *spare gun became available for installing in* Lord Clive *at Portsmouth Dockyard. The 149-ton gun was shipped on 7 September 1918 onto the athwartship mounting. The hydraulic cylinder near the base of the mainmast was capable of training the mounting 10° forward or aft.*

revolving mounting, the weight was reduced to 384 tons, made up as follows:—

	Tons
Gun	149
Gun carriage	19
Slide	60
Elevating and training gear	7
Loading and ramming gear	14
Side girders and cross members	68
Front and rear foundations	43
Gun shield, $^1/_2$-inch plating	24
Total	384

By October 1917, it was clear that there would be no chance of mounting the guns at Westende, so orders were given to proceed with the conversion of the two 12-inch monitors, followed by a third when *Furious*' second reconstruction released the third gun. The work at Elswick took far longer than expected, partly due to labour troubles. Although the first two guns had been sent to Portsmouth in January, trials of the mounting at Silloth were not completed until the end of May. The mounting was then despatched in pieces to Portsmouth where it arrived on 20 June for erection in *General Wolfe*. The actual gun shipped was Registered Number 2, which had previously been *Furious*' "A" gun. The gun in the second monitor, *Lord Clive*, was No. 3, *Furious*' spare, while *Prince Eugene* would have received *Furious*' "Y" gun, No. 1.

For bombardment purposes off the Belgian Coast, it was necessary to get every possible extra yard of range. The 15° increase of elevation added about 15% to the original range and a further 10% was obtained by using supercharges, in which one of the six part-charges was increased to 165lb, making a total of 690lb. The combined effect increased the range to about 36,500 yards using the existing 4 c.r.h. projectiles. Trials of *Wolfe*'s gun showed that firing the gun produced no self-inflicted damage on the ship; as the muzzle projected some 22 feet beyond the main hull, the blast was only felt right forward on the forecastle. New 8 c.r.h. H.E. projectiles with ballistic caps had been designed, adding another 10% to the range to give a maximum of about 40,100 yards.

In the 18-inch's few weeks of service, actual rounds fired against the enemy amounted to 81 by *Wolfe* and 4 by *Clive*. Exactly which type of projectile was fired is unknown; probably 4 c.r.h. A.P.C. from *Furious* modified with a ballistic cap to 8 c.r.h., since only two H.E. had been delivered by that time from Hadfield's. Wear of *Wolfe*'s gun was measured as about 0.37in after firing 161 e.f.c. (105 rounds including proof and practice, 57 being supercharges). These figures indicate that the gun would have been good for well over 300 e.f.c., comparable with most other British heavy ordnance using cordite MD. Its range of 20 miles made it a valuable if expensive, weapon for shore bombardment or coast defence work. Because of the small number of spots received on the few occasions that the gun was used, it is not possible to evaluate its capability thoroughly. Being so similar to the 15-inch, it would probably have been an equally effective performer, especially with its much heavier projectile and bursting charge. As a ship-to-ship weapon, its performance would have been much more questionable, despite an ability by the A.P.C. to penetrate about 18 inches of armour at 15,000 yards. The chances of hitting the enemy with only two guns, as *Furious* would have carried, would have been slight, even with the faster rate of fire of the turret mounting. While a single hit would have pulverised anything but a capital ship, it would probably have taken several hits to sink a well protected battleship — a difficult target from outside the normal range of the latter's guns and, from inside, a dangerous task for a very lightly protected battlecruiser.

The 18-inch guns were removed from the two monitors in December 1920 and, together with *Eugene*'s piece, continued to be of service. No. 1 was lined down to 16-inch calibre by Elswick in 1921 for use in cordite-proving

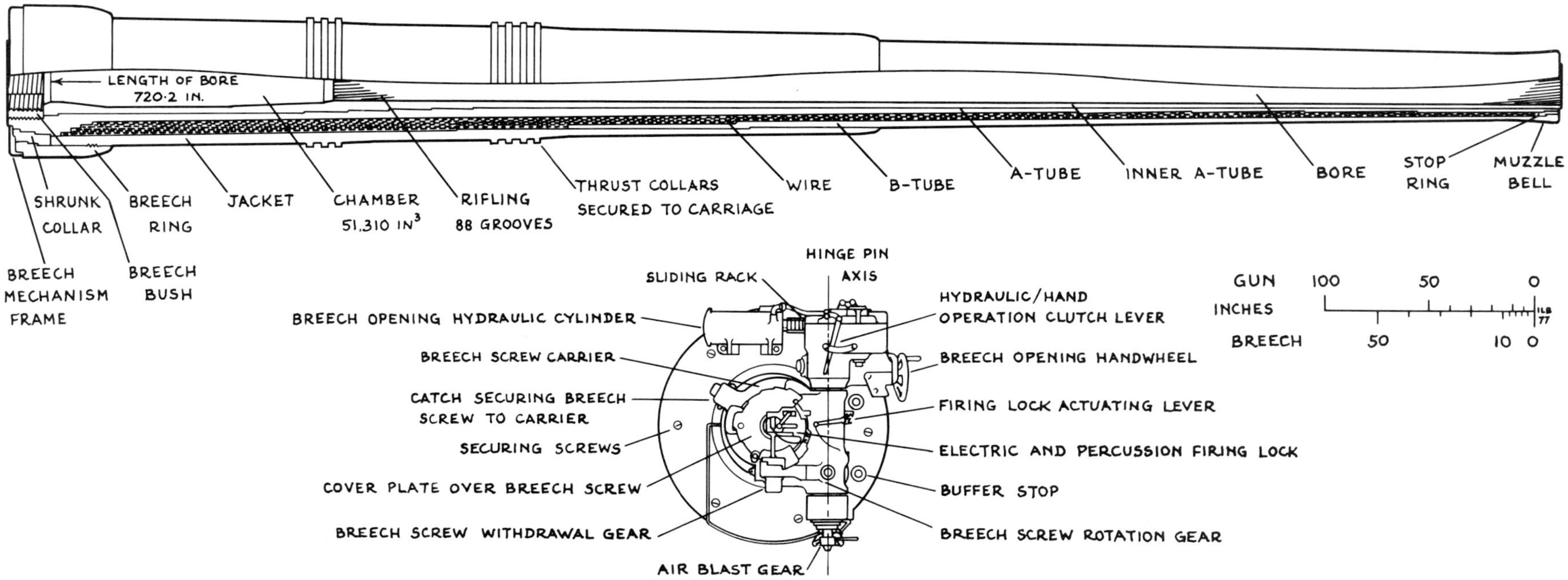

(Above) *Despite its impressive size, the 149-ton 40-calibre 18-inch Mk I gun was essentially only a scaled up 15-inch. The proportions and construction were typical of all large Brtish naval guns of the WW1 era. The gun was made of nickel steel apart from the carbon steel jacket and breech ring and over 200 miles of 0.25in × 0.06in high-tensile steel wire. The Welin type breech mechanism is illustrated to a 50% larger scale than the gun. Maximum range at 45° elevation using supercharges and 8 c.r.h. projectiles was 40,100 yards. The 2.8-ton weight of the breech mechanism excludes the securing frame.*

(Below) *The 18-inch single mounting officially known as the 15-inch B C.D., was designed by Elswick for the monitors on the lines of a land service model of the simplest type which simplified installation in* General Wolfe *and* Lord Clive. *Only 10° of training was permitted from dead abeam, while fixed 10° angle loading was arranged. Firing could only be carried out between elevations of 22° and 45° to distribute recoil forces evenly. A grid of additional bulkheads, pillars and girders was added between the forecastle deck and the inner bottom to take these forces. The drawing looking forward omits minor detail including access platforms and hydraulic piping to show the essential simplicity of the mounting. Projectiles were stowed on the upper deck, traversed by overhead rail to the hatch in the forecastle deck, then lifted by hydraulically powered winch and crane to a waiting tray on the left side of the breech. When the gun was ready to be loaded, the 1½-ton projectile was traversed across to the breech, landed on the loading tray and rammed home. The cordite charges were wheeled on a bogie along the forecastle deck, manhandled onto their waiting tray and then into the breech.*

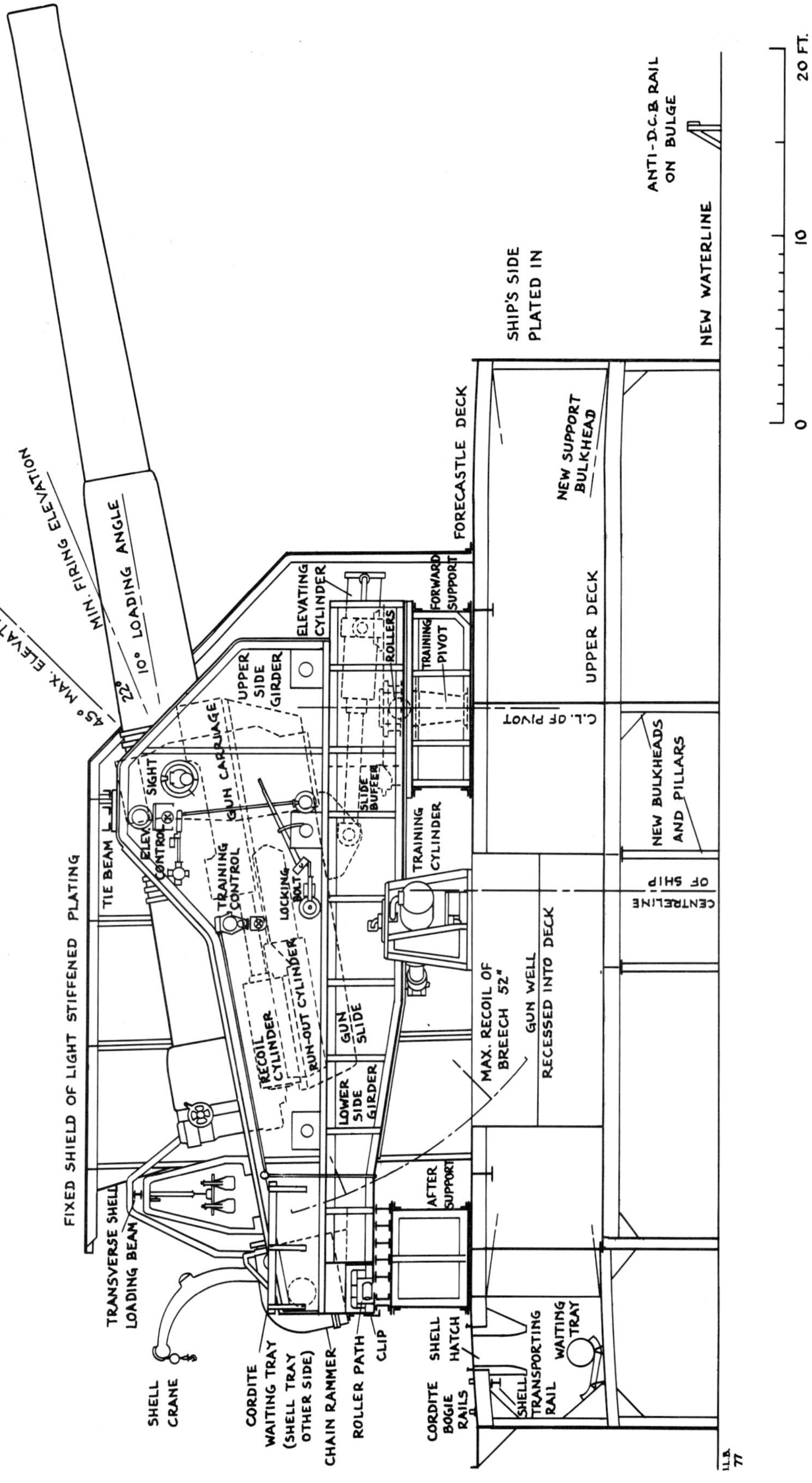
FIXED SHIELD OF LIGHT STIFFENED PLATING
TIE BEAM
45° MAX. ELEVATION
22°
MIN. FIRING ELEVATION
10° LOADING ANGLE
FORECASTLE DECK
SHIP'S SIDE PLATED IN
NEW WATERLINE
ANTI-D.C.B. RAIL ON BULGE
0
10
20 FT.
NEW SUPPORT BULKHEAD
UPPER DECK
C.L. OF PIVOT
NEW BULKHEADS AND PILLARS
CENTRELINE OF SHIP
ELEVATING CYLINDER
FORWARD SUPPORT
TRAINING PIVOT
ROLLERS
UPPER SIDE GIRDER
GUN CARRIAGE
SIGHT
ELEV. CONTROL
TRAINING CONTROL
LOCKING BOLT
SLIDE BUFFER
TRAINING CYLINDER
RECOIL CYLINDER
RUN-OUT CYLINDER
GUN SLIDE
LOWER SIDE GIRDER
MAX. RECOIL OF BREECH 52"
GUN WELL RECESSED INTO DECK
AFTER SUPPORT
TRANSVERSE SHELL LOADING BEAM
SHELL CRANE
CORDITE WAITING TRAY (SHELL TRAY OTHER SIDE)
CHAIN RAMMER
ROLLER PATH
CLIP
CORDITE BOGIE RAILS
SHELL HATCH
SHELL TRANSPORTING RAIL
WAITING TRAY
I.L.B. 77

18-INCH ORDNANCE — TECHNICAL PARTICULARS

Mark I Gun Length overall 744.2in; length of bore 40 calibres; length of rifling 585.4in; weight of gun including 2.8-ton breech mechanism 149.0 tons; recoil 52in.

B C.D. Single Mounting Total weight including gun 384 tons; maximum elevation 45°, minimum firing elevation 22°.

Ammunition Weight of projectile, 4 and 8 c.r.h. 3320lb; length of projectile, 4 c.r.h. C.P.C. 77.0in, 8 c.r.h. H.E. 84.7in; weight of bursting charge, 4 c.r.h. C.P.C. 243lb; weight of cordite MD 45 630lb, supercharge 690lb.

Performance Nominal muzzle velocity 2275ft/sec, supercharge 2425; range at 45° elevation, 4 c.r.h./8 c.r.h.: normal 32,700/36,000 yards, supercharge 36,500/40,100.

tests for the 45-calibre 16-inch which was to form the main armament of the four cancelled 1921 battlecruisers (see p.65) but which was actually installed in the battleships *Nelson* and *Rodney*. No. 1 remained in use for trials until 1942, being scrapped in 1947, while Nos. 2 and 3 lay in store until sold for scrap in 1933. The popular belief that they were mounted at Singapore as coast defence guns is incorrect — five 15-inch Mk I were the heaviest there. One of the mountings was used at Shoeburyness range, eventually going to Dover to mount a 14-inch Mk VII.

A rare close-up of the breech of Lord Clive*'s 18-inch gun. The 2.8-ton breech mechanism was hydraulically operated, although most of the work of ammunition supply was done manually. The angle bar framework supports the transverse loading beam for taking the weight of the projectile before ramming into the gun.*

§4 The 14-inch Mark II Gun

Until the WW2 *King George V* class battleships, the Royal Navy used no 14-inch guns of its own design, British requirements for this size of gun being satisfied by the 13.5-inch. The 14-inch Mk II and its twin mounting installed in the first large monitors was appreciably different in many respects from the 13.5-inch, although it was virtually identical to the U.S. Navy 14-inch 45 cal, which formed the principal armament of the battleships *New York* and *Texas*. Bethlehem had obtained the contract for the 14-inch guns for the Greek battlecruiser *Salamis* in 1912 and it was these guns which were ultimately mounted in the British monitors as described in Chapter II. The 45-calibre 63-ton guns were of all-steel construction, being built-up of ten shrunk-on hoops in a manner similar to British guns before wire-winding was introduced (see drawing of 9.2-inch Mk VI on p.193). Contrary to British practice, the rifling was made with an increasing angle of twist and a decreasing width of groove towards the muzzle. Such features had been tried in Britain but the resulting advantage of more gradual introduction of spin was not considered to outweigh the manufacturing difficulties; there were also other objections, such as copper deposited where the rifling increased in twist. The guns were designed to use nitro-cellulose tubular (N.C.T.) propellant, which produced considerably less erosion than the British cordite as its explosion temperature was lower. The propellant energy was correspondingly reduced, necessitating a heavier charge. The American 14-inch used a 350-lb charge to give a 1400-lb projectile a muzzle velocity of 2500ft/sec, while the British 13.5-inch Mk V required only 297lb cordite to achieve an identical performance. Partly on account of its greater weight, an N.C.T. charge cost about three times as much as the equivalent cordite charge.

The design of the mounting also differed considerably from normal British practice. Electric rather than hydraulic power was used, while the ammunition path to the guns and the corresponding hoists were arranged in different stages as illustrated on p.21. The projectiles were stowed vertically in the shell-room nose down, and travelled in this position in both the lower and upper hoists, only swinging to the horizontal within the gunhouse itself, for loading at zero elevation. The propellant was first lifted by hoists from the magazine, then delivered manually into the breech in four quarter-charges; the breech mechanism was then closed by hand. The mountings proved reliable and simple to operate, especially as the bombardment rate of fire was deliberately slow — about one round per turret per $2^1/_2$ minutes, which gave time for corrections to be made.

The first stocks of ammunition were all supplied from America, the projectiles being made to British specifications. Subsequently projectiles were manufactured in Britain, nose-fuzed 4 c.r.h. H.E. Propellant continued to be provided by the U.S. as no British ordnance factory manufactured suitable N.C.T., although towards the end of the war, alternative 233-lb cordite charges were supplied. N.C.T. was less stable and its performance less consistent than cordite and the stowage containers were sometimes not

14-INCH ORDNANCE — TECHNICAL PARTICULARS

Mark II Gun Length overall 642.5in; length of bore 44.5 calibres; length of rifling 536.8in; weight of gun 63.1 tons.

Twin Mounting Revolving weight 620 tons; maximum elevation 15°, minimum $-1\frac{1}{2}$°; total crew 67 men.

Ammunition Weight of 4 c.r.h. H.E. projectile 1400lb; weight of N.C.T. propellant 350lb.

Performance Nominal muzzle velocity 2500ft/sec; range at 15° elevation 19,900 yards.

airtight, so giving off a pungent odour. In order to obtain a predictable performance, care had to be taken to keep magazine temperatures constant and to select successive projectiles and charges of as nearly equal weight as possible for a particular operation. Even so, it was found that the guns never shot to their nominal muzzle velocity and range. Typically the loss in M.V. was about 150ft/sec, corresponding to a drop of about 2000 yards in maximum range. Although the gun did not fire A.P.C. in British service, its penetration would have been about 13 inches at 12,000 yards.

The accuracy of the guns varied from ship to ship. *Abercrombie*'s always shot well but *Raglan*'s performance often left much to be desired, with rounds sometimes dropping short. It was found that *Roberts*' guns always shot better when they had warmed up after a few rounds. Erratic performance was partly due to variation in the ammunition and to copper deposited in the bore from the driving bands, but mainly due to the construction of the gun, as it was difficult to lock together securely all the different hoops so that the gun would behave as a homogeneous mass of steel. Gaps between the hoops soon opened up, increasing steadily until there was a space of over 0.2in between them. A droop of up to $\frac{1}{4}$° occurred in some of the guns, causing them to whip considerably when fired and lose muzzle velocity. Apart from a loss in accuracy, more in distance than in direction, the range attainable fell off rapidly and replacement guns were needed to restore performance long before the bores were fully worn. Only the eight original guns were bought from Bethlehem but, as the company had no spares, the U.S. Navy supplied four guns which were basically similar, but designated Mk IV and Mk V by the R.N. as they had different breech mechanisms. Two Mk II were made at the R.G.F. in 1917 to wire-wound British design, which were fitted in *Abercrombie* at Malta in May 1918, so allowing her two original guns to be closely examined by ordnance experts at Woolwich.

The British assessment was not very favourable. The potentially long life was appreciated especially as, after about 250 rounds, the bore was found to be only about one-third worn (0.17in). The slack construction, poorly locked hoops and droop were particularly criticised, as was the thin A-tube and the low designed factor of safety. The general conclusion was that there were no particular advantages to be gained by copying U.S. practice in naval guns, mountings and propellants but that, if large forgings of good quality could be obtained, all-steel guns constructed of only two or three tubes would be preferable to wire-wound guns. From about 1930, all-steel construction was adopted for nearly all R.N. guns.

§5 The 9.2-inch Mark XII Gun

The 240-mm (9.45-inch) guns intended for *Nidaros* and *Björgvin* (see Chapter VI) were typical of Elswick designs of their period, consisting of inner and outer A-tubes, wire winding, B-tube over the muzzle portion and jacket over the rear portion. The single turret mountings were hydraulically operated, with the centre-line ammunition hoist cranked through the working chamber to deliver to the left side of the gun. The projectile was then moved onto a tray which swung round to the breech, in line with the hydraulic rammer. The original specification called for a gun capable of penetrating 8.75 inches of Krupp cemented armour at 7000 metres (7650 yards), using a 419-lb projectile, with 144lb of propellant giving a muzzle velocity of 2900ft/sec. Each gun cost about £6000, a single turret £26,000, a C.P.C. projectile about £15 and a charge £11.

When the two Norwegian ships were taken over by Britain in 1915, the guns were modified to 9.2-inch calibre so that standard service ammunition could be used, and designated Mk XII. A new thicker inner A-tube was fitted, making a slightly stronger gun. It was thus possible to reduce the volume of the chamber, resulting in a greater gas pressure and increased M.V. Using the existing 9.2-inch Mk XI $128\frac{1}{2}$-lb charge gave an extra 65ft/sec. The corresponding range at maximum elevation of 35° would have been about 28,500 yards, but the guns had not been installed or tested by the time work was suspended in May 1915. Plans to complete the ships were discussed in 1917, for use off the Belgian Coast where it was clearly desirable to obtain the greatest possible range. At a meeting in August between the Admiralty and Elswick, the possibility of increasing the elevation to 40° was discussed. Elswick were asked to provide this elevation and to include arrangements to handle a new long 8 c.r.h. projectile — a 4 c.r.h. with an added ballistic cap. To get the maximum possible range, 152-lb supercharges were also made available. The combined effect of increased M.V., increased elevation and 8 c.r.h. shells was to give the 9.2-inch Mk XII the prodigious range of 39,000 yards, only surpassed in the R.N. by the modified 18-inch.

During *Gorgon*'s brief period of active service, she fired about 200 rounds but, as many of these were supercharges, the guns were already half-worn by October 1918. After *Glatton*'s loss, *Gorgon*'s two guns were the only ones of that design in service and therefore of little practical value post-war, so they were removed from the ship in 1921 and scrapped in

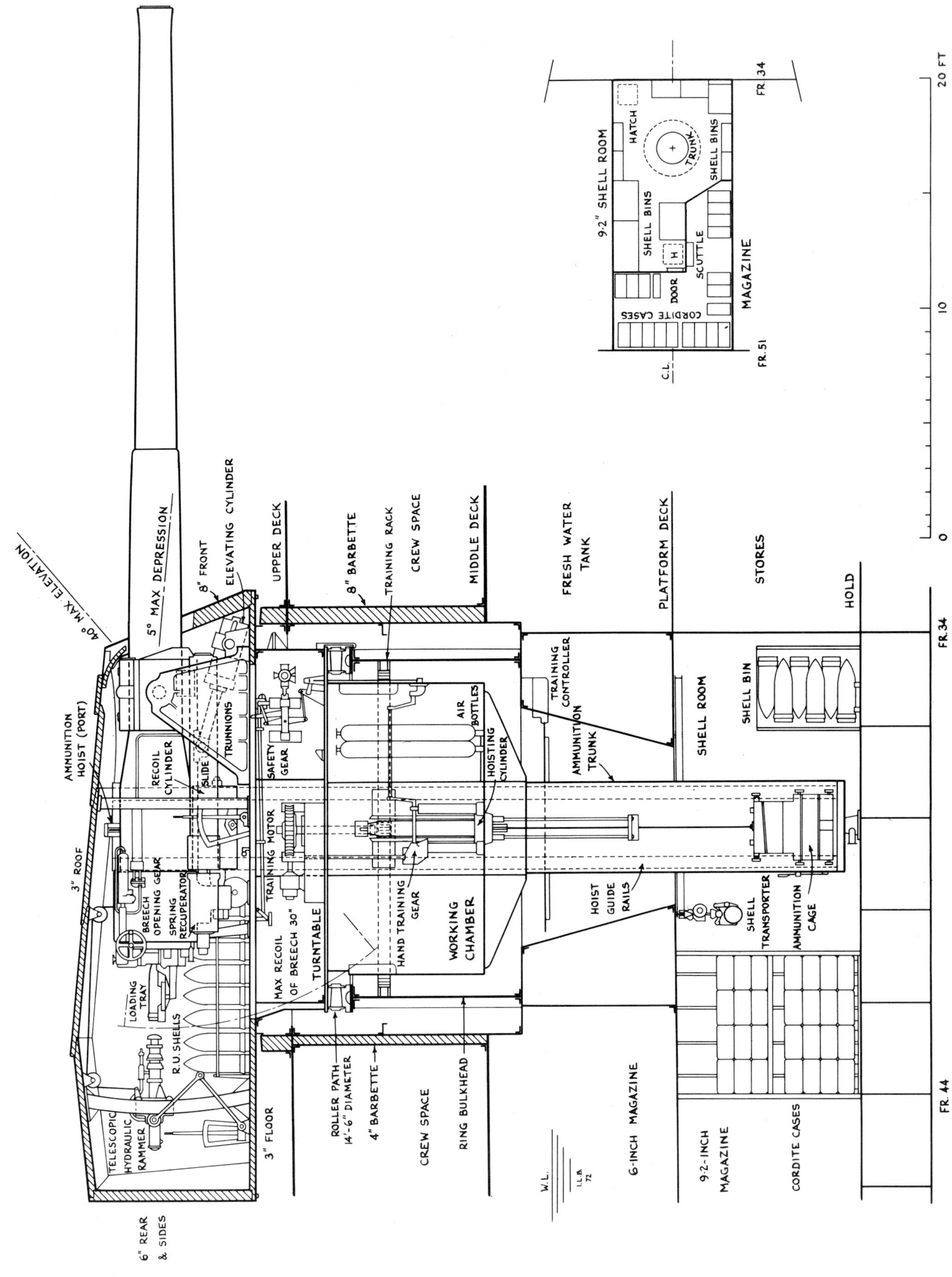

40° MAX. ELEVATION
5° MAX. DEPRESSION
8" FRONT
ELEVATING CYLINDER
UPPER DECK
8" BARBETTE
TRAINING RACK
CREW SPACE
MIDDLE DECK
FRESH WATER TANK
PLATFORM DECK
STORES
HOLD
FR. 34
AMMUNITION HOIST (PORT)
RECOIL CYLINDER
SLIDE
TRUNNIONS
SAFETY GEAR
AIR BOTTLES
HOISTING CYLINDER
TRAINING CONTROLLER
AMMUNITION TRUNK
SHELL ROOM
SHELL BIN
3" ROOF
BREECH OPENING GEAR
SPRING RECUPERATOR
TRAINING MOTOR
HAND TRAINING GEAR
WORKING CHAMBER
HOIST GUIDE RAILS
SHELL TRANSPORTER
AMMUNITION CAGE
LOADING TRAY
R.U. SHELLS
MAX RECOIL OF BREECH 30"
TURNTABLE
TELESCOPIC HYDRAULIC RAMMER
3" FLOOR
ROLLER PATH 14'-6" DIAMETER
4" BARBETTE
CREW SPACE
RING BULKHEAD
6-INCH MAGAZINE
9·2-INCH MAGAZINE
CORDITE CASES
FR. 44
6" REAR & SIDES
W.L.
I.L.B. 72
9·2" SHELL ROOM
HATCH
TRUNK
SHELL BINS
SHELL BINS
SCUTTLE
H
DOOR
CORDITE CASES
MAGAZINE
C.L.
FR. 51
FR. 34
0
10
20 FT

9.2-INCH ORDNANCE — TECHNICAL PARTICULARS

Mark XII Gun Length overall 485.4in; length of bore 51.4 calibres; length of rifling 403.0in; weight of gun 31.47 tons.

Mark IX Single Mounting Revolving weight 194.2 tons; maximum elevation 40°, minimum —5°.

Ammunition Weight of projectile, 4 c.r.h./8 c.r.h. H.E. 380/391lb; length of projectile, 4 c.r.h. H.E. 33.3in; weight of bursting charge 4 c.r.h. H.E. 40lb; weight of cordite MD 37, normal/supercharge 128½/152lb.

Performance Nominal muzzle velocity, normal/supercharge 2900/3060ft/sec; range at 40° elevation, 4 c.r.h. normal/8 c.r.h. supercharge 30,000/39,000 yards; maximum rate of fire 2 rounds per minute.

1923 — although two spare guns had been completed in 1921.

§6 Other Monitor Weapons

Under the press of wartime necessity, the monitors had to be fitted out with whatever guns could be obtained most readily. As a consequence, they mounted a miscellany of pieces, whose origins and other uses are too numerous to spell out in detail individually. Reference is made in the ship chapters to ordnance of particular interest, while the following Tables summarise the principal characteristics of the main armaments of the small monitors, the various secondary armaments and the anti-aircraft weapons. Wherever possible, data relates to the period in which the weapon was fitted in the monitors and the ammunition which they generally used; in other ships and at other times, different mountings, projectiles or propellants may have been used, giving a different performance, e.g. the 4-inch Q.F. V used different ammunition for low angle firing. Nearly all of the smaller calibres were standard weapons used in a wide range of other British ships. A few are still in service in various navies, such as the 4-inch Q.F. XVI*, 40-mm Bofors and 20-mm Oerlikon.

§7 Bombardment Techniques

Prior to 1914, gunnery techniques in the Royal Navy concentrated entirely on the problem of hitting an enemy ship — a directly visible target. The problem of indirect fire, where the target could not be seen, was considered to be the prerogative of the Royal Artillery. In order to hit an enemy ship, it was necessary to know the relative positions of the two vessels, predict their relative motion and, knowing the ballistic performance of the gun, translate this information into the appropriate angles for training and elevating the guns. Fire control instruments, the director system, the training of personnel, the gunnery exercises, the principal types of ammunition — all were devised to this end. On the rare occasions prior to WW1 that shore bombardment was undertaken, the target was usually visible from the ship, such as a fort, and the fire was controlled by direct observation as if at a stationary ship. The corresponding problem where the target was not visible was much more difficult to solve, so nearly four years of WW1 were to elapse before the R.N. developed a reliable system that could be used even under the most demanding conditions.

Successful shore bombardment requires that all of the following operations be accurately carried out:—

(i) Identification of the target and its location on a suitable map
(ii) Selection of a suitable firing position for the ship and accurate fixing of this position relative to the target
(iii) Selection of a suitable point of aim for laying and training the gun, which might not be in direct line with the target
(iv) Calculation of the exact range and height of the target, calculation of all the necessary ballistic corrections to allow for the current performance of the gun, and translation into gun elevation and training angle
(v) Laying, training and firing the gun in the required direction
(vi) Observation of the fall of shot
(vii) Communication of the results of the observation back to the ship
(viii) Application of the necessary corrections to bring the gun right on to the target.

This complex sequence often had to be carried out in the face of strong enemy opposition, while the key to success was accurate observation and communication. Given the inevitable slight inaccuracies of making and firing ordnance, it was virtually impossible to land the first round exactly on target, however carefully steps (i) to (v) had been carried out. In a general bombardment of a neutralising and harassing type, extreme accuracy was not so vital, but destructive fire to hit a precise target such as a shore battery or a lock gate from a dozen miles called for the highest standards of performance in every aspect. The individual techniques used for each step underwent progressive refinement as experience grew, from the makeshift arrangements off the Belgian Coast in October 1914, through the improvisations of the Dardanelles Campaign in 1915, to the sophistication off the Belgian Coast during 1918.

It is worth taking each of the eight steps in turn and tracing the changes that developed, particularly during WW1. Location of targets right on the coastline such as harbour installations presented no difficulty, as the

(Opposite) *The 9.2-inch single mounting in* Glatton *and* Gorgon *was converted from the 9.45-inch 35° elevation design prepared by Elswick for the Norwegians. The conical section round the trunk was necessary because the hoist was cranked to deliver to the left side of the gun. With elevation increased to 40°, supercharges and 8 c.r.h. projectiles giving 39,000 yards range, the Mk XII gun far outranged all other British WW1 ordnance except the 18-inch. The inset shows the compact arrangement of the forward magazine and shell-room (34ft × 19ft) for the 130 rounds of H.E. and 8 practice.*

MAIN ARMAMENT OF THE SMALL MONITORS

Gun						
Calibre	**9.2-inch**	**9.2-inch**	**7.5-inch**	**6-inch**	**6-inch**	**6-inch**
Mark	B.L. X	B.L. VI	B.L. III	B.L. XIV & XV	B.L. XII	B.L. VII
Length of bore, calibres	46.7	31.5	50	50	45	44.9
Length overall, in	442.5	310.0	388.2	309.7	279.7	279.2
Length of rifling, in	353.8	243.4	325.2	265.2	230.6	233.6
Construction	S. & W.	Steel hoop	S. & W.	S. & W.	S. & W.	S. & W.
Weight including breech mechanism, tons	28.3	22.0	15.75	8.10	6.90	7.51
Life, e.f.c.	450	350	500	ca1000	700	1200
Mounting						
Type	Turret	Vavasseur	Transferable	Vickers	Transferable	Transferable
Mark	V	C.P. III	P.III	Special Twin Turret	P. IX	P. III
Weight including gun and shield, tons	70 (R)	45 (T)	32 (T)	100 (R)	17.9 (T)	16.3 (T)
Maximum elevation, degrees	30	30	15	15	17½	15
Minimum elevation, degrees	0	−5	−5	−5	−7	−7
Ammunition						
Typical projectile	4 c.r.h. H.E.	2 c.r.h. C.P.	4 c.r.h. H.E.	4 c.r.h. H.E.	4 c.r.h. C.P.C.	4 c.r.h. H.E.
Weight, lb	380	380	200	100	100	100
Length, in	32.1	35.4	29.7	22.0	23.5	22.9
Weight of bursting charge, lb	33.0	30.0	23	ca11	7.5	13.3
Weight of propellant, lb	120 MD	53.5 C	54.25 MD	28.62 MD	27.12 MD	28.62 MD
Performance						
Nominal muzzle velocity, ft/sec	2700	2065	2700	2800	2750	2725
Range at max elevation, yards	25,000	16,300	15,000	14,000	14,700	13,500
Armour penetration by C.P.C.	5″ at 10,000yd	5″ at 6,000yd	4″ at 10,000yd	3½″ at 7500yd	3½″ at 7500 yd	3½″ at 7500 yd
Maximum rounds per minute	1	½	4	6	6	6
Fitted in	*M.15-M.18* (1915)	*M.19-M.28* (1915)	*M.26* (1916) *M.21, M.23* (1917) Mk IV in *M.24, M.25* (1916) See Note 2	*Severn, Humber, Mersey* (1914)	*M.29-M.33* (1915) *Abercrombie, Raglan, Picton* (1916)	*Severn, Humber, Mersey* (1915) *M.27* (1917) *Clive, Craufurd, Eugene, Moore, Rupert, Wolfe,* (1916-17) See Note 3

Notes
1. S. & W. = steel and wire; C = cordite Mk I; MD = cordite MD; R = revolving weight; T = transferable weight; P = pedestal (mounting); C.P. = centre pivot (mounting); C.P. = common, pointed (projectile). All mountings single except as indicated.
2. 7.5-inch Mk IV on Mk IV mounting generally similar to Mk III. Mk I gun in *M.26* from 1917.
3. Some 6-inch Mk VII had 20° elevation.

Anti-Aircraft Rocket Weapons

Designation	**3-inch U.P. Mark I**	**7-inch U.P. Mark I**
Type	Harvey Projector	Naval Wire Barrage
Projectile diameter, in	3	7
Weight of round, lb	56	35
Length of round, in	76	32
Type of projector	Single	20-barrel
Length of launcher, in	144	ca90
Weight of mounting, tons	0.5	4
Effective range, yards	1500	1000
Fitted in	*Erebus* (1941)	*Erebus* (1940)

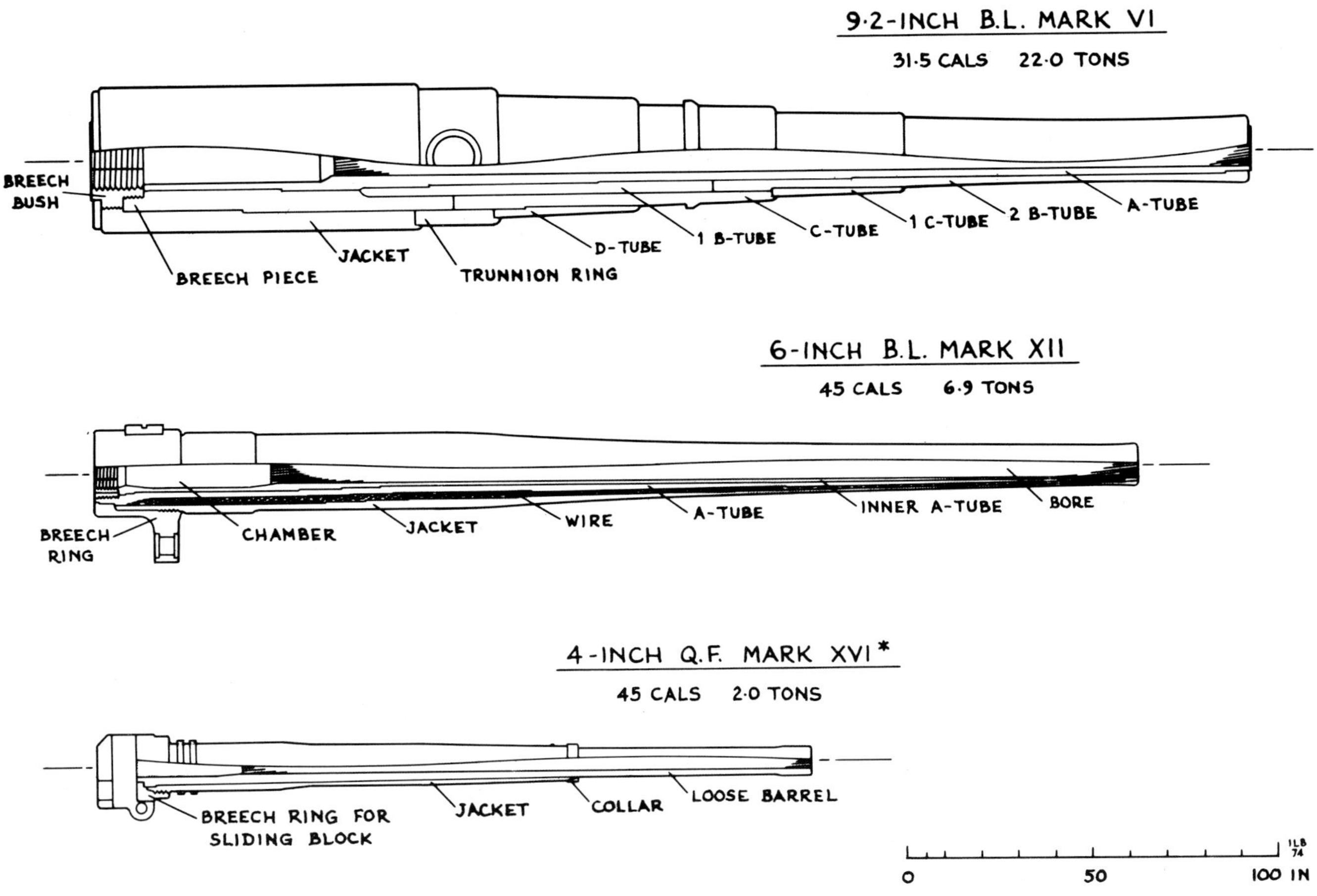

The monitors provided examples of three main stages of British naval ordnance development. The top illustration of the 9.2-inch Mk VI fitted in M.19 *to* M.28 *shows a design of the late 1880s, when heavy guns had to be built up of a large number of tubes and hoops. This basic type of construction was also used in the 14-inch monitors' Bethlehem guns. The stumpy profile with many shoulders gave rise to its nickname of the "soda-water bottle" gun. The construction of the 6-inch Mk XII used wire wound circumferentially to provide radial strength, and was typical of modern R.N. designs of the WW1 era. The gun was installed in* M.29 *to* M.33 *and as secondary armament in three of the large monitors. The lower illustration shows how an all-steel design was built up of fewer pieces, made possible by improvements in steel forgings and manufacturing techniques. The 4-inch Mk XVI* used as an H.A./L.A. gun in* Roberts *and* Abercrombie *was typical of medium calibre designs of the WW2 era. Breech blocks and other fittings are not shown.*

SECONDARY ARMAMENT IN THE MONITORS

Gun							
Calibre	**9.2-inch**	**6-inch**	**6-inch**	**6-inch**	**120-mm (4.72″)**	**4-inch**	**3-inch**
Mark	B.L. VIII	B.L. XVIII	B.L. XI	Q.F. II	Howitzer	B.L. IX	12pdr 18cwt Q.F. I
Length of bore, calibres	40	48.9	50	40	18	44.4	50
Length overall, in	384.0	303.9	309.7	249.3	89.9	184.6	154.7
Weight including breech mechanism, tons	25.0	8.65	8.70	7.00	0.57	2.12	0.90
Life, e.f.c.	250	1200	1000	1200		2350	1200
Mounting							
Mark	C.P. IV	IV	P. V	P. II	Vickers	C.P. I Triple I	P. IV
Weight including gun and shield, tons	79 (R)	65.7 (R)	16.2 (T)	15 (T)	4.65 (T)	5.4 (T) 18.5 (T)	1.71 (T)
Maximum elevation, degrees	13½	20	13	19	70	30 30	20
Minimum elevation, degrees	−5	−5	−7	−7	−5	−10 −10	−10
Ammunition							
Typical projectile	2 c.r.h. C.P.	4 c.r.h. C.P.C.	4 c.r.h. H.E.	2 c.r.h. C.P.	2 c.r.h. H.E.	3 c.r.h. H.E.	2 c.r.h. H.E.
Weight, lb	380	100	100	100	45	31	12.5
Weight of propellant, lb	66 C	28.62 MD	32.09 MD	13.25 C	1.78 MD	7.69 MD	2.75 MD
Performance							
Nominal muzzle velocity, ft/sec	2329	2800	2900	2154	1200	2600	2600
Range at max elevation, yards	12,000	16,000	13,600	11,000	ca9000 at 45°	13,700	9300
Maximum rounds per minute	1	3	6	6	ca10	10	15
Fitted in	*Ney* (1916)	*Glatton, Gorgon* (1918)	*Ney* (1917)	*Erebus, Terror, Wolfe, Moore, Craufurd, Soult, Ney,* (all Mk II 1916) *Roberts, Clive, M.26, M.27* (all Mk I 1916) See Note 2	*Severn, Humber, Mersey* (1914)	*Erebus, Terror, Soult, Clive, Moore* (1918) *M.27* triple (1919) See Note 3	All 14-inch, 12-inch and 15-inch (1915-16) *M.15-M.28* (1915) See Note 4

Notes

1. All guns hand-worked except 6-inch Mk XVIII. All mountings single except 4-inch triple.
2. 6-inch Q.F. I on C.P. I generally similar to Q.F. II on P. II. *Roberts*' gun on special H.A. mounting.
3. 4-inch Mk IX was B.L. version of 4-inch Q.F. Mk V.
4. 12pdr 18cwt mountings later converted for H.A. firing.

HIGH ANGLE GUNS IN THE MONITORS

Gun							
Calibre	**4-inch**	**4-inch**	**3-inch**	**57-mm (2.24″)**		**47-mm (1.85″)**	**47-mm (1.85″)**
Designation and Mark	Q.F. XVI*	Q.F. V	20cwt Q.F. I	Hotchkiss 6pdr Q.F. I		Hotchkiss 3pdr Q.F. I	Vickers 3pdr Q.F. I
Length of bore, calibres	45	45	45	40		40	50
Length overall, in	190.5	187.8	140.0	97.6		80.6	98.9
Weight including breech mechanism, tons	2.00	2.15	1.02	0.36		0.23	0.29
Life, e.f.c.	600	1600	1250	6000		6000	ca5000
Mounting							
Type	Twin H.A./L.A.	Single	Single	Single	Single	Single	Single
Mark	XIX	H.A. III & IV	H.A. II	H.A. IC	H.A. IV	H.A.IC	H.A. III
Weight including gun and shield, tons	15.2	6.8	2.83	0.84	0.93	0.58	0.70
Maximum elevation, degrees	80	80	90	60	90	60	80
Minimum elevation, degrees	−10	−5	−5	−8	−15	−8	−5
Ammunition							
Weight of H.E. projectile, lb	35.87	31.43	16	6		3.31	3.31
Weight of propellant, lb	9.0	5.87	2.12	0.54		0.45	0.83
Total weight of round including cartridge case, lb	63.5	54	27	9.7		5.7	6.6
Performance							
Nominal muzzle velocity, ft/sec	2600	2350	2000	1765		1873	2575
Range at 45° elevation, yards	19,600	16,300	11,200	8700		7900	5600 at 12°
Maximum A.A. ceiling, feet	39,000	29,000	23,000	ca10,000		ca10,000	ca15,000
Maximum rounds per minute per gun	16	10	20	20		20	25
Fitted in	*Roberts* (1941) *Abercrombie* (1943)	*Terror* (1939) *Erebus* (1940)	*Abercrombie*, *Havelock*, *Roberts* (1917) *Ney* (1915), *Soult* (1916) All 12-inch (1915-17) *Glatton*, *Gorgon* (1918) *Erebus*, *Terror* (1916) *Humber* (1919), *M.16*, *M.18*-*M.27*, *M.31*, *M.33* (1917-19) See Note 1	*M.15*-*M.33* (1915) See Note 2		*Severn*, *Humber*, *Mersey* (1915) See Note 2	All 14-inch (1915) *Soult* (1915) All 12-inch except *Eugene* (1915), *Glatton* (1918) *Severn*, *Humber*, *Mersey* (1914) *M.23*-*M.26* (1919) See Notes 2 & 3

Notes
1. 3-inch 20cwt originally fired a $12^1/_2$lb projectile at 2500ft/sec.
2. Effective A.A. range of Hotchkiss 3pdr and 6pdr about 1200yd, Vickers 3pdr about 2000yd.
3. Four Vickers 3pdr in *Severn* class were Mk II on low angle mountings.

CLOSE RANGE AUTOMATIC WEAPONS IN THE MONITORS

Gun								
Calibre	**40-mm (1.575″)**	**40-mm (1.575″)**		**40-mm (1.575″)**	**20-mm (0.787″)**		**0.5-inch**	**0.303-inch**
Designation	2pdr Vickers	2pdr Vickers H.V.		Bofors	Oerlikon		Vickers machine gun	Maxim M.G.
Mark	Q.F. I & II	VIII		N.1	II		III	I
Length of bore, calibres	39.4	39.4		56.25	70		62	94
Length overall, in	96.0	115.6 over guard		130	87		52	42.4
Weight, lb	572	850		423	141		56	60
Life, rounds	5000	7200		11,000	30,000			
Mounting								
Type	Single	Quadruple	Octuple	Single	Single	Twin	Quadruple	Single
Mark	H.A. I & II	'M' VII*	'M' VIA*	III*	IIA	V	'M' III	Pedestal
Weight including guns, tons	0.70	9.15	15.68	1.18	0.56	1.01	1.31	0.072
Maximum elevation, degrees	80	80	80	90	85	70	80	20
Minimum elevation, degrees	−10	−10	−10	−5	−5	−10	−10	−47
Ammunition								
Weight of H.E. projectile, lb	2.15	1.81		2.00	0.272		0.083	0.031
Weight of propellant, lb	0.21	0.26		0.56	0.061		ca0.015	0.0045
Total weight of round including cartridge case, lb	2.95	2.87		4.80	0.53		0.18	0.060
Performance								
Nominal muzzle velocity, ft/sec	1900	2300		2800	2725		2520	2060
Effective A.A. range, yards	ca1200	1700		2500	1000		800	500
Rounds per minute per barrel	200	115		120	480		700	450
Fitted in	All 14-inch (1915) All 12-inch (1915) *Ney, Soult* (1915) *Erebus, Terror* (1918) *Glatton, Gorgon* (1918) *M.23, M.24, M.26, M.27* (1918)	*Erebus* (1941) *Roberts* (1941) *Abercrombie* (1943) See Note 2		*Erebus* (1941) *Roberts* (1945)	*Erebus* (1941) *Roberts* (1941) *Abercrombie* (1943)		*Terror* (1939) *Erebus* (1940) See Note 3	All 14-inch, All 12-inch, All WW1 15-inch, *M.15-M.33* (1915-16) See Note 3

Notes
1. Maximum range four to six times effective range.
2. *Erebus* also had one 2pdr Mk VIII on single Mk VIII mounting, 1941. Weight 1.15 tons. H.V. = High velocity.
3. Fired solid projectiles, no burster.

This drawing by Stephen Bone shows Roberts' *spotting top during the Walcheren operation 1-2 November 1944. The Bombardment Liaison Officer, Captain S. W. T. Musto R.A., is standing at the plot; on his left is a map of Walcheren, through the window the island itself. Seated are the communication numbers, with the Gunnery Officer, Lieut-Commander H. S. Whittow R.N.V.R., in the duffle coat.*

normal navigational charts were sufficiently accurate in most cases. Targets inland were much more difficult to relate to the ship's position on a chart, which showed little detail of land features. Conversely land maps included few offshore features, while their grid system did not correspond with the chart's grid of latitude and longitude. Aircraft soon proved their worth in locating the position of hidden targets such as mobile batteries on the reverse slopes of hills so, by the end of 1915, almost any target at the Dardanelles could easily be referenced in relation to prominent landmarks. While the targets at the Belgian Coast were more clearly identifiable — dockyards, locks, batteries etc — resurveying was eventually necessary, to provide larger scale maps of the coast as well as to rechart those shallow areas of shifting sandbanks which had last been fully surveyed in the 1840s.

The second step also presented many problems: selecting and fixing accurately the ship's firing position. The position had to be chosen to give a good line to the target, to avoid if possible the fire of enemy shore batteries, to permit safe navigation, allowing for wind and tide. The ship's position then had to be fixed relative to the target location by sighting on prominent landmarks ashore — a difficult task off the low-lying, relatively featureless Belgian Coast, where German shore batteries drove the monitors almost out of sight of land. New methods were developed, such as that in which a destroyer would lay a buoy in advance at the firing position and drop two depth charges, one on each side of the buoy. Direction finding stations on the Kent coast would pick up the sound of the explosions on hydrophones, cross-plot the exact position to within a few yards and signal it to the monitors.

With the exact position of ship and target having been determined, the next step was to give the gun-sight a point to aim at. In the large monitors, the newly developed director system was used to aim the guns from aloft, the necessary elevation and training angles being transmitted electrically from the layer and trainer in the director to their counterparts in the turret, who had to match pointers to bring the turret on to the target. In the small monitors, layer and trainer used the normal telescope sights on the gun itself to sight the point of aim. There was little difficulty at the Dardanelles in finding a suitable aiming mark like a prominent rock more or less in line with the target. The angle between the mark and the target was then calculated and set on the horizontal deflection scale of the gun-sight so that, although the sights were pointing at the mark, the barrel was pointing at the target. Similarly, after the necessary angle of elevation for the range had been calculated (see p.198), the elevation to the mark was measured by sextant and subtracted from this angle to give the setting on the sights.

Off the Belgian Coast, conditions were much more difficult, especially after the monitors were driven out to firing positions ten miles or more offshore. The introduction of smokescreens to protect the ships finally ruled out any further use of shore marks. Bacon therefore used another ship as an aiming mark, generally one of the smaller monitors. Anchored out of range of the shore batteries, the ship burned a searchlight about four to six miles to seaward of the firing monitor. During 1916, Altham had rigged up in the 12-inch turret a repeater from the gyro compass which had been newly installed in *General Craufurd*, so that the turret could be trained on any true bearing to an accuracy of less than half a degree. The widespread installation during the summer of similar equipment in the monitors' directors called Gyro

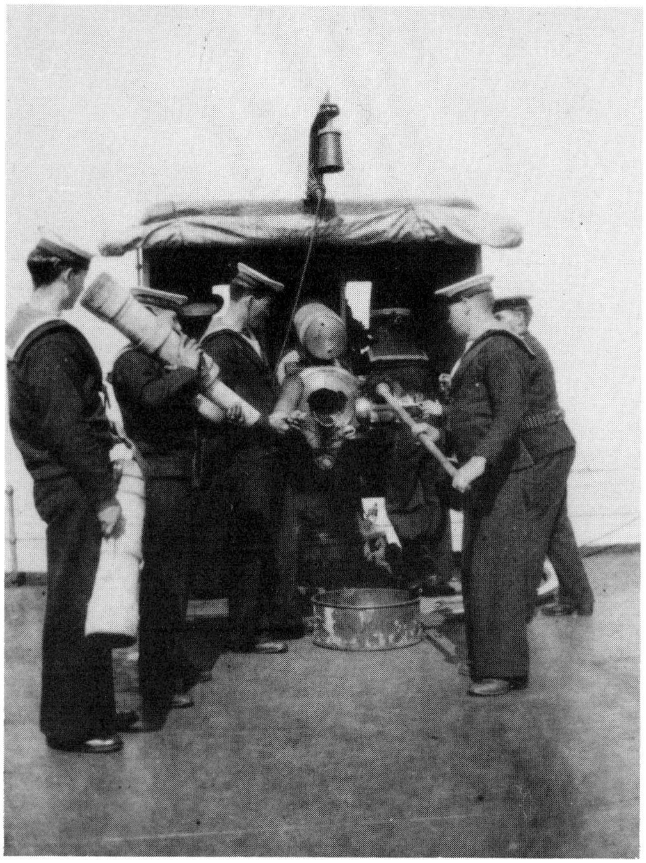

Director Training Gear enabled the Dover monitors to keep their guns on targets whilst underway, an operation which could otherwise only be undertaken by very special arrangements of buoys and subsidiary marks.

Calculation of the fourth step, the actual range to set on the sights, was complicated due to the great number of sources of potential error. For naval guns with high velocities and flat trajectories, inherent inaccuracies in bearing (or deflection) were relatively small, especially if both ship and target were stationary, as was usually the case. The most important sources of deflection error for long range firing were:—

(a) Wind across the line of fire
(b) Drift, i.e. the tendency of a spinning projectile to wander to one side, and rotation of the earth.

Possible sources of error in range and elevation were more serious, particularly anything that affected muzzle velocity, including:—

(c) Bore wear, with M.V. dropping appreciably as the gun became worn
(d) Type, quality and temperature of propellant and projectile
(e) Wind along the line of fire
(f) Air pressure and temperature
(g) Height of the target above sea level and curvature of the earth.

A number of these factors could be incorporated in the Range Table issued for the gun but for the others, estimated corrections had to be applied at the time of firing. Range Tables gave the necessary angle of elevation for a particular gun and specific ammunition to achieve a certain range under standard conditions, as well as time of flight, striking velocity of projectile, angle of descent and culminating point. Separate corrections were given for : bore wear, propellant temperature, muzzle velocity, drift and atmospheric conditions. A standard calculation form was used to convert the actual map range into the equivalent Range Table range, so that the elevation for the gun could be read off. Especially in a well-worn gun, the two range figures could easily differ by several thousand yards. Even after making all these corrections, there still remained a number of other

(Top) *All the early large monitors received one 3-pdr semi-automatic and one 2-pdr pom-pom as high angle armament. The photo shows* Sir John Moore*'s 50-calibre 3-pdr fitted with H.A. range dials. Elevation up to 80° was possible on this Vickers design, compared with only about 15-20° on the contemporary low angle mountings.*

(Middle) *Towards the end of WW1, the 6-inch secondary armament on the large Dover monitors was replaced by 4-inch B.L. Mk IX. The photograph shows the crew of one of* Sir John Moore*'s four guns at drill. The gun used separate ammunition: one man is holding the 31-lb projectile, two others are holding leather cartridge cases with cordite. The shaded light on top of the shield was for night action.*

(Bottom) *All the large Dover monitors received a 6-inch secondary armament in 1916.* Sir John Moore *was originally fitted with four 6-inch Q.F. on the forecastle deck abreast the funnel, two of which were replaced by 6-inch B.L. Mk VII. One of the latter is illustrated, having been allocated pre-war to the Royal Marine Artillery.*

sources of error which all contributed to an overall 'error of the gun', including:

— increase in temperature of the gun during firing
— droop of the gun as its tubes slackened with use
— inaccuracies of installation of mountings and sights, plus deflections of the hull at sea.

The fifth step of laying and training the gun to the required angles was relatively simple in calm weather. In any sort of a sea however, the gunlayer and trainer had a much harder job, as it was necessary to try to fire the gun at the instant that the motion of the ship brought the telescope crosswires exactly into line with the aiming mark. While it was sometimes possible to lay on the horizon, sophisticated types of spirit levels with telescopes such as clinometers proved more satisfactory. The task was simplified after the introduction of the Henderson gyro firing gear in 1918, which automatically fired the gun at the instant that the director sight was elevated for the correct range.

The existence of all these actual and potential sources of error meant that it was almost impossible to land the first round exactly on target. The first few rounds had therefore to be fired on what was in effect a trial and error basis, which placed great importance on the accurate observation and rapid reporting of the fall of shot, so permitting the necessary correction to be applied. During the "Race to the Sea", only very crude ground level spotting was possible in support of the Belgian troops, with rough corrections being laboriously telephoned to Nieuport for signalling by acetylene lamp out to the bombarding ships. Such a method could not possibly suffice for accurate sustained fire, so experiments were started using aircraft spotting and wireless communication. The preliminary bombardments of the Dardanelles forts early in 1915 had nearly all been made using only observation from the firing ships but, after the landings at Gallipoli, arrangements could be made for more effective methods. Early attempts were made at spotting from a kite-balloon tethered to a balloon ship. Although the balloon was not directly over the target, its height was sufficient to give a marked improvement over ground level observation. Communication was simple using a telephone with the wire running down the mooring cable, but the balloon was vulnerable to enemy aircraft. Early experiments with aircraft were not very successful. The first seaplanes were unreliable and had insufficient power to reach a good altitude, while their wireless sets were weak, temperamental and only capable of transmitting, not receiving. The observers were not sufficiently trained, whilst standard spotting codes had yet to be developed.

Gradually the difficulties were overcome. More powerful aircraft arrived, the observers became more experienced and the wireless sets were improved. By late 1915, the R.N.A.S. spotting service had developed into a reliable means of observing and controlling fire at Gallipoli. If the target was close to the front-line, shore observation was normally used, spots being telephoned back to the main Naval Observation Station and then relayed out to the monitors, e.g. by telephone to the moored Rabbit Island ships.

When the first large monitor arrived at Dover, Bacon's plans had been prepared on the basis of ground level observation. When firing near to the front-line, fire could be observed from vantage points in two or more high buildings, telephoned to a shore plotting station which drew out the bearings and then signalled the results to the ship. This was a slow procedure and not very accurate unless the observers were widely spaced with good lines of sight. Bombardment of targets well behind enemy lines, such as at Zeebrugge in August 1915, had to be observed by ships of the bombarding fleet, at first using the spotting tripods which were dropped into the sea offshore, as described on p.47. The observers on the vulnerable tripods had a poor view of the shell bursts from their position only a few feet above sea level, while their lamp signalling apparatus was inadequate, so the method had to be abandoned.

Despite some earlier failures with aircraft spotting, the experiments were continued. Those organised by Altham in November 1915 yielded a basic method which was to be refined into a very successful system by 1917-18; it enabled one observer to spot for several ships all firing at the same target. By this time, the Army clock spotting method was adopted, which was similar to rifle shooting in that several circles at standard distances from the target were imagined, in conjunction with bearings measured in 'hours' from the 12 o'clock position, which represented due north. A special Artillery Clock and Deflection Indicator was developed so that spots could be translated directly into changes of gun range and deflection.

It was usually necessary for the first ranging shots to be brought on to the target as quickly as possible, especially if the enemy was using defensive smokescreens to hide the target or was jamming W/T transmissions. Once the guns got on target, 'firing for effect' could take place more or less blind. Spotting services for the Dover monitors were generally provided by No. 1 Wing R.N.A.S., based at Dunkirk. Aeroplanes such as the Nieuport 12 soon replaced seaplanes owing to their better performance and endurance. After the corrections were received in the W/T office in the monitors, they were sent by telephone or voice-pipe to the Gunnery Officer and his team in the draughty spotting top, where the necessary alterations to gun elevation and deflection could be applied. After an operation, aircraft observation and photographs proved invaluable in assessing the results.

During WW2, the techniques established during WW1 and formalised in successive post-war editions of bombardment manuals were further refined, although more concerned with operational control and improved spotting methods than with changes in material. Radar was of little use for bombardment apart from assisting navigation and permitting the removal of rangefinders from bridge or spotting top — although the 15-foot rangefinder in each 15-inch turret was retained. Apart from improved projectiles, the 15-inch as used in WW2 differed very little from that in WW1. One technical improvement that did prove useful was the installation of a proper transmitting station with a fire control table, which simplified the problem of firing with the ship

This sketch by John Worsley shows Roberts' *turret during the Salerno bombardment on 10 September 1943. The breechworker is in the left foreground, like the others not wearing flashproof gear, probably owing to the heat and lack of serious enemy retaliation.*

underway, or stopped but drifting with tide or current. Other refinements included the introduction of gyro-stabilised director sights and, from 1943 onwards, the use of direct voice radio communication between observer and ship. The greatest changes occurred in observation and communication techniques, with most bombardments being in direct support of military operations rather than at predetermined coastal targets.

In the earlier Mediterranean operations, naval aircraft like Swordfish and Albacores were used for spotting as well as for dropping flares during night bombardments. For the later combined operations, new systems were devised to enable close support of the Army to be maintained during a landing. Forward Observer Bombardment teams of artillery officers and naval telegraphists signalled their spotting reports to the bombarding vessel, usually via an H.Q. ship, which were interpreted by the Bombardment Liaison Officer and the ship's Gunnery Officer to give the necessary corrections. With large numbers of ships allocated to bombardment duties and as many as 30 F.O.B.s, it was necessary to channel all requests for fire support through a Bombardment Control Organisation on board the H.Q. ship for a particular sector. The H.Q. ship was usually a specially converted merchant ship with a wide range of communications equipment plus accommodation for personnel from the three services. *Largs* served Force "S" at Normandy; others who served the monitors during 1943-44 included *Hilary*, U.S.S. *Ancon* and U.S.S. *Bayfield*. In response to requests from Army H.Q. ashore, the senior B.L.O. and Staff Gunnery Officer aboard the H.Q. ship allocated targets, F.O.B.s and spotting aircraft to a particular bombarding vessel, using special radio channels. The H.Q. ship had the latest tactical information on the front-line situation and air activity, and was an indispensable part of any combined operations fleet.

During the early stages of a landing operation, spotting was mainly by aircraft but, as the Armies pushed inland, the F.O.B. was used in preference wherever enemy targets were close to the front-line. When the F.O.B. made a call for fire giving the map reference and other details, the first round was on its way within about five minutes, usually landing within about 300 yards of the target in a position where it could be observed by the F.O.B., yet not alarming friendly troops. After two or three more rounds, the shells would be falling within 50 yards or so of the target; firing for effect required typically a further ten to twenty rounds. Nearly all of the monitor firings during the Sicilian and Italian landings were made under the control of F.O.B.s, although there were sometimes difficulties by their being in the wrong position or from radio communication problems.

Careful analysis of experiences in the Mediterranean during 1943 emphasised the importance of good communications and extensive training. The use of fighter reconnaissance aircraft for spotting, first used in Sicily, had been so successful that it soon became the principal means of observation thereafter, especially at Normandy. In addition to spotting fall of shot, the aircraft were invaluable in detecting tactical targets worthy of bombardment. Spotting by such fast aircraft was only effective if the pilot could devote his full attention, so it was necessary for him to be accompanied by another fighter as escort. The spotter would circle at about 5000 feet over the target, with his 'weaver' guarding his tail and ready to stand in should the former be brought down by A.A. fire. Owing to the distance from British airfields, the fighters could only spend about 45 minutes over the target in Normandy so, at any given time, there were two on station, two returning to base and two more approaching to relieve. Large numbers of aircraft with specially trained pilots were needed to sustain such an operation. Nine squadrons totalling about 170 aircraft participated on "Neptune" D-day: Fleet Air Arm Seafires of Nos. 808, 845, 886 and 897 Squadrons, R.A.F. Spitfires of Nos. 26 and 63, R.A.F. Mustangs of Nos. 2, 268 and 414, and U.S.N. Spitfires of VC S-7 Squadron. 435 sorties were flown on D-day alone, spotting for 135 shoots. After D-day, the Mustangs were withdrawn and the naval pilots based at Lee-on-Solent carried out the majority of the remaining 1700 sorties made during June 1944, covering some 400 shoots.

The American Shore Fire Control Parties operated slightly differently to the British F.O.B. system, which was basically an Army link between observer and ship. The S.F.C.P. itself interpreted the military requirements into naval terms and passed the corresponding orders to the ship; this put a great responsibility onto a team which might be under pressure in the field. The British considered that their system, in which there was a greater degree of centralised control, was more suitable for the conditions under which they operated. The experiences that the Americans learned in Europe were applied in the Pacific operations during 1945, when Wildcat fighters from escort carriers spotted many of the devastating bombardments of Iwo Jima and Okinawa.

CHAPTER XI

IN RETROSPECT

The Royal Navy was the only navy to build in significant numbers ships exclusively for coast offence purposes. Was its policy justified? The answer must certainly be yes. One has only to ask what other vessels it would have had to use in the absence of special purpose vessels and whether the resources required could have been more usefully deployed elsewhere. In answering the latter question, it is pertinent to consider some figures, which have been estimated from the published accounts of Britain's war expenditure. The WW1 fleet of 40 monitors, large and small, cost about £8 million to build. Each large monitor cost about £100,000 a year to run — payments for its crew, fuel, ammunition, stores, repairs etc — while a small monitor cost about £30,000 a year. The total cost of Britain having a monitor fleet during WW1 thus amounted to about £17 million, after making some allowance for 'overhead' costs of the naval establishment ashore. The total cost of the naval votes for 1914/15 to 1918/19 inclusive was £1080 million, so that the monitors accounted for only 1.6% of the total. The proportion of seagoing personnel serving in the monitors was also under 2%. As the monitors were nearly all built by merchant shipbuilders, there was no question of sacrificing construction of warships, although there was an appreciable effort required by the three main ordnance companies.

The WW2 fleet of two old and two new monitors absorbed fewer resources, even without allowing for the value of sterling having approximately halved between WW1 and WW2. The total cost of building and running the monitor fleet, with its average strength of only two ships available most of the time, amounted to about £11 million, out of a total for the R.N. of £3130 million for 1939/40 to 1945/46 inclusive, or only 0.35%. Building *Roberts* and *Abercrombie* in warship specialist yards did however mean the sacrifice of the equivalent of five destroyers, but this was not a large price to pay for two vessels who had made a major contribution to important amphibious operations.

The essential features of a monitor which no other vessel shared were the combination of hitting power and riskability. Compared with heavy land artillery, their principal attribute was mobility, and with aircraft bombing, accuracy and sustained fire. These potentialities were only realised to the full in later WW2 operations where, after the fiasco of Dieppe, no major British assault on any enemy European shore except Anzio took place without monitors in support. In most cases, it was necessary to supplement their limited number by battleships and cruisers, but the monitors were more cost-effective than such vessels. Compared with a battleship, they needed only about one-third the men and resources to provide a similar capability, as the battleship's greater number of guns was but a small advantage at the slow bombardment rate of firing. Their shallow draft and riskability enabled them to get closer to their target, so increasing their effective range inland, while their training for a single purpose ensured maximum efficiency in shore bombardment compared with ships for whom this was only a subsidiary role. Cruisers certainly made a major contribution in terms of rounds fired but lacked the range and hitting power of the big gun ships; their high speed and long endurance were of no particular value in this role.

With its vast resources during WW2, the U.S. Navy had less need than the R.N. to operate the most cost-effective vessels. Battleships and cruisers were used to lay down immense barrages as the American troops assaulted the succession of islands in the Pacific in 1943-45. The Japanese fleet having largely ceased to exist as a fighting force towards the end of WW2, the newest U.S. battleships as well as the oldest could be devoted primarily to bombardment duties, while their anti-aircraft batteries provided valuable close-range cover. The statistics of U.S. heavy calibre naval bombardments are staggering: 23,210 rounds of 12-inch and above plus 261,000 5-inch to 8-inch on Okinawa alone between March and June 1945, excluding heavy A.A. fire. This barrage was essentially for destruction which, in the absence of large numbers of heavy bombers within range, called for a much greater weight of fire than in the neutralisation role, which was that more commonly required in the European theatre. By comparison, bombardment expenditure at Normandy was 58,600 British rounds out of 141,000 Allied of 4-inch and above.

The monitors' role during WW1 was less clear cut. Churchill and Fisher's plans for a North Sea offensive supported by monitors were never put into effect, so the ships were used instead off the Dardanelles and Belgian Coast. In the Mediterranean, they relieved the Army of the necessity of deploying the heaviest artillery ashore, especially during the early stages of operations, and an equally important role was the substitution for more valuable vessels like battleships. After the evacuation of Gallipoli, the large and small monitors were useful as patrol vessels off enemy coasts, again relieving other

Sir John Moore*'s officers in full uniform play a genteel game with a medicine ball on the quarterdeck.*

Erebus' *officers relax more informally in WW2 style on the quarterdeck. Smoke canisters can be seen on the twin Oerlikon platform.*

more versatile ships like cruisers and destroyers for duties elsewhere. In terms of positive damage to the enemy, the Mediterranean monitors could point to no overwhelming successes, but their presence did certainly inhibit enemy freedom of manoeuvre on coastal front-lines such as Salonika, Palestine and the northern Adriatic. They and the other patrol vessels spared the Allies the need to devote resources to the defence of their own seaward flanks; in this role, the bulged monitor with its relative invulnerability to submarine attack proved most valuable. This latter attribute was demonstrated even better off the Belgian Coast, where British and French coastal defences were minimal compared with the heavily fortified German sector. The monitors patrolled with immunity only a few miles offshore, in effect constituting a mini-battle squadron with a considerable deterrent value on German surface ship operations in the area. It must be conceded however that their primary role of shore bombardment was less successful off the Belgian Coast. The exceptionally strong German coastal batteries and their accurate shooting made it difficult to destroy specific targets. It was never realistic to expect to put out of action the inland U-boat base at Bruges by gunfire alone, but it was possible to render the forward base at Ostende of little use to the Germans by the last year of the war.

Towards the end of WW1, the improvements in bombardment techniques enabled the monitors to make a more effective contribution, but only the newer faster vessels with longer range guns. The earlier vessels were of relatively little value by this time and could be deployed on guardship duties with no reduction in front-line offensive capability. The monitors' operations were always excellent morale boosters for the troops ashore. Even when their gunfire was not able to achieve much on the ground, their mere presence offshore, remaining on station in spite of all the enemy's attacks, was always welcome. Accounts and pictures of the monitors' bombardments were also good for civilian morale.

Of the 40 WW1 monitors, there is no doubt which vessels were the most valuable — *Erebus* and *Terror*. The 12-inch and 14-inch monitors were handicapped by their slow speed and comparatively short range guns. There was little that could have been done about the latter shortcoming; the early monitors were only built because the 12-inch and 14-inch guns were readily available — it was a question of those or nothing. The handicap of their slow speed is less excusable. The model experiments at A.E.W. clearly showed as early as December 1914 that the first monitors would never achieve their designed ten knots. While understandably Fisher would brook no delay in the construction of the four 14-inch ships, he was either pig-headed or badly advised by his D.N.C. when refusing to allow a modified hull form and more powerful machinery for the eight 12-inch and two 15-inch *Marshals*. There was time enough to draw new lines and order machinery of about double the power which would easily have given the required ten knots without delaying completion.

The decision to use diesels in the *Marshals* was also an error of judgement by Churchill and Fisher. Such new and untried machinery should never have been risked in vessels carrying the most powerful guns the Navy could provide. There is no time and little necessity in war to innovate in matters which are not vital to operational performance and for which adequate solutions already exist. Although *Soult*'s engines were not unsuccessful, the fiascoes with *Ney*'s engines contributed to the bad name that diesels generally obtained in the eyes of the R.N. Diesels had to be tolerated in vessels like submarines and in auxiliaries, which did not really count, but in surface combatant ships, the anti-diesel lobby remained strong up to WW2. In the case of the *Marshals*, it was not appreciated that their slow speed was due not so much to their type of machinery, but to their bluff lines, poor design of propellers and low installed horsepower.

As is so often the case, the most successful ship designs were those in which the principal features were well balanced: armament, speed, protection, seaworthiness. Insufficient performance in any one respect could jeopardise a design, but so too could 'excess' performance. The heaviest armed of the small monitors were by no means the most successful. The 9.2-inch gun was really too heavy for 600-ton vessels and the 6-inch monitors proved a better balanced design — despite the increased weight and reduced speed of *M.29* to *M.33* as completed. The use of a single turret in most of the monitors might be considered something of a risk, as one mishap could cripple the ship operationally, as was shown by *Erebus* on D-day. The alternative of two turrets was however not realistic, as the guns were always in short supply, so it was preferable to distribute those few available over as many hulls as possible.

In all the bulged designs, removal of the bulges would have added about two knots speed, but the loss in protection would not have been worth this increase, particularly after the bulged forms were properly designed. A slight relaxation of the specified shallow draft would also have improved speed by enabling finer lines to have been drawn. An increase of one or two feet would not have been a serious handicap even off the shallow Belgian Coast as, apart from *Marshal Ney*, there are no records of any of the monitors grounding. The long period between the wars when no monitors were built meant that the WW2 designs did not benefit much from the natural evolution that occurred in other ship types. Problems with steering were never properly overcome owing to lack of prolonged service experience. Design shortcomings like siting the turret too far aft in *Roberts* and *Abercrombie* would have been less likely to occur, as would the generally inadequate standard of outfit and equipment.

One great service the monitors performed during WW1 was to consolidate the increasing degree of professionalism in naval gunnery. Percy Scott had laid the groundwork before the war but it was the monitors' firing of large numbers of shells to maximum ranges that ensured that gunnery techniques and problems were fully appreciated, evaluated and developed. The operational conditions enabled proper care to be taken to estimate all the necessary corrections on as exact a basis as possible and to control the fire using the most accurate means — aircraft spotting and wireless reporting. Unlike ship targets, the monitors' targets could easily be photographed before and afterwards and a careful analysis made of every firing. The ability to fire at long range was recognised as an essential feature of a naval gun — before the WW1 monitors, no British large calibre gun had an elevation of more than 20°; after them, none had an elevation less than 40°.

Virtually every calibre of gun in the R.N. was used by the monitors and, with the large number of rounds fired compared with Fleet vessels, plenty of experience was obtained, especially of such factors as bore wear and corresponding loss of performance. Normally gun life was not a particularly important operational factor in most ships, but in the monitors, it sometimes had an influence, e.g. *Erebus* unable to participate at Salerno. All the guns mounted in the monitors were existing naval designs, i.e. high-velocity low-trajectory guns. Howitzers were never seriously considered after Churchill's suggestion in December 1914 (see p.41), although a design for a self-propelled Army-manned floating howitzer platform was proposed during WW2.

There must have been little anticipation of much monitor or even shore bombardment activity pre-WW2, as stocks of suitable shells were small in 1939 — 84% of the 23,210 15-inch held were A.P.C. By the end of the war, considerably more heavy shells, mostly H.E., had been fired at shore targets than ships. Aircraft bombing was certainly more effective in many roles, but its value was more restricted once the troops were ashore and requiring close support. It was reckoned that bombing accuracy was only about one-tenth that of naval gunfire and, while it was extremely rare for naval gunfire to fall on Allied troops, the same could not be said of aircraft bombing in close support. For saturation or general neutralisation fire, one 15-inch round was considered equivalent to about four 6-inch, whereas the ratio of shell weight was about 17 to 1. For destruction, especially of protected or distant targets, the 15-inch was the principal weapon as it could range about four miles further than a cruiser's guns.

Nearly every navy had coast defence vessels of one description or another, but the only one apart from the Royal Navy that made any attempt to build coast *offence* vessels was the Italian. A considerable fleet of hastily built and converted craft was pressed into service in 1916-18 for use on the Adriatic front (see p.62). The nation that had pioneered the original monitors had given up their construction after the completion of U.S.S. *Florida* in 1903; these designs were in any case only suitable for coast defence or river use. During the Vietnam War however, the U.S. Navy revived the monitor concept for riverine craft — specially built or converted vessels for inshore offensive operations. For example, some sixty L.C.M.s were converted to carry one 105-mm (4.1-inch) howitzer and several smaller guns in a well protected 80-ton hull. For work off the coast of Vietnam, the U.S.N. repeated its WW2 tactic by deploying cruisers and destroyers, supplemented during 1968-69 by the re-activated battleship *New Jersey*. Supplied with special ammunition, these vessels were capable of delivering a great weight of fire at ranges in excess of those possible with the same ordnance in WW2. Such was the nature of the war in Vietnam and the general lack of concentrated targets that the overall effect was not great, merely curtailing the enemy's use of the coastal strip.

The Royal Navy applied the term 'monitor' to one other design during the 20th Century but out of context with its previous use. The three modified K-class submarines of 1918, *M.1* to *M.3*, were described as 'monitor submarines', as they mounted one 40-calibre 12-inch Mk IX. This weapon was not however intended for coast offence purposes, but as a supplement to the normal torpedo armament in cases where the latter would not be effective; the concept was not a success. In planning for the invasion of Sicily, the idea of building a new fleet of small monitors was put forward. A design with two 6-inch guns was proposed in 1942 but it was found that the number required — a first batch of ten, followed by a further forty — could only be built at the expense of escort vessels or landing craft. Other means of providing fire support were therefore examined, including the conversion of some landing craft to carry

4.7-inch destroyer guns. A fleet of Landing Craft, Gun was therefore built in 1943-44, monitors in all but name. Typical vessels were the twenty or so L.C.G. (L)(3) converted from L.C.T.(3), carrying two single 4.7-inch Q.F. IX or B.L. I on a displacement of about 500 tons. In addition to providing gunfire support on amphibious operations, they also proved useful for other roles, particularly patrol work off the Normandy beaches.

Despite their impressive firepower, it was always recognised that the monitors were not of themselves able to disprove the old dictum about ships versus forts:[1]

> "Nothing has occurred to invalidate the maxim based on the experience of centuries that ships cannot engage properly armed and well designed shore defences with any hope of success unless the strength and equipment of the fort is greatly inferior to the armament carried by the ships."

The introduction of aircraft spotting did a little to even up the odds against the ship due to its relative degree of vulnerability — a single hit could sink a ship, but near direct hits on each main gun mounting were necessary to destroy permanently a fort's fighting ability. WW2 experience emphasised that the morale and experience of those manning the forts were perhaps the most important factors: there was no difficulty in inducing demoralised Italian coast defenders to surrender in 1943 but, at the same period, even relatively modest Japanese defences could only be overcome by total annihilation.

When time and resources permit, purpose-built designs always prove superior to adaptations. The ex-Brazilian river monitors and ex-Norwegian coast defence battleships were welcome 'windfalls' and were able to contribute usefully to particular operations, but were discarded as soon as WW1 was over, while *Erebus* and *Terror* were retained. Only the largest navies can afford to build ships for limited roles; the others must make do with general purpose designs. When those special purpose vessels have few peacetime uses, it becomes more attractive to add the specialist role to some existing design. Indeed the gunfire support role is one of the main reasons for retaining guns of 4-inch to 5-inch calibre in modern destroyers and frigates, so that a bombardment capability is available from more or less any significant vessel taking part in an operation. The role of the long range heavy calibre gun against ship or shore targets has now been taken over by the air or surface launched precision guided missile.

The British monitors were not normally thought of as regular Navy ships. Their crews were largely reservists and many of their officers were either older men passed over for further promotion, or relatively junior. Apart from Ramsay and Tweedie, no ex-monitor C.O. rose to flag rank in the Royal Navy, but this did not mean that the monitors were not well run and efficiently handled. The monitors and those who manned them have never been given the credit they deserve, especially the small monitors with their additional handicap of numbers instead of easily remembered names. It is hoped that this account of the origins, activities and ultimate fates of the 42 British monitors, whose life spanned half a century from 1914 to 1965 and who played an important role in both World Wars, will help put the record straight; the Royal Navy will never build their like again.

[1] *The Gunnery Manual,* Vol. 1, 1922. ADM 186/171

BIBLIOGRAPHY AND SOURCES

Published Sources

There are not many published works that give monitors more than a passing mention. Among those that I have found helpful are:—

E. Altham, *Monitors in Modern Naval Warfare*. Journal of the Royal United Service Institution, Vol. LXIX, 1924

E. Altham, *The Dwina Campaign*. J. R.U.S.I., Vol. LXVIII, 1923

R. H. Bacon, *The Dover Patrol 1915-1917*, 2 vols. (Hutchinson, 1919)

R. H. Bacon, *From 1900 Onward*. (Hutchinson, 1940)

The Belgian Shiplover, *British Monitors, Class "M"*. No. 127, Jan/Feb 1969

F. C. Bowen, *Ships of the Monitor Type*. Shipbuilding and Shipping Record, 30 Aug 1945

Brassey's Naval Annual. Various years, e.g. 1921

E. K. Chatterton, *"Severn's" Saga*. (Hurst & Blackett, 1938)

E. K. Chatterton, *Seas of Adventures*. (Hurst & Blackett, 1936)

W. S. Churchill, *The World Crisis: 1911-14; 1915*. (Thornton Butterworth, 1923)

J. S. Corbett and H. Newbolt, *Naval Operations*, 5 vols. (Longmans, 1920-31)

R. H. Davis, *Deep Diving*. (St Catherine Press, n.d.)

K. G. B. Dewar, *The Navy From Within*. (Gollancz, 1939)

K. Edwards, *Operation Neptune*. (Collins, 1946)

The Engineer, *The British Monitors*. 14 Feb 1919
Some Notes on the Vickers Diesel Engine. 22 Aug 1919

M. Gilbert, *Winston S. Churchill*, Volume III and Companion Volume III. (Heinemann, 1971)

J. G. Hamilton, *Naval Bombardment*. J. R.U.S.I., Vol. XC, 1945

J. Iron, *Keeper of the Gate*. (Sampson, Low, n.d.)

A. D. Jacobsen, *Trutzig und Treu*. (Behrs Verlag, Berlin, 1935)

Jane's Fighting Ships. Various years, e.g. 1919

H. A. Jones and W. Raleigh, *The War in the Air*, 6 vols. (Oxford, 1922-37)

R. Keyes, *The Naval Memoirs of Admiral of the Fleet Sir Roger Keyes. Scapa Flow to the Dover Straits 1916-1918*. (Thornton Butterworth, 1935)

Der Krieg zur See: Die Mittelmeer Division. H. Lorey (Mittler, Berlin, 1928); *Der Krieg in der Nordsee*, 7 vols. D. Groos; W. Gladisch (Mittler, Berlin, 1920-37; Frankfurt 1965); *Die Kämpfe der Kaiserliche Marine in den Deutschen Kolonien*. K. Assman (Mittler, Berlin, 1935)

The Marine Engineer and Naval Architect, *The New Navy*. January, February 1919, July 1920

S. E. Morison, *History of U.S. Naval Operations in World War II*. Vol. 9: *Sicily-Salerno-Anzio;* Vol. 11: *The Invasion of France and Germany*. (Little Brown, 1954 & 1957)

S. W. Roskill, *The War at Sea*, 3 vols. (H.M.S.O., 1954-61)

The Shipbuilder, *The White Diesel Marine Oil Engine*. January 1920

G. Smith, *Britain's Clandestine Submarines*. (Yale U.P., 1965)

B. Stjernfelt, *Alarm i Atlantvallen*. (Hörsta Förlag, Stockholm, 1953)

R. H. Thompson, *The Rise and Fall of the Monitor 1862-1973*. Mariner's Mirror, August 1974

H. Tweedie, *The Story of a Naval Life*. (Rich & Cowan, 1939)

Unpublished Sources

The bulk of the sources I have used comprise official records held primarily by the following institutions:—

Public Record Office

Among many hundreds of records consulted, the following contained the most useful information:

Histories and Reports of Proceedings (WW1) ADM 137/177, 398, 496, 507, 630, 774, 782-3, 1565-6, 1668, 1684, 1700, 1734, 1741-3, 2095, 2112-3, 2168, 2170, 2215, 2236, 2268, 2272, 3329, 3791

Cases and Reports of Proceedings (WW2) ADM 199/360, 426, 904, 946-7, 949, 1386, 1598, 1645, 1655, 1661

Naval Historical Monographs (WW1) ADM 186/ 606, 611, 613

Ship's Logs ADM 53 series

Ship's Books ADM 136/23 (*Terror*)

Cases (miscellaneous reports, e.g. losses) ADM 116/1348-9, 1433, 1625, 2461, 3584, 5053

Secretary's Papers (miscellaneous reports, e.g. *Erebus* transfer) ADM 1/ 8513-4, 8547, 8557, 9832, 9876, 10543, 11292

Pink Lists (ship's movements) ADM 187 series

Navy Lists ADM 177 series

Armament Lists ADM 186 series, e.g. 170

Quarterly Appropriation of Gun Mountings ADM 186 series, e.g. 197

Range Tables ADM 186 series, e.g. 181

Gunnery Handbooks ADM 186 series, e.g. 171, 315, 329

National Maritime Museum

Ship's Covers (D.N.C. design files) ADM 138/ 433 (*Severn, Humber & Mersey*); 436 (*Erebus & Terror*); 502 (Oilers); 600 (*Glatton & Gorgon*); 647 (Small monitors)

Admiralty Drawings (all WW1 monitors)

Gunnery Handbooks

Vickers and Armstrong's ordnance drawings

D'Eyncourt Papers

Diary of C.P.O. Bass

Naval Library

Includes many naval historical references, some also in the P.R.O., N.M.M. and I.W.M.

Records of Warship Construction During the War (WW1)

Technical History of the War (WW1) especially Nos. 28, 33, 34

Naval Historical Monographs (WW1) e.g. Dover Command

Battle Summaries (WW2) B.R. 1736 series

Pink Lists

Navy Lists

Steamships of England (WW1)

War Vessels and Aircraft

Gunnery Handbooks (O.U. and B.R. series)

Range Tables

Ship's Log Summary Cards (WW1)

Details of Estimates (WW1 costs)

Admiralty Fleet Orders

Ministry of Defence

War Diary (WW2 chronology, Naval Historical Branch)
Damage Reports (e.g. *Abercrombie*)
Lillicrap Workbooks 188/1-3 (Bath)
Gun Registers (Priddy's Hard)
Ship's Cover, Ship's Book and Drawings (*Roberts* and *Abercrombie*)
Range Tables (Ordnance Board)
Model Test Records (Admiralty Experiment Works)

Imperial War Museum

Gunnery Handbooks
Books of Reference (B.R.)
General and historical works

ACKNOWLEDGEMENTS

Since so little has been previously published about monitors, I have particularly appreciated the help and information provided by a very large number of individuals and organisations. With a correspondence file extending to well over a thousand letters, it is not possible to acknowledge everyone by name, but nevertheless, I am grateful to all who have helped, some alas no longer alive to see the result.
In particular to those who served in monitors:
Cdr L. G. Addington, Capt Sir J. M. Alleyne, Mr A. J. Brunsdon, Capt N. D. Campbell, Cdr P. J. Cardale, Cdr A. W. M. Collyer, Capt R. E. C. Dunbar, Capt R. H. Errington, Rev D. A. Farquharson-Roberts, Cdr C. J. Gordon, Capt G. Lydekker, Capt N. C. Moore, Cdr H. L. Morgan, Capt H. F. Nalder, Cdr L. F. Robinson, Major C. R. J. Scott, Capt L. A. W. Spooner, Cdr P. H. B. Taylor, Mr G. Watson, Capt K. U. White, Lt Cdr H. S. Whittow, Capt M. F. Wilson.

To those whose knowledge of naval matters filled many gaps: Mr A. D. Baker III, Mr J. G. Bedford, Mr D. K. Brown, Dr N. J. M. Campbell, Mr D. B. Cochrane, Mr R. J. Coleman, Col R. A. Colenso, Mr. J. J. Colledge, Mr J. David, Mr J. Dixon, Lt Cdr R. O. Dulin, Mr M. C. Dunstan, Mr R. H. Gibson, Mr J. W. Goss, Mr W. G. Hall, Mr P. H. Judd, Mr D. J. Lyon, Mr P. S. Millington, Mr G. A. Osbon, Mr A. W. H. Pearsall, Mr A. M. Preston, Mr G. Ransome, Mr H. C. Rayner, Mr V. C. Richards, Lt Cdr D. Trimingham.

To the staff of the following companies who were most helpful in providing information or access to records and photographs (the company names are those appropriate at the time consulted, although some have since changed, or ceased operation):
Bolinders Company, John Brown (Clydebank), Dunford-Hadfield, Eisen und Metall, Harland & Wolff, Hawthorn Leslie (Engineers), McKie & Baxter, Lithgows, Palmers Hebburn, Scott's Shipbuilding & Engineering, Shell International Marine, Swan Hunter Shipbuilders, Vickers Shipbuilding Group (Barrow), Vickers Engineering Group (Elswick), T. W. Ward, J. S. White,
and not forgetting the staff of the North Tyneside and South Tyneside Public Libraries.

But no adequate history of British warships can be written which does not make full use of the resources and records of those institutions whose staff made such efforts to see that the monitor history was given every assistance:

Public Record Office
National Maritime Museum
The Naval Library
Imperial War Museum

and the Ministry of Defence, including the Admiralty Experiment Works; H.M. Dockyard, Chatham; H.M. Dockyard, Portsmouth; H.M.S. *Excellent*; Naval Home Division; the Ordnance Board; Royal Armament Research and Development Establishment; Royal Naval Armament Depot, Priddy's Hard.

I owe a particular debt to the University of Newcastle upon Tyne, who have provided financial assistance, and to the World Ship Society, both of whom recognised the importance of publishing a history of monitors. The latter's knowledgeable members pointed to many sources of information, not least their own and the Society's records. I am especially grateful to my wife and my mother who have given support and assistance during the long years of research.

Illustrations

Compared with more numerous and more publicised warship types, there are not many photographs of monitors, as their active careers were short and surrounded by security restrictions at the time. I am therefore especially grateful to the following for permission to reproduce illustrations on the pages listed.

A & A Plans 60-1; John Brown Ltd. 10, 27, 44, 83, 151, 152, 153, 155; A. J. Brunsdon 134; Capt. R. E. C. Dunbar 65, 181 (left), 200; *The Engineer* 76 (lower); Rev. D. A. Farquharson-Roberts 143, 202 (right); Harland & Wolff Ltd. 22, 24, 48, 59, 105, 126; Hutchinson Group 51, 108; Imperial War Museum 28, 29, 31, 32, 33, 36, 49, 50, 52, 54, 56, 57, 58, 62, 64, 65, 72, 73, 74, 75, 79, 85, 87, 89, 90, 95, 96, 103, 104, 107, 108 (top), 110, 113, 116, 117, 129, 130, 156, 157, 164, 165, 197; McKie & Baxter 47; Ministry of Defence 136, 137, 138, 168; Capt. N. C. Moore 53, 181 (right), 198, 202 (left); National Maritime Museum 86, 92-3, 114, 127; G. A. Osbon 80; A. & J. Pavia 120 (top), 135, 168; Public Record Office 66 (right), 119; Cdr. L. F. Robinson 185, 188; *Shipping World & Shipbuilder* 76 (upper); W. P. Trotter and the Oscar Parkes Society 66 (left), 76, 77, 78, 96 (bottom), 98, 115; U. S. National Archives 160, 161; P. A. Vicary 30, 35, 112, 118; Vickers Ltd. 70, 155, 175, 176; World Ship Society 63; Wright and Logan 39, 132, 133.

Other illustrations are my own or from my collection.

INDEX

The index is arranged to include the most important subjects, but excludes passing references to people, places and ships, e.g. names of vessels escorting monitors. Illustrations are indicated by italic type.